MATT KRAMER'S
NEW CALIFORNIA
WINE

MATT KRAMER'S
NEW CALIFORNIA
WINE

MAKING SENSE *of* NAPA VALLEY, SONOMA, CENTRAL COAST, *and* BEYOND

BY MATT KRAMER

RUNNING PRESS
PHILADELPHIA • LONDON

Library of Congress Control Number: 2004092617

ISBN 0-7624-1964-4

Cover and interior design by Serrin Bodmer
Cover photograph: CEPHAS / R & K Muschenetz
Edited by Alison Trulock
Typography: ACaslon, Trajan, and TradeGothic

This book may be ordered by mail from the publisher.
Please include $2.50 for postage and handling.
But try your bookstore first!

Running Press Book Publishers
125 South Twenty-second Street
Philadelphia, Pennsylvania 19103-4399

Visit us on the web!
www.runningpress.com

CONTENTS

For Stuart, for everything.

PREFACE

I asked how can you ever be sure
that what you write is really
any good at all and he said you can't
you can't you can never be sure
you die without knowing
whether anything you wrote was any good
if you have to be sure don't write
　　　　　　　　—*Opening the Hand*, W.S. Merwin

I n revising *Making Sense of California Wine*, the obvious question is: What
has changed? This book first appeared in 1992. At that time, the now-
famous "explosion" in prices and marketing—the invention of "cult" Cabernets; the proliferation of tiny labels selling for $50 to $100 a bottle—had not
yet occurred.

All of that was mostly fashion, fueled by economics. But beneath the
glossy surface were real, substantive changes. California's vineyards were
undergoing massive revision, thanks to the changes forced upon them by the
widespread infestation of phylloxera.

Phylloxera (a microscopic, sap-sucking root louse) required growers in
many parts of California—and especially in densely planted Napa and
Sonoma counties—to uproot their existing vines and start all over again. The
cost, over the decade-long span of the 1990s, was at least $1 billion, accord-
ing to the University of California at Davis Department of Viticulture and
Enology.

That this replanting occurred at the same moment as the longest economic boom in American history was no small thing. The 1990s saw four
consecutive years in which the gross domestic product growth exceeded 4
percent annually, among other economic markers.

Had phylloxera occurred during a less economically buoyant time, California vineyards would look very different than they do today. And California wines would *taste* different too.

One of the most significant additions to this edition of *Making Sense of California Wine* is its chapters on how California's viticulture (grape-growing practices) changed. And how that, in turn, altered the taste of California's best wines.

Some things have not changed in California wine. For example, ten years ago the most lucrative California wines were Cabernet Sauvignon, Chardonnay and Merlot. That's still true today.

Cabernet Sauvignon acreage more than doubled between 1992 and 2002. Chardonnay plantings increased almost 40 percent. Merlot acreage saw a fivefold increase in the same time period, from 10,000 acres to more than 50,000 acres.

That said, we *have* seen a significant expansion in other varieties, such as Pinot Noir, which more than doubled in acreage, reaching almost 24,000 acres by 2002. Syrah exploded in popularity, mushrooming from little more than 500 acres to more than 16,000 acres.

These are the easily grasped facts. But the most significant change of all is less easily seen. It's a profound change—a cultural shift really—in the mentality of California's best winemakers and grape growers. For the first time ever, California fine-wine producers are seeing the land—dare I say it?—as if they were French.

For decades, California winegrowers proudly pursued a mechanistic view of grape-growing and winemaking. Everything had to be scientifically—which is to say, mathematically—verifiable. If it couldn't be verified, it didn't exist. It was an engineer's view of wine.

The importance of soil is a choice example. For decades, California winegrowers almost literally ignored the land. The effects of different soil types were of little or no concern.

Today, though, you would think that, like in a science fiction story, a race of Burgundians had secretly penetrated the minds of California's fine-wine ambition winegrowers, the now-numerous producers who have sought for the past few decades to raise the quality of California wine from the ordinary to something previously achieved only by the greatest European producers.

Everywhere, the talk is about matching just the right rootstocks to every soil type in their vineyard.

They will trot out detailed, multicolored maps of the vineyards showing sometimes dozens of different rootstocks keyed to the mosaic of soils (clay, sandy, gravelly) in often surprisingly small vineyard sites. "Nuance" is the word most frequently, and reverently, voiced.

This is wonderful and speaks of a genuine cultural shift. Where previously a kind of interventionist muscularity was the mode, today the attitude—and the action—is more deferential. This can only help create finer wines, which indeed is already occurring.

Of course, much remains to be pursued in California winemaking. There's still far too much oakiness in California wine (although thankfully less than there used to be).

There's still too much reliance on technology to overcome questionable aesthetic decisions (such as using devices like spinning cones or reverse osmosis to remove excess alcohol from wines made from intentionally overripe grapes). And there are still far too many boring, taste-alike Cabernets and Chardonnays chasing the same few customers.

That said, it's also equally clear that California is setting the stage for a new kind of Golden Age of fine wine. We are seeing already—and will see many more examples in the next decade—wines of considerable originality. We are seeing wines of much greater finesse and, yes, nuance.

Above all, the once-absolute dominance of Napa Valley and Sonoma County is giving way to a greater equality of recognition to districts in Santa Barbara County, Paso Robles and Monterey County, among other locales.

Certainly, Napa and Sonoma will continue to get the lion's share of tourism and publicity. After all, they've got the critical mass of wineries and vineyards. But Napa and Sonoma's monopoly on fine-wine quality is now legitimately challenged by others. A new recognition of the equal quality (and ambition) of other winegrowing districts is beginning to dawn.

This second edition of *Making Sense of California Wine* seeks to identify and explicate these changes, as well as highlight some of the latest wine achievements. One thing is certain: Now, more than ever, it's really all about vineyards. Because of that, a disproportionate amount of attention is given to wineries that grow their own grapes. These are the wineries that can deliver consistency.

The newest appellations—Santa Lucia Highlands, Santa Rita Hills, the westernmost section of Sonoma Coast, the west-of-Highway-101 portion of Paso Robles—are all, in effect, pursuits of place. Where once blending from numerous sources was considered the ideal, California's finest wines are now openly all about "somewhereness."

It's a good bet that, fifty years from now, California wine historians will look back upon the exciting last decades of the twentieth century as only prefatory to the substantive achievements now only just under way.

A new fine-wine culture is emerging, one not based on hype, hope, and commercial hoopla but on an originality of taste and the sort of patient devotion to site that have long distinguished Europe's greatest wines.

But can you be sure? *You can't you can never be sure*. The importance of somewhereness in a wine is not that you can identify it, label unseen, with unerring accuracy. That's not the point. But what is true for fine wine everywhere else in the world also is true for California: Its best wines are revelations of place. Of this I am sure. As for the particulars of my observations, inevitably they will have to be confirmed by your experience. *If you have to be sure don't write*. I have written, anyway.

INTRODUCTION

I was talking about music with a friend of my teenage daughter. I asked,
'Can you play the piano?' She replied, 'I don't know. I've never tried.'
It was then that I realized what it meant to be an American.
—Michel Salgues, Founding Winemaker, Roederer Estate

To those familiar with California today it seems inevitable that California be a winegrowing state. After all, it is so Mediterranean: Its coastal hills are so contoured, sunlit, so amenable to cultivation of all kinds. Yet wine was not inevitable, at least not fine wine.

It is important to underscore this distinction between mere "wine" and "fine wine." They are kin, but not twins. Virtually any temperate zone can create some sort of wine. It needn't even be from grapes. But the leap to "fine wine" is something else again. At that moment, the ambition becomes more than agrarian. It becomes more than just preserving and reducing a bulky fruit. Not least, it becomes more than a vehicle for intoxication.

Fine wine is a different ambition. It is a refinement, an amalgam of urban and rural. Fine wine is to fruit what the refined English country house is to rural living: a hybridization of studied pleasure with raw nature. As in the English countryside, this does not come about casually. It is the result of economic, cultural, and social forces.

Although it rarely is discussed, one of the underlying elements in the creation of fine wines is an engagement with the future. This phrase, "engagement with the future," refers to several ingredients. Foremost among them is money. Fine wine is capital-intensive. Grapevines require three years before they bear fruit. Tanks, barrels, filters, presses, and bottling lines all chew up capital. Many wines require at least two years of aging in tank, barrel or bottle before being released. Then there are labor costs. Vineyards are labor-intensive: planting, pruning, spraying, and harvesting. In the cellar, there's the actual winemaking, the transfer of wines from vat to barrel to bottle. Clearly, an "engagement with the future" requires a belief that there will be a return on one's investment. With fine wine comes a magnification: You need more and better.

But this engagement is more than monetary. The political and cultural climates must be conducive. There must be a sense of political stability. And there must be a cultural sensibility that fine wine is a socially endorsed pursuit. This is not just a matter of wine being fashionable, but actually important. Fine wine must be seen as being an expression of civilization. It has to be a vehicle of local pride.

When these elements of finance, politics, and culture coalesce, you will discover a blossoming of fine wines. When just one of these same ingredients is absent, fine wine is suffocated. The examples are numerous. From the Middle Ages to the present, France has issued an unrivaled array of fine wines. It also has been a nation of considerable and continuing wealth that has functioned, for the most part, with a sense of stability since at least the 1400s. Not least, it shares a common cultural vision of the importance of fine wine as a national cultural aesthetic.

The importance of stability can be seen in the ancient fine wine tradition of Germany. Until about 1870, Germany was in a state of almost constant political flux. Politically, it could not be described as stable. But it was for wine. The reason was the presence of the powerful and rich Benedictine and Cistercian orders in the Mosel-Saar-Ruwer and the Rheingau. Their enduring presence meant that an engagement with the future could be made. The monastic example also spurred the ambitions of the local nobility for their own vineyards, thereby furthering the social and cultural prestige of fine wine.

In comparison, Italy has seen the quality—and the public estimation—of its wines vary dramatically over the same period. As a nation, it lacked the widespread wealth of France, cultural unification, monastic presence, or even a national government until the Risorgimento in the 1860s. Even then, Italy remained a collection of isolated regions with little sense of national pride until the mid-twentieth century. What sort of engagement with the future could evolve out of such a circumstance? Who would risk capital on such instability?

California's first such engagement with the future appeared in the 1870s. Not only had a wine industry become widespread, but an ambition for fine wine was revealed. Witness the creation of the Vina Ranch by railroad baron, California governor, and United States senator Leland Stanford. After travelling to France in 1880, Stanford returned to California fired with the fine-wine ambition. The following year, he began buying land along the Sacramento River between the towns of Red Bluff and Chico, an area in central northern California that once had a minor winegrowing history. Today, it is confined to crops such as rice and olives.

Stanford announced that he would create wines that would rival the best of France; planted more than 1,000 irrigated acres in one year; imported French vineyard workers; built a brandy distillery; and by 1885 had amassed a whopping 55,000 acres of pasture and farmland. By 1887, Stanford's Vina Ranch had 3,575 acres of vines and a wine cellar with a two-million-gallon capacity. As if this were not enough, in 1888 Stanford built yet another winery to handle the grapes grown farther south on his ranch in Palo Alto, the site of which is today Stanford University. (I am indebted to Thomas Pinney's superb book, *A History of Wine in America: From the Beginnings to Prohibition*, for these details.)

Yet where is the Vina Ranch and the residue of Stanford's ambition today? Gone. It dwindled upon his death in 1893 and then was swallowed utterly with the advent of Prohibition. Vina Ranch became part of the endowment of Stanford University, along with the Palo Alto vineyard. (Ironically, Stanford University's first president was an ardent prohibitionist.) Its final harvest was in 1915, after which the vines were uprooted. By that date, already two-thirds of the 48 states were "dry." Four years later national Prohibition would be enacted by amending the Constitution of the United States. The political stability upon which this nation has long prided itself actually was absent for wine.

Nor was Stanford's undertaking unique. Instead, it was emblematic. Apart from knowing that they existed, what do we retain of such ambitions as the 2,000-acre Fountain Grove winery near Santa Rosa? Or the 2,000-acre St. George Vineyard in Fresno? Or the 1,600-acre Natoma Vineyard near Sacramento? The list of smaller, but still significant, wineries that disappeared numbers in the hundreds. Although a few winery names from this first "civilization" remain, such as Schramsberg, Gundlach-Bundschu, and Inglenook, they scarcely represent a continuity. Nearly all are either revivals of something previously defunct (such as Schramsberg) or wineries that soldiered on by selling the grapes or bulk wines demanded by the market.

Stanford's Vina Ranch is worth noting because the very obscurity today of so high-flown an ambition reveals the degree of loss of California's original fine wine culture. The loss represents more than just a passing amnesia. It does not figure in our collective cultural memory today because we have no authentic linkage to the original ambition, except for a few shards of documentary evidence. When the fine-wine ambition was revived in the late 1960s and early 1970s, it had no memory of prior efforts. There were only scraps of evidence of the ambition, as the few winegrowers who survived Prohibition of necessity were devoted or resigned to making bulk wines. The exceptions that existed by way of wines or men were too few to reconstitute a real memory, let alone a tradition. After all, the fine-wine ambition had only just been forming before the prohibitionist campaign gained momentum in the early 1900s.

Nevertheless, starting in the late 1960s (1968 marks the first year when table wine production exceeded dessert wines) and continuing to this day, all of the ingredients coalesced in California for an "engagement with the future." The state's economy boomed, creating widespread wealth. The local population increased dramatically, making California virtually a nation unto itself. Politically, the memory of Prohibition faded. An individual California culture emerged, which valued and celebrated fine wine as a statement of civilization and refinement. All of the ingredients were present: capital, politics, and culture. California erupted with wineries: In 1966, California had 227 wineries, mostly concentrating on bulk wines. By 1989, California counted 771 wineries, most of which pursue fine wines.

California wine historians have labored mightily to establish a record of winegrowing in California. But their work is closer to archaeology than history. The telling point is the absence of tradition. The effect of California's original fine-wine ambition is as lost to us today as the Etruscans are to modern-day Tuscans. We, like them, have various remains from which we can extrapolate—and identify with—but as in post-Etruscan Tuscany, the modern culture has been built entirely from scratch. We know that others passed this way before, but the path—if discernible at all—leads nowhere.

But this lack of tradition extends beyond the trauma of Prohibition. An absence of another sort of tradition also preceded it. Unlike the fine wine regions of Europe, California never experienced what might be called "true primitivism." This phrase is deliberately chosen. With respect to wine, "true primitivism" means a fixity on the land, an anchoring to place. Nearly all of the great wine districts of Europe came into being as a result of generations of vine-tenders being anchored to their spot, unable to relocate due to economic, political, or social reasons. However unpromising their spot of earth, they had to make it work. There was no choice. If, as in Southern Italy, only grapes could grow in dry, sun-drenched, and otherwise barren spots, then grapes would be planted. If the wine is good, all the better. If not, what was the alternative?

It is this "true primitivism," this adhesion to a place, however unpromising, that accounts for the creation of wines such as Côte-Rôtie in France's Rhône Valley and Bernkastel in Germany's Mosel Valley. There, the hillsides are so steep that no farmer who had any choice in the matter would consider cultivating such sites. As it happens, they turned out to be supreme on the planet for their wine types. But that was just happenstance. It was all the local farmers had to work with, so they tried to make it work.

Yet California winegrowing never was as primitive as European. This was not necessarily for the better. If a piece of land looked the least bit unpromising for grapegrowing, the California winegrower either moved on or moved in grapes grown somewhere else. The scale of the land, and the ability to move at will, meant that almost no one chose difficult vineyard locations. And when such sites were chosen, almost invariably you could find a madman or a visionary behind the search. Anyone who has visited Chalone Vineyard perched 2,000 feet in the Gavilan Range just under the Pinnacles National Monument cannot help but be awed that this dry, impossibly remote hermitage of a vineyard was first founded in the late 1800s. Its unnamed discoverer was known to be a Frenchman, probably a Burgundian. (For that matter, he was probably a reincarnated Cistercian monk, so austere is the site.)

That said, it must also be pointed out that easily cultivated sites are not necessarily the lesser for being so. But ease of cultivation extends beyond the application of the plow. With fine wine it extends to the very applicability of the area for winegrowing at all. The European example has great wines emerging from "marginal" locales—marginal, that is, for the grape variety in question. Pinot Noir planted in the Bordeaux region of southwest France undoubtedly would thrive—as a plant. But the resulting wine just as undoubtedly would lack the character achieved farther north in the Côte d'Or. There, the reach of the grape matches perfectly the grasp of the wine. When Pinot Noir reaches farther north—such as in Champagne—the grasp is weakened. The wine is too thin, too light, too acid for greatness. In California, ease of cultivation means more than choosing between fertile valley floors and rocky hillside slopes. The absence of a "true primitivism" meant that implausible places would be explored episodically, if at all, because there was no reason to do so.

Ironically, it is only now that such a "primitivism" is emerging. The driving force is economics. As land prices increased dramatically in California since the mid-1970s, aspiring grape growers and winery owners began to look beyond the borders of the most established areas. The pattern was largely centrifugal, spinning off from the center point of Napa Valley. It was in Napa Valley, after all, that the fine-wine ambition was born anew in the late 1960s and early 1970s. Anyone newly interested in pursuing an ambition to make fine wine looked there first—and then settled. There was no need to look farther.

For example, in 1973, the French Champagne house of Moët-Hennessy (now LVMH Moët Hennessy LouisVuitton) decided to establish an outpost in Napa Valley. It purchased 900 acres of unplanted vineyard land in the Carneros district for $1,500 an acre. Subsequently, it bought an additional 800 acres, paying $4,000 an acre. But when, in 1986, Joseph E. Seagram & Sons purchased René di Rosa's already-planted Carneros vineyard called Winery Lake, it paid ten times as much: a reported $42,500 per acre of vineyard. In the decade between Moët's bold stroke and Seagram's belated one, only players with deep pockets could afford to locate there.

Also in that intervening decade, vineyard prices elsewhere in Napa Valley saw similar increases. Many aspiring winegrowers who originally looked at Napa found themselves examining other neighborhoods, namely nearby Sonoma County. And then the same escalation in land values occurred there. So the circle of investigation became wider.

At the same time, the fine-wine ambition was emerging elsewhere in the state. The ambition took hold of well-heeled professionals never previously involved with winegrowing: doctors, lawyers, aerospace engineers. They began to plant vines on land they happened to own—whether it was suitable for fine wine grapes or not. It happened in Mendocino County in the north, the Santa Cruz mountains south of San Francisco, and into Santa Barbara. What's more, corporate executives exercised similar options, using corporate money, often with no greater knowledge than the wine hobbyists. The vast—and often ill-advised—plantings in Monterey County are the most dramatic example of that.

Some of these ambitions grew. Home winemakers became professionals. Sometimes they stayed put; often they left for more promising or at least recognized vineyard locations. Land still was cheap enough and sufficiently plentiful for such fluidity. But by the mid-1980s, the opportunities for movement were severely reduced. Housing costs skyrocketed. Vineyard land became both expensive and scarce. Development costs increased dramatically, as the simple-to-cultivate sites in sought-after districts were all snapped up or were affordable only to the likes of Seagram.

For the first time since the revival of the fine-wine ambition, Californians found themselves stuck in whatever chair they were sitting when the music stopped. The California and the national wine market stagnated or contracted in the 1980s. Yet the number of wineries increased, spawned in part by the inability of grape growers to find an outlet for their grapes. In desperation they entered the processing business and hung out a winery shingle.

Some were happy; others felt thwarted. Economics fixed them to their place—and continues to do so. For the first time ever, "true primitivism" appeared in California winegrowing. And it is typically Californian in its creation. Where in Europe the forced adhesion to place occurred because of a deficit—of money, social and political freedom, or just knowledge—in California it occurred because of a surfeit: too much money, too many people, even too much ambition.

The result is a forced rethinking of what works best for one's spot. This would have occurred anyway, but the new immobility—like a hanging—clears the mind. There's nowhere to look except inward: perhaps only to a local audience; perhaps to a greater degree of specialization; perhaps to a renewed determination to find one's opportunities within one's new limits.

It cannot be said now what the outcome will be. But the likelihood is strong that the economic motivation of this new "primitivism" will lead to more specialized wineries and wine districts. It will likely lead to redefined ambitions. Not every fine wine producer will strive to make ever more expensive wines. Or even try to outdo some other producer's ballyhooed Cabernet or Chardonnay. Producers will be content to find reliable, lucrative niche markets. This, of course, is what long ago happened in Europe.

To the outside observer, it seems a promising development. The investigation of this book—to view California wine from the perspective of the land—makes evident that many relatively young districts already have found, or are on the verge of finding, true vocations of place. It now is apparent that certain grape varieties do perform particularly well in certain places. The new limitations can act to magnify this. The greater focus will lead to social and economic rewards that come from shared identity. It is far easier to sell your previously unwanted Cabernet Franc or Gewürztraminer if your place on the map gains recognition as being the place for that wine. This already is happening: sparkling wine and Pinot Noir in Carneros; Cabernet Sauvignon in Stags' Leap; and Chardonnay in Santa Maria Valley, to name but a few.

Only now is California wine approaching a sensibility of place. The fine-wine ambition has taken root. So, too, have the vines. The combination means a new steadiness of accomplishment. The poet Jack Gilbert captures it: "The marriage, not the month's rapture. Not the exception. The beauty of many days. Steady and clear. It is the normal excellence, of long accomplishment."

A CAUTIONARY WORD
ABOUT APPELLATIONS

To name a thing is to make it real.
—Albert Camus

Throughout much of this book is a recurring acronym: AVA. It stands for American Viticultural Area. Note the absence of the word "appellation," which is commonly used everywhere else where wine boundaries are defined, such as France, Italy, and Spain. Its absence is not by chance.

Much can be said about these American Viticultural Areas. Indeed, much has been said—and only rarely has it been favorable. This is not the place to get into the wrongheadedness of the AVA system. Suffice it to say that it is simple fence building. Unlike the appellation regulations of France and Italy, the American version makes no effort to regulate which grapes can be grown in which areas, how the vines must be trained, or the way the wines are made. All of this, and more, is part of the European appellation system. This is one reason why the term "appellation" has been avoided.

The notion of an American Viticultural Area was adopted in 1978. Vineyard and winery owners anywhere in the nation can apply to the former Bureau of Alcohol, Tobacco and Firearms (BATF)[1] for such a designation. The application must propose a name for the AVA and make a case for why the area deserves a separate status. The application process can cost tens of thousands of dollars, as applicants hire lawyers to draft the proposal and researchers to prove—or pretend to prove—that the area has a long and distinguished grapegrowing history.

[1] In January 2003, as a result of the creation of the U.S. Department of Homeland Security, the former Bureau of Alcohol, Tobacco, and Firearms (BATF) saw its responsibilities altered. A new bureau was established called the Alcohol and Tobacco Tax and Trade Bureau, commonly abbreviated to TTB. It now has the same functions as the former BATF.

Mostly it's hokum. The BATF went to great lengths to ensure that no one think that its approval of an AVA implies an endorsement. In fact, every BATF approval had—and still has—has a disclaimer such as this: "ATF does not wish to give the impression by approving 'Wild Horse Valley' as a viticultural area that it is approving or endorsing the quality of the wine derived from this area. ATF is approving this area as being distinct and not better than other areas." Actually, it's a good thing it says this. Wild Horse Valley AVA is a sub-appellation of Napa Valley. The BATF approved an area of 3,300 acres on the basis of just 73 acres of vineyard.

The fact is—and it is a fact—that the BATF—and now the newly-named TTB—will approve just about any area proposed as long as no one else objects. Usually there are objections, almost invariably from landowners outside of the proposed boundaries. Virtually without exception, they are always accommodated. I cannot think of any significant AVA boundary dispute in which the parties who were excluded subsequently were not invited in.

That said, a number of AVAs have merit. Whether the adopted boundaries are as rigorous as they should be is beside the point. It's too early for that. Economic reality has frog-marched the process forward, never mind whether any of the parties involved—let alone outside kibitzers such as wine writers—really know where the lines should be drawn. If the name "Napa Valley" fetches a premium on the shelf—which it does—then who's and who's out is a pocketbook issue. And lines will be drawn.

Besides, you've got to start somewhere. It is safe to say that virtually all AVAs are too big. Someday, the process will be refined. As in France and Italy, we will eventually discover which grapes do best in which districts. A *de facto*, if not legal, restriction on grape varieties will emerge. For example, the Stags Leap District in Napa Valley already is edging closer to growing only Cabernet Sauvignon and its blending cohorts. Carneros increasingly is planted only to Chardonnay and Pinot Noir. Sections of Carneros sympathetic to other varieties eventually will become appellations—excuse me, AVAs—unto themselves. This is how it has happened everywhere else.

Already, many California AVA names have fallen from use. Sometimes it has been because the one vineyard in the AVA has been abandoned. Or because wineries are reluctant to cite an obscure or unheralded name on their labels. But when the AVA has *wine meaning*, such as Howell Mountain AVA or Anderson Valley AVA, the tendency is for both producers and consumers to pursue it ever more avidly. This is because the AVA "works."

By the way, in terms of legal niceties, a wine using an AVA name on the label, such as Stags Leap District, need only be 85 percent from the AVA named. If it has a vineyard designation, such as Martha's Vineyard, it must be 95 percent from the vineyard cited. Also, take care not to be seduced by the phrase "Made and Bottled By." All that is legally required for this phrase is that the winery ferment "not less than ten percent" of the wine. In other words, ninety percent of the wine in the bottle could have been—and probably was—made by some other producer. The phrase "Vinted and Bottled By" is better yet: It's not even legal. (For that matter, *vinted* is not even a legitimate word.) Yet you see it all the time on wine labels.

All of these delicious quibbles aside, the creation of appellations, whether called American Viticultural Areas or any other term, is necessary and desirable. Moreover, the interested wine fancier is well served to pay attention to an AVA name on a label. When specific, it can be a clue to continuing wine satisfaction. This assumes that the AVA has genuine wine meaning. A surprising number do. The intent of this book is to assist in finding some of the meaningful ones.

ACKNOWLEDGMENTS

When faced with a blank page, let alone the yawning maw of a not-yet-written book, a writer feels alone. No bear cub on an ice floe could feel more stranded. Yet it's not so. No one writes alone, even though the act itself certainly is solitary. All books reflect the material help and psychological support of others. This one is no different.

I am indebted to the editor of the first edition of this book, Maria Guarnaschelli. Without her courage and confidence, none of the original *Making Sense* books would have appeared. And today, this same occurrence could not have happened without the comparable courage and confidence of Carlo DeVito, to whom I am most grateful.

I am deeply indebted for everything my good friend Brian St. Pierre has gave me then and now: encouragement, knowledge, an occasional raised eyebrow when necessary, and above all, unswerving support. Without him, writing this book would have been far more arduous.

A grateful word must be (happily) added for all the help so generously given by Vic Motto of Motto, Kryla, and Fisher.

You get the picture. A writer's acknowledgments—this writer's, anyway—give a glimpse into the shadow world of his professional life. Suffice it to say that if the following people did not inhabit—sometimes quite vocally—my shadow world, this book would look very different. Many thanks to: Sao Anash, Todd Bacon, Jean T. Barrett, Roger Boulton, Karen Brooks, Geoffrey Bruce, Barbara Edelman, Matt Elsen, Bill Failing, Tom Ferrell, the late Stephen Gilbertson, Stuart Harrison, Agustin Huneeus, Pam Hunter, Jim Laube, Robert Lescher, Bob Liner, Tom Matthews, Don Moore, John and Ann Nicholas, Kyle O'Brien, Tom Passavant, Jeff and Ellie Patterson, Sandy Rowe, Marvin Shanken, Bob and Nonie Travers, and Ed Wetschler.

Last, and never least, is my wife, Karen. I am endlessly grateful to her above all others.

THINKING
CALIFORNIA

THE MACHINE IN THE MIND

To this day many an American is breaking his life on an excessive demand for the perfect, the absolute, and the boundless in realms where it is accorded to few ... The injunction to be content with your lot and in the situation where God has placed you is not an expression of New World thinking.

—Thornton Wilder, "The American Loneliness,"
Atlantic Monthly (August 1952)

To see California through its wine alone is to miss the source of its wineworld stature. This is to say that the greatness of California winegrowing is found as much in how it *pursues* wine as in how the wines actually taste. Whether California wines are universally recognized as "superior" is mostly gamesmanship—and salesmanship. What is more important, and less disputed, is that no other winegrowing area is more influential to the fine-wine ambition everywhere.

Why should this be? How could a fine-wine ambition little more than three decades old be so influential? To be sure, California's influence has been buttressed by triumphant results in various blind tastings of its wines against those of Bordeaux or Burgundy. But these alone do not account for California's unlikely leadership role. After all, if it were only a matter of wine, no upstart winegrowing area, no matter how newly accomplished, could dislodge France or Italy from positions of preeminence. Yet both nations now follow the California lead. Italians freely acknowledge the California example as a model for their own extraordinary revitalization. The French are, perhaps, more grudging, but no less indebted. Areas new to the fine-wine ambition, such as Australia, are openly imitative.

The source of California's extraordinary influence—and its own achievements—comes from a persuasive vision: agriculture shaped by the machine.

This transforming vision began in the mid-1800s as an inevitable outgrowth of the Industrial Revolution. But nowhere was the urge to transform farm craft into machine regularity greater than in the United States. Partly this was due to the sheer size of American farms, especially in the Midwest. Partly it lent itself to a national pastime for tinkering and a fascination with machinery. As the Dutch historian B. H. Slicher Van Bath observed in *The Agrarian History of Western Europe A.D. 500–1850*:

> England and the United States were the countries that took the lead in the invention and application of new farm machinery in the eighteenth and nineteenth centuries. Western Europe followed in the nineteenth century, but only hesitantly. This was not due to conservatism, but because the typical farm of continental western Europe was little suited to increased mechanization. In most countries the farmers were tenants, not owners. Rent was still often levied in kind, in the form of share-cropping; tithes, too, had to be paid in kind. As both rent and tithes took their share of any rise in production, there was no inducement for the farmer to increase his yield at the cost of heavy investment.

Not least is the American urge to transform landscape into something more to one's liking. This last element, although the most abstract, is also the most powerful. As Thornton Wilder observed, "The injunction to be content with your lot and in the situation where God has placed you is not an expression of New World thinking." This, in itself, is a radical departure for winegrowing—more so even than for wheat, corn, or cattle.

The difference with winegrowing is that it is a long-term venture. Expensive to establish, vineyards traditionally are not easily tinkered with. Given the expense, grape growers traditionally have been unsympathetic to change. This is especially so with fine-wine vineyards, as their tradition is more than simply monetary. With fine wine, the challenge is to push grapevines to their limits: How cool or warm before it's too cool or warm? How dry before it's too dry? How extreme a soil type? All this is characterized as "stress."

Until California's fine-wine ambition, "stress" was achieved largely from naturally occurring conditions. In Europe, grapevines were planted in a non-methodical fashion along a wavelength of locations, as if tuning a radio until you lock on to the strongest signal. The "signal" is not just flavor. It also includes grape yields, disease resistance, winter hardiness, summer heat, drought resistance, and soil suitability. Hindsight makes the process seem deliberate, but much of it was haphazard. Over the centuries, the tradition congealed into articles of hard faith.

This approach was challenged when California bulk winegrowing began anew immediately upon Repeal in 1933. What became the transforming vision of California winegrowing—agriculture shaped by the machine— arrived through the agency of California's preeminent agricultural college, the University of California at Davis. Located in a small farming town about twenty miles east of Sacramento, the state capital, UC Davis expanded on the efforts of the state's first college of agriculture established in 1868 at the University of California at Berkeley. There, a viticulture and enology department was created in 1880. Only in the late 1930s did the program gradually drift from the Berkeley campus to Davis, where the wine and grape-growing program is known as the School of Viticulture and Enology.

This new vision of winegrowing was itself an outgrowth of a larger social and academic movement. Agricultural colleges everywhere were locked in a battle with farmers. Professors at agricultural colleges were dedicated to applying to agriculture the same principles of "systemization" that was the *idée fixe* of America from the 1870s to the 1920s. The idea of systemization was applied to virtually all business and social endeavors. Farming was no exception. "These systematic agriculturists . . . assumed that farming was composed of numerous discrete operations and that success was the consequence of rationally conceived and pursued methods."[2]

The shock troops of this systemization movement were agricultural colleges. They, in turn, were subsidized by those businesses with an interest in the benefits to be reaped by large-scale farming performed with mechanical reliability and predictability. As Marcus and Segal point out, "The bestowal of collegial sanction often led others to adopt the practices, which tended to standardize farm operations. Application of systematic farming techniques only sometimes increased farm profits and reduced drudgery, but its partisans

[2] Alan I. Marcus and Howard P. Segal, *Technology in America—A Brief History*, (New York: Harcourt Brace Jovanovich, 1989), p. 189

always identified themselves as progressive."[3] When bulk winegrowing returned to California's vast, flat, irrigated Central Valley, the systemization of American agriculture and the dominance of agricultural colleges was already in place. Of all the major crops in America, wine grapes was one of the last to be addressed.

For their part, agricultural college professors had a point, nowhere more so than with winegrowing. Precisely because of its ancient heritage, winegrowing practice in Europe changed grudgingly, if at all. Although it was exclusively Europeans who first established that yeasts caused fermentation (Louis Pasteur in 1859); that bacteria in the presence of oxygen caused wine to turn to vinegar (Pasteur in 1866); and that enzymes were the agency by which the fermentation was achieved (Eduard and Hans Buchner in 1897), European winegrowing practices were mostly unmoved by the revelations.

In this, America had its one advantage. Because of Prohibition, no ingrained tradition presented resistance. The UC Davis enology and viticulture professors could fashion a new "scientific" vision of how and where grapes should be grown and, even more importantly, how wine should be made. Their influence was assured not only because of the ignorance caused by the wholesale collapse of winegrowing during the thirteen years of Prohibition, but also because by then the authority of agricultural colleges was unchallenged.

The absence of a fine-wine ambition was a benefit to UC Davis. Otherwise, the pull of European tradition would have weakened the sway of the college professors. (Which is precisely what occurred in the 1980s and 1990s.) Where such as Leland Stanford looked automatically—and longingly—to Europe, those concerned with bulk wines felt no such pull. Their interest was proper farm management in order to extract the highest yields and the healthiest vines. Stress, so called, was not the issue, as the finer gradations of quality that emerge from it are of no concern to bulk wine production.

Just how basic winegrowing in California was after Prohibition is revealed by the enormous influence of the notion of heat summations or degree-days, a vision of the land propounded by UC Davis. The idea of degree-days for crops is not new. But its application to grapevines, although discussed in Europe as far back as 1872, was largely academic. By then Europe was covered in vines and mired in tradition.

[3] Ibid., p. 192

The degree-day concept is straightforward. With grapevines, growth proceeds only when the temperature achieves fifty degrees Fahrenheit. Every degree above that is counted as one degree-day. When these degree-days are totaled over the several-month span between the beginning of vine growth and the harvest of ripe grapes, the total is called temperature summation. At a glance, one can establish the coolness or warmth of a site or district.

Building on the work of Frederic T. Bioletti, the influential director of the UC Berkeley wine science program, viticulturist A. J. Winkler embarked upon a statewide investigation of temperature summations in the 1920s. Subsequently, his student and later distinguished colleague Maynard A. Amerine, in collaboration with Winkler, categorized these heat summations in brackets labeled Regions I (the coolest) through V (the hottest). To this day, California winegrowers still talk about their vineyards as being "high Region I" or "low Region II." This simple but useful scale was made more graphic, literally, by a map of the entire state showing various pools of temperature, each categorized as Region I through V. It was first published in 1944.

For the first time, vineyards could be established not by unthinking tradition or gut instinct, but by scientific methodology. It was rational; it was systematic. And it provided a basis upon which to proceed to revitalize an industry. Above all, it became the basis of an *American* vision of winegrowing: quantitative, methodical, verifiable. For bulk winegrowing, this vision was sufficient. That the university never subsequently offered a methodology of greater nuance speaks volumes: The bulk winegrowers who funded its research had no need for one.

For the fine-wine ambition, degree-days is crude. It measures only heat and that only in the aggregate. What if a site is hot in the morning but cooled rapidly by fog or winds in the afternoon? Numerically, the site may be considered warm or cool, depending upon the degree-day total for the growing season. But it tells us little about how the *grapevine* reacts to the swings in temperature. Or about sunlight intensity. Or about the effects of wind, rain, humidity, or night temperatures on the grapevine. The insight extends only to how well and regularly a grape variety is likely to ripen its grapes properly. What the ripe grape delivers in terms of the flavor shadings that distinguish fine wine from ordinary is another matter entirely.

It should be noted that vineyard plantings in California, to this day, are not entirely rational, despite the veracity of the degree-days vision, however limited. Rationality has to compete with the marketplace. With Chardonnay, the most lucrative grape variety, the competition is almost one-sided. As late as 1988 there still were 2,164 acres of Chardonnay planted in grossly too-warm Regions IV and V, according to the California Agricultural Statistics Service. More telling yet is that 10,380 acres are planted in Region III sites, which is warm for Chardonnay. The lure of Chardonnay in the marketplace clearly is too enticing to be resisted. Nevertheless, the influence of the degree-days vision is strongly felt. Three-quarters of California's Chardonnay vineyards are planted in areas classed as Region I (3,077 acres) or Region II (26,249 acres).

The surprisingly small acreage of Region I sites is revealing: What California considers cool is relative—and limited. Region I is 2,500 degree-days or fewer. Burgundy's Côte d'Or registers 2,120 degree-days, which would put it just barely above a hypothetical Region 0. (Each climate region is delineated by 500 degree-days.)

That the UC Davis scale effectively *begins* at 2,500 degree-days tells us not only how warm are many of California's traditional vineyard areas, but also the limitation of the vision that places so much emphasis on climatic zones. Precisely because grapes do not ripen regularly or easily in cool sites, to identify such sites was to legitimize them. This was not possible, as those sites can never achieve the machine regularity fundamental to scientific winegrowing.

This commitment to machine regularity is further evidenced by the vast labor of Harold P. Olmo, a UC Davis professor with a Ph.D. in genetics who for decades specialized in creating new wine grape hybrids. Nearly all of his twenty-five hybrid varieties were invented to deliver decent acidity and flavors while baking in hot Region V climates. In 1989, only two Olmo-created high-yielding hybrid varieties occupied significant acreage in the Central Valley: Ruby Cabernet (7,037 acres) and Rubired (7,030 acres). Nearly all of the others have fallen into disuse, partly because of a decline in bulk wine consumption and partly because of an embrace of traditional, "classic" varieties such as Chardonnay and Cabernet Sauvignon.

For the machine in the mind, it is a far better thing to add acidity to a "flabby" wine grown in a too-warm location—or to laboriously "design" a new grape variety—than to plant a grape variety in a place where it might not ripen fully every vintage. More than economics is at work here. Equally powerful is a determined interventionism. The offense of European winegrowing was its passivity. The machine in the mind offers a more muscular approach.

A special contempt is reserved by the machine in the mind for the influence of soil on wine. The importance of soil for fine wine has been so abundantly demonstrated *by the wines themselves* in Europe, most convincingly in France, that it would seem evident that soil plays a significant role. One need only taste a great Meursault or Chablis to be convinced. But soil, more than even climate itself, cannot easily be altered. The only practical intervention is of the most superficial sort, such as fertilizer or topsoil. (Even here, the machine in the mind is tempting. Randall Grahm of Bonny Doon Vineyard in Santa Cruz decided that Burgundy's limestone-rich soil was indispensable for growing Pinot Noir. So he "planted" the soil of his vineyard with ten tons of limestone per acre.)

Reproducible, "scientific" verification of the role of soil is unavailable: Soil is far more ambiguous than neatly quantified temperature summations. That its role cannot be pinpointed, let alone measured, wrenches the machine in the mind. The degree of discomfort, even scorn, is displayed by Maynard A. Amerine and Philip M. Wagner in their chapter, "The Vine and Its Environments," in *The University of California/Sotheby Book of California Wine* (1984):

> Many popular commentators and almost all vineyard owners attribute some magical property to vineyard soils. As indicated in the preceding sections, there are differences between regions and localized areas (exposure, valley floor versus hillsides, and so forth). Some of these differences are due to variations in temperature, some perhaps also to moisture (and thus related to soil temperature), soil microorganisms, and vineyard and ecological practices. How many of the differences are due purely to soil factors has not, to our satisfaction, been scientifically determined.

Note the use of the word "magical," a derisive term in scientific circles if ever there was one. The premise is clear: Neither people who taste wine ("popular commentators"), nor people who grow grapes and make wine ("vineyard owners"), can know anything about what informs a wine with a particular character. The reason is not because they fail to be properly disinterested parties (which cannot always be said for university researchers either), but because their conclusions are not couched in scientific terms.

"Scientific" in this instance is peculiarly narrow. It is not just a matter of proper methodology, by which all scientific assumptions must be explored. Instead it is narrow in its insistence upon a vocabulary largely mathematical in voice and content. The machine in the mind proceeds from a definition of science such as that offered by the behavioral psychologist Clark L. Hull in *Principles of Behavior* (1943): "All deductions [should] take place according to the explicitly formulated rules stating the functional relationships of A to X and of X to B. This latter is the essence of the scientifically objective."

Such a purely mathematical vision of "objectivity" can be seen in *Wines: Their Sensory Evaluation* (1976), by Maynard A. Amerine and Edward B. Roessler, two former UC Davis professors, and intended for a popular readership. Of the book's 204 pages of text, nearly half is devoted to statistical procedures. The authors make no apology. On the contrary, in the Preface they state forthrightly, "We recommend these procedures to both amateurs and professionals." Their posture is this:

> We are certain . . . that an understanding of such procedures will instill a healthy skepticism about the claims of quality differences that we find in the popular literature, and about the price tags that we find on some wines. Our basic premise is that wine consumers and professional enologists alike will enjoy their wines more and will make more intelligent decisions about wine quality and wine value if they understand how and why they make such decisions and how to determine, when necessary, the statistical significance of those decisions.

That wine drinkers will "enjoy their wines more" when they examine the "statistical significance" of their judgement boggles the mind—unless there's a machine in it.

The unseen hand of industry funding also played a role in the rejection of soil as a factor in wine quality. Here again, the bulk winegrowing that constituted nearly all of California wine—and certainly virtually all of its prof-itability—until the 1970s had no use for painstaking soil research. If you're growing ten tons to the acre of Thompson Seedless or Chenin Blanc grapes in a Region V climate—or making bulk wines in Napa and Sonoma as was commonplace—the niceties of soil distinctions are of little use.

Now, for the first time, the university has ascribed some importance to soil. Not coincidentally, the research was performed under the auspices of a grant from winegrowers, only this time it was the fine-wine ambition wine-growers of the Stags Leap District in Napa Valley. They wanted evidence of the distinction of their area to establish a federally administered legal bound-ary known as an American Viticultural Area. Funded by a grant, Deborah Elliot-Fisk, an associate professor of geography at UC Davis, analyzed the soils of twenty vineyards in the proposed district. The result: "The Stags Leap District is the first viticultural area in the United States to be so approved based on the distinctiveness of its soils," she reported.

To ascribe the machine in the mind solely to the exertions of agriculture college professors would be misleading. They, too, drew inspiration from their place, just as the winegrowers themselves did. The "campus" of California itself cannot be ignored. Irrigation is a choice example. Traditionally—which is to say, from the European experience—vineyards were planted wherever vines stood a chance of growing. Drought-resistant, they take well to dry cli-mates such as are found in southern France, Spain, Greece, and southern Italy. Grapevines do need some water, though, especially at certain moments in the growing season. The trick is the right amount of water at the right time. Among the many fine calibrations that result in fine wine, only climate is more influential.

Controlling water to create fine wine was nonexistent in traditional winegrowing, except on the smallest possible scale, such as a grower digging a culvert to divert localized runoff. Only one notable exception to the old tradition exists: Bordeaux's Médoc region. Alone among the acknowledged great wine districts of Europe, the Médoc has a machine in the land. Unlike California, the machine is used not to irrigate, but to drain.

The Médoc is that section of Bordeaux that today houses nearly all of the famous châteaux whose wines fetch such remarkable prices. It is a sixty-mile-long, triangular peninsula bounded on the west by the Atlantic Ocean and on the east by the Gironde estuary, with little more than sixty low-lying miles at its widest point.

The reputation of the famous Médoc châteaux is such that it might surprise casual onlookers to discover that these properties once were waterlogged marshes. The ancient fame of Bordeaux originally rested with the areas across the Gironde: Côtes de Blaye, Côtes de Bourg, and, especially, Saint-Émilion. For centuries, winegrowers in these districts gazed across the water at the Médoc viewing worthless land. That what they saw would someday be proclaimed the source of the world's greatest red wines would have struck them as preposterous.

But in the late 1600s, Dutch civil engineers—at the request of the *parlementaires*, a local aristocracy of land owners and lawyers of the powerful Bordeaux law court called the *Parlement*—drained the swampy Médoc marshes. Soon afterward, it was discovered that vines planted in sites close to the gravelly banks of the Gironde created unusually good wines, in large part thanks to effective drainage.

They also discovered that drainage was not a one-time exercise. It required continuous assistance. Bordeaux is a rainy place, with storms sweeping in from the Atlantic. The Médoc is low-lying. Elaborate systems of tile drains were installed in the vineyards—mostly in the 1800s—carrying off the excess water into nearby streams or canals that drain into the Gironde. Today, nearly all of the great and not-so-great Médoc chateaux maintain extensive subterranean drainage works, using large plastic pipes.

The drainage of the Médoc and, especially, the installation of vineyard drainage systems, was the first instance of the machine in the mind applied to the fine-wine ambition. It was the first instance of the fine-wine ambition being applied to a site implausible without the machine in the mind. It was the first instance of a large-scale fine wine area where success requires continuous, albeit passive, machine assistance. This assistance is so sub rosa—in every sense—that it goes unnoticed by outsiders, like a heart pacemaker. Still, it was the earliest demonstration of the possibilities of the machine in the mind.

Irrigation, on the other hand, is active. It is so extensive in California that, were it eliminated, many of the state's vineyards would either disappear altogether or be vastly reduced in scale and production. In this, California agriculture shares the same plight as California urbanism: Almost everyone is dependent upon vast quantities of water being sluiced from elsewhere. With vines, the water comes either from the state's elaborate network of aqueducts or from deep wells drilled on the property tapping an aquifer.

Whole winegrowing regions in California would not exist were it not for irrigation: 28,000 acres in Monterey County; 9,400 acres in Santa Barbara County; 7,000 acres in San Luis Obispo County; and most dramatic of all, 430,000 acres of wine grapes in the vast Central Valley (San Joaquin, Stanislaus, Merced, Madera, Fresno, Tulare, and Kern counties). Many, if not most, of the vineyards in Napa and Sonoma counties would be curtailed in size or yield without irrigation.

Of course, this is not about to happen, despite the repeated droughts that California suffers. Moreover, improved irrigation systems that economize on water by use of "drip emitters" (originally developed in Israel) are replacing more wasteful overhead sprinklers. This is occurring most in Napa and Sonoma, as well as in Santa Barbara and Monterey counties, where the reward is sufficient to justify the expense of such systems. Drip irrigation is a matter of plastic tubes threaded through the vines, on or just above the ground, with drip emitters stationed at each vine. Nutrients also can be precisely metered to the vines, along with the water.

First introduced in California in the early 1970s, drip irrigation expanded the commercial frontier of fine wine. Vineyard areas without the massive water supply required for overhead sprinkler irrigation, or on hillside sites where overhead sprinklers are impractical, suddenly became potentially profitable. Grape yields could be commercially viable in previously marginal locations. Above all, a machine regularity of growth and harvest could be assured.

It was no coincidence that, in the 1880s, so many vineyards and wineries emerged along the Russian River in Sonoma County, virtually lining its banks. The plenitude of water is one reason so many pre-Prohibition wineries and vineyards, such as Italian Swiss Colony, Korbel, Simi, Geyser Peak, Foppiano, and Martini & Prati, were able to survive: They could achieve yields competitive with the big Central Valley growers. Until the 1970s, all of these wineries, as well as others that appeared immediately after Repeal, such as Cambiaso (now Domaine St. George) and Pedroncelli, engaged in bulk winegrowing. In a brutal price-oriented bulk market, yields are everything—

and abundant water was the key, thanks to the high water table and easy irrigation afforded by the Russian River.

However, fine wine makes irrigation trickier. The grower seeks a more precise calibration—stress, again. Too little water, and you have immature or dehydrated grapes. Worse, there's little or no development of the many compounds that create flavor and aroma. The same absence of character results from too much water: Grapes are bloated and the vine happily devotes its energy to foliage rather than fruit. Not only is water quantity a concern, but equally critical is *when* the water is applied.

For example, in the 1970s, Monterey County winegrowers discovered to their dismay that the extreme vegetalness of their Cabernet Sauvignon—evidenced by an offensively intense odor of bell pepper—was in part due to applying water to the vines too late in the growing season. When they eased off, so, too, did the awful bell pepper smell. Now, the general view everywhere is that vines should be irrigated in the winter and spring. And like addicts, they should be weaned from their supply starting in July, the better to create the desired stress deemed essential for the development of character.

Some of California's fine-wine ambition vineyards are so dependent upon irrigation that they are one step removed from hydroponics. This suggestion of vines being rooted in a soilless medium (hydroponics) is abetted by the fact that the soils in parts of Monterey County and in the Santa Maria Valley of Santa Barbara County are extremely sandy. Drainage is fast and absolute. Far from being a drawback, it adds to the degree of control. The vineyard manager can predict almost exactly how much water is needed; how long it will remain in the soil and thus within reach of the vine; and when more water will need to be applied.

Once a seat-of-the-pants procedure, irrigation technique today is guided by such devices as tensiometers and neutron probes (both measure soil moisture); autopyrometers (measures leaf moisture); infrared thermometers (measures leaf temperature); and computer models that mathematically calculate such variables as wind, light, and grapevine leaf canopy to predict future water needs.

The hip-bone-connected-to-the-leg-bone quality of interventionism is demonstrated by a heightened degree of interest in trellising techniques and vine spacing formulas. The grapevine has always been subject to various pruning and training techniques. Left to its own devices it will either sprawl over the ground or clamber, tendril by tendril, up the nearest available tree or shrub.

Domesticating the grapevine, like training a house dog to fetch the newspaper, is a patient, methodical exercise. Three elements are involved: spacing, trellising, and pruning. Each affects growth, vigor, yield, and grape quality. How you space, trellis, and prune depends upon what you seek to achieve. Not least, it depends upon how much money you can command for the grapes.

Not until the 1980s did the discussion of vine spacing assume major philosophical proportions. The needs of bulk winegrowing determined the scope of the discussion, such as it was. Various pruning techniques had by then evolved. But spacing and trellising were largely standardized, the prototype having long ago been shaped on the template of Central Valley grape-growing.

Until the 1980s, virtually all California vineyards, whether in Napa, Sonoma, or San Joaquin, had eight-by-twelve spacing: eight feet between vines and twelve feet between rows. This works out to 454 vines per acre. It was promulgated as ideal by Professor A. J. Winkler of UC Davis and indeed it was ideal—for the bulk winegrowing that was California wine everywhere in the 1940s, 1950s, and 1960s. Its sensibility was prosaic: The row spacing was recommended, in large part, because growers needed twelve feet between rows to get their tractors through the vines. In the 1970s it was advised for machine harvesting.

The eight-foot distance between each vine also was sensible. Vines cost money; every vine has to be pruned individually; more vines per acre means significantly higher costs. Also, land was cheap. There was plenty of room to spread out. Moreover, until the late 1960s, the single most widely planted wine grape, so called, actually was Thompson Seedless. The extent of its planting was such that it was singularly influential. A neutral white grape, Thompson Seedless was ideal for Central Valley growers because if the grapes couldn't be sold for the sweet bulk wines then popular, they could be dried and sold profitably as raisins. Close spacing for Thompson Seedless is like a logger asking advice from a bonsai master.

When the fine-wine ambition took hold, spacing and trellising practices came under new scrutiny. With grape prices rising, the overriding requirement of high yields no longer drove the market. Concerns about quality appeared. This, in turn, gave fine-wine growers pause: Perhaps the traditional

Bordeaux and Burgundy spacing offered something by way of quality gradations lacking in California's big-as-all-outdoors approach?

In both Burgundy and Bordeaux, the vines are dramatically more closely
bunched. In Bordeaux the spacing is often one meter by two meters (three
feet between vines; six feet between rows). This works out to 2,023 vines per
acre. In Burgundy (and frequently in Bordeaux, too) the spacing is even
closer: one meter by one meter, resulting in 4,046 vines per acre. The thinking is that vine vigor can be reduced by crowding (stress again). The idea is
that although the yield per acre is unchanged, the few clusters per vine
means that greater character and nuance can be acquired. Of course, this is
not quantifiable.

What is quantifiable is the cost. At today's prices, a grafted cutting with
no established roots runs about $2.00 per vine. An eight-by-twelve-foot spac-
ing requires an outlay of roughly $1,135 in vines. A meter-by-meter density
costs nearly nine times as much: $10,115 an acre. Then you have to add the
cost of more trellising and significantly increased labor for pruning and harvesting. All that for a mere *hope* of improved quality. No wonder UC Davis
professors look upon close spacing like high school monitors clucking over
close dancing—nothing good can come of it. Nevertheless, producers such as
Robert Mondavi, Simi, and Sterling, among many others, are determined to
try—looking east to Europe rather than next door to Davis.

But this apparent embrace of old methods has a new twist: radical trellising devices. Grapevines are like any other climbing plant, such as roses—
you've got to put the shoots somewhere. With grapevine canes, as they're
called, the answer is a trellis. A worker ties individual canes to wires strung
between posts. The grapevine leafs out, clusters form, and in the fall, pickers
or harvesting machines make their way along the rows, relieving the
grapevines of their fruit. The vine can be shaped to grow pretty much however the vineyard owner desires. Not surprisingly, theories abound as to the
ideal trellising system.

Trellising may seem to be of little account to the wine drinker, but it is
part of the machine in the mind. The tie-in involves irrigation. Precisely
because the grower can control the water given to the vine, its growth is now
dramatically more under control than it might be otherwise. This, in turn,
offers the grower the opportunity to further alter the vine's production, much

in the same way that a chicken breeder can affect the growth or laying patterns of the bird by keeping it closely cooped, controlling light and feed. California winegrowing still is far from such a "greenhouse" environment, but near-ubiquitous irrigation has afforded California growers more control than is allowed winegrowers almost anywhere else in the world. Keep in mind that in French vineyards entitled to appellation designations—the finest wines—are forbidden to use irrigation.

As a result, there is a rethinking of trellising techniques. The buzzword of the moment is "canopy management." This is a fancy way of talking about leaf growth. The problem is vigor. A vigorous grapevine prefers to spend its energy producing more foliage than fruit. The art of pruning and trellising is to redirect this vigor toward fruitfulness. With water now available as needed, the vines are vigorous, especially in rich, deep soils such as the Napa Valley floor or in areas of strong light intensity, such as Monterey. Before irrigation, the site itself provided a built-in equilibrium. It was sites of near-perfect equilibrium, such as the best parts of Rutherford and Oakville in Napa Valley, that were deemed superior. They received enough natural rainfall and the soil drained—or retained—only as much water as was necessary for restrained growth. A harmony of vine and site emerged.

Trellising determines how much leaf canopy is created and where it will grow. This, in turn, affects how much sunlight plays upon the grape clusters. If desired, a vine can be trellised in such a way as to produce more clusters per vine, in other words, a higher yield. At present, the fine-wine ambition of some California winegrowers is to achieve higher yields through "canopy management" aided, in some cases, by radical new trellising designs. Many of these trellising designs have been formulated elsewhere, notably Switzerland, Australia, and New Zealand. But the degree of control afforded by irrigation amplifies the possibilities.

Irrigation plays a role in another form of vineyard control: frost protection. One of the banes of winegrowing everywhere is the possibility of a spring frost just as the vines are at their most tender: while budding or, later in the spring, flowering. A frost while budding can result in a damaged vine; if it occurs during flowering the crop could be severely reduced or lost altogether. Each grape flower, once pollinated (called "set") creates a single berry. Grapes come in clusters only because the flowers form in those same clusters.

The original frost control devices are known as smudge pots: oil-burning devices set among the vines that exude dense black smoke. The idea is that these smudge pots can raise the vineyard temperature. Their efficacy is limited, at best. Somewhat more useful are windmills, airplane-size propellers mounted on towers set in the vineyards. The idea is that cold air settling on a valley floor can be mixed with warmer air in a layer thirty to sixty feet above it. Windmills are a common site in Napa Valley, the narrow shape of which invites such "inversions." They are considered only marginally useful, such as when the cold air layer is not especially frigid.

The most effective frost protection involves the availability of irrigation. Known as "aspersion," it is simply a matter of spraying the vines with water, creating a thin cloak of ice on the vines. This "hair-of-the-dog" approach to frost protection is elegantly effective. In the process of freezing, water radiates heat, thus protecting the buds. The ice also offers some degree of insulation if the cold weather persists.

This technique, by the way, was originally devised in the 1920s by Washington State cranberry growers. It is by no means a foolproof system (wind can play havoc with it), but it is perhaps the single most effective frost protection available. Aspersion is now widely used in many California vineyards.

The machine in the mind is perhaps most dramatic with the practice of "grafting over." Traditionally, once a vineyard was planted, there was no changing it, short of uprooting the vines. Because of the expense of preparing the soil, buying the cuttings, planting them, nurturing them, and then waiting three or four years to see the first crop, a vineyard was—if not forever—then something good for your professional lifetime. Short of catastrophic vineyard diseases or infestations such as phylloxera, any changes would be the concern of your children.

In the late 1970s, a technique known as "field grafting" was perfected. A grape variety is determined not by its rootstock, but by its budwood. Pears of all varieties are grafted onto quince rootstocks; roses of every hue are attached to briar roots. Field grafting allows a grower to use an existing vine, already long since rooted and bearing, to change its stripes. A fifteen-year-old Cabernet vine can, in just two years, become a fully bearing Chardonnay vine. The winegrower need no longer be patient and forebearing. Almost by waving a magic wand (actually it's first a chainsaw and then a surgically sharp knife) an existing vineyard can be transformed literally overnight.

The technique of field grafting is a revolutionary development. Grafting grapevines is nothing new. But previously, successful grafts could only be performed with brand-new vines *before* they were planted in the vineyard. This is known as "bench grafting." It still is performed for nearly all new grapevines before they are planted in a vineyard.

The trickiness in grafting, whether on a workbench or in the field, lies in matching up the microscopically thin cambium layer in whatever rootstock you're using with whatever "budwood" you chose. Like tunnelers burrowing from opposite directions, the cambium layers of both parts must meet precisely if the graft is to succeed. Joining the microscopically thin cambium layers of both rootstock and budwood is essential, as this layer of cells just below the bark serves as the supplier of new growth for both the wood of the vine as well as the tissues that transport the nutrients up and down the plant. If they fail to marry, the vine will die.

Previously, this was an exacting procedure best performed in greenhouses with young rootstock and budwood. But in the late 1970s, a new grafting technique was perfected called T-budding, which allowed new budwood to be joined to a mature, already planted vine. The success rate varies with the skill of the worker, as well as the timing of the grafting, but successful "takes" of up to 95 percent are now common.

The machine in the mind implications of field grafting are significant. Historically, winegrowing was a craft of almost inhuman patience, the grower slowly, arduously discovering which varieties work best in which sites. The decades-long span of time insured that the insights would be enduring and abundantly proved. The vineyard was beyond the reach of fashion, in the same way that a federal judge is appointed for life. The grower had no choice, short of impeachment by uprooting, but to learn to make the vines work for the site.

California vineyards now are ephemeral. A vineyard that once issued unprofitable Gewürztraminer now spurts cash-flow Chardonnay. Whether the Gewürztraminer was any good was beside the point; it just didn't pay. European growers, in comparison, cannot avail themselves of this "off with their heads" approach. They are constrained by wine regulations that insist on adherence to certain grape varieties in certain districts, at least those that have a tradition of fine wine. Now, for the first time, vineyards sway with fashion like football fans in a choreographed "wave."

Yet another element contributes to the machine in the mind: California's longstanding division between grape-growing and winemaking. Traditionally, wines were made on the spot where the grapes were grown. At most, grapes were hauled by horse-drawn cart to a nearby village. The fragility of ripe grapes coupled with poor or nonexistent roads and slow modes of transport made this a necessity. In the Médoc, for example, wines were "finished" in the vast warehouses along the waterfront in downtown Bordeaux, called the Quai des Chartrons. But the winemaking itself occurred on the estates. Even the twenty or thirty miles from some of the châteaux to Bordeaux was prohibitively distant. A separation between grape-growing and winemaking was unimaginable.

Although prior to Prohibition many vineyards contained at least rudimentary wineries on-site, the pattern of shipping large quantities of wine— and later, grapes—over long distances became characteristic of California winegrowing. In 1902, according to Thomas Pinney's *A History of Wine in America*, the awe-inspiring California Wine Association, a consortium of wine merchants, owned more than fifty wineries that together accounted for two-thirds of all of California's wine production. Its vineyards and wineries stretched as far south as Cucamonga in San Bernadino County and as far north as Yolo County. Yet all of the thirty million gallons of wine annually produced by this vast enterprise eventually was funneled to a central cellar in San Francisco to be fashioned into a single, brand-named wine called Calwa.

Since Repeal, however, grape-growing in California has been a separate pursuit from winemaking. With the reconstruction of the industry after Prohibition, the segregation of grape-growing and winemaking accelerated. Two causes are contributory. One is truck transport. Before paved roads became common, the possibility of shipping grapes, rather than wines, was limited. Speed is essential, as is pinpoint delivery. Water transport and railroads simply are too slow for all but the toughest, most thick-skinned grape varieties. This is one reason why Alicante-Bouschet and Zinfandel, especially tough grapes, were the varieties of choice for home winemakers in the East during the Prohibition years. Boxcars of grapes were shipped by train from California, arriving in Chicago and New York a week or more later with relatively little damage.

Paved roads and powerful trucks allowed a centralization of winemaking facilities. Where before it was a matter of blending already-made wines, such as at the California Wine Association's ten-million gallon facility called Winehaven on the shoreline of San Francisco Bay, the new facilities performed the complete winemaking function, from grapes to bottling.

Today, shipping grapes over long distances is taken for granted. A fine-wine ambition winery such as Ridge Vineyards, reachable only by traversing a winding mountain road high above Cupertino in the Santa Cruz Mountains, thinks nothing of reaching to a half-dozen different vineyard sites, some of them hundreds of miles from the winery. Modern trucking makes it feasible, along with such technological niceties as blanketing the grapes with an inert gas such as nitrogen as a prophylactic against oxidation while in transport.

The other contributing cause was the loss of the original fine-wine ambition. With California relegated to bulk wine production from 1933 to the 1960s, the sense of authorship essential to fine wine was absent. The only market for grapes was not for finished wine of a particular character, but for grapes of a specified (high) sugar content and general soundness. Wineries saw grapes from a Shakespearean premise: "Ripeness is all." Until very recently, a grape grower's efforts weren't really related to wine, except in a kissing-cousin sort of way. Well into the 1970s, growers still had their crops assessed simply by degrees Brix, a measurement of sugar content. Only later did wineries employ more nuanced evaluation, such as a greater reliance on pH, total acidity, and even just tasting the grapes.

The absence of the fine-wine ambition—and a market that would encourage its flowering—amplified this separation between vineyard and winery. California wine language reflects this. California winegrowers at all levels of quality still talk about tons (of grapes) to the acre. European growers, in comparison, talk about hectoliters (of wine) per hectare. They see their vineyards as producing wine rather than grapes. The difference in vision is telling. Only now do winemakers in California talk about grapes and wines as inseparable. Before the 1990s, it was still the exception rather than the rule. Happily, a more "European" vision has taken hold.

This was originally reinforced by university training. Students at the UC Davis Department of Viticulture and Enology were previously required to choose between the two subjects, as if grape-growing somehow is separate from winemaking. This, too, has changed. Today, the university recognizes that the division between the two fields was not only artificial but pernicious. Coursework and departmental requirements have changed significantly to reflect this. (The original reasoning was that the UC Davis program was meant to teach science and its methodologies, rather than actually train potential winegrowers in their craft. Different scientific disciplines apply to grape-growing and winemaking.)

The machine in the mind presupposes a certain mastery. Its interventionism makes this irresistible. This is more than just a matter of trucks or grafting or drip irrigation. All of these, and many more, such as mechanical harvesters, are tools. In themselves they are admirable, even desirable. But how they are used can alter one's vision of the land and the relationship to it. For centuries, the winegrower was subservient to site. The received message of the land was just that—received, rather than imposed.

The machine in the mind is more assertive. It lends itself most readily to the achievement of predictability and reliability. It can corral unruly influences in the vineyard and winery to achieve a brand (and bland) uniformity. The greater the degree of financial investment, the stronger will be the push in that direction.

Whether one applauds this is beside the point. It is an inevitable twentieth-century—and now, twenty-first-century—development. California simply helped make it more appealing, as well as showed its potential. No group of winegrowers anywhere could have pursued it more openly, adventurously, even innocently than in California. In fact, it was this American openness—nowhere more practiced than in California—that helped propel its influence. That, coupled with a fine-wine ambition as fierce and determined as anybody's, along with huge economic resources, is what makes California so influential.

Ultimately, the influence is because the machine in the mind is applied to fine wine. It's easy enough to see its applicability to bulk winegrowing. But to apply its leverage to the delicate calibrations of fine wine is something else again. This, perhaps, is the innocence—in the best sense of the word—that no ancient fine-wine culture could bring itself to. The burden of valid traditions would prevent it—or at least strongly inhibit it.

Also, the economic persuasiveness cannot be ignored. That fine wine could be created on a scale never before accomplished in Europe has made the machine in the mind irresistible to both wine fanciers and corporations seeking new opportunities. Not least, it helps answer the profound cultural need of our time, to put our signature on our achievements.

Still, the machine in the mind has reached a turning point. It now must grapple with a more subtle challenge. The challenge today can be summed up in one word: ambiguity. As it comes closer to the European aesthetic standards of "fineness," the machine in the mind must wrestle with the ambiguity that underlies the finest wines. California's ambition is heading that way. This is why, for the first time, the supremely ambiguous French notion of *terroir* is being used by many California winegrowers. This is why the ambiguous matter of soil and subsoil is so much more investigated now than before. This is why, increasingly, so many winemaking subtleties, such as using wild yeasts, are being explored. The propulsion of the machine in the mind has slowed. The fog of ambiguity makes it a less penetrating methodology, at least until a few verities within each ambiguity can be confirmed. Then it will again pick up speed.

For the first time since the original fine-wine ambition of the 1880s, California winegrowers are passionately probing the old European fine-wine traditions. This began first with winemaking technique, such as leaving young Chardonnay on its sediment in small oak barrels. This ancient Burgundian practice flies in the face of the machine in the mind teachings of UC Davis, whose winemaking professors opposed such "dirty" practices. Indeed, it does leave open the possibility of microbial infection. The winemaker must exercise extreme care—and personal attention. This, in turn, does not lend itself easily to the pantograph approach.

California's determination to create ever-finer wines will continue to power its influence.

No doubt, someone will figure out a way to monitor hundreds of barrels at a time of vulnerable Chardonnay wines on their lees. Maybe it will involve sensors inserted into each barrel tied to a computer, like an intensive care patient with electrodes taped to his chest. The influence of the machine in the mind is that this sort of accommodation is plausible. The willingness to accept that an old practice still is worthwhile shows the peculiarly Californian flavor that makes its example so appealing.

Above all, California offers a genuinely new vision of wine. The old European aesthetic standards for fine-wine will likely continue. The European insight is acknowledged by all. But how these insights are achieved, how one arrives at the fine-wine pinnacle, that now is California's prerogative.

Whatever happens, California has permanently altered how fine wine is pursued. Its winegrowers are happily "breaking their lives" (and sometimes their bank accounts) pursuing "the perfect, the absolute, and the boundless in realms where it is accorded to few." That it is worth doing, indeed that it can be done, is what makes modern-day California so significant in the millennia-old history of winegrowing.

CALIFORNIA'S COMING OF AGE— THE NEW MENTALITY OF NUANCE

He could not always see, could not always hear. He was not what he
made his mind up to be. A man was the sum of his limits; freedom only
made him see how much so. America was no America.

       —Gish Jen, *Typical American*

As chronicled in the preceding chapter, "The Machine in the Mind," the underpinning of California winegrowing is a deep-rooted American belief that we can *act*. Not for us is the seeming passivity of European wine-growing, with its patient acceptance of things as they are given to you. The real motto of America is not "E Pluribus Unum" (out of many, one) but rather, "Accept No Limits."

This is surely one of the qualities that make America great. After all, "accept no limits" powered California wine from banal bulk production to superb fine wines in a shorter span than any nation at any time in history.

Nevertheless, starting in the 1990s, limitations began to be felt. Everybody had small, new French oak barrels and knew how to use them. Everybody had computer-controlled presses. Everybody had comparable wine-science edu-cations. The winemaking playing field was almost level—indeed, not just in California, but around the world.

The distinction between winemaking and wine itself is comparable to the difference between talking about the mechanics of writing and actually writ-ing something good. A glance at writers' magazines reveals the distinction. You'll find such articles as "Hearing Your Writer's Voice;" "Nonfiction That Touches Readers Right Where They Live;" and "How To Create Damn Good Characters." (I did not invent these. All three have appeared in *Writer's Yearbook*, published by *Writer's Digest* magazine.)

I use this analogy of writing because, until recently, the discussion of wine in California was couched in similar terms. All you had to do to create "damn good character" in Chardonnay was choose the right blend of French oak barrels, employ lees contact and obtain the right clone. Never mind that neither writer nor winemaker can create damn good characters unless it's already in them. With the writer, it's in the mind; with the winemaker, it's in the site.

However, a "machine in the mind" mentality pursued character through technique alone. The idea is that you can "hear your writer's voice" by sheer know-how. Or, more to the point, that great wines are *made*—much in the same way that if you construct your sentences like James Joyce, you too will be a great writer.

Joe Heitz didn't first look for his "winemaker's voice" and then make Martha's Vineyard Cabernet. He just made it—and then discovered what emerged only shortly before the rest of us. The same is true for Randy Dunn on Howell Mountain, and many others whose wines have "damn good characters." The aspiring winemaker (or questing wine critic) turns to these fellows and asks, "How'd you do it?" The honest ones shrug. The kind ones offer a few tips, as a gesture of encouragement. The self-deluding (or outright liars) lay out all sorts of methodologies and techniques, pretending that they—rather than the site—were responsible.

The machine in the mind belief in technique has deceived enology school students into thinking that they know *wine* because they know how to "make" it. (The analogy also holds true for students in creative writing programs.) Both groups emerge, degrees in hand, confident in their grasp of their subjects.

The fledging winemakers do know how to *make* wine, just as the newly credentialed graduate of a creative writing program knows how to type, craft a grammatical sentence and write "nonfiction that touches readers right where they live." Command of such things is not unimportant. But anyone who has tried to write even a simple letter knows that technique is an empty vessel.

Such matters are raised not to be censorious. Post-Prohibition wine had to start somewhere. You do have to know how to write a clear, grammatical sentence if you intend to say anything comprehensible to others. The professors at UC Davis were clear-eyed in their assessment of California's needs at the time.

But today, the need goes way beyond technique. The "machine in the mind" mentality had crippled the pursuit of quality in California wines. It defined "quality" far too narrowly, much in the same way that a successful term paper is a different accomplishment than a successful novel. One is easily graded by conforming to certain norms; the other is successful precisely because it breaks norms.

The exhilaration of the 1970s and 1980s—all those dramatic, impressive, attention-getting, "the-dog-can-talk!" achievements—were over. California's best wines were acknowledged as truly fine. But *now* how could they get better?

"Accept no limits" is a powerful motivating force. California's fine-wine ambition winegrowers were stalled in their drive toward perfectibility. So they changed their own culture—not, in this observer's opinion, out of conviction but out of necessity. They knew that the next level wasn't going to be either easy or quick. And that it was going to be a matter of nuance, which meant one thing: the vineyard.

For decades everyone in California paid lip service to the truism "wine is made in the vineyard." But winemaking was a lot more fun. You could intervene. You could make things happen. With the swoop of a signature on a check, you could transform a winery almost overnight. Winemaking—with all its tools and gizmos—is inherently technological, which suits Americans just fine. And it offers near-instant gratification, which suits Californians especially well.

Vineyards, on the other hand, are inherently slow-paced. Vines take three years just to bear fruit and fifteen to twenty years to arrive at full maturity with deep roots and characterful fruit. What's more, the results are incremental, taking years, even decades, to become fully apparent. No matter how rich you are, or how impatient, vines cannot be rushed.

Not least, vineyards have a separate, living existence. Ask any vineyard owner and he or she will tell you that their vineyard is its own life form. You can't "make" La Tâche or Hermitage. You plant your vines and hope that, by sheer good fortune, the confluence of the soil *in that one spot* with the microclimate *in that one spot* results in something wonderful. And if it isn't, the truth is that there's not a helluva lot you can do about it. You can't change the soil, after all. Nor can you modify the microclimate. The definition of "quality" only now is being revised. For the first time ever, winegrowers are acknowledging the importance—not the impotence—of soil.

That said, a grower's relationship to his or her vineyard is far from passive. The grower chooses which varieties are planted. Vineyards that seemingly had no distinction with one variety can, like a drab brown rock under a black light, come alive when planted to a different grape variety. This is precisely what happened in certain parts of Sonoma County's Russian River Valley when Pinot Noir began to be more widely planted.

Then, deciding how the vines are spaced—between rows and between vines—can make a difference. Then there are questions about rootstocks (vigorous or devigorating). Not least are decisions about how much and when to irrigate—or whether to irrigate at all.

Equally influential is how you train your vines. You can choose from numerous trellising methods. That, in turn, affects your intended yield—how many clusters per vine you're seeking.

Yield is really where you make your money. But no one disputes that for each grape variety (and each site, too) there's a critical "tipping point" between too high a yield for real quality and too low a yield for profitability.

California's new mentality of nuance was jump-started in the late 1980s with the broad-scale invasion of phylloxera. A new mutation of this root louse infested many California vineyards (although not all, as Monterey and Santa Barbara counties are still largely phylloxera-free). Even though most vineyards were little more than twenty years old, if that, growers had no choice. They *had* to replant. Phylloxera was killing their vines.

But to see phylloxera as the sole instigator of the new mentality of nuance does not give sufficient credit to California's restless fine-wine ambition. Phylloxera only accelerated the process.

What's happening now in California—and will continue for decades to come—is an expensive, almost obsessive, focus on refining fruit. Already, you can taste the difference. More advances will appear as the new vines mature and further refinements suggest themselves.

The Transformation of the Vineyards

When you visit California wineries today, especially the smaller ones where your tour is more personal, you will hear all sorts of vineyard details. Most of these are esoteric, at least to those of us who don't own vineyards. But the reason we hear these details, especially now, is because the producer really is trying to explain why his or her wines are better.

The Nuance of Rootstocks

If it weren't for phylloxera, we wouldn't be hearing about rootstocks at all. Prior to the inadvertent export of the phylloxera root louse from the southern United States to Europe in 1863 (some native American vines were exported to an English nursery with soil clinging to the roots) every grapevine in Europe grew on its own roots. These vines are all of the *Vitis vinifera* species; the native American vines are wholly different, such as *Vitis rupestris* and *Vitis riparia*, among others. They had developed a natural resistance to the root louse. The European grapevines had none.

The consequences of the infestation of phylloxera in Europe were catastrophic. Over decades nearly every grapevine died, except those growing on very sandy or extremely stony soil, which the root louse finds inhospitable.

Winegrowers were desperate beyond description. They tried everything: flooding the vineyards, fumigation, and sprays of every sort. Nothing worked. The last resort was grafting roots of the phylloxera-resistant native American grapevines onto their *Vitis vinifera* vines. It seemed to Europeans to be a genuine miscegenation. However, it worked. It was the most expensive solution, as well as the least welcome. But they had no choice.

Today, virtually all grapevines in Europe—and most vines elsewhere in the world—have grafted rootstocks. Some vines are "own-rooted," i.e., a Riesling grapevine growing on its own Riesling roots, as certain areas of California (Monterey and Santa Barbara counties), Oregon, and New Zealand, had no history of phylloxera. Slowly, though, even these zones are now seeing an infestation.

As soon as it was accepted, however grudgingly, that grafted rootstocks were the only way to restore Europe's vineyards, a new industry arose to develop better rootstocks by crossing or hybridizing various native American grapevines. It was discovered that certain species grew better (or worse) in limestone soils or clay soils.

Today, a grape grower can order dozens of different rootstocks, each proclaimed to have one or another virtue. A rootstock can be "devigorating," which means that it throttles back a vine's tendency toward vigorous growth. You want a devigorating rootstock if your vineyard has rich, deep soil that encourages a lot of growth and abundant grapes.

A vineyard might have an unusual amount of calcareous material such as limestone or chalk (common in France and Italy, but rare in California). Such soil creates wines with an attractive stony or minerally scent and taste. But it's tough on the grapevine as calcareous soil encourages chlorosis, where the high lime content causes yellowing of leaves and retards growth.

Yet other rootstocks are more or less drought-resistant (very important in many California sites). Some rootstocks are more or less resistant to nematodes, which are microscopic worms that invade the roots and impair plant function. They're a big problem in California, as well as many European vineyards.

Some rootstocks tolerate high-acid soils. Some are tolerant to salt. Yet others are better or worse at assimilating mineral trace elements such as potassium and magnesium. (Potassium is important for sugar development in the grape and helps promote even ripening; magnesium is important for photosynthesis.) Some grape varieties, such as Cabernet Sauvignon, Merlot, and Syrah, demand more potassium. Putting them on a rootstock that inhibits its uptake is a poor choice.

Ultimately, the real nuance is matching the "right" rootstock to a particular soil type. Keep in mind that no vineyard has uniform soils. Even a site as small as just a few acres typically has multiple topsoils and sub-soils, especially if it's on a hillside, where drainage, erosion, and geological effects typically create a jumble of soil types.

So what does a fine-wine ambition California winegrower do? Something they never did before: painstakingly map their vineyards. This is achieved with some dazzling technology including satellite imagery.

This mapping is called a geographic information system, which is a computerized graphics application that allows "layers" of information to be assembled on a map: soils, topography, drainage, streams, etc. The information can be as complicated or as simple as the owner cares to pay for. Usually the information is color-coded.

First, a global positioning system establishes vineyard boundaries, watercourses and the like. Then the data are piled on. A tractor might drag a harrow-like device over the soil at one-foot and three-foot depths in a grid pattern to determine soil electroconductivity. The electrical conductivity of the soil (essentially a matter of more or less water-holding capacity) gives an overall picture of soil transitions, as sandy spots have a different conductivity than clay. This is especially useful for getting a sense of soil variations in large vineyard sites.

More commonly, soil cores or pits are dug, again in a methodical pattern such as a grid. Soil samples are then analyzed for structure and chemical composition and the information is precisely plotted on the map.

All of this, in turn, provides the basis for deciding which rootstocks to use for which grape variety in which spot. Numerous California wineries can show you maps of their new vineyards where they have employed as many as two dozen different rootstocks in, say, a forty-acre vineyard, all keyed to variations in soil composition, grape variety, and slope.

Such apparent precision suggests that growers actually *know* which rootstock works best. Actually, it's all a guessing game—which growers freely concede. What's occurred in California starting in the 1990s is a vast experiment in nuance: seeking a deft, informed touch in aligning the right rootstock to the right vine in the right soil for both. It will take at least a decade, if not longer, for the results of this vast, statewide experiment to become fully apparent.

The Nuance of Soil

An appreciation for the subtleties of soil is perhaps the most revolutionary element of California's new mentality. It is revolutionary because, as previously detailed in "The Machine in the Mind," the old California mindset was more than just uninterested in the influence of soil on wine: It was dismissive, even derisive.

During the decades when California winegrowing struggled to recover from the catastrophe of Prohibition—effectively from the 1930s to the 1980s—the overriding concern was selecting the right places to grow grapevines. That meant climate and temperature.

It must be noted that nothing is more influential to successful grape growing than climate. You can have the most desirable soil in the world for a certain grape variety, but if the climate is inappropriate (too cool, too warm) then it's for naught. Nothing good, let alone fine, will ever come of your efforts.

So it made sense for UC Davis to pursue its degree-day measurements and to promulgate its climate categories of Regions I through V. They had to start somewhere. And that absolutely was the best place to begin.

However, by the 1980s—when vineyards were installed throughout the state and a new audience for fine wine was established—a different need was felt. First, the original climate categories were too broad to achieve the gradations of wine quality now being sought (and never dreamed of even a decade earlier).

So growers began to fine-tune their selection of vineyard sites, looking at ever smaller and often more "extreme" (at least under the old formulations) climates. The vineyards just a few miles inland from the Pacific Ocean on the Sonoma County coast are just one example of this pursuit; the ocean-influenced western reaches of Santa Barbara County and Paso Robles are two others.

Concurrent with this came an awareness of the importance of soil on wine quality. It is an inevitable progression. First you start planting vineyards. It's pure prospecting. You and your neighbors hit pay dirt, so to speak. The varieties you planted respond beautifully and your wines are lovely. Then you engage in the small, accretive details—in both winemaking and grape-growing—that make good wine into fine wine and, if possible, truly great wine.

Finally, you arrive at soil. All other things being equal—the right vines planted in the right climate—what makes wines really *distinctive* is soil. Soil takes wine beyond fruit. Everything must already be in place (including the right winemaking techniques) for soil to show its informing influence. This is precisely what happened in California in the 1990s.

Hearing California winegrowers proclaim the fundamental importance of soil in the 1990s was like listening to someone who devoted his life to making money suddenly going on about the finer points of Impressionist brushstrokes. It was startling. And welcome.

Today, the word "*terroir*" is on everyone's lips. Terroir has insinuated itself into the American wine vocabulary. That's no small step, as even using the word, however little understood, is a tacit acknowledgment that it exists.

Terroir is a French word, a concept really, that's still pretty fuzzy to most Americans. We are, after all, a precise people. (One-quarter of all Caucasian

Americans come originally from Germany, a culture of precision.) We like things exact, scientific, and verifiable. Terroir is none of that.

What, exactly, is terroir? Narrowly speaking, it's a one-word recognition of the relationship between plant and site, with us as cultivators. Terroir embraces everything that affects a plant in a particular site: sunlight; air and water drainage; soil structure composition; rainfall and so on.

You can have a broad-scale terroir, which is to say a large area with a common characteristic. Carneros is a good example. Most growers in Carneros have a pretty similar soil (sandy loam topsoil with dense hardpan clay underneath) and a common climate (ocean-influenced cool). So you can refer, however vaguely, to the "terroir of Carneros."

More usefully, terroir is used to convey the distinctions of smaller, individual vineyards—or even subplots with a vineyard. (In Burgundy, such subplots are referred to as a *climat*.) Much depends on which grape varieties are planted (Pinot Noir is famously sensitive to fine gradations of difference) and how diverse the soils and exposures might be, such as a hillside that intersects a geological jumble of subsoils.

California (and by extension, America) was ready for "terroir" by the 1990s. After all, the last two decades of twentieth-century American life were all about seeing things "new." This led to a lot of mystical nonsense such as crystals, zodiacs, and the like. Still, the intent was sincere.

We also perceived the limitations of science, namely that its insistence on the mathematically verifiable, failed to acknowledge delicate and ambiguous "truths" that do not lend themselves easily, if at all, to quantification. Still, these truths were powerful and insistently present—if you looked. Fine wine was itself such a "looking."

California winegrowers, for their part, found their scientific certainties called into question simply by the experience of their own wines. Why did this Cabernet Sauvignon from here taste consistently different from another grown only a few hundred yards away? Science held few, if any, answers.

Once the quantifiable certainties were eliminated—winemaking technique, rainfall, wind, exposure, soil type, and so on—questions still remained. There had to be something that at least accounts for, if not explains, the differences we could all taste. This is disturbing to rational minds. There has been no other choice: We must *see* differently.

Terroir is all about observation. Every caretaker of plants knows, if he or she works a certain plot long enough, tending the right plants in the right place, that the Earth speaks.

Think of how profound your knowledge would be if, for example, your family grew the same ultra-sensitive crop (wine grapes) in your family's two-acre backyard for, say, ten generations. Every square inch of your backyard would be known to you. And not just from your own tending of the plot, but also from the received wisdom and experience of generations of your forebears.

That's what exists in all the great European vineyard areas, especially places growing ultrasensitive grapes such as Burgundy (Pinot Noir), Piedmont (Nebbiolo) and Germany (Riesling). This is why the concept of terroir is so natural to them, so obviously inevitable. Theirs is intimacy with grape and site—terroir, if you like—that California is only now just beginning to acquire.

This new awareness of, and appreciation for, the nuance of soil is not a final step in California's accelerated march toward wine greatness. Rather, it is a beginning step, like a martial artist of technical accomplishment who searches for more refined, even spiritual, sources for true mastery.

The Nuance of Growing Grapes

When you look at a vineyard today, the most important thing to remember is that its architecture is artificial. Grapevines in the wild sprawl on the ground and clamber upward toward sunlight only when their tendrils can grasp on to a bush or tree and hoist up the plant.

Even the orderly appearance of vineyards is relatively new, dating only to the late 1800s. This is important because it underscores how—in the millennia-long span of winegrowing—our knowledge of training grapevines is still nascent.

Before phylloxera arrived in Europe in the early 1860s, no vineyards anywhere looked orderly. This was because of how the grapevines were propagated. Today, you buy a grapevine cutting, dig a hole and plant it. You attach the cutting to a stake to keep it upright and put a protective tubular "grow tube" (or simply an empty cardboard milk carton) at the base of the tender cutting to keep critters from nibbling on it.

These vines are planted in straight rows and, as they grow, their tendrils grasp the wires that run the length of the row that is your "trellising system."

The size and shape of your trellis determines how you prune the vine. And that, in turn, determines the quantity and quality of your fruit.

But all of these decisions are relatively new. In the old days, vineyards were planted in rows. But they didn't have any trellising. The universal practice in Europe before phylloxera was a hugely labor-intensive system known as "layering." A vine cutting is planted and staked. After a few years, the grower takes a long shoot from that vine, bends it while it is still attached to the parent vine, and buries it in a shallow trench nearby. He leaves just a few buds showing above the earth, from which leaves and shoots will emerge.

This bent and "layered" shoot grows into a separate new vine with its own roots growing from the part of the shoot beneath the earth. Then, after a few years, it too is allowed to grow a long shoot which is, in turn, buried in a nearby trench to grow yet another vine.

The layered vineyard was, in effect, a vast subterranean "hive" of roots, all connected, as growers often did not sever the newly rooted shoot from the parent plant. Where one plant began and another ended did not, in effect, exist. It was a viticultural version of Wordsworth's "child is the father of the man."

In time, what with all the trenches dug in every direction, vineyards were chaotic, as well as densely planted. Layered vineyards, when fully cultivated, had some 10,000 vines per acre, each vine about one and one-half feet apart from the others in all directions. Such vineyards could only be cultivated by hand or with a horse; only biped and quadruped could tiptoe through the disarray.

What this meant for grape-growing was that you had a field of thin vine trunks, each about three to five feet tall when fifteen to twenty years old. These "trunks" were not self-supporting, so each vine was tied to a tall wood stake. (The stakes were removed every winter to prevent them from rotting in the ground.)

Every vine was severely pruned so it might bear only a few clusters or even just one. The yield depended on the grape variety grown. Pinot Noir in Burgundy, for example, yielded just one ton an acre—from 10,000 vines! Today, in Burgundy you have two to four tons an acre from just 4,000 vines.

All this changed radically when phylloxera infested Europe's vineyards. You couldn't have a vast, interconnected root system when an implacable root louse was the cause of the destruction. Because each vine had to be grafted on to a phylloxera-resistant (American) rootstock, each vine had to exist independently from the others.

That, in turn, meant that each vineyard had far fewer vines per acre, as grafting rootstocks was expensive. You couldn't simply bend a shoot from a neighboring vine into the earth, as it would have been "own-rooted"—and soon dead from phylloxera.

So growers had to rationalize their grape growing. From the late 1800s onward, they devised different methodologies for trellising and pruning their vines. Economics dictated many of their decisions and still do.

California vineyards never really had "layering" except in the long-gone vineyards of the early Spanish missions and in the earliest commercial plantings prior to about 1865. But they were heirs to European theories and methodologies about grape growing. After all, most of the early winegrowers were German, French, and Italian.

By the time of California's first Golden Age of wine in the 1880s, scientific agriculture was already in vogue, as previously discussed in the chapter, "The Machine in the Mind." And the effect of phylloxera in Europe was already well known.

Phylloxera arrived in California in 1873, a decade after it had reached Europe. The effects of phylloxera in California were fully felt by the 1880s. Ironically, this was precisely the same moment that California also saw the dawning of its first Golden Age. Exactly 100 years later, the same two events repeated themselves.

California vineyards did not "rationalize" its vineyards all that much after phylloxera. French vineyards adopted a system where vines were shaped to drape across a wire trellis (the Guyot system, named after its French inventor, Jules Guyot).

California vines, for their part, were frequently "head-trained," where pruning created a free-standing, sturdy trunk from which gnarled spurs formed. These spurs sprouted shoots on which leaves and clusters formed. It was literally self-supporting. You still see many head-trained Zinfandel vines today. Head-training takes a lot of space for each vine, something European growers didn't have.

Until the early 1970s vineyard land cost little, even in California's most expensive vineyard location, Napa Valley. For example:

In 1960 an acre of planted vineyard in Napa Valley cost an average of $2,000 (equivalent to $11,600 in 2000).

In 1970, it was $5,000 an acre (equivalent to $22,100 in 2000).

By the year 2000, however, the average price of an acre of planted vineyard in Napa Valley skyrocketed to $92,500.

The key was grape prices. Unless you could sustain your vineyard by inherited wealth or profits from another business (which occurred frequently in Napa Valley especially in the 1970s and 1980s), recouping the cost of lower yields or improved trellising techniques from higher grape prices was unavailable.

In 1980 the average price in Napa Valley for a ton of Cabernet Sauvignon grapes was $616. A decade later, in 1990, a ton of Napa Cabernet nearly tripled to $1,606. And a decade after that, in 2000, it almost doubled again to $3,168 a ton. Prices elsewhere in California had a similar trajectory, although not as stratospheric.

What these rising prices meant was that growers had every incentive—and reward—for doing whatever it took to improve grape quality. Forced by phylloxera to replant anyway, it was a golden opportunity to rethink their vineyard techniques and pursue the most rigorous techniques, no matter how expensive.

For decades, UC Davis recommended (based on cheap land and low grape prices) vineyard spacing of eight feet apart between vines and twelve feet wide between rows. This eight-by-twelve spacing worked out to an economical 454 vines per acre. Big American tractors could fit easily between those spacious rows, which is no small consideration.

Trellising was recommended. But it was a simple, economical T-shaped trellis, where the shoots created an arching canopy of shoots and leaves cascading over both sides of the wires strung on each side of the horizontal bar of the "T." It worked; it was simple and not least, it was economical. But then the vines themselves changed.

Until the 1970s most California vineyards were dry-farmed, which is to say that no water was applied to the vineyard. This served to diminish the vigor and productivity of the grapevine. But with the advent of inexpensive drip irrigation, the vines suddenly became much more vigorous, with abundant vegetation and grape clusters.

Virus infections, which once stunted growth and grape yield, were largely eliminated through propagation of virus-free stock. Improved nutrition and fungicides created bigger vines and more usable grape clusters at harvest. Weed control improved, leaving more moisture and nutrients to the vine.

All of these factors converged almost simultaneously in the 1970s and early 1980s. Grapevines, like overfed kids, grew huge. The vine shoots were immense, cascading over the sides of the T-shaped trellis to create twin arches that touched the ground and nearly filled the space between the twelve-foot rows. This became known as "California sprawl."

What resulted was a huge, dense "canopy" of leaves. It was dark inside that canopy and grape clusters were shielded from sunlight. The ratio of vegetation (leaves and shoots) to fruit was unbalanced, creating fruit with poor color and noticeable herbaceous or vegetative flavors in the resulting wine. In effect, the seemingly ripe fruit (based on sugar measurements) really wasn't ripe at all.

What emerged was a radical rethinking of what grapes *really* needed in this new world of drip irrigation, virus-free stock and better nutrition. What resulted is called vertical shoot positioning.

This new vine-training approach (coupled with the installation of new clones, about which more in a moment) dramatically changed the taste of California's best wines. Because of vertical shoot positioning, wines today taste riper, bolder, and richer, as well as darker (for red wines). They're also more alcoholic, as grapes are allowed to get riper than before, with a corresponding rise in sugar content.

Today, you see almost everywhere a tall (six feet high) support structure. A set of parallel wires face each other on either side of the support, with little more than a foot-wide space separating them. Because the supports are so high, you typically see three sets of parallel wires running on each side. This is the vertical shoot positioning trellis.

The key is that foot-wide space between the opposite sets of wires. Today, instead of a bushy haystack canopy of leaves and shoots, the idea is to create a tall, thin canopy through which sunlight, air, and sprays can pass through easily.

Now come the literal vertical shoot positioning. This sort of tall trellis is not in itself new. But the idea of taking young, flexible shoots—which by nature prefer to grow sideways or diagonally—and weaving them upward into this narrow, vertical structure *is* new. It's also hugely labor-intensive, as workers must go through the vineyard several times during the growing season to individually attach each shoot to the next (higher) set of wires as the shoots grow.

It's all about sunlight. Previously, sunlight was seen as something a grape cluster, like a fair-skinned child, needed protection from. Now, the theory says the grapes should be *exposed* to direct sunlight—or gently dappled light at most.

Today you see something almost shocking: grape clusters denuded of surrounding foliage. They hang from the vine fully exposed to sunlight. What about sunburn? Grapes do get sunburned and it affects the resulting wine (more oxidation, lower acidity).

But evidence is mounting that, if the grapes are exposed to sunlight at just the right (early) moment in the growing season, they get the equivalent of a protective tan. Their skins get thicker and become sunburn-resistant. The notion of exposing grapes fully to sunlight is that they will ripen evenly and more fully throughout the cluster, as no part is shaded.

To do this, though, entails yet another expensive, labor-intensive effort where vineyard workers go through the vineyard to remove all or most of the leaves surrounding each cluster. This has to happen only during a few-weeks-long window of opportunity in the spring after the fruit has "set" (when the flowers are successfully pollinated and small berries form).

One other noteworthy element of vertical shoot positioning is that you can install more vines in each row. Imagine a row of children standing side by side, all with their arms raised upward. A lot more kids can fit in the row that way than if they're standing side by side with their arms positioned horizontally. What's more, you can have more rows of vines, too.

The idea is not to create more crop, but to have each vine delivering its resources to fewer clusters. The overall yield—two tons an acre, four tons an acre—will be the same. But, as in a service-intensive restaurant, the number of servers (vines) per customer (grape clusters) is considerably increased.

Theories abound as to the ideal vineyard spacing: How many vines per acre? It comes down to economics. The traditional model in Burgundy and Bordeaux is meter by meter or roughly three feet between vines with rows just three feet apart (the width of a horse). That works out to 4,046 vines an acre. Vines are trained low (about three feet high) and the soils, after centuries of intensive cultivation, are low in nutrients. Such density seemed wide-open after the congested chaos of the old layered vineyards.

This is a very different environment than California, where soils tend to be rich and comparatively virginal and no historical memory of the old ways remains. But in the 1990s the European density model beckoned. Could higher vineyard densities improve California wine quality? No one knew.

Curiosity and capital were abundant. Vineyards had to be replanted anyway, thanks to phylloxera. So the great vine density experiment ensued. Newly replanted vineyards were treated to varying vine densities, ranging from the meter-by-meter spacing (4,046 vines an acre) to lesser—but still considerable—densities such as 1,800 and 2,400 vines an acre.[4]

So far, the results are unclear. Interestingly, no one appears to now endorse the European meter-by-meter spacing. Such extreme high density seems to create in Cabernets and Pinot Noirs noticeable vegetal/weedy/herbaceous flavors. These unwanted characteristics are reported to diminish or simply not exist at lesser densities.

But the jury is still out. So much depends upon so many variables: topography, soil and subsoil, microclimate, rootstocks, timing and amount of irrigation, clones, grape variety, vine age, pruning, trellising, and winemaking. It will take decades before California winegrowers can have assured knowledge about ideal vine density levels.

The Nuance of Clones

The other great transformation of California wine today is literally in the grapes themselves. Choosing the right clones or strains for each grape variety you plant is one of the more significant decisions a grower can make today.

Every grape variety has multiple strains or variations. Since grapes do not reproduce genetically identical versions of themselves when grown from seed, to get an exact duplicate of a particular strain, a cutting must be taken, encouraged to root and voilà!, you've got a duplicate. This reproduced vine is

[4]If you want to figure out the number of vines in various spacing densities, the formula is to divide 43,560 (the number of square feet in one acre) by the vine and row spacing. For example, a density of 4 feet by 4 feet would be 43,560 ÷ 4 (10,890) ÷ 4 = 2,722 vines.

called a clone. (My grandmother used to do this all the time by taking a leaf stem from a friend's African violet.)

A word about terminology: A "clone" is what scientists call asexually reproduced plant material. "Cloning" refers to the methodology of reproducing the original plant material. What is being reproduced is a mutation or strain. However, colloquially the word "clone" has become synonymous with "strain."

Slight genetic variations occur spontaneously within shoots of all sorts of plants, grapevines included. These mutations might be in response to certain soils or even microclimates. No one really knows what causes them. Growers call such mutations "sports." For millennia, observant growers kept an eye out for such "sports," hoping for a variant with better size, color, flavor, or disease resistance.

Since the European wine grape, *Vitis vinifera*, has been cultivated for thousands of years, a vast array of mutations within a variety was inevitable. Old vineyards throughout Europe host numerous strains of their local grapes.

But it was only in the late twentieth century that an effort was made to methodically identify, catalog, and discriminate among the thousands of strains identified among hundreds of grape varieties. Then virus-free stock was propagated by cloning and eventually made available to nurseries, which commercialized these cataloged clones.

The French government was in the forefront of this decades-long academic effort, although the Germans, Italians, and Spanish, among others, are now comparably diligent. These efforts are continuing today everywhere grapevines are found, including California.

The importance of clonal distinctions—and their commercial availability—to California winegrowers cannot be overstated. This is because clonal selection can make an astonishing difference to the taste of wines, at least if the grape is grown in a suitable zone and soil. If you plant a cool-climate grape variety in an overly hot climate, it won't matter which clones you use. It would be like fine-tuning a radio signal that's all static. It won't help.

But if a grape variety *is* grown in a spot sympathetic to it, then clonal differences can be major. You can really taste the differences. Much depends upon the grape variety. Pinot Noir, for example, is famously subject to numerous, quite different strains or clones. Not only is Pinot Noir subject to an unusual amount of spontaneous genetic mutation (thus creating hundreds of strains), but the resulting strains can taste very different from each other. Some clones taste strongly of red fruits, such as raspberries. Others emphasize black fruits, such as black currant or cassis.

Still, many grape varieties are less susceptible to mutation or their mutations do not reveal significant differences. Much depends not only on the grape variety, but also on the cultural ambition applied to it.

Sangiovese, for example, has more than 200 strains. But until recently, Italian winegrowers paid little methodical attention to them. Growers were once lackadaisical about creating truly fine Sangiovese wines, such as Chianti. Today, though, they're paying very close attention, as their ambition to create superb wine is equally intense. An exhaustive selection and propagation of the best Sangiovese clones is now ongoing in a decades-long project.

Differences among clones go beyond taste. Growers look for disease resistance, yields, color, berry and cluster size, and how early or late the fruit ripens. All of these can vary, sometimes to a surprising degree.

In the 1990s—and continuing today—California saw a widespread overhaul of its basic plant material. New, better, or simply different clones were installed almost everywhere.

Some grape varieties were affected more than others. Cabernet Sauvignon, for example, had previously received considerable clonal attention from Professor Harold Olmo of UC Davis. He differentiated among numerous strains starting in the 1950s. As a result, much of California's commercial Cabernet Sauvignon nursery stock derived from Olmo's selections, leaving a legacy of high-quality Cabernet plant material when plantings increased in the 1970s and 1980s.

Lately, some new clones from Bordeaux have become commercially available, adding greater diversity. But whatever recent taste changes in Cabernet Sauvignon might exist is probably less from clonal selections than vineyard management and winemaking.

However, with Chardonnay, Pinot Noir, and Syrah the changes in clonal selection have been dramatic and are easily tasted. All three varieties grown from newly available clones are very different from the vine material available in the 1970s and 1980s.

This doesn't mean, one hastens to add, that all the originally available clones for these varieties were bad. But they were often selected for suitability to growing areas considerably warmer than what are today some of California's best winegrowing districts.

Chardonnay Clones

The classic California Chardonnay clone, selected and recommended by UC Davis, is called clone 108. It's a good clone, with disease resistance, respectable yields, and good flavors. But clone 108 tends to ripen relatively late, which suits warm (for Chardonnay) zones—which is where nearly all of the vineyards in California once were back when clone 108 was considered ideal.

But when planted in cooler areas, such as Russian River Valley, Carneros, or Anderson Valley (or farther north in Oregon's Willamette Valley), clone 108 Chardonnays are lackluster because they mature too late for their growing seasons. Clone 108 Chardonnays grown in cool climates achieve true ripeness only in unnaturally warm vintages.

Today you hear about the so-called "Dijon clones," a term used for both Chardonnay and Pinot Noir. It refers to the strains selected by Raymond Bernard, the Burgundy region director of the French government agency ONIVIN (*Office National Interprofessionnel des Vins*). Starting in the 1970s, Bernard cataloged hundreds of Chardonnay and Pinot Noir strains in Burgundy's ancient vineyards. He subsequently identified a number of strains that returned good results for yield, disease resistance, and flavor. These "winners" were eventually made available to other universities and, through them, commercial nurseries.

With Chardonnay, you hear about Dijon clones 75, 76, 78, 95, and 96, among others. Each has certain flavor notes and different cluster sizes.

California, for its part, also has some "traditional" Chardonnay clones that are sought after and, in the right spots, highly desirable. They typically are named after the person who went to Europe, brought back some cuttings, and grew them in his vineyard. New growers came along and asked if they could obtain some "budwood" or cuttings of the vines to propagate in their vineyard.

Hence, we now have such (good) California Chardonnay clones as the "Wente clone," "Martini clone," and "Martin Ray clone," among others. Growers continue to import such cuttings illegally, although now they do it at some genuine risk, as well as a certain amount of collegial disapproval as so much new nursery stock is now legally available. These illegally imported cuttings are jocularly called "suitcase clones." Their owners boast about how they came from famous vineyards such as La Tâche (Pinot Noir) or Château Lafite-Rothschild (Cabernet Sauvignon).

What is worth remembering is that, although clonal selection is significant, every clone will perform differently in each new site in which it's planted. A Chardonnay clone tested in Burgundy doesn't always deliver the same flavor characteristics when grown in, say, Carneros.

What's more, over time, the vine itself subtly modifies itself in reaction to the soil in which it's rooted and the climate in which it matures. Thus, fruit from the mature vine can taste different than the fruit from the same vine when it was younger. In time, even the Dijon clones will become truly native and become, in effect, "California clones." Maybe someday, perhaps a century from now, we'll even ship some of these same long-since-evolved "Cal-Dijon clones" back to Burgundy as new strains for them!

Pinot Noir

No grape variety has more identified strains than Pinot Noir. It's unusually unstable genetically. Also, because it's been grown continuously for so many centuries in Burgundy, it has received exceptionally long-term attention. Not least, no red wine reveals more flavor shadings, with the result that clonal differences are easier to taste with Pinot Noir than any other red grape.

All of which means that anyone growing Pinot Noir in California or anywhere else is obsessed with choosing desirable strains of Pinot Noir for their site. No grape variety is more finicky as to site, either, which means that not every good clone is necessarily good for your particular site. Pinot Noir is a form of madness, for both producer and drinker alike. Both persist because a great Pinot Noir brings you as close to God as any wine can.

Here again, the new "Dijon clones" have transformed California Pinot Noirs (and Oregon too). Although California and Oregon were already in possession of a few good Pinot Noir clones, notably the "Pommard clone," much of the other material, such as the "Wadenswil clone" from Switzerland (also known as Clone 2A), has proved problematic in many areas. Another, the "Martini clone" is now widely seen as less desirable.

The Dijon clones for Pinot Noir, like those for Chardonnay, go by the numbers. You have clones 113, 114, and 115 (all exhibiting strong "red fruit" flavors such as raspberry and cherry), as well as 667 and 777 (which have "black fruits" such as black raspberry and black cherry, as well as some cola notes).

Making matters more complicated yet, Burgundy's experience reveals that for Pinot Noir, even more than for Chardonnay, you really want a mix of clones in your vineyard, rather than just one or two. The best Pinot Noir vineyards today will have as many as a dozen or more clones, in various proportions. In Burgundy, this clonal mix is ancient and intermixed in the vineyard itself. In California, growers more scientifically and methodically plant each clone in blocks, each made into segregated batches of wine to be blended together later.

The effect of the new Dijon clones on California Pinot Noirs has been dramatic. Where California was seen, only fifteen years ago, as unsuitable for growing fine Pinot Noir, today—thanks to choosing cooler sites—California now makes America's most diverse range of Pinot Noirs. The Dijon clones, coupled with such stalwarts as the "Pommard clone," the "Martin Ray clone," and the "Hanzell clone," among others, have brought California Pinot Noir alive.

Ironically, the next challenge will be for growers to acquire more subtlety and differentiation among their Pinot Noirs. However fine the Dijon clones are, they also tend toward a certain stridency and intensity of just a few flavors. They're almost too pure, too intense. The next challenge will be to modulate this, the better to achieve the flavor shadings, subtlety, and taste transparency that distinguishes great Pinot Noir from merely good. This will be achieved by site selection as well as extensive clonal variety, along with deft winemaking and blending among various clonal lots.

Syrah

No other grape variety in California, except Pinot Noir, has benefited from the nuance of clones as much as Syrah.

If the catchword for Chardonnay and Pinot Noir is "Dijon clones," then the key word for Syrah is "ENTAV": the *Establissement National Technique pour l'Amélioration de la Viticulture* or the National Technical Association for Viticultural Improvement.

ENTAV is a government-supported French agency created in 1962 that has become a clearinghouse and coordinator for identifying, preserving, and commercializing France's vast grapevine patrimony. A subsidiary licenses the reproduction of their plant material to licensees all over the world. It works closely with the French government agency called INRA (the *Institut National de la Recherche Agronomique* or the National Institute for Agricultural Research), hence the frequently seen term ENTAV-INRA.

California has only a scant history with Syrah. Instead, it has a long history with a similar variety it calls Petite Sirah. (The first Petite Sirah labeled as such only appeared in 1961 from Concannon Vineyards.)

In the 1990s, former UC Davis geneticist Carole Meredith identified Petite Sirah as grape variety called Durif. It was created in the 1880s by Dr. Jacques Durif of the University of Montpellier to offer resistance to powdery mildew, which was plaguing France at the time and to which Syrah is particularly susceptible.

When California growers went to France in the 1880s looking for vines, including Syrah, some did indeed bring back the true Syrah. But others returned with Durif, either knowingly or inadvertently. When phylloxera wiped out California's vineyards in the 1890s, they were replanted mostly with Durif, Peloursin, and very likely some Syrah. But it was a literal jumble, and Syrah got lost in the crowd.

Many growers thought that Petite Sirah and Syrah were one and the same. So it was a bit of shock when Dr. Meredith announced that 90 percent of California's Petite Sirah plantings are not Syrah but Durif, which is a hybrid of Syrah and another variety called Peloursin. The remaining 10 percent of the Petite Sirah plantings in California vines are pure Peloursin.

As a result, California has no significant history, unlike Australia, of growing Syrah. The first commercial release of Syrah labeled as such came from Napa Valley's Joseph Phelps winery from the 1974 vintage (released in 1977). Phelps, who had been searching for Syrah cuttings in France, found that neighboring Christian Brothers winery had four acres of Syrah, which they planted in 1959 as an experiment. Phelps bought ten tons of grapes and secured some vine cuttings to start his own Syrah planting.

Even then, Syrah was slow in coming. To see just how recent Syrah is in California, consider the following:

Total Syrah Acres Planted in California
1993—741 acres
1994—987 acres
1995—1,331 acres
1996—2,084 acres
1997—4,277 acres
1998—7,194 acres
1999—10,299 acres
2000—12,699 acres (48 percent of which was not yet bearing)
2001—14,735 acres
2002—16,054 acres (26 percent of which was not yet bearing)
(Source: California Agricultural Statistics Service)

Nearly *half* of all the Syrah grown in California is in the Central Valley, which grows grapes for inexpensive or bulk wine production. In comparison, San Luis Obispo County has 12 percent of the Syrah acreage; Sonoma County 11 percent; Santa Barbara County 8 percent; Napa County 5 percent; Mendocino County 4 percent; and Amador, El Dorado, and Lake counties have about 1 percent each.

As you can see, it was only in the late 1990s that Syrah really began to take off. In 2000, almost half of everything planted was so recent that it wasn't even bearing (it takes three years for a vine to bear fruit).

California is only just now beginning to explore its potential for Syrah. The early returns are more than just promising. They are exhilarating. Already, some extraordinary Syrahs are appearing. What's more, the most promising spots are not, as might be expected, Napa or Sonoma counties, but farther south, in San Luis Obispo (Paso Robles) and Santa Barbara counties. But almost every locale, including Central Valley, has potential for at least good-quality Syrah.

Syrah has benefited mightily from the availability of the new ENTAV clones. ENTAV has cataloged and selected seventeen Syrah clones, many of which are available in California through UC Davis and its Foundation Plant Material Service, which propagates certified virus-free clones.

In addition, there are the so-called Shiraz clones, which are strains imported from Australia, which has been growing Syrah (they call it Shiraz) for 150 years. These Shiraz clones generally have larger clusters and bigger yields than the ENTAV clones, as well as different flavor characteristics. Typically they come from Australia's Barossa field station and are numbered one through seven.

One of the more widely planted clones is the Estrella clone, named after Estrella River Winery in Paso Robles, which started its Syrah vineyard in 1975 with a clone from cuttings from the Chapoutier family vineyard in Hermitage. The Estrella clone has berry and jam fruit characteristics, while yet a different strain, called the "Durell clone" (from the Durell Vineyard in Sonoma County) is thought to add blueberry and coffee notes. Yet other clones are notable for imparting leather scents.

Such descriptors inevitably will vary from site to site, so generalizations are more treacherous than usual. Syrah, unlike Pinot Noir, is an unusually accommodating grape variety, performing equally well (if differently) in both warm and cool sites. Cool-site Syrah has a signature blueberry scent; warm-site Syrah is more about spice and leather notes. Choosing the "right" clones for the right site can make a significant difference.

THE PRICE OF SUCCESS

Follow the money.
—Bob Woodward and Carl Bernstein,
All the President's Men

One of the fascinations of California's fine-wine ambition is its sheer newness. To those who follow its wines closely, this quality may not be so apparent, like a new-car smell to its everyday driver. But seen from even a slight distance, the gloss still shines. The paint barely seems dry, let alone any sort of patina having developed.

Nevertheless, some features already are prominent. One in particular stands out: money. A fantastic amount of money has fueled California's fine-wine ambition. The showplace wineries that line Napa Valley are only the most visible evidence. Even more money has been applied to land acquisition and vineyard development. No authoritative dollar figure has been put forth, but it easily runs into the hundreds of millions. This, mind you, only for fine wine.

Obviously, such financial extravagance can emerge only from an enormous pool of wealth. Anyone who has even glanced at the California economy in the past thirty years already knows how broad and deep is the state's economic reservoir. Then, there's money brought in from elsewhere: East Coast, Europe, Japan. Outsiders have made California's fine-wine ambition their own. Everyone loves a winner.

Any book that purports to view California wine from the perspective of the land must confront one uncomfortable fact: Too many California vineyards are planted to Chardonnay and Cabernet Sauvignon. Only the most egregious booster could deny that a disconcerting number of California Chardonnays and Cabernets lack distinction. That too many are lookalikes. That too few display real character, as opposed to winemaking quality.

Such assertions are hardly eye-opening. In fact, they now are common-place. But, once past the repetitiveness of tasting 150 Chardonnays or Cabernets of seemingly slight difference—and no real interest to begin with—is a key question: Why are there so many? Why do Chardonnay and Cabernet Sauvignon *still* account for more than half of all the 2002 vineyard acreage in Napa County (56 percent) and Sonoma County (47 percent)? The same proportions applied twelve years earlier in 1990, when Cabernet and Chardonnay collectively occupied 56 percent of Napa's plantings and 53 per-cent of Sonoma's.

Nor is this domination of Chardonnay and Cabernet Sauvignon confined to Napa and Sonoma. Chardonnay remains triumphant in Santa Barbara County, with 49 percent of its acreage (down from 55 percent in 1990); Cabernet Sauvignon adds another 7 percent (down from 10 percent in 1990). In Monterey County, however, Chardonnay and Cabernet combined for 55 percent of the total (up from 43 percent in 1990). In Mendocino County, they now total 43 percent of the plantings (up from one-third of the plantings in 1990).

Clearly, these two grape varieties are the fine wines the public persistently wants and—this is critical—for which it's willing to pay a premium. This is why we will continue to see Chardonnay and Cabernet Sauvignon still being grown almost without regard to the appropriateness of the site or even the result of the wine. That said, growers are slowly navigating toward growing the right grapes in the right place. But economics skews the compass. The purpose of this chapter is to show why, to reveal how economics continues to squint the vision of the California fine-wine ambition.

If you've got high-priced land, grape-growers and winemakers have little choice: They *have* to produce grapes that command a premium. This still means Cabernet and Chardonnay, at least in the aggregate. The only two grape varieties gaining on the Cabernet-Chardonnay axis are Pinot Noir and Syrah. While Pinot Noir can fetch a comparably high price, its yields (for top quality) are less that of comparably good quality Cabernet Sauvignon. So economically it's not an ideal contender. Besides, it's extremely site-finicky.

Syrah, for its part, looks to be the only grape variety that might conceiv-ably challenge Cabernet's red wine hegemony. From a paltry 548 acres planted throughout California in 1990, Syrah has exploded to 16,054 acres in

2002. The best bottlings achieve invitingly high prices for producers, although still less than the priciest Cabernets. Not least, Syrah can grow successfully with lucratively high yields in numerous climates and soils, making it a serious rival to Cabernet Sauvignon.

It's still the case that whole winegrowing areas, such as Napa Valley, can no longer afford to lead the market, to take risks. The stakes are too high for adventurism of any sort, such as alternate grape varieties. In Napa Valley in 2002, for example, even Syrah was only 1.9 percent of its plantings (or 850 acres). Even such progressive marketing experiments such as screw caps or synthetic corks are seen as prohibitive. California has, for the moment, become a victim of its own economic success. It is the unexpected, even ironic, result of too much ambition.

This "excess" of ambition was spurred by a drive to command prices comparable to famous European wines, especially red Bordeaux. Make no mistake: It was—and is—a necessary pursuit. No fine wine anywhere is achieved without an almost profligate expenditure of money. This is not just a matter of lavish wineries. Instead, you need financial resources for such critical considerations as eliminating substandard batches of wine; risking a late harvest in the face of threatening weather; lowering yields to achieve greater character; and, of course, the acquisition of necessary winemaking items such as new barrels, presses, tanks, bottling lines, and the like. Although hundreds of California winery owners have money acquired elsewhere, only the exceedingly wealthy can afford to stanch an outflow of capital indefinitely—and they are not about to.

When "outsiders" were gripped by the fine-wine ambition in the late 1960s and through the 1970s, they willingly invested their money. But the riptide of economics was quickly at crosscurrents with their ambition. Although the ambition was both fierce and focused, the economics could not be got around: California wines had to command a higher price or the ambition would bankrupt itself. They had to convince previously skeptical—if not outright contemptuous—Americans that California wines are every bit as fine as the great properties of Europe. More to the point, they had to convince them to pay a comparable price. Only then could their ambition be self-sustaining.

Those who reported on California wines during this time—the 1970s and early 1980s—will not soon forget the endless rounds of comparison tastings.

These were conducted by the wineries, wine writers, magazines, newspapers, and not least, by private wine buyers. Arguments seesawed over the presumed superiority of red Bordeaux over California Cabernets. Old vintages of each were exhumed, to refute the doubters who asserted that California wines do not age well compared to red Bordeaux. The outcome of the story now is well known. By being as unrelenting as the economics that impelled them, the fine-wine-ambition Californians, aided by ever-better wines, eventually convinced—or at least silenced—the doubters.

Partly it was a victory of chauvinism, especially on the West Coast, where everyone was rooting for the home team. Partly it was aesthetics: California Cabernets and Chardonnays did show well in blind tastings against red Bordeaux and white Burgundies. Not least, victory was helped in the late 1970s and early 1980s by an unusually weak dollar against the French franc. Prices of French wines soared. Where California had only nibbled at a once-reluctant market (especially on the East Coast), it soon began gulping whole chunks of it. Virtues were discovered in California wines that previously went unnoticed. Wine sales increased significantly, as eventually did prices.

Here, we arrive at the hidden element of California's fine wine economics: Its pricing is still pegged to Europe. Even buyers with exclusive fidelity to California wines still assess "value" based upon what Bordeaux and Burgundies cost. Californian growers recognized this from the start—and still do. It is well to recall the prices of the finest French wines in the late 1960s and early 1970s. Although today the prices seem laughably cheap (the tears *are* from laughter, aren't they?), the fact is that, at the time, such prices gave even the European wineries only a meager return on investment. Europeans had the advantage of inheriting mortgage-free estates; Californians were, for the most part, starting from scratch.

For example, in 1966, five years after Joe Heitz courageously set out to make fine wines under his own label, Heitz was asking a then-boggling $9 a bottle at the winery for his 1962 Pinot Chardonnay Lot C-22 (the wine actually came from Hanzell Vineyards). Why was this such an extraordinary price? Because in 1966 you could purchase Montrachet 1962, Domaine Comtes Lafon for $10. And that was two bucks a bottle more than Baron Thenard's 1962 Montrachet. Heitz's regular 1962 Chardonnay was selling for $6, which then was the second-highest price asked for a California Chardonnay. (These prices, and the others to follow, are drawn from catalogs from the now-defunct Draper & Esquin Wine Merchants in San Francisco.)

In 1968, the year Freemark Abbey was founded, you could buy 1966 red Bordeaux on futures—to be delivered only six months later—as follows: 1966 Ch. Léoville-Las-Cases ($4.07 a bottle); 1966 Ch. Trotonoy ($4.15); 1966 Ch. Palmer ($4.77); 1966 Ch. Latour ($9.03); 1966 Ch. Mouton-Rothschild ($10.23); 1966 Ch. Petrus ($10.64); and 1966 Ch. Lafite-Rothschild ($11.10).

In comparison, one of California's then-recognized great red wines, Charles Krug Cabernet Sauvignon "Vintage Selection" 1963, commanded $3.50 a bottle. The equally well-regarded Beaulieu "Georges de Latour Private Reserve" Cabernet Sauvignon 1964 sold for $4.25. Inglenook Cabernet Sauvignon "Cask" 1966 sold for $5.75. Lee Stewart's old Souverain Cellars (now the site of Burgess Cellars) sold its superb 1966 Cabernet Sauvignon for $4. These prices were twice or more what most California red wines sold for at the time.

In 1970, four years after Robert Mondavi started his own winery, Mondavi's 1968 Chardonnay sold for $3.50. Freemark Abbey 1968 Chardonnay asked $5. Chalone 1969 Pinot Blanc sold for $4.50. Hanzell 1967 Chardonnay commanded a premium: $6 a bottle, the same as for their 1965 Pinot Noir. To put this in perspective, a Chardonnay fan could buy Chassagne-Montrachet "Les Rouchottes" *premier cru* 1966, Domaine Ramonet-Prudhon for $6.72 a bottle. Batard-Montrachet 1966, a *grand cru*, went for $7.85. A Pinot Noir fan could pick up Vosne-Romanée 1966, Domaine Mongeard-Mugneret for $5.46 a bottle. In comparison, Joe Heitz fought vigorously to get $3.50 for his 1963 Pinot Noir.

Another price-breaking winery at the time was Schramsberg, a Napa Valley sparkling wine producer started in 1965. Then, as now, French Champagne was considered preeminent. In 1969, Krug Champagne, one of the great French labels, sold for $6.69 a bottle. Yet that year Schramsberg was able to ask $6.40 a bottle for their 1966 Blanc de Blancs. It was a rare instance of parity. These wineries were the trailblazers. They argued their cause, virtually demanded their price. They had chutzpah.

What it Really Costs to Produce a Bottle of Wine

To listen to California winegrowers, theirs is a business fraught with expense. They battle against business-destroying vineyard pests such as phylloxera and Pierce's disease.[5] Many California winegrowers have had to replant at huge expense.

Then, of course, there is the neverending marketplace battle, where wine producers are buffeted by competition not only from neighbors, but also from massive influxes of imported wines. This is no small competition and it is increasing considerably. Imports increased by 28 percent in just four years. A quick look at the numbers is revealing:

Total U.S. Wine Imports
2002—67.7 million cases of wine
2001—59.1 million cases of wine
1999—48.5 million cases of wine

The source of these imports is equally illuminating:
2002
Italy—37 percent (22.1 million cases of wine)
France—18 percent (12.48 million cases of wine)
Australia—18 percent (12.44 million cases of wine)

1999
Italy—32 percent (16.8 million cases of wine)
France—24 percent (12.4 million cases of wine)
Australia—11.6 percent (4.5 million cases of wine)
(Source: Wine Institute)

[5] Pierce's disease is a lethal grapevine disease caused by the bacterium *Xylella fastidiosa* spread by certain kinds of leafhoppers known as "sharpshooters." The bacterium affects only the xylem or water-conducting tissue of the vine. Insects with piercing/sucking mouthparts such as sharpshooters feed on xylem sap and thus transmit the bacterium from diseased vines to healthy ones. The vine's water-conducting system becomes blocked and it slowly dies. There is no known cure. Grape-growers instead seek to reduce or eliminate the habitat for the vector (the sharpshooter), which is the foliage in moist or wet areas such as creeks or streambeds. Pierce's disease is named for Newton B. Pierce, who was California's first professionally trained plant pathologist and was the first to describe the disease in an 1892 Department of Agriculture bulletin, "The California Vine Disease." He was unable to identify its cause, though.

Australia is the big winner, with a 176 percent increase in imports to the United States in just four years. France, in comparison, has effectively declined by remaining stagnant while the imported wine market grew by 28 percent.

In the meantime, total U.S. wine consumption has increased only slightly. In 2002, Americans consumed 245 million cases of wine, a 5.6 percent increase over 1999, when consumption was 232 million cases.

Equally revealing is the fact that while California wine sales have increased only about 8 percent in case volume between 1998 and 2002, the dollar value of those sales increased by 28 percent. People are drinking a little more, but drinking better—assuming more expensive does, in fact, mean better.

All of this underscores that the wine business is a ferociously competitive environment. Being a winegrower is no cakewalk. That said, don't cry too much for them either, especially those producers selling at the upper end of the market. Much of the hand-wringing about winery bankruptcies has occurred with vineyard owners and wineries serving the much less lucrative bulk and low-price parts of the wine market. They have been hit hard, especially by inexpensive imports from Australia, Italy, Chile, and Argentina, among other countries.

But at the high end, it's another story. Here's what it *really* costs to produce a bottle of wine. Look at the following and you'll see just how lucrative high-priced wines can be—*if* you're successful in the admittedly fierce competition.

The Cost of One Ton of Grapes

Everything in California wine pricing ultimately relates to the cost of one ton of grapes, whether it's what it costs you as a grower to produce that ton or you as a winery to buy it.

The cost of a ton of grapes for a grower comes down to five powerful elements:

What did your land cost?

What did it cost to develop that land into a vineyard?

What is your annual cultivation cost?

Which grape varieties are you growing?

What is your yield?

Two recent studies, *Vineyard Economics: An MKF Research Report Including the Updated MKF Vineyard Cost Study* (2000) and the University of California Cooperative Extension's *2003 Sample Costs to Establish A Vineyard and Produce Wine Grapes*, offer detailed examinations of the business of grape growing in Napa and Sonoma counties. The following data are drawn from the exceptionally comprehensive report from Motto, Kryla and Fisher (MKF), a Napa Valley-based consulting and accounting company.

What Did Your Land Cost?

No single expense is greater than your land. Today, in Napa and Sonoma counties, which have the highest-priced vineyard land in California, you will pay $120,000 to $140,000 an acre for undeveloped vineyard land.

What Does it Cost to Develop that Land into a Vineyard?

The major decision with a new vineyard (apart from grape variety) is your choice of vine density.

Low-Density Planting: A vineyard with eight feet between rows and six feet between vines (8 x 6) or 907 vines an acre. Cost: $26,412 an acre.

Medium-Density Planting: A vineyard with six feet between rows and four feet between vines (6 x 4) or 1,815 vines an acre. Cost: $33,315 an acre.

High-Density Planting: A vineyard with four feet between rows and four feet between vines or 2,722 vines an acre. Cost: $41,916 an acre.

A high-density vineyard costs 1.6 times as much to develop as a lower-density planting. Yet so far, no one has been able to prove that high-density plantings are consistently superior, although differences will likely appear over time and will likely differ among grape varieties. Right now, it's all experimental.

How it Breaks Down Annually

You've bought your land and developed a vineyard. Every year, regardless of the size of your crop, you will spend between $8,467 (low density) to $21,230 (high density) an acre to pay your interest costs (calculated at 7 percent); account for depreciation (5 percent); cultivate your vineyard, pay your property taxes, insurance, and office expenses, and harvest your grapes, among other annual expenses. Your actual harvesting cost will be $120 to $150 a ton for hand harvesting. One picker can harvest one ton of grapes in an eight-hour day. Annual cost per acre including harvesting:

Low Density: $8,467 an acre

High Density: $21,230 an acre

Clearly, the burden is the cost of land. At $140,000 an acre, it accounts for 68 percent of your vineyard cost. The higher the cost of the land, the higher the price per ton you must command simply to recover your costs, especially if you're seeking the highest quality achieved only at lower yields.

When land is this expensive, a relatively high-density vineyard is proportionately inexpensive. This explains, in part, the willingness of many California growers to pursue expensive vertical-shoot trellising, as well as high-density plantings. Compared to their land costs, it's no big deal. However, if your land is only $15,000 an acre, spending nearly twice that to establish a vineyard can seem extravagant.

What You Need to Get for a Ton of Grapes to Break Even

This is what developed vineyards (land + vineyard development per acre) must obtain per ton of grapes simply to break even:

A vineyard with a land cost of $140,000 an acre at five tons/acre = $4,246 a ton
A vineyard with a land cost of $140,000 an acre at four tons/acre = $5,307 a ton
A vineyard with a land cost of $140,000 an acre at three tons/acre = $7,076 a ton

A vineyard with a land cost of $70,000 an acre at five tons/acre = $2,123 a ton
A vineyard with a land cost of $70,000 an acre at four tons/acre = $2,653 a ton
A vineyard with a land cost of $70,000 an acre at three tons/acre = $3,538 a ton

A vineyard with a land cost of $10,000 an acre at five tons/acre = $1,693 a ton
A vineyard with a land cost of $10,000 an acre at four tons/acre = $2,116 a ton
A vineyard with a land cost of $10,000 an acre at three tons/acre = $2,822 a ton

What these numbers make clear is the supreme importance of vineyard yield. You would think that land costing a mere $10,000 an acre would be able to break even at a far lower cost than another piece of land costing $140,000. But it's not so.

For example, if you grow Pinot Noir, your yields will be between two and three tons an acre. That's a typical Pinot Noir yield. But if you grow Cabernet Sauvignon on the Napa Valley floor, you can easily get five tons an acre. That, in fact, is what many growers (as opposed to wineries) seek and achieve.

At $10,000 an acre—a pittance—you will still need $2,822 a ton to break even at three tons an acre. *Yet at five tons an acre, you need only half again as much to break even on land costing fourteen times as much.* This explains why land prices in places such as Napa Valley can continue to skyrocket seemingly without limit. (Francis Ford Coppola, owner of Niebaum-Coppola winery, bought the adjacent Cohn Vineyard property for more than $300,000 an acre, which is the record price so far. And he'll have to spend another $50,000 to $75,000 an acre to replant.)

As long as growers can command a high price per ton, land prices can easily be recouped—if you've got the bucks (or access to them) to start with.

Keep in mind that viewing wine through the "price per ton" lens does not fully reflect other financial realities of the wine business. For example, you can make much more money by successfully processing your own grapes, in other words, becoming a winery rather than just a grower.

This explains how (and why) some producers can—and do—keep their yields low on high-priced land and still offer their finished wines at a price lower than what they would have to charge if they bought such supremely expensive grapes. They make up their "lost" profit through access to another profit source, namely selling a more lucrative finished bottle of wine rather than just the raw material. Every student of agricultural economics knows that the *real* money is in value-added finished products rather than in raw materials.

The Inevitability of Chardonnay and Cabernet Sauvignon

All of which brings us back to square one: which grape varieties to plant? You looked at the nature of the site; at what other growers in the area had planted; and at forecasts of market trends. But really, you looked at the numbers. This is what they told you:

In Napa Valley in 2002, Chardonnay commanded an average of $2,295 a ton. Sauvignon Blanc, in comparison, fetched $1,586 a ton. Gewürztraminer

$1,083 a ton; Riesling $1,782; Chenin Blanc $796; and Viognier $2,127.

Among red wine grapes, Cabernet Sauvignon achieved $3,921 a ton in 2002. Cabernet Franc got $3,685 a ton, while Merlot achieved $2,790 a ton. Pinot Noir trailed at $2,191 a ton. Zinfandel sold for $1,895 a ton. Syrah fetched $2,752 a ton. Petit Verdot got a whopping $4,915.

The decision is obvious. Among the white wine varieties, Chardonnay can make your "nut" most easily as it can grow acceptably well in many vineyard sites at economic yields. Viognier is more site-finicky and buyers are more demanding about quality. It's a niche market.

Among the red varieties, there are more choices. Still, although Cabernet Franc, Merlot, Syrah, and Pinot Noir all fetch good prices, the demand for these is not as intense as for Cabernet Sauvignon. Not least, none of them is as qualitatively successful in as wide a variety of sites as Cabernet Sauvignon. Also, none—except Syrah—performs as well when pushed to higher yield levels. Pinot Noir, for example, is qualitatively inferior when pushed much beyond three tons per acre.

But what if you inherited the vineyard outright? Or what if you bought your land years before the boom, when the prices were minimal? Couldn't you plant what you wanted, at whatever yield you liked? True, you can do what you want without bankers breathing down your neck. But vineyards are a business like any other. And every business has to operate on what's known as "market value cost accounting." What this means is simply that you cannot look at your property based on what it originally cost (known as historical cost accounting). You've got to operate it based on its current worth.

This notion of contemporary value cannot be ignored, except by the foolish. Even the most passionate winegrowers understand that their vineyard is an asset. It is something you can borrow against, something you eventually sell or pass on to your children. Whatever happens, its current worth or potential value must be acknowledged. For example, a vineyard where the land alone is worth $100,000, which is planted to a variety fetching just $1,000 a ton, such as Gewürztraminer in Napa Valley, actually is decreased in value.

From a business point of view, the historical cost of a vineyard is irrelevant if land values are increasing or are already commanding nosebleed prices. For example, the section of the old To-Kalon vineyard in the Oakville area of Napa Valley now owned the Robert Mondavi Winery achieved its original fame in the 1880s from its production of Refosco, a red wine grape. (It was called Crabb's Black Burgundy.) No doubt, it was top-notch Refosco. Still, if Mondavi borrowed against the vineyard or tried to sell it, how much could he command if To-Kalon remained planted to Refosco?

Today, the To-Kalon vineyard is the primary source for Mondavi's acclaimed Reserve Cabernet Sauvignon. Would a Refosco wine deliver the $100 a bottle that Mondavi's Reserve Cabernet Sauvignon does today? Would it add to the value of the property? Planting expensive land to produce a wine of incommensurate value is like purchasing a house in an expensive neighborhood only to knock it down to build a garage.

Intrinsic to the escalation of vineyard land value is a chicken-and-egg issue: Do values rise because certain sites do well with Cabernet and Chardonnay? Or are Cabernet and Chardonnay grown because the land is so expensive? The answer, not surprisingly, varies with the location.

Napa Valley, for example, is subject to non-wine-related pressures from its proximity to the Bay Area. Potential vineyard buyers who made (and kept) their bundle in the computer businesses of nearby Silicon Valley are willing, and able, to pay a premium for the privilege of living in a country environment graced with city amenities.

Moreover, its fame has brought dramatic financial pressures—and resources—from afar. However expensive Napa vineyard land might seem, it still looks cheap to European or Japanese investors for whom vineyard land is simply unavailable, such as in Champagne or Burgundy, or is prohibitively expensive.

Will we see less Cabernet and Chardonnay? Unless the market changes, rendering these two varieties less lucrative than they are now—or other varieties equally rewarding—the answer is "no."

In *Making Sense of California Wine*, I wrote: "Certainly, we shall see more plantings of Rhône and Italian varieties such as Syrah, Mourvèdre, Sangiovese, and Viognier than currently are planted—even in high-priced districts. (This wouldn't take much. In 1990 these four grape varieties occupied just 852 acres statewide.) But the overall proportion of Cabernet and Chardonnay is, if anything, likely to increase."

I was only partially correct. Syrah most certainly saw an enormous increase (16,054 acres planted in 2002), although much of that was in Central Valley. Mourvèdre was a non-starter. It still has only 653 acres in 2002. Viognier did a bit better with 2,001 acres planted in 2002. But you can't really say that it took off—or looks likely to, either.

Today's grape-growing reality *has* changed somewhat, but not very much. A few grape varieties other than Cabernet Sauvignon and Chardonnay can command the high prices needed in expensive precincts such as Napa and Sonoma. Syrah and Pinot Noir are the candidates, along with Merlot and such blending varieties as Petit Verdot.

But the facts still remain depressingly similar to those a dozen years ago: Cabernet Sauvignon and Chardonnay still rule. Any wine adventurism where land is expensive and varietal yields must be low is still the exception. The figures previously examined demonstrate that growers, at least in districts where land prices are high and likely to continue to rise, still have little choice but to follow the money.

DRINKING
CALIFORNIA

NAPA VALLEY

In California, where nature has combined Italy and Greece, the spirit of man responds to the invitation of nature and a more sensuous pleasure-loving life characterizes the society—in spite of its practical materialism . . . Here American society may dream as well as work.

—Frederick Jackson Turner,
The Development of American Society (1908)

From the perspective of wine, Napa Valley does not exist. This is to say that no one can taste a wine and declare with plausible certainty, "This has got to be from Napa Valley." It's too big for that. For that matter, so is Bordeaux. Instead, Napa Valley is a calling card, a foot-in-the-door selling point.

So where *is* Napa Valley, if it doesn't exist in wine? In the mind, is one answer. Napa Valley has become a symbol. No winegrowing area is so famously competitive. Nowhere is money so publicly spent to celebrate wine and promote it. This is why so many foreign investors, as well as wealthy Americans, choose Napa Valley. They identify with what Napa Valley symbolizes and want, in turn, to be identified with it. Few wine areas are so publicly symbolic of success. Bordeaux, Burgundy, and Champagne come most quickly to mind, but land acquisition there is virtually impossible for outsiders, to say nothing of social acceptance.

Nowhere has California dreamed and worked as in Napa Valley. The dream is pure 20th-century romanticism: to improve on nature. But the challenge is peculiarly hard when that dream also is an unflinching pursuit of fine wine.

As a result, Napa Valley has taken on a life separate from its original wine achievement, in the same way that Gucci, Tiffany, and Maxim's represent more than leather, jewelry, or good food. Because of this, the knowledgeable wine lover looking for good wine does not look to "Napa Valley." Instead, one is well advised to look to the smaller districts it comprises.

This is why Napa Valley is slowly subdividing. Fine wines come from somewhere. This is true everywhere in the world and not even California, not even Napa Valley, is exempt. Its best producers know that it's no longer enough to grow Riesling cheek by jowl with Cabernet merely to make an acceptable wine.

Now, the new question is: What can you do really well? What is the true vocation of place? The best winegrowers acknowledge, even in the sharp-pencil business that is Napa Valley winemaking, that it's not the brand that makes the wine. It's the land. If you think about the best Napa Valley wines you ever drank, the odds are that they came from particular places; some as small as a single vineyard, but none larger than a choice subdistrict such as the AVAs of Howell Mountain, Carneros, Mount Veeder, Stags Leap, Oakville, Rutherford, Spring Mountain, Diamond Mountain, and, recently, Oak Knoll. Yet other such districts are sure to come, such as Calistoga. They give "Napa Valley" substance. "Napa Valley," in turn, gives them customers.

The other compelling reason to look for smaller district names is the enormous amount of blending performed by many Napa Valley wineries. Because of this, Napa Valley has too many wines of no distinguishing character. They are nearly all well made, but many, if not most, are interchangeable. This is especially so with the white wines. With the large-scale exception of the Carneros district, and a few very small areas high in the hills, Napa Valley is not a source of consistently distinctive white wines.

But Napa Valley *is* a magnificent reservoir of memorable red wines, none better than Cabernet Sauvignon. Here, multiple sites, on the valley floor as well as in the hills, have what can only be called pride of place. The taste memory lingers lovingly in recalling Cabernets from the Stags Leap District, Oakville/Rutherford, Howell Mountain, various Yountville vineyards, and any number of stops along the way.

The Pinot Noirs from Carneros grow more persuasive every year. Successful Zinfandels are spottier, but by no means rare.

Sangiovese has yet to make a case for itself, although a handful of growers persist. Someday their perseverance may pay off, but the early expectations of Sangiovese stardom (my own included) have not yet been borne out.

Carneros AVA

If, by some tourist magic, you could simply take wing from downtown San Francisco and fly about thirty miles in a straight, northeasterly shot from Fisherman's Wharf, you would land, exhilarated and chilly, on the flat shore of Carneros or Los Carneros (both names are allowed). It would be a trip with the wind at your back, entirely over water, as Carneros abuts San Pablo Bay, which is the northern third of an inland sea, the rest of which is San Francisco Bay.

A glance at a map of California shows that the Pacific Ocean knocks everywhere against the California coastal mountains, but is not allowed in. Only moisture and ocean breezes get through, a good example being the narrow Anderson Valley in Mendocino County, which admits the ocean influence, but not the ocean itself. The only breach in this bulwark—in fact, the only one along the entire length of California—is the Golden Gate. The Pacific surges in between portals formed by opposing headlands, a two-mile gap spanned by the famous suspension bridge.

Everything about Carneros—its soil, temperature, and moisture—is determined and explained by these cold Pacific waters spilling in. On a map, Carneros straddles both Napa and Sonoma counties, one of the few California AVAs to cross political boundaries. On a wine label, Napa or Sonoma are only for appearances, a marriage of marketing convenience. (If a wine comes from both counties it can only be called Carneros.) Neither of these inland empires has any significance to Carneros vineyards. Like a whaler's wife, Carneros is instead looking forever out to sea.

As the pathway for cold Pacific waters, San Pablo Bay is the reason for the wind, cool temperatures, and fog of Carneros. It also explains the Carneros soil: a massive slab of clay and silt left behind five million years ago as a vast inland sea drained, of which San Francisco and San Pablo bays are the remnants. Carneros soils can be summed up in two words: clay and loam. Soil sophisticates toss around such terms as Bale clay loam, Clear Lake clay, Huichica loam, Cole silt loam, Diablo clay, and Zamora silty clay loam. But really, it's dense, hard clay covered by a scrawny layer of silty/gravelly topsoil. The clay makes for difficult drainage, which, in turn, explains why nearly all of Carneros' 6,200 acres of vines are drip-irrigated. Clay will hold water but not readily release it. Carneros vines can get by without irrigation, but the yields are considered uneconomic.

Topographically, Carneros barely made it ashore. Part of Carneros is just above sea level, with more secure hills as you go farther inland. Anyone who has seen Dutch *polders*, those flat farmlands reclaimed from the sea, already knows what Carneros-by-the-sea looks like. The difference in elevation between the flats of Carneros and the inland hills is not dramatic, but still significant. It's too soon to say with assurance, but it strikes this observer that over time, Carneros will subdivide into two zones. The hilly inland area will continue to produce Pinot Noir, but will also reward red wines such as Cabernet Franc and, especially, Merlot. The bayside vineyards will most likely continue to find their destiny only in the Pinot Noir and Chardonnay already planted. Such a pattern is over-neat, to be sure, but a tantalizing few examples point to such a possibility.

Just why this division might occur rests with the effects of wind and fog. These, in turn, affect temperature. To listen to Californians talk about Carneros is to conclude that the place is frigid. "Cool" in California is a relative thing. By California standards, Carneros *is* cool. The local growers dutifully trot out the UC Davis degree-day charts that show most of Carneros to be Region I, which is 2,500 degree-days or fewer. These same charts also portray vineyards in Burgundy and Germany as identically cool, at least if you paint your vineyard picture by numbers.

Yet when you taste Carneros wines, you get a different story. One discovers excellent acidity and an admirable leanness. But also plenty of fruit. You can taste the sun. Carneros is "California cool," which is different than European cool. The difference is sunlight intensity. The light simply is brighter in California, including Carneros.

Sunlight intensity is a function of latitude. Carneros gets its cool from fog and wind, rather than, as in Burgundy, from reduced intensity. Beaune is at 47 degrees latitude, which makes it as northerly as Quebec. Carneros, in comparison, is at 38 degrees latitude, the same as Sicily. Twelve hours of sunlight in Beaune is different from twelve hours of sunlight in Carneros, even if the ambient temperatures are identical.

Sunlight intensity is only a piece of the puzzle. Elevation moderates its effects, as does the angle and exposure of a hillside. In Carneros, morning fogs frequently dim the sunshine, no matter how intense. Sometimes incessant wind from the bay can make the grapevines "shut down" as they struggle to prevent excess water loss from the leaves.

The timing and quantity of drip irrigation plays its role. How the vines are trained, which affects how much sunlight reaches the grape clusters and how much foliage is present, is critical. Not least is the grape variety planted. After all, what's cool for Cabernet can be warm for Riesling.

Carneros wines, red and white, have a lovely kernel of warm sun wrapped by a lean, almost austere fruit. They display a finesse absent in many other Napa Valley and Sonoma sites. This is especially evident with Pinot Noir. Here the relative coolness makes itself known. They have flavor intensity allied to leanness.

Carneros is notable for yet another attribute: It's Napa Valley's cash cow. Certainly it prefers not to be seen as such, yet it is so. The Carneros district does straddle the Napa/Sonoma county line, almost equally divided between the two. And it does serve Sonoma wineries as generously as it does Napa Valley's.

But really, it's Napa Valley that benefits from Carneros and its more than 3,000 acres of Chardonnay. This is because the Napa Valley name is golden, both on the label and, especially, for tourism. Napa's wineries need "product," as they (crudely) say in business parlance.

Many Napa Valley wineries made their original reputations (and achieved high prices) with fine, limited-production bottlings of Cabernet Sauvignon. However, consumer demand often outstrips the supply of these original fame-creating wines. This is where Carneros fits in.

Napa's wineries seek to capitalize on their potent brand names by expanding their product lines, in the same way that high-end fashion houses sell perfumes, scarves, handbags, and trinkets emblazoned with their lustrous brands. Many Napa Valley tourists want white wine, especially Chardonnay. But what might be called Napa Valley *classico*—the valley floor between Napa and Calistoga—isn't noteworthy for white wine production.

Carneros allows Napa Valley to have its Cabernet cake and eat its Chardonnay profits, too. This explains why so many Napa Valley wineries buy Chardonnay fruit or wines from Carneros. They can still legally proclaim the wine as "Napa Valley" (if it came from Napa County's half of the district) or, if necessary, sidestep the matter by simply identifying it as "Carneros," which the law also allows. Thanks to the number of Napa wineries using its fruit, "Carneros" has become closely associated with "Napa Valley." So the fact that half of Carneros is in Sonoma County is largely irrelevant.

Most Carneros grapes are handled by wineries outside of the district, with perhaps a majority of the fruit still finding its way into sparkling wines, notably those of Domaine Carneros, Domaine Chandon, Domaine Mumm, and Gloria Ferrer.

This sparkling wine-destiny may no longer be the case. Grapes once meant for bubbly are increasingly sold as Pinot Noir or Chardonnay table wines, as the market for sparkling wine has contracted dramatically.

And what of the quality of Carneros wines, especially the Chardonnay? "Mixed" is probably the best description. Too many Carneros-grown Chardonnays are bland. They are "correct," but only rarely are they compelling. Partly this is because of overly generous yields, thanks to ample irrigation. And partly it's due to older clones unsuited to Carneros' cool climate, a problem largely being resolved with new plantings of Dijon clones originally selected in Burgundy precisely because of their affinity for cooler sites.

"Chunky" and "meaty" never leap to mind when tasting Carneros wines. Rather, they are silky. This is as true for Merlot (unexpected) as for Pinot Noir (expected). Chardonnays *can* be plumped up by late-harvesting or barrel fermentation, but a "fat" Carneros Chardonnay, like an overfed cat, seems somehow wrong—a slender frame with a paunch.

But even when yields are low and clones are appropriate, there's no getting around soil. Chardonnay is a site-transparent grape variety and very revealing of the particularities of where it's grown. Coolness ensures a desirable purity of fruit flavor. This is Carneros' strong suit. But soil composition, preferably something calcareous like chalk or limestone, vaults Chardonnay to a different flavor dimension. This, regrettably, is what Carneros lacks.

Carneros' coolness does serve Pinot Noir to more rewarding effect. Its coolness teases out Pinot Noir's berryishness, making the Pinot Noirs collectively more rewarding than the Chardonnays. That said, Pinot Noir also comes up against the limit of soil, as it's a grape variety universally acknowledged as the most soil-susceptible of all red wine grapes.

As the late Louis P. Martini, who pioneered Carneros as a winegrowing zone in the 1940s, once lamented to me in an interview, "Carneros has an ideal climate but, because of all the clay, it doesn't have an ideal soil." His dream, he said, would be the coolness of Carneros with the limestone soil of a site such as Chalone Vineyard.

As you might imagine, this is not what Carneros boosters would like you to read. Napa's and Sonoma's biggest wineries have a powerful vested interest in proclaiming the glories of Carneros-grown Chardonnay.

On the scale they need, Carneros is easily the best local Chardonnay source they've got. So they try sincerely to make it succeed. And every vintage does offer slightly better wines, thanks to the influence of proper clones and more deft winemaking techniques. But profound Chardonnay distinction—a leap beyond an appetizing fruitiness—is unlikely to appear, as it's not in the "bone of the land."

Stags Leap District AVA

That there is no such place as Napa Valley, from the perspective of wine, is because so many of its vineyards are on the valley floor. There, the soils are mostly rich and deep, which is swell for plant growth, but makes stand-out distinction all the harder. Geographers and geologists can (and do) trot out all sorts of names for the ostensibly distinctive soil types of the valley floor, but the fact is that its soils are mostly just what you'd expect from an ancient river floodplain: a lot of clay, some gravel, some sand, and plenty of good rich dirt.

This does not mean that the Napa Valley floor cannot deliver good wines. Quite the opposite. What it does mean is that it's harder to create *distinctive* wines. Most Napa Valley floor wines are interchangeable: "There isn't any there there," as Gertrude Stein put it. This is what makes the Stags Leap District (and the Oakville/Rutherford stretch) so impressive.

More than anywhere else on the valley floor, to say Stags Leap is to assume Cabernet Sauvignon. Although a little Chardonnay is grown there, it has failed to make a mark and is dwindling to nothingness. Stags Leap is an ideal example for demonstrating that certain grape varieties can be immensely expressive, while other plausible varieties planted in the same spot come up speechless. What Stags Leap has to say is heard (at least by this taster) only through Cabernet Sauvignon. Its *courtier* grapes, Cabernet Franc, and Merlot, pipe up with interesting asides, but only that.

Stags Leap Cabernets display a distinguishing style, the most publicized description of which is "an iron fist in a velvet glove." But that misses the mark. It fails to capture the soft luxuriance of the fruit. Stags Leap Cabernets have what might be called a corseted voluptuousness. Fanciful as that description is, I can only say that it has proved surprisingly helpful in blind tastings. The Stags Leap Cabernets do stand out.

The fruit has another distinguishing feature. Where Oakville/Rutherford Cabernets are notable for mintiness and a sinewy muscularity, Stags Leap Cabernets are compounded of chocolate, black currant, raspberry, and black cherry flavors that are delivered solidly but gently. Such tip-toe gentility is largely absent in Oakville/Rutherford Cabernets.

Just why Stags Leap wines have such qualities is, as always, the compelling question. That they exist has been confirmed to my own satisfaction, thanks to two tastings. One was composed exclusively of Stags Leap District Cabernets. The other comprised Cabernets from vineyards all over Napa Valley, all made at the Robert Mondavi Winery. Both tastings were blind. A recognizable Stags Leap character was evident on both occasions. In the Stags Leap-only tasting it was revealed by a powerful family resemblance. When grouped together for a family portrait, the commonality was instantly recognizable. In the Mondavi free-for-all, proof came from it the opposite perspective: Stags Leap wines resembled no others. (Given the wide range of vineyard sources in that tasting, it also served as testimony to the accuracy of Mondavi's winemaking.)

Two elements appear to contribute to the Stags Leap Cabernet character: topography and soil. Topography is critical in that it serves to route cooling afternoon breezes from San Pablo Bay into a narrow channel, providing a stronger cooling effect than might otherwise occur. The breeze reaches a small but significant set of knolls on the valley floor about seven miles past the city of Napa. The highest point on any of them is just 611 feet. Little more than a mile separates these knolls from the foothills of the Vaca Range, which are perpendicular enough to be better described as a palisade. Some Stags Leap Cabernets can display a vegetal quality, which may be a result of these cooling breezes, as it is for Cabernets in the Carneros district. Then again, it could be due to irrigation or picking times.

The Stags Leap vineyards are found on the terraced hillsides of the knolls, the valley floor of what might be called the Stags Leap funnel (actually it's the Silverado Trail) and carved into the sharp uplift of the mountains. The cooling is thought to affect all three sites, as the breeze swirls and eddies its way like a pinball through the knolls. Considerable sunshine is received, especially on the southeast-facing hillsides against the Vaca Range palisade.

As for soil, growers in the district point to a study performed by Deborah Elliot-Fisk of the UC Davis Department of Geography. She reports, "We have not seen any valley floor soils elsewhere in Napa Valley similar to the Stags Leap District floor soils. They are in a remnant channel of the Napa River and thus time has significantly altered them as compared to the contemporary floodplain soils of the river." Not all Stags Leap District wines come from floor vineyards, which are largely clay loams. Those on the hillsides have different soils (gravel over volcanic bedrock) yet still, to this taster, retain strong familial character to the floor-grown wines. This leads me to suspect that soil is not as powerful an informing element in Stags Leap Cabernet character as climate. Surely it plays a role, though.

Something should be said about the amusing (if aggravating to its participants) saga of Stags Leap District nomenclature. First, it revolved around the use of the name "Stags Leap" at all; second came a controversy over the employment of a critical apostrophe.

The origin of Stags Leap as a local geographical name is traced to Horace B. Chase, a San Francisco businessman who, in 1893, established a winery in the area. He christened it Stags Leap, the same name he gave his manor house. (Note the absence of an apostrophe). The winery failed in the late 1800s with the appearance of phylloxera.

Seventy-nine years later, in 1972, two new wineries issued their first wines, one calling itself Stag's Leap Wine Cellars (owned by Warren Winiarski) and the other Stags' Leap Winery (originally owned by Carl Doumani, who sold it to Beringer Blass in 1997). No sooner had they released their wines, however, than the two owners wrangled over the legal right to the "Stag's (or Stags') Leap" name. It seesawed in the courts, with Stag's Leap Wine Cellars winning the first round, as the judge decided in its favor. Upon appeals from Stags' Leap Winery, another judge overturned that ruling, declaring that both wineries could use the name, as well as an also-disputed portrayal of a stag on their respective labels.

Matters stood there until the appellation movement gained momentum in the mid-1980s. With about a dozen new wineries in the area and a clutch of new vintages seeming to confirm a sense of place (as opposed to trademark), local winery and vineyard owners agitated for a Stags Leap appellation. Like a science fiction saga where an alien invader unites previously warring nations, suddenly Stags' Leap Winery and Stag's Leap Wine Cellars found themselves allied in a Gang of Two fight against a perceived usurpation of their Stag's/Stags' Leap name.

The preciousness of the name had by then become apparent, thanks to a Stag's Leap Wine Cellars Cabernet having come in first in a widely reported France versus United States wine tasting held in Paris in 1976. The result was immediate and lasting fame, along with higher prices. The effect was so dramatic that even arch rival Carl Doumani of Stags' Leap Winery benefited, which he acknowledged in 1985 in an interview in *Wine Spectator*. "Our phone rang off the hook when Warren won that thing," he conceded. No sooner graciously said, however, than undone. "Winning that was worth a lot of money and it's brought a lot of recognition to this area. But if people are trying to capitalize on that name then I don't like it."

They lost. The appellation juggernaut was too powerful to be stopped. Their right to the Stags Leap name was found, at least by others, to be too tenuous for trademark exclusivity. After much haggling, the two combatants did, however, come up triumphantly holding the wiggly tail of an apostrophe. The new AVA would be named Stags Leap District, *sans* apostrophe. Stag's Leap Wine Cellars and Stags' Leap Winery kept their orthographic integrity.

One can only imagine what Jonathan Swift could have done with such material.

Oakville and Rutherford AVAs

No vineyard area anywhere in California is more controversial than Oakville/Rutherford. Ironically, it's not a matter of legitimacy. Virtually everyone acknowledges that a certain stretch of land, about six miles long and maybe two and one half miles wide, issues Cabernet Sauvignon of uncommon distinction. Other grapes are planted there, but its claim to (considerable) fame is due solely to Cabernet. So why the controversy? The answer is Shakespearean:

Who loses and who wins, who's in, who's out—
And take upon us the mystery of things . . . [6]

The mystery of things in Oakville/Rutherford, the nerve-nibbling dispute, is "who's in, who's out." This, in turn, determines "who loses and who wins." No vineyard land anywhere in California is more expensive than that clustered around the valley floor hamlets of Oakville and Rutherford.

This is where Beaulieu and Inglenook first secured their eminence. Later came the fame and fortune of such wines as Heitz Martha's Vineyard and Bella Oaks Cabernets, Robert Mondavi's Reserve Cabernet, Freemark Abbey Bosche Cabernet and many others. It is the Sutton Place, the 16th *arrondissement*, the Mayfair of California vineyard neighborhoods. And just as in those money-plumped precincts, who belongs is *everything*.

The first skirmish began with the name itself. Somehow the name "Rutherford Bench" gained currency. It probably was the work of pesky wine writers. That no one could find a bench (except right in front of Franciscan Vineyards, which drolly had built a Brobdingnagian wooden bench inscribed "Rutherford") didn't matter. It sounded good. Despite the absence of any geological justification, a surprising number of wineries in the area insisted that there really was such a place as the Rutherford Bench.

Applications for both a Rutherford Bench AVA and an Oakville Bench AVA were completed and submitted, reportedly at a cost of $100,000. When growers in the Oakville and Rutherford townships saw the proposed boundaries, everything but the noon whistle blew. It was the old story: Somebody was going to be left out. The problem was that these somebodies were powerhouses, namely, everyone who owned vineyards east of the Napa River, such as Caymus, Groth, Silver Oak, Girard, Swanson, Rutherford Hill, Beringer, Freemark Abbey, and Franciscan Vineyards, among others. They were going to be unseated from the nonexistent Bench and instead be given only an Oakville AVA or a Rutherford AVA.

In the ensuing brawl, the Bench got benched. Instead, a backup proposal for creating valley-wide AVAs was substituted. Fearful of having the valley carved up into a confusing jumble of overlapping AVAs as happened in

---

[6] *King Lear*, Act V, Scene III

Sonoma County, this same committee also proposed creating AVAs based on townships. The idea is identical to that functioning in Bordeaux. Like the communes of St-Estèphe or Pauillac, there would be a Rutherford AVA, Oakville AVA, Calistoga AVA, Yountville AVA, and so forth. All of Napa Valley would be divvied up. This process is nearly completed as of this writing, with Oakville and Rutherford already having their own approved AVAs. (Calistoga is still pending at this writing, but approval is inevitable.)

Collectively, is there a difference between Oakville and Rutherford? Not that I can tell. The fact is that much of the valley-floor vineyards of both appellations are more alike than not. Both have pockets of dense, clayey soil, typically near the Napa River, but not always so. Both have similar, flat, valley-floor exposures. Both grow a lot of Cabernet that inevitably gets treated differently by different wineries. So it's hard to generalize.

But what one *can* say with certainty is that both Oakville and Rutherford have a vocation of place for Cabernet. Yes, some fine Sauvigon Blanc is grown there, but no one disputes the primacy of Cabernet. And the Cabernets do tend to reveal certain attributes: They're meaty, rich wines with uncommon balance and benchmark Cabernet tastes of black currants, olives, herbs, and the like. These are the benchmark Cabernets to trot out for a novice taster and say, "*This* is what a good Cabernet tastes like."

What both districts share is equilibrium. The Cabernets have unusual balance, as if poised on the tip of a fulcrum. This is prominent precisely because of their scale: Oakville/Rutherford Cabernets are husky. The vines enjoy just the right admixture of warmth, water and sunshine, as if being metered out by an exquisitely sensitive injection system.

This is why, more than anywhere else in Napa Valley, Oakville/Rutherford can be described as "traditional." This derives not from its history, but from its intrinsic equilibrium. This same attribute is found in virtually every famous European vineyard area. Such areas represent what might be called a nexus, an alignment of natural advantages made apparent to us via the grapevine. It is a competency of place. Only cultivation is needed, rather than alteration.

What results is not just ease of grape-growing, but of something not duplicable elsewhere, no matter how apparent the similarities. You may be sure that other valley-floor producers would be scrambling to replicate Oakville/Rutherford if they could, just as neighboring growers in Burgundy would love to reproduce Vosne-Romanée or Gevrey-Chambertin. But it cannot be done.

Just how well-calibrated the area—if not necessarily its boundaries—is demonstrated by the fact that most Napa valley-floor vineyards generally share similar attributes: a widespread presence of rich, deep soils, similar exposures, virtually identical elevations, and comparable rainfalls. These make more for commonalities than differences. Yet Oakville/Rutherford Cabernets clearly taste different from others on the valley floor.

Much of the difference between, say, a Yountville Cabernet and one from Calistoga is probably due more to temperature than to soil, exposure or elevation. Yountville is cooler because it is closer to San Pablo Bay and its fogs and breezes; Calistoga is tucked farthest away and consequently is warmer. But the stretch between Rutherford and Oakville has the sheer luck of being—so the wines themselves tell us—at an ideal point along the valley's cool-to-warm progression.

Another element of the equilibrium does involve soil. Here, the vineyards west of Highway 29, the ones up against the Mayacamas foothills, do seem to have an advantage. These sites—Mondavi's To-Kalon Vineyard, Far Niente, Martha's Vineyard, Bella Oaks, various Beaulieu and Inglenook sites, and Niebaum-Coppola, among others—enjoy soils that need little tinkering. Keep in mind the Médoc's extensive vineyard drainage systems and California's vast reliance upon irrigation.

Yet when you walk through Mondavi's To-Kalon Vineyard, which has been one of Napa Valley's best vineyards since Hiram Crabb created and named it in the 1870s, the first thing you notice is the absence of irrigation. Given both California's severe drought and its near-addiction to irrigation wherever vines are planted, this is revealing. When asked why, one of Mondavi's viticulturists replied "It simply doesn't need it." The best stretch of Oakville/Rutherford probably *is* west of Highway 29. The soils are less susceptible to the poor-draining clay spots more commonly found along the Napa River. But the advantage does not seem overwhelming.

Regardless of the soil, what all good Oakville/Rutherford wines have—or should have—is a noticeable mintiness allied with a muscular, substantial fruit. Rarely are they wines of elegance. Instead, they are wines of—dare I say it?—masculine strength. Not for Oakville/Rutherford is the soft voluptuousness of Stags Leap District or the detailed austerity of Howell Mountain. Instead, the Oakville/Rutherford Cabernets are forthright wines, filled with a declarative fruit.

Other grapes are, of course, grown in the area, the most notable among them being Sauvignon Blanc. But however good the Sauvignon Blancs—and they are good—they do not strike this taster as being anywhere near as distinctive as the Cabernets.

A word should be said about the famous mintiness of Oakville/Rutherford Cabernets. It is a defining flavor element in nearly all of the best examples. That said, a few bottlings, most famously Heitz Martha's Vineyard, are so intensely minty that the scent is better described as eucalyptus. This, in fact, is the near-universal description. Martha's Vineyard abuts a sizable grove of eucalyptus trees. Anyone who has stood under, let alone downwind, of a eucalyptus tree can attest to the carrying power of its pungent volatile oils. The likelihood is strong that these volatile oils adhere to ripening grapes growing nearby. And that they will flavor the resulting wine.

Robert Mondavi Winery has pursued this theory, because part of its To-Kalon Vineyard adjoins Martha's Vineyard. What separates the two is the Martha's Vineyard eucalyptus grove. The Mondavi experiment segregated the 1990 harvest of a plot of Cabernet grapes growing from the eucalyptus grove to a distance 100 feet from the trees. These grapes were vinified separately. Another batch of grapes, grown beyond the 100-foot marker, also were vinified separately. The result? The winery reports that the wine grown closer to the trees displayed an intense eucalyptus scent and taste; that from beyond the 100-foot marker was devoid of it.

Oakville AVA

Cynics of the AVA process—they are legion—point to the artificiality of most of California's wine boundaries. Largely, they are correct. But what the naysayers are (wrongly) reluctant to accept is that you've got to start somewhere.

Appellation boundaries everywhere in the world, even including seemingly precise zones such as in Burgundy's Côte d'Or or Germany's Mosel-Saar-Ruwer, are rarely all that exact, even now. They too went through the same recalibrations that Napa Valley is only just beginning to wrestle with today.

Oakville is a good case in point. As previously described, the push was on simply to create the Oakville and Rutherford appellations, never mind particularities of wine distinction. The names were already worth too much money. It was, in effect, trademark protection.

But now that the Oakville and Rutherford brands have been corralled, what next? As elsewhere, distinctions of place (if they exist at all) mount only with a critical mass of wines and vintages.

Unlike most places in California, there's already no dispute about what grows best in Oakville and Rutherford: it's Cabernet Sauvignon. More than anywhere else in Napa Valley, to say Oakville or Rutherford is to presume Cabernet Sauvignon.

However, it's already apparent—at least to this observer—that the east-west breadth of the Oakville AVA encompasses a greater range and distinction of place than this single appellation signals.

As previously noted, the original urge was simply to distinguish Oakville from Rutherford. So the boundary barons looked north to south. Now, however, it's become apparent that there is in Oakville an easily tasted division between what might be called Oakville East and Oakville West.

"Oakville West"—the section abutting the Mayacamas Range incorporating such vineyards as To-Kalon (Mondavi, Beckstoffer), Far Niente, Martha's Vineyard, Opus One, Harlan—is different from "Oakville East,"which probably starts on the valley floor just west of the Silverado Trail and reaches high up into the Vaca Range. Vineyards there, such as Rudd (on the valley floor), Dalla Valle, Miner, and Showket, among others, are much newer, dating only to the 1980s.

The difference between Oakville West and Oakville East is apparent to both eye and palate. Oakville West Cabernets offer, at their best, a dusty, gravelly scent and taste with an almost lacy texture. This is thought to derive from the alluvial fans that cascade from the Mayacamas Range onto the valley floor. Not every wine has these features (winemaking can emphasize it or obscure it), but they're present often enough to be considered characteristic.

Oakville East, in comparison, is about dramatic, intense Cabernet of penetrating strength that's thick on the tongue. You couldn't create a lacy-textured Cabernet no matter how hard you tried. The upper elevations in the

Vaca Range, where Dalla Valle, Showket, and Miner vineyards are located, have the rockiest soil in all of Napa Valley. Indeed, there almost isn't any soil, at least as one commonly thinks about dirt. Boulders abound and rock walls line the road, simply because they had to put the rocks from their vineyards somewhere.

You can see these same (smaller) rocks on the valley floor in Rudd Vineyard just west of the Silverado Trail. But there, on the valley floor, it's better-described as soil mixed with rocks, as opposed to the hillsides, which is rocks with a little soil added almost as an afterthought.

This valley-floor rocky soil turns into tender topsoil as you shade west toward the vineyard leased by Plumpjack Vineyard, contiguous to Rudd. These rocks signal a terroir marker of some sort.

Exposure plays a significant role as well. Oakville West has what's called a "three o'clock shadow," when the sun begins setting and certain pockets of vines hugging the base of the Mayacamas are plunged into shade. Oakville East, in comparison, is subjected to fierce afternoon sunlight, which floods the vineyards and bakes the rocks, which retain the sun's warmth well into the evening, like a cooling pizza oven.

Not surprisingly, Oakville East Cabernets deliver a fruit intensity and strength unlike anything grown in Oakville West. The wines are texturally different: Oakville East is denser, more tannic and jammy, almost syrupy; Oakville West has more finesse, better acidity, and great flavor refinement.

These characteristics reflect their respective extremes. Indeed, the closer you get to the middle of the valley floor (Groth, Silver Oak, Franciscan) the less pronounced are either sets of characteristics. This is not to say that this valley-floor "heart of Oakville" lacks its own attributes, but the wines tend to be less individual. They are simply (but hardly merely) exceptionally good.

Unlike Oakville, which has a noteworthy concentration of highly distinctive east-side vineyards clinging to the face of the Vaca Range, the Rutherford AVA is more homogenous.

Like Oakville, you have the same base-of-the-Mayacamas hugging vineyards located on alluvial fans west of Highway 29. This includes such famous sites as Beaulieu Vineyard Number One, Bosché, Sycamore, Niebaum-Coppola (the former Inglenook Vineyard), and Bella Oaks, among others.

On the east side of the Rutherford AVA, the Vaca Range is too steep for vineyard development. Most of Rutherford is all about a generous expanse of enviably good dirt on a broad valley floor. It's land an Iowa farmer could love.

Mount Veeder AVA

As you tramp inland from the flat shores of Carneros, you can go about eight miles straight north without much huffing and puffing. Then the shoreline flats give over to undulating hills, the sort that cows and sheep enjoy everywhere in the world, and still do in Carneros. Then, all of a sudden, the going gets tough. You have reached the southern tip of the Mayacamas Mountains. This is how you would see the Mayacamas Mountains if you simply came ashore or if you inhabited the Napa "wine mind." To their way of thinking, the Mayacamas Range starts from the flats of Carneros.

A better, more encompassing perspective is the proverbial bird's-eye view—way up. The Pacific Ocean is to the west. It slams against a coastal range of relatively low mountains, the "ridge family": Inverness Ridge, Bolinas Ridge, Miller Ridge, Beatty Ridge, etc. These give way, about twelve miles inland to the east, to a broad, flat valley in the middle of Sonoma County. This is where (and why) Santa Rosa is found. Actually, Santa Rosa lies in the mid-point of the valley's length. At its northern end you'll find Healdsburg. You can seemingly skateboard the length of the valley, past Santa Rosa and then Petaluma, all the way to the lapping waters of San Pablo Bay.

Still looking east, we then see the flanks of the Sonoma Mountains. Almost immediately is spied a narrow little valley called Sonoma Valley. It lies in the cleavage formed between the Sonoma and Mayacamas mountains. At the ridge of the Mayacamas Mountains is the county line dividing Napa and Sonoma.

The Mayacamas are high, volcanic, and rugged. Once over the range you look down upon the famous Napa Valley. And on the other side of the valley you see another mountain range, which is the Vaca Range. (Some erroneously think it also is part of the Mayacamas range, but it's not so.) The layout looks like nothing so much as a huge tuning fork, with the narrow Napa Valley between the tines.

Napa Valley has long had a vague sense of a place colloquially referred to as "Mayacamas." As mentioned previously, in this local vision it comes not from Sonoma County, but from its own Carneros flats. It extends north only for about eight miles, to Bald Mountain, which is midway between Napa and St. Helena. Just why this vague sense of "Mayacamas" should stop mid-valley at St. Helena is hard to explain. Probably, this folkloric impression of "Mayacamas" is due to the longtime presence of the winery known as Mayacamas Vineyards, which was restarted in 1941 (it actually dates to the 1880s), perched on the slope of Mount Veeder itself. Actually, the Mayacamas range continues unbroken to Calistoga, which is another ten miles north of St. Helena.

This is why when the time came, in March 1990, to baptize this vague sense of "Mayacamas" the newly created AVA was instead named "Mount Veeder," after the 2,677-foot volcanic peak, the most prominent in the range. The Mount Veeder AVA extends from the sharp, high ridgeline, i.e., the Napa County line, down the flanks to 400 feet above the Napa Valley floor, from the inland edge of Carneros to Bald Mountain.

If you've been following this, a question probably has occurred: Why does the Mount Veeder AVA stop at the Napa County line at the top of the ridge? What about the "Mayacamas" vineyards on the Sonoma side, such as Louis Martini's Monte Rosso Vineyard, or the vineyards of the Carmenet, Kistler, and Hanzell wineries? Don't they have similar volcanic soil? (They do.) Don't they share similar elevations? (They do.) Don't they have more in common with the Mount Veeder AVA than with the Sonoma Valley AVA, which includes all sorts of valley-floor vineyards? (They do.)

So why is "Mount Veeder" only on the Napa Valley side? The answer is politics. The then-new BATF knows no more about wine than it does zoology. But it did know politics. And in Napa Valley, wine politics has become as much a full-time occupation as wine itself. Many Napa Valley winery and vineyard owners are concerned about the dilution of the Napa Valley name.

The diluting influence, in their view, is the appearance of appellation names such as Howell Mountain and Stags Leap District. Because so much wine gets blended in Napa Valley, the trading name "Napa Valley" far exceeds any other in value in this view. (In reality, certain sub-appellation names such as Oakville, Rutherford, and Stags Leap command higher prices for their grapes than simple "Napa Valley.") Any diminution of that name, or attention diverted from it, is considered ill-advised. This view is held by many, if not most, of the large wineries in Napa Valley, as well as some small ones. Their vested interest lies in the sanctity of the market rather than of vineyards.

The flash point came with the creation of the Carneros AVA in September 1985. The BATF allowed the Carneros AVA to cross political boundaries. Roughly half of Carneros is in Napa County and half in Sonoma County. The labels need only state "Carneros," with no additional mention of either Napa or Sonoma. That it makes viticultural sense, no one disputes: Carneros is a true wine appellation. Subsequently, "Carneros," rather than "Napa Valley" reaped massive publicity for its wines. Many Napa Valley winegrowers resented this, their reaction being along the lines of "We wuz robbed."

As a result, in 1989 this contingent got the California state legislature to pass a law, *applicable to Napa Valley only*, mandating that all present and future AVAs in Napa Valley display the Napa Valley name on the label. An exception had to be made for Carneros, because it had already become a BATF-approved viticultural area. In effect, all other Napa Valley AVAs—Wild Horse Valley, Stags Leap District, Howell Mountain, Oakville, Rutherford, Mount Veeder, Spring Mountain, and so on—really are *sub*-appellations. This is why Mount Veeder stays on its own side of the (political) fence.

To be sure, the Sonoma flank of the Mayacamas Mountains is not identical to Napa's. The iron-rich red soil of the Carmenet and Monte Rosso Vineyards on the Sonoma side is absent on the Napa side, where it's white/gray volcanic soils mixed with sedimentary soils.

More significantly, the rainfall is different. The Sonoma side gets twenty-five inches to thirty inches of rain annually; the Napa side gets fifty to sixty inches. The rain comes from the moisture-laden ocean air from the west.

At first glance this doesn't make sense. The Napa flank is on what should be the lee or "rain shadow" side of the range. Yet it gets more rain than the Sonoma flank.

The reason is that the Mayacamas Range is not high enough to create a barrier. In fact, it's just high enough, at about 2,000 feet, to actually *increase* the rainfall on the Napa flank. Air cools as it rises. Moisture condenses more readily from cooling air. If the Mayacamas were higher, the upwardly moving air would make it, say, only halfway up the slope before condensing. Instead, the air makes it over the top with most of its moisture intact and then condenses just as it starts down the Napa flanks.

Sunlight is different on the two sides as well. The Sonoma side gets almost perpendicular, westerly afternoon sun. The Napa side gets more morning sun, thanks to the east-facing slopes.

Nevertheless, the two Mayacamas Mountain flanks have more in common with each other than with their respective valley-floor associates. One supposes that, over time, viticultural realities will supercede political ones. Whether that will result in a two-flanked Mount Veeder AVA or an entirely new "Mayacamas" AVA remains to be seen—or rather, tasted.

Politics aside, is there such a place, *in the wine*, as Mount Veeder? Unquestionably. The volcanic soils and high elevations (up to 2,000 feet) are the contributing elements to Mount Veeder wine distinction, both red and white. What set the Cabernets apart from nearly all other Napa Valley versions is not their intensity, but their pungency. Many other good Napa Cabernets deliver intensity of flavor, such as those in Oakville/Rutherford, Howell Mountain, Stags Leap District, and not least, the neighboring hillsides of Spring Mountain and Diamond Mountain. Yet none of these districts—not even Spring and Diamond mountains—offers quite the same *smack* of intensity allied with earth. One can easily believe claims of tiny berries and low yields. The texture is rich but not thick, saved by the compensatory acidity built in by the high elevations.

Given its lengthy history, it would seem that Mount Veeder is destined for Cabernet Sauvignon. Indeed, when they are good, they are uniquely so. No other place in Napa Valley—indeed, nowhere else along the Mayacamas Range—creates Cabernets that taste quite like those from Mount Veeder. The giveaway is a minerality utterly absent in Cabernets from either Spring Mountain or Diamond Mountain.

Yet often overlooked is the fact that Mount Veeder, like many hillside appellations, is far from homogenous. Much depends upon exposure. This explains, in part, why less successful Mount Veeder-grown Cabernets can sometimes be too weedy or vegetal. It's easy to forget just how close Mount Veeder is to San Pablo Bay and its cooling effects. Mount Veeder is the coolest of the three Mayacamas Range AVAs.

A possibility exists, so far based on too few examples, that Mount Veeder might be as well—or even better—suited for Syrah than Cabernet Sauvignon. Again, much depends upon individual sites. The stellar Syrahs created by Lagier Meredith Vineyards demonstrate a previously unsuspected vocation of place for Syrah on Mount Veeder. If its experience is repeatable elsewhere, then it's entirely possible that someday Mount Veeder will be synonymous with Syrah rather than Cabernet Sauvignon.

That said, there's no denying the austere, minerally goodness of Mount Veeder-area Cabernets. At first glance, they would seem to be the sort that wine tasters derisively call "competition wines" because of their husky scale. Yet typically they do not show well when paraded with other Cabernets. Against more polished, but less site-specific Cabernets, their very character sets them uncomfortably apart, like a wild fish in a school of tank-raised trout. They show best in the surroundings of comparably pungent tastes such as pesto, well-aged lamb, and anything abundantly redolent of fresh garlic. Then they fit like no other.

Chardonnay shares a similar intensity: strong, buttery fruit and a noticeable earthiness. A mineral tang in the finish always is present. Unlike the Cabernets, the fruit intensity and earthiness do not stand alone quite as well. White wines, more than reds, trade on finesse—how the flavors get delivered. By themselves, the Mount Veeder Chardonnays can seem a little lumpish, as texturally they can be almost unctuous, reminiscent of an Alsatian Pinot Gris. (One wonders why Pinot Gris is not planted along the Mayacamas ridge. It should do beautifully.)

Nevertheless, Mount Veeder-area Chardonnays have character: They clearly come from somewhere. For that reason alone, they are well ahead of California's large contingent of "nowhere" Chardonnays. Their textural thickness, combined with an earthy richness of fruit, makes them a more specialized wine than most of California's one-size-fits-all Chardonnays. This is the Chardonnay to serve with bouillabaise or cioppino, as well as more strongly flavored cheeses such as aged fontina or ripe soft-rind cheeses. It then becomes newly compelling, like a sudden insight into a once-difficult painting. Characterful wines, like difficult paintings, require discovery.

Spring Mountain AVA

The power of wine to reveal distinctions of place is persuasively revealed in Spring Mountain. There is no actual Spring Mountain. Instead, it's a colloquial term long used in Napa Valley to refer to a section of the Mayacamas Range at the midpoint of the valley just west and north of St. Helena. The name derives from the numerous springs and creeks on the mountainside.

Like Mount Veeder (but unlike neighboring Diamond Mountain), Spring Mountain has a long history of winegrowing. Indeed, it may have the longest history of any hillside zone in Napa Valley, with the earliest plantings thought to date to the 1860s, right at the ridge line where Pride Vineyard now is located. The first documented planting, however, dates to 1874, the La Perla Vineyard, which is now part of Spring Mountain Vineyards.

As elsewhere along the Mayacamas Range, red wine reigns, especially—but not exclusively—Cabernet Sauvignon. Spring Mountain is clearly warmer than Mount Veeder, although it's just cool enough to share a common challenge of selecting appropriate exposures to achieve full ripeness.

In a blind tasting of representative Cabernets from the trinity of Mayacamas Range AVAs—Mount Veeder, Spring Mountain, and Diamond Mountain—the odds are good that you'll spot the Spring Mountain Cabernet with little difficulty. While all three districts create substantial Cabernets, those from Spring Mountain are typically the darkest-hued, with almost aggressive tannins and a powerful density. Absent is the signature mineraliness of Mount Veeder and, fascinatingly, the characteristic dark chocolate scent and comparatively soft tannins that distinguish Diamond Mountain Cabernets.

Just why is, as always, the recurring question. Of course, no definitive answers are found, but differences among the three AVAs are traceable. For example, the soils of Spring Mountain are frequently an equal mix of sedimentary soils such as sandstone and various conglomerates along with iron-red volcanic soil.

In comparison, Diamond Mountain, contiguous with Spring Mountain to the north, is composed almost exclusively of volcanic soil. Mount Veeder, in comparison, has mostly sedimentary soils.

As always, the soil component is thrown into play with temperature differences. Here again, Spring Mountain is decidedly warmer than Mount Veeder, which is twelve miles to the south and thus closer to the cooling effect of San Pablo Bay. But Spring Mountain is cooler than Diamond Mountain during the afternoons thanks to ocean-derived breezes coming from the west, at least according the Spring Mountain growers.

They assert that only Spring Mountain, among the three Mayacamas Range AVAs, receives this cool ocean-derived effect, thanks to a topography that distributes the westerly winds blowing in from the Pacific Ocean. Much depends upon elevation, as Constant Winery, at the peak of Diamond Mountain, also gets this afternoon cooling. (Howell Mountain, across the valley, also feels the effect of afternoon ocean breezes.)

All three Mayacamas Range AVAs, though, get a similar amount of ocean-influenced rainfall in the winter. A quick glance at the towering redwoods and gurgling streams in all three districts leaves no doubt about the sixty inches of rainfall each gets every winter. That's about twice what falls on the valley floor.

Somehow, all of these details (and yet others particular to individual sites and exposures) combine to create a Spring Mountain distinctiveness. Spring Mountain reds are almost implacably fierce, yet its tannic ferocity is tempered by a fruit density like no other in Napa Valley. Spring Mountain creates Napa Valley's richest, strongest, most pungent red wines.

This is not confined only to Cabernet Sauvignon, either. Some of Napa's most powerful and persuasive Merlot is grown on Spring Mountain. This is Merlot country every bit as much as it is Cabernet.

White wines are less commonly seen, yet the few Sauvignon Blancs found on Spring Mountain are superb, filled with an earthy dimension just like the reds. Riesling, championed by Smith-Madrone Vineyards near the top of the mountain, is one of California's finest, again exhibiting that "smack of the earth," as Robert Louis Stevenson so poetically put it in *Silverado Squatters* (1883). At the base of the Spring Mountain AVA is pioneering Stony Hill Vineyard (founded in 1952), which creates superb Chardonnay, as well as good Gewürztraminer.

Diamond Mountain AVA

What makes Diamond Mountain interesting is that, on a map, it appears to be simply a continuation of the Spring Mountain AVA. They are contiguous, separated only by the valley through which Ritchie Creek runs. Yet the Cabernets from Diamond Mountain are strikingly different from those of Spring Mountain. Really, you can tell them apart in a blind tasting without much difficulty, if you get good examples of each. The giveaway is a signature scent and taste of dark chocolate.

From outward appearances the landscape doesn't look different from Spring Mountain: the same dense forest, spooky with redwoods, rich, red volcanic soil, and rainfall. Yet the wines offer different tastes and textures.

As elsewhere along the Mayacamas Range, it's really red wines, above all Cabernet Sauvignon, that define the area. But Diamond Mountain, alone among the three AVAS, delivers its Cabernet with a striking whiff and taste of dark chocolate. Neither Spring Mountain nor Mount Veeder have this.

What's more—and rather baffling—is that when you compare the Cabernets of these three zones, those from Diamond Mountain always have the softest tannins. Mount Veeder Cabs have hard, almost green tannins (the coolness makes itself felt); Spring Mountain Cabs also have hard tannins, but wrapped in intense fruit.

Diamond Mountain Cabernets are far from wishy-washy—they *are* big wines—but the compounding of softer tannins with that chocolate note makes them less pungent than Spring Mountain's and riper-tasting than Mount Veeder's.

Regrettably, not much white wine is grown on Diamond Mountain today, although Sterling Vineyards once issued a series of Diamond Mountain-grown Chardonnays that were among Napa Valley's most characterful, in an earthy, long-aging way. They failed to persuade most tasters though, so Chardonnay is now rarely issued. However, a tiny planting of Roussanne at Reverie Winery was extraordinary enough to make one a believer in its possibilities on Diamond Mountain.

Howell Mountain AVA

When it comes to so-called "mountain wines" the temptation is to believe Tolstoy's assertion that "All happy families resemble one another." While it is true that many wines grown at high elevations or on steep hillsides do resemble one another in matters such as lower yields, higher acidities, and firmer tannins compared to softer, lusher valley-floor wines, such resemblances are superficial. There's more to a genuine (wine) family than that. Howell Mountain, in the Vaca Range on the east side of Napa Valley, proves the point.

By the measures of "mountain wines," Howell Mountain should be indistinguishable—or at least interchangeable—with Diamond Mountain, Spring Mountain, or Mount Veeder. It shares an ostensible family resemblance in such features as elevation, temperature, and soils. Yet Howell Mountain wines, red and white, are dramatically different from those of any of these three Mayacamas Range districts (or vice versa). The firm tannins and unyielding fruit when young, so often pointed to as "mountain wine" characteristics, are makeup rather than "bones."

What sets Howell Mountain Cabernets apart is a distinctive "watery" texture—in the best sense of the term. Also present is a certain spiciness. They bring to mind an end-of-dinner conversation I had years ago with my colleague Hugh Johnson. Hugh is a "claret man," which is to say that, left to his own devices (and against the tide of his powerful curiosity), he would as soon drink a red Bordeaux as any wine. I, on the other hand, am a Burgundy sort. I pressed Hugh about why he so liked Bordeaux wines—especially as compared to my beloved Burgundies. "What I so like about them," he replied, "is that they go down like water." Howell Mountain Cabernets have that quality.

Elevation is the key. The impact of elevation for Howell Mountain wines is far-reaching. Howell Mountain occupies a volcanic plateau in the Vaca Range on the east side high above the Napa Valley floor. It looks across the valley to the Mayacamas range on the west side. Established as an AVA effective in 1984 (the first sub-appellation after Napa Valley itself became an AVA effective in 1983), Howell Mountain *begins* at the 1,400-foot elevation. Many of its vineyards are well above this, at between 1,600 feet and 2,000 feet.

One element of this 1,400-foot demarcation is that the vineyards are not subject to the inversion layer that blankets the Napa Valley floor during summer mornings until about eleven o'clock. An inversion is where warm air lies above cold. Cold fog from San Pablo Bay seeps into the valley during the summer, dissipating by late morning. Howell Mountain is literally above all that. As a result, it receives more morning sun than the valley floor. In fact, it gets sunshine all day.

By itself, this full measure of sunshine would normally result in an excessively warm environment for fine wine. Instead, Howell Mountain is warmer in the morning, cooler in midday, and ten to fifteen degrees warmer at night than the Napa Valley floor. Overall, it is cooler than the valley floor vineyards at its base, which lie just north of St. Helena. Partly this coolness is due to sheer altitude: Temperature drops as altitude rises. The usual rate of decrease (known in meteorological jargon as the normal lapse rate) is three and one-half degrees Fahrenheit for every 1,000 feet. This can make a real difference to something as sensitive as a grapevine.

But what really cools down Howell Mountain, despite all its received sunshine, is afternoon wind. This is why it is cooler at midday. The flattened crest of Howell Mountain is scoured by wind every summer afternoon starting at about two o'clock. Some vineyards feel the full brunt; others are in protected pockets. But the wind affects the temperature almost everywhere, as it cools the mountain.

Its source is maritime, an emissary from the Pacific. The breeze first circulates through Sonoma's Russian River Valley, then heads across the Sonoma valley floor south of Healdsburg, escaping over the low end (1,000 feet) of the Mayacamas range near Calistoga. Eventually, it reaches Howell Mountain.

This susceptibility to ocean winds so far inland helps explain why the Las Posadas State Forest on the southeastern flank of Howell Mountain contains a grove of what is classed as "coastal redwoods." Nurtured by the moisture-bearing winter winds, this grove is farther inland than any other "coastal redwoods" in California. Howell Mountain rainfall is similar to that of the Mayacamas at about forty-one inches a year, although still about one-third less than Mayacamas' sixty-plus inches a year. Still, it's twice as much as, say, the city of Napa on the valley floor, which sees just twenty-four inches of rain annually.

The soils of Howell Mountain are not, by geologists' standards anyway, very much different from those of the Mayacamas Mountains, yet its Cabernets are nowhere near as earthy-tasting. Two distinct soils are present, both volcanic in origin, but from different volcanic effects. The north side of Howell Mountain has a dark red soil called Aiken loam, the same as is also found in the Mayacamas Mountains. It comes from lava outpourings. The south side has a gray/white soil, known in geological parlance as Kidd, Boomer, and Forward loams. It is created by explosive material lofted from volcanic explosions—in other words, ash. The difference between the two soils is that between basalt and pumice. Drainage is different: slower in the denser red; faster in the more porous white. Neither is especially nutritious, partly due to runoff over the eons from the steep slopes.

Howell Mountain creates wines of detail. Absent is the pungency of Mount Veeder and Spring Mountain Cabernets, as well as the earth and chocolate notes found in Diamond Mountain Cabernets. Instead, its Cabernets are leaner, spicier, and more austere, although equally intense and tannic. But the "goes down like water" quality gives them grace. The Zinfandels are equally distinctive, but less articulate. Comparing the Howell Mountain renditions of these two grapes gives meaning to the term "breed." The Cabernet has it; the Zinfandel doesn't. Still, the Zinfandels are among the most rewarding and detailed of any in the state.

The white wines are more problematic. Howell Mountain Chardonnays are few in number and almost ultrasonic in pitch: One feels them as much as tastes them. They are lean, verging on skeletal. So far, Chardonnay does not appear to be as expressive a vehicle as either Cabernet or Zinfandel. Viognier, however, responds well, although probably more to the mountain's incessant sunshine than to anything else. Its aromatic qualities are well-displayed, but the grape is not known for much more anywhere in the world.

Napa Valley Producers
Worth Seeking Out (And Some Not)

Acacia Winery—One of the linchpin wineries of Carneros. Typical (in the best sense), indisputably Carneros Pinot Noirs and Chardonnays from various named-vineyard sites nearly all in the Napa half of Carneros. Among the named-vineyard Pinot Noirs, that from ten-acre St. Clair Vineyard is the most long-lived and rewarding. Acacia prefers a noticeably oaky style, but both the Pinot Noirs still shine with Carneros fruitiness.

Araujo Estate Wines—When Bart and Daphne Araujo bought the former Eisele Vineyard in 1989, made famous by Joseph Phelps winery, they secured as close to a sure thing as a vineyard can get in Napa Valley. To their credit (and profit), they have made this "sure thing" better than ever, thanks to painstaking, respectful vineyard cultivation and first-rate winemaking. The meaty flavor density for which Eisele Vineyard (the Araujos respectfully still use the name on their label) was famous is still present, but in a more polished, more "transparent" fashion. It is now one of the great estates of California and worth the top dollar the new owners are asking (and getting).

Arieta—See *Kongsgaard.*

Artesa Vineyards and Winery—The new name for the former Cordorniu sparkling wine facility in Carneros. When the sparkling wine bubble popped, some producers around the state simply went out of business (Piper-Heidsick, Maison Deutz). Others channeled their Chardonnay and Pinot Noir supply into still wines, while producing a smaller amount of bubbly. Artesa Winery, for its part, simply renamed itself altogether and set up shop as a winery specializing in Chardonnay and Pinot Noir on their original 172 acres of Carneros vines, as well as another 100 acres of Chardonnay in the coolish Sonoma Coast AVA. The new winery also has 150 acres of vines in Alexander Valley, twenty-five acres of which is Tempranillo, the classic Spanish red wine grape. Since it's a new venture, it's too early to comment with certainty on its wines. So far, so very Carneros—which is to say good, true Chards and Pinots of no soul-stirring quality yet.

Atlas Peak Vineyards—Located in the Vaca Range midway between Oakville and Napa, Atlas Peak Vineyards was originally a vastly ambitious undertaking of three foreign companies: the Tuscan wine company L. & P. Antinori (5 percent ownership); the Bollinger Champagne house in France (10 percent ownership); and the big money Allied Lyons of England (85 percent ownership), through its subsidiary, Hiram Walker-Allied Vintners.

This trio of investors purchased land planted to vines by William Hill high in the mountains in 1986, with 500 acres of vineyard in steep terrain that had to be painstakingly terraced. The development cost was reported to be a then-staggering $35 million—before building a winery. These original owners were adventurous: The partnership planted Sangiovese, Zinfandel, and Refosco in addition to the expected Cabernet Sauvignon, Chardonnay, and Sauvignon Blanc. The vineyard picture is rounded out with Pinot Noir, Petite Verdot, Sémillon, Merlot, and Pinot Blanc.

Since then, the partnership foundered. Today, Atlas Peak Vineyards is owned by Allied Domecq and Antinori. The wines, regrettably, do not seem to have fulfilled the early high expectations of this singular site. Sangiovese, once thought to be a sure thing, has so far proved ho-hum. The Cabernet Sauvignon is certainly good, but hardly outstanding, especially in contrast to the admittedly fierce competition elsewhere in Napa Valley. Perhaps more time will allow the owners to tease out the originality of this high-elevation site, but so far, nothing heart-stirring has emerged. As the Italians would say, *peccato* (a pity).

Barnett Vineyards—Located near the peak of Spring Mountain, Barnett Vineyards issues some of the most refined, elegant wines on a hillside famous for the aggressive pungency of its (profound) Cabernets and Merlots. From its terraced hillside vineyards, Barnett offers two Cabernets, both in small quantities as yields are painfully low. The Spring Mountain District Cabernet is all berryish elegance; the rarer Rattlesnake Hill Cabernet (production is just 200 cases a year) is strikingly dense in the mid-palate yet delivers its strength with Pinot Noir-like finesse. Also excellent are Spring Mountain-grown Merlot (mostly from York Creek Vineyard) and lovely Pinot Noir from Sleepy Hollow Vineyard in Monterey County's Santa Lucia Highlands district.

Beaulieu Vineyard—The proverbial keeper of the flame. Despite an old-fashioned "full line" of wines, which include some decent Chardonnay and, especially, Cabernet, under the Beautour brand, there really is only one significant B.V. wine: the famous Private Reserve Cabernet Sauvignon. It is an exemplar of Oakville/Rutherford, coming exclusively from Beaulieu's romantically named vineyards: B.V. No. 1 and B.V. No. 2. Vineyard No. 1 is in Rutherford; Vineyard No. 2 is near Oakville. The consistency over decades of vintages is overwhelming proof of Oakville/Rutherford having a "there there." For this taster, only the strong vanilla scent of American oak intrudes. But unlike the Alexander Valley fruit of Silver Oak's Cabernet (q.v.), the muscularity and depth of Oakville/Rutherford Cabernet can better withstand the overlay of vanilla that is the giveaway to the traditionally treated American oak barrels used by both wineries.

Beringer Blass—Probably no big-scale corporate winery has succeeded in pleasing nearly all folks all the time the way Beringer Blass has. Keep in mind that this winery has been passed around to several big-buck owners, all of them admirable in their day. First came Nestlé in 1972, which put the then-shabby winery back on its feet with admirable investment and long-term planning. It really set the tone and the standard. Then came the Texas Pacific investment group, which bought it as a frank investment, but had the wit to stay with Nestlé's original vision. They, in turn, sold it for $1.2 billion in 2000 to the Australian beer giant Foster's which, for its part, astutely recognized that what they bought shouldn't be tinkered with. The name changed with this last purchase to Beringer Blass, to reflect Foster's ownership of the Australian winery Wolf Blass.

In the meantime, Beringer has proceeded to successfully appeal to all levels of California wine buyers. Its cash cow is its white Zinfandel, which accounts for about 40 percent of Beringer's entire case production. As the second most popular white Zinfandel (after Sutter Home) in the nation, it pays the bills.

At the high end, Beringer issues a series of named-vineyard Napa Valley Cabernets that take a back seat to no one in Napa Valley. Considering the price-no-object competition among Napa's ultra-rich "boutique" wineries, that's no small achievement. Ask anyone in Napa Valley and they'll tell you that Beringer's own vineyards are among the best and most scrupulously managed of any in Napa Valley.

Some tasters prefer the Private Reserve Cabernet, which is a blend of several vineyards. It is indeed superb. But for this taster, the singular flavors exhibited by the Chabot Vineyard Cabernet, with its punch of chocolate/cassis is more original tasting. (Chabot always makes its way into the Private Reserve blend, where you can find the same chocolate/cassis flavors.)

High on Howell Mountain is the Tre Colline (three hills) vineyard, which produces a lean, dusty, flavorful Cabernet that delivers the characteristic "goes down like water" quality of good Howell Mountain Cabs.

Elsewhere on Howell Mountain is Bancroft Ranch (under long-term lease and management by Beringer), which creates the now-famous Bancroft Ranch Merlot. It is arguably the finest Merlot in California, offering the signature dark chocolate scent and taste of top-quality Merlot with the sort of character and detail that usually are found only in Howell Mountain Cabernets. It can rightly be said to be one of the world's great Merlots.

Not everything is stellar: A Cabernet from Knight's Valley in Sonoma County has never impressed. It's pleasant, but no more than that. And, as is so often the case in Napa Valley, the Chardonnays are well made but ho-hum. That Napa Valley is red wine country is never better proved than by Beringer's Private Reserve Chardonnay: Qualitatively, it's not a patch on the Private Reserve Cabernet.

Blankiet Winery—Located in Yountville, on the hillside directly behind and above the vineyard of Dominus, this new winery has attracted considerable attention thanks to its prominent winemaking consultants, Helen Turley and John Wetlaufer. They almost always receive high praise from a handful of wine critics for the richness and intensity of the wines under their care. Whether Blankiet will justify its acclamation remains to be seen, as too few vintages have been released for legitimate analysis. That said, the chances are awfully good that something special should emerge from this sixteen-acre hillside site planted to Cabernet Sauvignon and Merlot. Time will tell.

Bond—This is the new venture of Harlan Estate, with 1999 as the first vintage. Bill Harlan, owner of Harlan Estate, had an enviable problem: Your name is golden for your namesake wine, but you can't expand your own estate vineyard in the foothills of the Mayacamas Mountains. Demand far exceeds supply. How do you capitalize on a market when you don't have any more wine to sell?

Enter Bond—and not as in "James Bond." Rather, as in gilt-edged bond. The almost Freudian giveaway to Bond is the label itself: It's a literal copy of the blackish-green fine engraving of an old-fashioned stock market bond certificate.

When I visited Harlan for the purposes of this book, Bill Harlan elaborately explained the thinking behind Bond. According to him, the notion of both the word ("bond") and the act was to create partnerships between himself and a handful of vineyard owners in Napa Valley. They would enter into detailed, extensive written contracts in which Harlan would make the wine from their grapes, and they would mutually create a proprietary named under the Bond label. Neither party could subsequently employ the name if one or other party later withdrew from the contract.

To listen to Harlan, this was a unique undertaking. It's nothing of the sort. Numerous California wineries engage in just such single-vineyard designated undertakings. Rather, Bond is a variation on a (legitimate) theme. In fairness, there's no reason to doubt that the vineyards selected by Harlan are—or will be, as it expands—anything less than first-rate. Harlan has too much reputation to lose by allying his name with less than superb wines.

Early offerings of brand-name wines Melbury (1999 and 2000) and Vecina (1999 and 2000) are indeed lovely bottlings, both made in Harlan's signature ultra-glossy, "juicy," oaky winemaking style. Like the flagship Harlan Estate wine, these are sure to excite attention and praise, as the style is frankly seductive and the quality genuine (See also *Harlan Estates*).

Bryant Family Vineyard—Few Napa Valley wines are richer, lusher, more opulent, or more acclaimed than Bryant Family Vineyard. Located on Pritchard Hill near Chappellet, this ten-acre vineyard really is a wine apart. As one of the indisputable "cult Cabernets," it's hard to separate the hype from the substance. But that's not Bryant's fault. They not-so-simply make a spectacular—if a bit overripe and oaky—Cabernet Sauvignon and they've gotten their reward in print and profit. This was another of the wines crafted by consultants Helen Turley and John Wetlaufer—until the arrangement became fractious and then litigious. They are no longer consulting to Bryant. If you get a chance to taste this wine, you should—especially if someone else is paying.

Buehler Vineyards—This is the source of dramatic, bold Cabernet and Zinfandel from Buehler's twenty-six-acre vineyard high up in the Vaca Range. In past vintages, a rather heavy hand with oak has been modulated to something more reasonable. What's more, in Napa Valley's often Alice-In-Wonderland pricing environment where producers will insist with a straight face that $100 for a bottle is "reasonable," Buehler has indeed kept its prices genuinely fair. This is a winery that has settled into admirable consistency, high quality, and fair pricing. Bravo!

Burgess Cellars—Although located on Howell Mountain, the Burgess vineyard around the winery is at the 900-foot elevation, well below the beginning of the Howell Mountain AVA which starts at 1,400 feet. Nor do the Burgess wines evoke Howell Mountain. Cabernet is the signature wine, with powerful punch of almost overripe flavor. What is missing is the "goes down like water" grace found in the Cabernets grown higher up on Howell Mountain. The wine to look for is the Vintage Selection Cabernet.

Cain Vineyard and Winery—If you follow narrow Langtry Road on Spring Mountain you will pass two of Napa Valley's greatest estates. They are contiguous: Fritz Maytag's York Creek Vineyard and, at the end of the road, Cain Vineyard. Cain is one of the most spectacularly sited vineyards anywhere in California and is now, after a decade of replanting, emerging as the source of superbly characterful Cabernet.

Two wines stand out. One is an exceptional value, called Cain Cuvée. It is sourced from several vineyards in Napa Valley (including Cain Vineyard's own grapes) and is perhaps the best-value Cabernet I know from Napa Valley.

Superior, and more expensive, is Cain's signature wine called Cain Five. The name refers to the classic five Bordeaux grape varieties from which it is composed: Cabernet Sauvignon, Cabernet Franc, Merlot, Petit Verdot, and Malbec. As the new post-phylloxera estate vineyard matures, Cain Five will likely eventually be a pure Spring Mountain expression. (It's already more than half estate-grown.) Exceptional in its intense spicy/herbal qualities with a licorice/anise scent that is characteristic of Spring Mountain Cabernet, Cain Five is one of Napa Valley's most distinctive, rewarding Cabernets.

Cakebread Cellars—This winery has stayed the course better than many longtime Napa Valley producers. Where others have skewed their winemaking to follow the latest fashion trends toward ultraripe, blatantly oaky/sweet wines, Cakebread's winemaking is as plain and sincerely good as Mom's homemade apple pie. The wines stand or fall on the intrinsic goodness of their grapes.

As always, there's a range of wines to choose from. And, as is typical in Napa Valley, the reds are better than the whites. Really, the wines to look for are the small-lot Cabernets, especially the Benchland Select and the Three Sisters bottling. Benchland Select is equally divided between Oakville and Rutherford and is a textbook example of the lacy texture and dusty/gravelly qualities that everybody points to (but aren't always delivered) as classic Oakville/Rutherford attributes.

Three Sisters, for its part, comes from the eastern side of Napa Valley and is fatter and richer than Benchland Select, but lacks its finesse. Worth noting is Cakebread's "plain" Cabernet Sauvignon. It's an exemplar of Napa Valley Cabernet as it should be; pure, free of obvious winemaking distortions, and straightforward in the best sense—a wine version of the boy you'd want your daughter to marry.

Carneros Creek Winery—A longtime proponent of Carneros-grown Pinot Noir, Carneros Creek Winery has never quite vaulted itself into the top rank of California Pinot Noir producers. Is it the limitations of Carneros Pinot Noir? Winemaking? Management? Opinions differ. Suffice it to say that this is a winery that, so far, has not delivered on its promise or potential, in this observer's opinion.

Carver Sutro Winery—Good, hearty, rewarding Petite Sirah comes from this old sixteen-acre Calistoga vineyard now owned by married couple Anne

Carver and Dennis Sutro. With Napa Valley obsessing over Cabernet Sauvignon, it's rewarding to see a Napa winery devoting itself to Petite Sirah—and to such a good end, too. It's a superb Petite Sirah: burly, intense, focused, and just plain delicious. Winemaker Gary Brookman is, by the way, the winemaker for Miner Family Vineyards and Grace Family Vineyards. He's a real pro. Worth seeking out.

Casa Nuestra Winery—This might well be Napa Valley's most endearing small winery. Owned by Gene Kirkham since 1968, Casa Nuestra has somehow kept itself snug inside its own 1970s time capsule. For example, it remains devoted to nurturing the forty-plus-year-old Chenin Blanc vines in front of its funky little winery on the Silverado Trail just south of Calistoga. The dry Chenin Blanc created by Casa Nuestra is spectacular, displaying the variety's signature anise/licorice scent and taste. Very likely it is California's finest and truest Chenin Blanc.

Then there's Casa Nuestra's almost preposterous—considering its location—Tinto Classico Old Vine Oakville. This is a red wine blend of eight red grape varieties grown in a tiny plot of seventy-year-old vines in Oakville, hard up against the Mayacamas Range. Its nearest neighbor? High-priced Harlan Estate. It makes no economic sense, but owner Gene Kirkham doesn't care. A regular Tinto, grown elsewhere in Napa Valley, is literally cloned from all the varieties grown in the ancient Tinto Classico site in Oakville.

Prices are, by Napa Valley's inflated standards, ridiculously cheap. Truth be told, Casa Nuestra is almost a museum piece of an old Napa Valley that soon no one will remember and will certainly not be resurrected. Get it while you can.

Caymus Vineyards—No winery has received more hoopla in recent years than Caymus. Yet when you look at the extensive offerings, it all comes down to just one wine: the Special Selection. While the regular Cabernet bottling is an exemplar of Oakville/Rutherford, it's the Special Selection that gets everyone excited because it's more resonant than the regular bottling and has a classic Oakville/Rutherford character. So much for the Rutherford Bench business: Caymus' vineyards are east of the Napa River, well away from what would have been the boundaries of the Rutherford Bench. Extended barrel aging makes the Caymus Cabernets a bit oaky, but the fruit quality is dramatic. White wines from the Mer Soleil vineyard in Monterey County have caused considerable stir in recent years, as the wines are good, in a dramatic fashion.

Chappellet Vineyard—Tucked in the Vaca Range, Chappellet has been beavering away making quintessential "mountain wine" since the 1968 vintage. Originally, the winery issued hard, tight Cabernets that never seemed to blossom, or at least unfurl. More recent vintages, starting in the mid-1990s, have seen not so much softer wines as more dimensional and resonant ones. Few wineries have had a longer haul before arriving at a stylistic "sweet spot" than Chappellet. But arrived they have. The prospects are likely that the next decade will vault Chappellet Cabernets into Napa Valley's top rank. It's been a long time coming.

Worth noting is this same dogged perseverance with Chenin Blanc, which has kept its austere faith to a more rewarding end. Chenin Blanc needs bottle aging and here, unlike with the older Cabernets, this high-elevation site shows its intrinsic worth for this underrated variety.

Château Montelena—It's tempting to say that in recent years Château Montelena hasn't gotten the huzzahs it deserves. That isn't quite true, as evidenced by the fact that its Cabernet and Chardonnay are sold on an allocated basis. Clearly, plenty of people still are clued in. But this sense of Château Montelena being out of the limelight is no doubt because, in the 1970s, it was on everyone's lips.

Château Montelena was the paradigm Napa Valley winery. It still is, even if newer wineries have shouldered it aside at the public relations trough. Since the 1978 vintage, the Cabernet comes exclusively from a seventy-acre vineyard in Calistoga. It is Napa Valley Cabernet at its best: opulent, long-lived, and elegant. It also shows just what the Calistoga area can do, an area that has frequently been written off as too warm for greatness. Few California Cabernets have been as consistent or as elegant. Simply put, Château Montelena creates one of California's greatest Cabernets—as well as one of its most successfully long-lived.

Although the Chardonnays are noteworthy, they simply are not as good as the Cabernets. Two sources are employed in separate bottlings: Alexander Valley in Sonoma County and Napa Valley. The Alexander Valley is the better of the two. The winemaking philosophy is not to fiddle: no lees contact, no malolactic fermentation, no barrel fermentation. They do last, but are not anywhere near as profound as the Cabernet.

Chimney Rock—This winery still has not found its focus, despite an enviable location in the choice Stags Leap District. This strikingly designed winery, modeled on a (South African) Cape Dutch manor house design, still has yet to establish itself as anything noteworthy. Like so many other Napa Valley wineries, its blended wines from grapes purchased here and there are of no distinct or consistent quality. Only the Stags Leap District-designated Cabernet provides real character. But even that wine is not up to others in the same category such as Shafer or Pine Ridge.

Clark-Claudon Vineyards—Napa Valley increasingly offers small lots of distinctive Cabernets grown by people who are in it for more than just the social cachet or even the money (although that's always nice). Clark-Claudon is one such winery. Located on what might be called the "other side" of Howell Mountain—which is to say the as-yet-undelineated stretch of hillside and valley that lies between the eastern base of Howell Mountain and the western boundary of Pope Valley. It's something of an undiscovered zone, at least by tourists.

Cabernet Sauvignon is the ticket at Clark-Claudon and what an exceptional wine it is: dense, filled with red currant/grenadine scents and tastes, and quite supple in texture. Production is small at 2,500 cases. Worth seeking out.

Clos du Val—One of the earliest French-influenced wineries in Napa Valley (owned by John Goelet; the original and still-current winemaker is Bernard Portet). Clos du Val's original claim to fame actually was Zinfandel. Today it has branched out to other varieties, but really, it's the Cabernet that's got it. The reason is simple: Clos du Val Cabernet comes from the Stags Leap District (since the 1987 vintage, the label so states).

Located at the southern end of the Stags Leap District at the base of the Vaca Range palisade, Clos du Val had the misfortune of having poor soil drainage. This resulted in wines that too often displayed a vegetal or herbaceous note. Phylloxera proved to be an expensive blessing. Because the vines had to be replanted, the winery had the opportunity to install an always-needed drainage system. This will very likely usher in a new (and better) era of Clos du Val Cabernets.

Clos Pegase Winery—A winery where architecture, rather than wine, is the *raison d'être*. Located across Dunaweal Lane from Sterling Vineyards, Clos Pegase put itself literally on the map thanks to its Michael Graves-designed winery. (Owner Jan Schrem sponsored a design competition through a San Francisco museum; Graves won.) The wines, however, are ho-hum—and always have been, come to think of it. The winery, however, is very much worth visiting.

Constant Winery—Located at the ridge-line peak of Diamond Mountain, this somewhat unheralded winery has yet to fully make its mark. But it's a good bet that it will, as the vineyard—called Diamond Mountain Vineyard—is surely among Napa Valley's most singular hillside sites. Like other Diamond Mountain producers, Cabernet is the vehicle and Constant Cabernet exhibits Diamond Mountain's signature chocolate scent allied to the surprisingly soft, round tannins that this AVA seems to enjoy. Fred and Mary Constant prefer their Cabernets blended with about two-thirds Cabernet Sauvignon and roughly one-third Merlot, sometimes with a bit of Cabernet Franc included. This is a winery that, after a bit of stylistic indirection, has now found its true voice and will very likely become a prominent name in Napa Valley.

Cuvaison Vineyard—Cuvaison is one of those Napa Valley wines that might be best described as "good enough." A winery that has frequently sourced its grapes, especially Chardonnay and Merlot from Carneros, it has yet to establish a signature wine that sets it apart from dozens of other equally acceptable, if commercial, operations. Since the winery has had decades to find and refine its identity, it's now fair to say that this is who they are and what they're about: good but not great, plausible but not impressive.

Dalla Valle Vineyards—This is the winery that effectively created what I call "Oakville East." Located in the rock-strewn hills of the Vaca Range but technically in the Oakville AVA, the late Gustavo Dalla Valle defied conventional wisdom and installed his vineyard in a spot that had never previously seen vineyards. It was too rocky, they said. Too dry. Too extreme. "They" were right on all counts except for one: What emerged was a Cabernet Sauvignon unlike any in Napa Valley—or anywhere else in the world, for that matter.

Happily, acclaim soon followed. (It's nice when that happens, isn't it?) Dalla Valle makes two wines: a regular (and very fine Cabernet) and a richer, bigger, fuller, more dramatic version from a subplot in their vineyard called Maya. The Maya bottling has gotten most of the attention, and yes, it is superior. But the regular Dalla Valle Cabernet is unfairly overshadowed by it.

Really, it's like a fraternal twin that, as first glance, looks almost—but not quite—identical. Both Cabernets provide an uncommon textural density characteristic of "Oakville East," with a rich, sappy fruitiness and firm but not harsh tannin. They are structured wines built (by the land itself) to last. You could no more make a light, flimsy wine from this sun-drenched, rocky site than Beethoven could have written a simple nursery rhyme.

Darioush Winery—Installed in Stags Leap District, this relative newcomer to the area is still groping to find its way. So far, nothing especially distinctive has emerged from a winery found in one of Napa's most distinguished (and distinctive) zones. But it's still early days. To watch.

Diamond Creek Vineyards—Diamond Creek Vineyards is one of the heroic wineries of Napa Valley. Where other supposedly "personal" wineries in the area have cast a wide and changing net for grapes, and have pandered to changing styles in public taste (remember "food wines?"), Al Brounstein's Diamond Creek Vineyards has remained true to its school. The "school" in this case is Diamond Mountain, out of which Brounstein carved four vineyards: Volcanic Hill, Red Rock Terrace, Gravelly Meadow, and Lake Vineyard. The one-acre Lake Vineyard is only rarely bottled separately; the other three almost invariably are. The differences are noticeable, although not dramatic. All are richly earthy, profoundly Diamond Mountain.

For a long time, the style of the winemaking was rustic. But recent vintages have been much more refined, without any loss of character. Quite the opposite: Diamond Mountain shines through more brightly and clearly today than ever before, thanks to better winemaking "faceting." They age with grace, and have more intrinsic character than almost any other Napa Valley Cabernets.

Diamond Mountain Terrace—A tiny winery (250 cases annually) located, of course, on Diamond Mountain. Their first vintage was 1999, and already, they're off to a superb start issuing intense, rich, classic Diamond Mountain Cabernets compounded of dark chocolate, soft tannins, and impressive intensity. One would be fortunate indeed to be on their mailing list, as this winery offers Diamond Mountain Cabernet of truly top quality.

Dolce Winery—In 1991, Far Niente's owner, the late Gil Nickel, decided that he wished to re-create, as best as possible, a Sauternes-style wine in Napa Valley. Much to everyone's astonishment—my own included—he has succeeded. I confess that I couldn't have been more surprised. Napa Valley has long issued various late-harvest wines, a number of which see significant amounts of *Botrytis cinerea* or noble rot, the mold that gives Sauternes its spicy taste and syrupy texture. (The late Myron Nightingale, the longtime winemaker of Beringer Vineyards, pursued botrytised wines ardently. Beringer still makes one called, in homage, Nightingale.)

Nickel fashioned an entirely separate winery from Far Niente and in his cost-no-object manner instructed the winemaker and vineyardists responsible for Dolce to do what had to be done. By definition, that means money, as a great Sauternes-style wine requires tremendous rigor in limiting yields, waiting for noble rot to appear (it doesn't always) and then employing yet more rigor in selecting only the best lots on a barrel by barrel basis. It's a labor of love even if you can command the $100-a-bottle price Dolce asks.

What's impressive is just how good the latest bottlings of Dolce are. The early attempts, inevitably, were hit and miss. But starting with the 1999 vintage, Dolce has become a dead-ringer for a really good Sauternes—yet with a distinction all its own.

For one thing, it's almost as acidic as Sauternes itself, a necessary element in a sweet wine. For another, there's a fruit dimension present that's absent in lesser-quality Sauternes. But the balance, the botrytis, and the sheer "breed" found in the best Sauternes are now found in Dolce too. You'll find an apricot hue and that spicy pineapple scent and taste frequently found in Sauternes. The wine, at least in the turning point 1999 vintage bottling, is 95 percent Sémillon and only 5 percent Sauvignon Blanc grown in the cool Coombsville zone near the city of Napa. Earlier, less successful bottlings saw more Sauvignon Blanc. Now the question is: How frequently can the success of the 1999 bottling be repeated? Even Sauternes doesn't bat better than four vintages out of ten.

Domaine Carneros—Created by the French Champagne house Taittinger in the 1980s in hot pursuit of what was expected to become a huge American sparkling wine market, Domaine Carneros—like most others— found itself becalmed in a glutted sea of taste-alike sparkling wines. It certainly has a physical presence in the Carneros district, as you can't miss the Disneyland-like replica of Taittinger's seventeenth-century brick and stone Champagne château.

Today, Domaine Carneros continues to issue good, but hardly exceptional, sparkling wines. Now, it is diverting some of the Pinot Noir once meant for bubbly into still wines. The still wine program will take time, as the fruit from Pinot Noir vines intended for still wine must come from vines trained and pruned (and harvested) differently than for sparkling wine. Then, of course, there are the usual vinification challenges that, no matter how broad the knowledge base of your neighbors (and no matter how generous they are in sharing it), you still have to learn anew for yourself. All this is part of Domaine Carneros' new mission to restructure itself as a winery that creates both sparkling and still wines.

Domaine Chandon—California's sparkling wine king. Others, such as Korbel and Schramsberg, are older. But, really, it was Domaine Chandon that put California sparkling wine front and center when Moët & Chandon first arrived in Napa Valley in the early 1970s. By getting in early they paid a pittance for land (as little as $600 an undeveloped acre). And they built a showcase California-inspired winery that still looks good today (and isn't a touristy French knick-knack like Domaine Carneros' *faux château*).

And the wines? Reliable, good, occasionally something better than that in selected bottlings that see more aging before release. But really, like every other sparkling wine producer relying heavily (as Domaine Chandon does) on Carneros-grown Chardonnay and Pinot Noir, there's only so much you can achieve by winemaking and cellaring techniques. After all, France's Champagne region has intensely chalky soil, while Carneros is more about gravel and clay. Soil *does* make a difference.

Worth noting is that, while other California sparkling wine producers have either faltered, failed altogether, or transformed into conventional wineries, Domaine Chandon remains serenely secure as a sparkling wine producer. (Although it, too, is now issuing more still wine.)

The reason? Simple economics. Moët invested so long ago, and so cheaply compared to its competitors, that Domaine Chandon could lower its prices to whatever level it took to meet its competition and still make a profit, while the competition financially bled the death. No one dared take that head-to-head route during the California sparkling wine wars, but the threat was always there.

Consequently, although retail prices remained mostly proportionate to production costs, Domaine Chandon always had higher profits per bottle because their investment was far less than those of later arrivals. Unless the market expanded, which it didn't sufficiently, Chandon was in the catbird seat, as no one dared try to beat it on price, while everybody's quality (except Roederer Estate in Anderson Valley) was pretty much the same. Point, game, set.

Dominus Estate—Dominus is the proprietary name of a blend of Cabernet Sauvignon (about 70 percent), Merlot (20 percent), and Cabernet Franc (10 percent). The vineyard, west of Yountville called Napanook, was originally owned by the daughters of the late John Daniel, whose family owned Inglenook until 1964. They went into partnership with Christian Moueix, the owner of Pomerol's Château Petrus. It was his portrait that appeared on the original Dominus label—a declaration of vanity unthinkable in Pomerol and virtually unprecedented even in California, where one's name on the label was usually thought to suffice. That label has since changed and now sports Moueix's almost illegible, John Hancock-sized signature instead.

Moueix is now the sole owner of Dominus and created an ultramodern winery (not open to the public). Since the original 1983 vintage bottling, Dominus wine has been intense and sometimes affected by a herbaceous note, as Yountville is a relatively cool locale. The early bottlings were heavy-handed. Because of this, Dominus did not become the runaway market success its owners expected.

Dominus has become a more accessible wine, more supple yet still resonantly flavorful. This surely is due to winemaking technique, yet also is likely characteristic of Yountville Cabernets in general (see Grgich Hills, Markham, and Charles Krug). This is one of those conjectures that needs more producers, vintages, and identified sources for an informed judgment. Still, Dominus is clearly a wine of impressive place.

That said, the winemaking style is increasingly "old-fashioned" in its preference for austerity and willingness to display herbaceous notes. If anything, Dominus now creates more classically Bordeaux-type wine than, ironically, Bordeaux itself.

Duckhorn Vineyards—A winery that shows just what blending *can't* do in Napa Valley: It can't create wines of distinctive character. Duckhorn wines, across the board, are pleasant, but one misses a sense of source. The Cabernets should be distinctive, yet by the time other grapes are blended in, all that results is a pleasantly "correct" Cabernet. Duckhorn's signature wine is Merlot, which is similarly "correct," but bland to the point of banality—for as much as $80 a bottle. Go figure.

Dunn Vineyards—Randy Dunn is the uncrowned king of the (Howell) mountain. It was his site-specific Cabernets, starting with the 1979 vintage, that first brought attention, then acclaim, and finally a shower of money on Howell Mountain Cabernets. Usually, when such sagas are recounted, the ending has the visionary pioneer trampled by a mob of better-financed followers. Not so this time. In 1991, Randy Dunn purchased the forty-seven-acre Park-Muscatine vineyard (fifteen acres of which were planted, mostly to Petite Sirah and Zinfandel), which is close to his own vineyard. He has replanted it entirely to Cabernet Sauvignon.

Dunn has made enough money to build a 250-foot-long tunnel to house his barrels. All this from a $62,000 purchase in 1979 (from his former employer, Charles Wagner of Caymus Vineyard) of a fourteen-acre spread that included a six-acre already-planted vineyard.

Dunn also issues a Cabernet identified as "Napa Valley" from purchased grapes. Although it is excellent wine, it's really the Howell Mountain Cabernet that makes Dunn so sought after. Since the inaugural 1979 bottling, Dunn Howell Mountain Cabernet has consistently proved to be one of California's most accomplished and characterful wines.

Dyer Vineyard—This is the tiny, personal vineyard (and home) of two former winemakers, Dawnine Dyer (former head winemaker of Domaine Chandon) and Bill Dyer (formerly head winemaker of Sterling Vineyards). They own a scant four acres of Cabernet Sauvignon, Cabernet Franc, Merlot, and Petit Verdot on Diamond Mountain. Located in what might be called Diamond Mountain's "golden enclave" where Diamond Creek, Von Strasser, Reverie, and Dyer are virtually cheek to cheek, Dyer delivers the real goods. Simply put, these are great Cabernets. They brim with the characteristic cocoa and blueberry scent of Diamond Mountain Cabernet/Merlot. Ditto for the soft, ripe tannins. Quantity is obviously minute; quality superb. If you can find it, get it.

Eagle and Rose Winery—A newcomer to the Napa scene, Eagle and Rose is really an expression of Pope Valley, where its vineyards are located. So far, the array of wines does not impress. They are well made, but conventional-tasting. However much various Napa Valley powers (Louis M. Martini winery, Saint-Supéry) insist that Pope Valley really *is* a legitimate part of the Napa Valley appellation—which it legally is—the wines tell us differently.

Emilio's Terrace/Gargiulo Vineyard—The Gargiulo family (based in Los Angeles) owns a small Oakville vineyard in a choice location. Various wines are issued (Pinot Grigio, Rosé, etc.), all in tiny quantities, but the one really worthwhile wine is—no prizes for guessing—the Cabernet Sauvignon designated Emilio's Terrace, after their vineyard manager. This is lovely Oakville-grown Cabernet: rich, meaty, beautifully balanced with a hint of mint.

Far Niente Winery—No winery is more baffling, at least to me, than Far Niente. Despite the prime location of its vineyard in the heart of Oakville/Rutherford hard up against the Mayacamas foothills (Mondavi's To-Kalon Vineyard surrounds it), the Far Niente Cabernet has yet to equal the achievements of neighboring vineyards. It should be one of California's supreme Cabernets. It isn't. Oddly, this is not because of late owner Gil Nickel's lack of ambition or resources. (He died of cancer in October 2003 at age sixty-four.) While it displays Oakville/Rutherford characteristics, the Cabernet so far has lacked the focus, backbone, and above all, articulation, that one can expect from the location.

Far Niente Chardonnay is blended from a vast array of lots (as many as sixty) from the Oakville/Rutherford site and two cooler vineyards east of the city of Napa. Also, it does not see malolactic fermentation, giving it a brighter acidity than many other Napa Valley Chardonnays. Still, it's more a winemaking achievement than a vineyard one. The Oakville/Rutherford Cabernet, in comparison, has a known identity that has yet to be fully revealed. A Cabernet more revealing of its source, rather than of winemaking, still has yet to emerge. It's certainly good. It should be flat-out great. For this taster, it isn't.

Fife Vineyards—A small vineyard located on Spring Mountain, Fife is really more of a label for which various lots of wines bought from as far north as Mendocino are sold by owner Dennis Fife. The estate vineyard creates a good, but not yet exceptional, Cabernet.

Franciscan Vineyards—The comeback champion of Napa Valley, maybe even of all California. From 1971 through 1975, it went through two owners only to wind up in bankruptcy, although still retaining 450 acres of vineyards. Purchased in 1975 by the late Justin Meyer and a Colorado investor, the winery expanded its vineyard holdings by an additional 1,000 acres. At the same time, Meyer created a separate, higher-priced brand called Silver Oak Wine Cellars. In 1979, Franciscan was again sold, to a family-owned German firm, the Peter Eckes Co.

After floundering for several years, in 1986 Eckes brought in Agustin Huneeus, Sr., a longtime winery management professional, as a fifty-fifty partner. He proved to be, literally, the saving grace of Franciscan Vineyards. Huneeus, Sr. established the direction, stability, and standards that were previously lacking. A low-priced brand called Estancia was created, originally as an outlet for Franciscan's 240 acres in Sonoma's Alexander Valley. It immediately offered, and still does, good values in Cabernet, Chardonnay, and Sauvignon Blanc. Later, the Estancia brand switched its source to Monterey County as a result of new vineyard purchases.

The purchase of the 1,200-acre Pinnacles Vineyard in Monterey County has led to an adeqnate Pinot Noir and Pinot Gris. Franciscan purchased Mount Veeder Winery in 1989 (q.v.), which operates separately.

Finally, in 1999, Franciscan was bought by the former Canandaigua Wine Company—since renamed Constellation Brands—for a reported $240 million. Huneeus, Sr. retained ownership of Quintessa, his personal high-end estate in Oakville.

Today, Franciscan has become a true powerhouse winery, with the capital and marketing muscle of Constellation offering unprecedented propulsion. It is expanding its vineyard holdings while at the same time steadily ratcheting up its quality at all price levels.

Freemark Abbey Winery—The notion of Oakville/Rutherford is embodied in Freemark Abbey Winery almost as much as is in Beaulieu and Inglenook wineries. Originally founded in 1935, it really dates to 1967 when it was revived by Charles Carpy and seven other investors. (Carpy is old Napa Valley stock. His French-born grandfather owned the Greystone winery of Christian Brothers—now the West Coast campus of the Culinary Institute of America—until 1895.)

Although Freemark Abbey issues the usual line of Chardonnay, Riesling, and Merlot, it's really just two single-vineyard Cabernets, both from Oakville/Rutherford, that give it luster: Bosché and Sycamore. These two vineyards put Freemark Abbey on the map—and keep it there. They are among the finest expressions of place in Napa Valley, with no stylistic flourishes or razzmatazz.

Godspeed Vineyard—This is a twenty-two-acre, family-owned-and run-vineyard on Mount Veeder that issues fine Chardonnay and disappointing Cabernet. (They are made at Monticello Winery.) The Cabernet is true to its Mount Veeder origins, but fails to wow, as it lacks mid-palate density. The Chardonnay, an increasingly rare item on Howell Mountain, is more distinctive. It sees no malolactic fermentation and only 25 percent new oak. What results is buttery, with a characteristic Mount Veeder stoniness. It's worth seeking out.

Grace Family Vineyards—Grace Family Vineyards deserves mention, even though the odds of coming across a bottle from this two-acre vineyard are next to impossible. Is it good wine? Yes, it's very good. Classic Napa Valley Cabernet, in fact. But it's no snappier than any of a couple dozen other top-ranked valley-floor Cabernets. Rarity and curiosity drive the price as much as quality. Still, if you see it and someone else is paying . . .

Grgich Hills Cellar—It says something about Grgich Hills Cellar (and above all, about Croatia-born co-owner/winemaker Miljenko "Mike" Grgich) that at a time when even the lowliest Napa Valley wineries charge tasting-room fees for sampling third-rate offerings, the funky tasting room of Grgich Hills asks nothing. What's more, the wines offered typically are Grgich's *best* wines. It's safe to say that Grgich Hills is now unique in Napa Valley in humility, hospitality, and just plain perspective.

Happily, the wines are equally endearing. Grgich Hills is synonymous with large-scale, intense Chardonnay and rightly so. They are astonishingly consistent. The consistency is achieved by blending from among the winery's 165 acres of Chardonnay vines spread across Rutherford, Yountville, Napa, and Carneros. It is a brand supreme. That said, the quality is exceptionally high and the style bull's-eye in its intent to create intense, almost tropical Chardonnay every year.

Something should also be said about the Grgich Cabernet, a variety not usually associated with Grgich Hills. For this taster, the Grgich Cabernets are probably the greatest "unknown" Cabernets in Napa Valley. Here, consistency is achieved by almost exclusive reliance upon a single, prime source: Grgich Hills' forty-three-acre vineyard in Yountville, which lies hard by the

Napanook vineyard of Dominus. What appear to be Yountville characteristics of leanness, suppleness, roundness, and a hint of mint are present in the Grgich Cabernet as well. It is an impressive wine that could not come from just anywhere.

Groth Vineyards and Winery—Groth was put on the wine map by a then-unprecedented score of 100 points from Robert M. Parker, Jr.'s *The Wine Advocate* for its 1985 Reserve Cabernet Sauvignon. All of a sudden, it was *the* Napa Valley Cabernet. Regrettably, Groth has never since created a wine quite as good as that now-legendary 1985. Too many of the recent Cabernets have exhibited off-putting vegetal notes such as asparagus. The estate vineyard in Oakville is in center-valley, near the clayey, cold-soil banks of the Napa River. A concerted effort to reduce this vegetalness is under way, with efforts at canopy management techniques and leaf-pulling to reduce vegetalness in the fruit. The Reserve Cabernets are better than the regular bottlings, but this is a winery that has somehow stumbled from a pinnacle. Since the vineyard has a known competency of place, it is entirely possible—even likely—that Groth can return to form.

Guilliams Winery—A small Spring Mountain District producer of uneven quality issuing Cabernet Sauvignon and Merlot. Although the wines have quality, they seem to lack refinement and consistency. One gets the sense of a small family winery still searching for its style.

Harlan Estate—Few wineries anywhere in the world, let alone Napa Valley, have been showered with more unstinting acclaim than Harlan Estate. Located smack in one of the choicest spots possible in the foothills of the Mayacamas Mountains near Mondavi's To-Kalon Vineyard, Far Niente, Martha's Vineyard, and other big names in Oakville, Harlan is staking a claim to greatness.

Created by Bill Harlan, who also owns Meadowood Country Club near St. Helena, everything has been done in a spare-no-expense fashion. Two wines are offered, both Cabernets. The flagship wine is simply labeled Harlan Estate; the second label is called The Maiden. Both wines are intensively sought after and frequently appear at auction soon after release, selling for three or four times (or more) the winery's original asking price. (You have to be on Harlan's long-closed mailing list to obtain the wines; there are no sales to retailers or restaurants.)

Inevitably, when supplies are so small (between 1,500 and 2,500 cases a year are made of the Harlan Estate with The Maiden adding at least another 700 cases) and the praise and scores are so lavish, a mythical quality enshrines a wine. In fairness, this was not artificially created by Harlan. Rather, it was a gift from the wine-writing gods—maybe even a bit of a curse. After all, when expectations run so high from readers' fantasies, can any winery fulfill them?

So what *does* Harlan Cabernet taste like? And why has it received such uncommon acclaim? Harlan Cabernet tastes just like it should, given the vineyard location. This is to say that it is a meaty, rich, intense Cabernet that exhibits a noticeable gravelly/dusty soil quality that characterizes the best Cabernets from Oakville/Rutherford. Any doubts about the much-heralded distinction of place of the so-called Rutherford Bench can be easily resolved upon tasting a Harlan Cabernet. This wine could not have come from anywhere. It's mighty fine.

Still, such quality does not fully explain the Harlan's luster. That derives, in the taster's opinion, more from the *style* of the wine. Harlan Estate is like nothing so much as a very attractive woman who, unnecessarily, wears too much makeup. Harlan Cabernet is dramatically oaky in scent and taste, as well as smooth as a politician. There are no abrasive tannins here. The fruit is lush, "juicy," and massive.

Harlan is the quintessential "low-cut dress wine," with a lot on offer, as it were. Not surprisingly, it leaps out in a blind tasting because of its lush, soft, rich, oaky intensity—as well as its legitimate intrinsic quality. Like that beautiful woman, one only wishes that all the sluttish makeup was removed and the intrinsic beauty more fully revealed. But then it wouldn't attract quite so much panting attention, would it?

Hartwell Vineyards—This is a new Stags Leap District winery that is still sorting out its standards. The wine is good, true Stags Leap District Cabernet in its rich, soft gentility. Unfortunately, there's been some variation in matters of fruit density, a clear indication of less than ideal rigor when it comes to yields. If that gets attended to, then Hartwell is on its way to becoming an exemplary Stags Leap District producer, as their vines are well-sited.

Herb Lamb Vineyards—An excellent small producer that first came to considerable public attention through Colgin Cellars, which first issued a vineyard-designated bottling from Herb Lamb Vineyards and still is the main producer. Meaty, slightly minty Cabernet from a seven-acre vineyard at the 800- to 1000-foot level of Howell Mountain, it's fine wine, if difficult to secure as production is limited.

Heitz Wine Cellars—The importance of source is never better revealed than with Heitz Wine Cellars, founded in 1961. The wine that launched Heitz to early attention, the 1962 Chardonnay Lot C-22, came from Hanzell Vineyard, a source long since unavailable to Heitz. Although the winery has always made Chardonnay, along with many other wines, the fact is that Heitz is notable only for two wines: Martha's Vineyard and Bella Oaks. Both are single-vineyard Cabernets from Oakville/Rutherford and both are superb. Neither vineyard is owned by Heitz, but the winery has an exclusivity on the grapes. Martha's Vineyard is owned by Tom and Martha May; Bella Oaks is owned by Belle and Barney Rhodes. The reason, as James Laube explains in his detailed book, *California's Great Cabernets*, is that both the Mays and the Rhodeses are shareholders in Heitz Wine Cellars. (Another single-vineyard Cabernet, Fay Vineyard in the Stags Leap District, was sold by Nathan Fay in 1986 to Stag's Leap Wine Cellars.)

A regular Cabernet bottling also is issued, from grapes from Heitz's seventy-acre vineyard near the Silverado Trail. It is notably good Cabernet, but never as distinctive or characterful as the two named-vineyard versions. The latest versions of Heitz Cabernets show a more refined, polished style than previously seen from this winery. Indeed, the latest vintages of Martha's Vineyard are as buffed as a show car.

Hess Collection Winery—Swiss water magnate Donald Hess has slowly amassed an extraordinary amount of vineyard acreage in Napa Valley, as well as elsewhere in California, to build a powerhouse winery. Located on Mount Veeder, the Hess Collection Winery issues multiple levels of wine quality at varying prices. Wines are sourced from as far away as Monterey County and as close as Hess' 280 acres of vines on Mount Veeder itself. The lesser wines, labeled Hess Select, are pleasant and well made but undistinctive. The signature bottlings that give the Hess Collection its luster are the Hess Estate wines and the real goods, the Mount Veeder-grown The Hess Collection wines. In The Hess Collection level of wines, you can find the pungent, earthy/minerally distinction of Mount Veeder-grown Cabernet Sauvignon. Overall, the Hess Collection Winery is a mixed, and increasingly large, bag.

Most of the wines are blended from multiple vineyard sources, creating a decent standard but only rarely an outstanding, truly individual wine.

Honig Vineyard and Winery—Honig's claim to fame is its Sauvignon Blanc, which is indeed mighty fine. Made in a slightly oaky Bordeaux style (as opposed to a steely, crisp Sancerre style), Honig's Sauvignon Blanc is a sure bet in almost any vintage I can think of.

Howell Mountain Vineyards—This is one of the great, unheralded estates of Napa Valley located high atop Howell Mountain, as the name suggests. Started in 1988, Howell Mountain Vineyard was originally known for its Zinfandel, which was the red wine grape of choice on Howell Mountain until Randy Dunn of Dunn Vineyards made a case for Cabernet in the 1980s.

Today, Howell Mountain Vineyards makes both Zinfandel and Cabernet Sauvignon. Both are outstanding: pure, true expressions of Howell Mountain place, as well as superb examples of their respective grape varieties. Two vineyard names are used: Beatty Vineyard is the actual vineyard of Howell Mountain Vineyards; Black Sears is another vineyard at a slightly lower elevation owned by Joyce Black Sears and Jerre Sears, who are co-owners of Howell Mountain Vineyards with Mike Beatty.

The differences between the two wines, both for Cabernet and Zinfandel, are noticeable, but not dramatically so. Both deliver a dusty, metallic scent and taste, along with deep, rich fruit. Beatty Ranch seems to have more of an iron note, while Black Sears is richer and denser, but not quite as characterfully pungent as Beatty Ranch.

A third wine, labeled Old Vines, is used for both a Zinfandel as well as a Cabernet Sauvignon. The label signals a blend of both vineyards and both are superb, marrying the qualities of the two vineyards admirably. This is a winery that deserves far more acclaim than it seems to have received. Seek it out.

Jarvis Wines—William Jarvis, an Annapolis graduate, left the Navy early in his career and went to what is now called the Silicon Valley in the 1950s. After working for Hewlett-Packard, he set out on his own and created his own electronics company that he subsequently sold for a tidy sum. An autodidact, Jarvis then traveled to Europe and lived for long periods in Champagne, the Loire Valley, and Spain. There, he acquired an interest in wine, although not one that compelled him to return to California to start a winery.

Instead, he purchased a large, historic ranch high in the hills above the city of Napa simply to live a country life. But this "country" was in Napa Valley, and you know what happened next. Jarvis got the wine bug. He planted thirty-seven acres of vines and proceeded to install a largely self-designed, entirely underground (including the offices) winery that cannot fail to impress. It's easily one of Napa Valley's most lavish sets of tunnels.

Jarvis set out to sell his wines, all estate-grown, at relatively high prices for an unknown winery growing grapes in an unproved location. The wines, each with individual plot designations such as Lake William and Lake Leticia (named after family members), are powerful, strong Cabernet blends that, so far, do not show much pedigree. They are certainly good wines. But as yet, they are not great wines. They lack distinction, "breed," call it what you like. That (regretfully) said, this is a winery that may someday deliver far more impressive goods than it has so far, as Jarvis' ambition is genuine and sustained.

Robert Keenan Winery—One of the early arrivals on Spring Mountain (1977), Keenan has seen something of a rocky road that has only now started smoothing out. It's an odd story in a way, if only because Keenan wines enjoyed early acclaim and success. But the original owner, Robert Keenan, is a cantankerous sort, and he discovered that he didn't particularly care for some of the attendant nonsense and superficiality that accompanies the wine business, especially in a chichi locale like Napa Valley. So he lit out for Hawaii and tried to run his winery long-distance. It really didn't work.

Eventually, the time came where Robert Keenan had to decide to either sell his winery or, alternatively, allow his son, Michael (who had long had a separate career away from wine), to run the winery with complete independence. Robert Keenan chose the latter.

The results are already impressive and bode extremely well for the future. Keenan wines from the late 1990s and early 2000s are simply superb: dense, rich, strong, classically powerful Spring Mountain-grown reds. Merlot is a standout—one of California's finest, in fact. Cabernet Sauvignon is pure Spring Mountain in its brawny intensity and blackish hue. A mostly estate-grown Chardonnay (30 percent comes from Trefethen Vineyard) is a powerful, earthy Chardonnay that has real appeal. Keenan is on the comeback trail big-time.

Kongsgaard/Arietta—The source of some of Napa Valley's most distinctive white wines. John Kongsgaard has strong convictions about how his wines, at least, should be made. He uses very little sulfur dioxide, employs older barrels and believes in using wild, rather than cultured, yeasts. Kongsgaard Chardonnay is sourced almost entirely from the eastern hills within the city of Napa, a relatively cool location. (The vineyard is adjacent to his parents' home; the Kongsgaards are an old and distinguished Napa family.) A small amount, perhaps 10 percent, is sourced from Hudson Vineyard in Carneros. The result is an intense, lemony, dense Chardonnay that is more than reminiscent of a *grand cru* Chablis—which is no small achievement.

Also worthwhile is a Roussanne (66 percent)/Viognier (34 percent) blend, again from the family vineyard in Napa. Red wines derive mostly from Hudson Vineyard in Carneros, including a fine Cabernet Franc (75 percent)/Merlot (25 percent) blend that delivers a pleasing "cool climate" berryishness. Less persuasive is a Merlot/Syrah blend. But quite impressive is a clearly cool-climate 100 percent Syrah, again from Hudson Vineyard. These are sold under the Arietta label (which is co-owned by wine auctioneer Fritz Hatton).

Overall, Kongsgaard makes some of Napa Valley's most original-tasting white wines that do not follow the conventional tastes of sweet oakiness and bland fruitiness. These are wines of real character and distinction.

Charles Krug Winery—Although always promising to return to its original pre-1970s greatness, there's no getting around the fact that Charles Krug Winery has settled into a comfortable, apparently profitable, mediocrity. As is well known, Charles Krug is owned by the "other Mondavi," namely Peter Mondavi. Krug's numerous offerings are strictly commercial, save one: the Vintage Selection Cabernet. Throughout the 1960s and earlier, Krug took a back seat to no one with what was then labeled Cesare Mondavi Vintage Selection Cabernet Sauvignon. I still savor memories of vintages back to the early 1960s. But in the 1970s the backbone of the Vintage Selection wine was broken, in part due to Robert Mondavi having received the To-Kalon Vineyard as part of his settlement after breaking away from the family business. Since then the Vintage Selection has wandered both geographically and stylistically.

One of Napa Valley's biggest vineyard owners, Charles Krug could return to noteworthy quality whenever it wishes, but so far it appears to be content to issue well made if uninspiring wines on a large scale.

Ladera—The newly renamed Château Woltner, this winery has every possibility of becoming one of the stars of Howell Mountain once its vineyards—transformed from Château Woltner's unsuccessful pursuit of Chardonnay—are fully reconstituted with Cabernet Sauvignon. The historic old winery has been beautifully restored and its new Midwestern owners, Pat and Anne Stotesbery, seem to be genuinely committed to winegrowing, rather than Napa Valley social hobnobbing. Releases from the 2000 vintage reveal a lithe yet fully ripe style: "black cherries rolled in dust" is how my notes describe one (successful) Cabernet.

Lagier Meredith—One of the attractions of California wine is that even a vineyard as small as four acres cannot only create legitimate excitement, but is even capable of revising how an entire district might reconsider its potential. This is, in effect, the story of Lagier Meredith.

Stephen Lagier was a longtime employee of Robert Mondavi Winery; Carole Meredith recently retired as a professor at the UC Davis School of Viticulture and Enology and is famous for her work in grapevine genetics. They installed a four-acre vineyard next to their home on Mount Veeder, planting it themselves entirely to Syrah. To the best of my knowledge, theirs is the first Syrah planting on Mount Veeder. And if it's not, in fact, the first, it's certainly one of the earliest. They were also able to take advantage of the newly commercialized ENTAV clones from France. (See page 68.)

What has resulted in just a few years—the first vintage was 1998—has been nothing less than revelatory. Lagier Meredith Syrah is consistently impressive in every vintage they've made so far, exhibiting classic Syrah elements such as a scent and taste of white pepper married to the blueberry fragrance and taste that signals when this variety is grown in a cool (for Syrah) climate. Tannins are fine-grained rather than coarse.

In the space of just a handful of vintages, one is forced to reconsider whether Mount Veeder—long devoted to Cabernet Sauvignon—might in fact be better suited to Syrah. Keep in mind Mount Veeder's proximity to San Pablo Bay. It's cooler than any of the other Mayacamas Mountain sites and, depending upon the vineyard exposure, can sometimes have difficulty fully ripening Cabernet Sauvignon, resulting in sometimes vegetal Cabs with hard tannins. (Other exposures do just fine, though.)

Lagier Meredith Syrahs are superb. And the fact that they can—and probably should—cause a wholesale rethinking of just what best serves a winegrowing district as old as Mount Veeder (it dates to the 1880s) shows just how new California winegrowing really is, even in a spot as long-established as Napa Valley.

Lamborn Family Vineyard—It's hard not to admire stubborn winegrowers working in difficult sites. "Labor of love" is the tired but true description. In a world clamoring to pay for Cabernet Sauvignon, especially if it's entitled to say "Howell Mountain," the Lamborn Family doggedly pursues Zinfandel from an eight-acre vineyard on Howell Mountain. And what a Zinfandel it is. Here, Howell Mountain makes itself felt. The Zin is usually concentrated, beautifully defined, and often quite tannic, with a dusty note abetted by cherry/chocolate fruit. Although not as detailed as a Howell Mountain Cabernet, it surely is more so than most Zinfandels from almost anywhere else.

Markham Vineyards—Another example of the promise of Yountville as a source of distinctive Cabernets. The wine to look for is the single-vineyard Cabernet identified as the Cabernet Reserve, which is from Yountville Ranch, a 100-acre (planted) vineyard bracketed between Grgich Hills' Cabernet vineyard and Dominus' Napanook. The Markham Cabernet is of a piece with its running mates: supple, concentrated, and distinctive. Original owner Bruce Markham sold the winery in 1988 to the Japanese winemaking company Sanraku, which still owns it. Markham Vineyards purchased La Jota Vineyard on Howell Mountain in 2001 and is making considerable investments in upgrading the winery.

Louis M. Martini—The sad saga of Louis M. Martini winery finally reached its denouement in 2002 when this old-line Napa Valley family wine was purchased by E. & J. Gallo. For the Gallos, this was their first venture in Napa Valley, although the winery had bought massive amounts of Napa Valley fruit over the decades. But it had never previously ventured into actually owning a Napa Valley-based winery.

Just why the Louis M. Martini winery faltered at the same time that Napa Valley itself climbed ever higher on the success ladder is the stuff of business-school case studies. After all, the winery owned choice vineyards in Carneros (which it pioneered in the 1940s), as well as a famous site on the Sonoma flank of the Mayacamas Mountains (Monte Rosso Vineyard).

What happens now is anybody's guess. But observing the increasingly fine wines of Gallo of Sonoma leads one to believe that the Gallo money and winemaking standards will infuse new life into the tired Louis M. Martini brand, as well as revivify some of Martini's best vineyards. Chances are good that this will indeed happen—and not a moment too soon.

Mayacamas Vineyards—The source of some of Napa Valley's most significant wines, both red and white. Anyone who doubts that California wines can convey a sense of somewhereness need only wander the long trail of Mayacamas Vineyards vintages. The taste is pure Mount Veeder: earthy, pungent, structured to last. For once, the Chardonnays are equally as impressive as the Cabernet, although the voice of the land does seem better amplified through the red than the white. Still, you can't miss it either way.

Worth noting is the exceptional Sauvignon Blanc, which is one of California's very best. It is pure Mount Veeder in its stony austerity and density of fruit, thanks to preposterously low yields (one ton an acre) from old vines. Mayacamas Vineyards represents the best of California in its willingness to avoid using new oak, in its California tradition of eschewing malolactic fermentation for its white wines, and for its sheer tenacity of purpose in creating profound expressions of its high-elevation Mount Veeder place. The wines require patience, as they are notoriously long-lived, but they are very much worth the wait. Really, you can't do better than Mayacamas Vineyards for California wine profoundness.

Miner Family Vineyards—One of the vehicles that demonstrates the separate existence of "Oakville East." The Miner family made its bundle from Silicon Valley (Dave Miner's uncle was one of the original partners of Sun Microsystems; Dave Miner also had his own computer industry ventures). Anyway, Miner's claim to fame is Cabernet Sauvignon, which comes from Oakville Ranch (owned by Dave Miner's aunt, Mary Miner). Located high in the Vaca Range, it is one of the most spectacularly sited vineyards anywhere in California. Like its neighbors Showket and Dalla Valle, the Oakville Ranch vineyard is strewn with rocks and boulders.

Miner Family Vineyards purchases fruit from Oakville Ranch (which now has its own label as well, called Oakville Ranch Vineyards). This fruit creates superb Cabernet Sauvignon. Dave Miner has crafted the wines with great respect and integrity, allowing it to display an intrinsic dried-cherry scent and taste allied to the textural density that distinguishes all the Cabernets from "Oakville East."

Other Miner wines, such as Viognier, Sauvignon Blanc, Chardonnay, Merlot, Syrah, and Pinot Noir are made from purchased fruit. Quality varies (the Viognier is especially good, especially considering its unlikely source: Simpson Vineyard in Madera, which is in the Central Valley). Really, it is the Cabernet that puts Miner on the wine map.

Robert Mondavi Winery—Unlike Louis M. Martini, where the family saga ended in a sale to E. & J. Gallo, the Robert Mondavi Winery saga continues. The story is so well known by now it hardly bears retelling. Patriarch Robert Mondavi, who turned ninety years old in 2003, long ago turned over the management reins to sons Michael and Tim, as well as daughter Marci. They, in turn, with their father's active consent, took the winery public, making them all quite rich while still retaining a majority share of the voting stock.

In the meantime, fueled by capital from its public stock offering, Mondavi expanded its operations, especially in its enormous Woodbridge line of inexpensive wines. In the meantime, despite having engaged in an expensive and much-ballyhooed renovation of its namesake Oakville winery, the prestige wines such Mondavi's Cabernet Reserve failed to impress some critics. The Chardonnay is good in a rich, oaky, opulent way. Pinot Noirs, after repeated "this time we've really done it" assertions, still fail to impress, although the wines are indeed better than before.

So what's real and what's public relations smoke? What's real is that Mondavi owns some of Napa Valley's choicest vineyards, none more so than the 593-acre To-Kalon Vineyard on the valley floor on the western side near the Mayacamas Mountains in Oakville. It is one of Napa Valley's supreme vineyard sites. When you've got a resource such as that, you are, by definition, always "in the game."

That said, there *has* been a loss of focus at Mondavi. Partly it was a calculated insistence upon a certain winemaking style characterized as "traditional" by winemaker Tim Mondavi. Too often, it led to rather thin, unsatisfying Cabernets. But partly it's due to a nagging sense that Mondavi is now run by a bunch of "suits" rather than what used to be called "wine men."

One suspects that, in consequence of going public, the intense, quarterly attention to the bottom line created a different focus than when the winery was still privately held and Mondavi did what it had to do to create exceptional wines. Corporate "suits" move "boxes," as business parlance refers to cases of wine; wine men and women, however, make and sell *wine*. The two are not mutually exclusive, but they're not the same, either. However good and ambitious a businessman Robert Mondavi was in his prime, you always knew he was a "wine man" before anything else.

In the meantime, Mondavi still makes some pretty fine wine. After all, it creates, in partnership with Baroness Philippine de Rothschild, the Opus One wine. And its To-Kalon Sauvignon Blanc is one of California's best. And it does own Byron Winery in Santa Barbara County, which issues lovely Chardonnays and Pinot Noirs. It's a big operation and was well before it went public. So scale is not the issue. They've done "big" before and done it well. Very likely, they'll return to form (and rigor) and do it well again—if they secure a sense of wine focus and mission.

More than any other winery (and wine family) in California, much is expected of Mondavi. Thanks to the ambition, achievement, vision, and sheer generosity of namesake Robert Mondavi, this winery is more than a business. It's a symbol. And when it stumbles, however briefly, attention gets paid.

Mount Veeder Winery—Purchased in 1989 by the Franciscan winery partnership of Agustin Huneeus and the Peter Eckes Co., Mount Veeder Winery is now part of the extensive portfolio of Constellation. Run by Constellation's Franciscan Estates group, the original hillside vineyards of Mount Veeder Winery have undergone extensive replanting as a result of phylloxera. In the interim, Franciscan necessarily blended valley-floor Cabernet with the Mount Veeder-grown Cabernet. One suspects that in this necessity they found a virtue, namely a broader market. The old Mount Veeder Winery Cabernets, made from 100 percent estate fruit, were massive, characterful wines that didn't always appeal to a broad array of palates. Ameliorating the pungent, earthy fruitiness of the Mount Veeder-grown Cabernet with gentler, more conventional-tasting valley-floor fruit made the wine more accessible.

Today, the Mount Veeder Winery Cabernet is still, however, an expression of place, as its estate fruit takes a back seat to no grape from anywhere. It is more polished than before, as well. What will emerge in the next decade, as the new plantings mature, is anyone's guess, but it's a great property that has been respectfully rehabilitated, so the prospects are good.

Neal Family Vineyards—Mark Neal runs one of Napa Valley's biggest vineyard management companies. He knows where all the good grapes are buried, as it were. In 1997, he decided to build his own underground winery next to the family home on Howell Mountain. Production is small at present, using purchased Cabernet grapes, mostly from Rutherford. The new wines, tasted mostly from barrel, are well made and promising. To watch.

Napa Redwoods Estate—One of the oldest vineyards (and wineries) on Mount Veeder, dating back to the 1880s with some of the original winemaking equipment found in an old barn and now on display, Napa Redwoods Estate is still a work in progress. For decades its grapes were cared for by a local caretaker and were sold to local wineries. (The owners are a San Francisco-area family that simply used the property as a summer retreat.)

Recently, the owners have decided to renew the vines and establish a winery, starting with the 1999 vintage. The vineyard itself was long known as Castle Rock Vineyard, but that brand had already been claimed by another, so they use the Castle Rock Vineyard as a vineyard designation applied to the Napa Redwoods Estate label. Quality so far is middling. But the location of the site is promising. And the historic quality to the ancient property is something special. To watch.

Newton Vineyard—Another of the great vineyard estates of Spring Mountain, Newton Vineyard originally made its mark under the aegis of winemaker Ric Forman, who eventually left and started his own winery. Like so many others on Spring Mountain, the strength of Newton's wines rests with its rich, succulent Cabernet Sauvignon. Over the years, Newton has shown itself a consistent Cabernet performer and certainly one of the Spring Mountain standard-bearers.

Today, though, the winery has new company (and competition) from new or reinvigorated Spring Mountain estates such as Keenan, Cain, Spring Mountain Vineyards, Paloma, Pride Mountain Vineyards, Terra Valentine, Schweiger, Smith-Madrone, and others. Among all the hillside locations in Napa Valley, none promises greatness or is more intensely competitive today than Spring Mountain District.

Niebaum-Coppola Estate—Movie director Francis Ford Coppola has become enthralled with the legacy of the old Inglenook winery, once the source of what some consider Napa Valley's grandest Cabernets from the

1940s and 1950s. First, Coppola bought the old Gustave Niebaum estate formerly owned by Inglenook. (Niebaum, a Finnish sea captain, founded Inglenook in the 1880s.) That initial sixty-three-acre vineyard on the foothills of the Mayacamas Mountains near Rutherford created Coppola's original wine called Rubicon. It was an unusually robust, even old-fashioned wine when it first appeared in 1978, with characteristic Rutherford mintiness. Considerable winemaking tinkering has given it more polish, but Rubicon remains, to this day, a rather burly wine.

Then Coppola's ambitions expanded to include more vineyard acreage, which required a much bigger wine portfolio to help pay for it. The winery now issues 300,000 cases of wine. In effect, Coppola sought to reclaim virtually all of the original vineyard holding that created the original great Inglenook wines. To that end, he not only purchased the original old Inglenook winery structure, but in 2002 bought a seventy-eight-acre parcel of land contiguous with his Niebaum-Coppola estate, the J.J. Cohn Vineyard, for a record-breaking $400,000 an acre. Virtually all of this new acquisition will require replanting, as the existing vines were poorly cared for. (Fittingly, the J.J. Cohn Vineyard was owned by the estate of Joseph Judson Cohen, who was co-founder of Metro-Goldwyn-Mayer, the Hollywood studio. Coppola's partner in the purchase was Cohen's grandson and heir, Bret Lopez, who will retain twenty-four acres of vines and the family home.)

For all its ambition, Niebaum-Coppola is still a winery very much in transition. While it is now, thanks to its land holdings, one of Napa Valley's foremost estates, the wines still do not fulfill the undoubted capacity of the site to create unequivocal greatness. Both the Cask Cabernet and the Rubicon bottlings are certainly good, but not outstanding. The estate-bottled Cabernet Franc is, if anything, more consistently rewarding than the Cabernet Sauvignons. An estate-bottled white wine blend called Blancaneaux (41 percent Chardonnay with 26 percent each Roussanne and Marsanne) is ho-hum.

Perhaps when the new land acquisition is replanted and incorporated into the winery mix, Coppola will achieve his dream of channeling Inglenook's old Cabernet wine into new Niebaum-Coppola bottles. So far, however, this is a great property dreaming of a glorious past that is not yet within its present grasp.

Opus One—A common misconception about Opus One should be clarified from the outset: Opus One has never been a single-vineyard wine. It may be someday, but not for a while. In fact, part of its own recently planted vineyard, directly in front of its newly completed Mayan temple-like winery on Highway 29, was replanted because of phylloxera. The winery, built at a rumored cost of $23 million (the official line was $15 million), has air-conditioned cellars, despite their underground location. It seems that the winery is sited on a geothermal hot spot.

No California wine has seen more hype than Opus One, a Cabernet blend proprietary label jointly created by the late Baron Philippe Rothschild of Château Mouton-Rothschild and Robert Mondavi. From the first vintage in 1979, it has been a wine intentionally created for expense-account dining. From a winemaking standpoint, the idea behind Opus One is consistent with the Mondavi blending approach: the primacy of winemaking over site. This helps explain the early uneven quality and style of the wines.

That said, Opus One has finally settled into a genuine consistency. It is a glossy, rich wine with a full measure of the Oakville/Rutherford meatiness and mintiness. There's also plenty of new French oak. It's the sort of wine where even a newcomer to Cabernet Sauvignon can say with assurance, "Now, *this* tastes like an expensive wine." And that, of course, was precisely what Mondavi/Rothschild set out to achieve. Considering that Opus One now makes about 30,000 cases a year, and sells at a retail price of $150 a bottle, it cannot be called anything other than a grand success.

Pahlmeyer—Jason Pahlmeyer first released wines under the name Five Palms, changing it to Pahlmeyer in 1987. Randy Dunn of Dunn Vineyards makes the wine, from purchased grapes grown in the Caldwell Vineyard located in the comparatively cool Coombsville area east of the city of Napa. This is unusual in that Coombsville is planted more to Chardonnay than the Bordeaux-type red wine varieties used for the Pahlmeyer blend.

Paloma Vineyard—A small family-run winery on Spring Mountain, Paloma is yet another of the stellar performers currently working with Spring Mountain fruit. Paloma's well-chosen specialty is Merlot, which seems to have a vocation of place on Spring Mountain. Paloma's rendition is dense, rich, chocolatey, and flat-out impressive. If you're a Merlot lover seeking a wine of real distinction (as opposed to merely easy Merlot drinking), then Paloma Vineyard is your place.

Pepi Winery—Formerly known as Robert Pepi Winery, it was sold by its namesake to Kendall-Jackson, which renamed it Pepi Winery and refocused the winery to Italian varietals such as Sangiovese, as well as Sauvignon Blanc. The new wines are good, but by no means stellar. Quality is improving, as Pepi gropes to find its voice. Besides, so far, nobody has yet found the secret to Sangiovese success in California, so Pepi remains in the running, like everyone else.

Joseph Phelps Vineyards—No winery is more prodigious in issuing a variety of wines than Joseph Phelps. They're two excellent Cabernets, a single-vineyard bottling called Backus and Phelps' famous proprietary Cabernet called Insignia. These are in addition to a regular Cabernet bottling. Then there's a regular Chardonnay called Ovation (mostly from Phelps' Los Carneros vineyard and blended with other Carneros sources) as well as a Los Carneros Vineyard Chardonnay entirely from that estate-owned vineyard.

Then there are Merlot, Syrah, a Rhône blend called Le Mistral, Sauvignon Blanc, Viognier, and a proprietary-named dessert wine called Eisrebe (92 percent Scheurebe and 8 percent Muscat).

Only the most assiduous taster could keep up with all of these wines from every vintage. The winning wines, almost without exception, seem to be the Backus and Insignia Cabernets. Phelps was famous for its Eisele Vineyard Cabernet, which was a twenty-six-acre vineyard formerly owned by Milt Eisele. It was sold in 1989 to Bart and Daphne Araujo, who now make an impressive Cabernet from it under their own label.

The Backus Cabernet comes from a forty-five-acre site off the Silverado Trail, right by the Oakville Crossroad in Oakville. It offers the usual Oakville/Rutherford suspects of cassis, mint, and textural muscle.

The proprietary-named Insignia, which is probably Phelps' most famous wine, is a blend that differs with every vintage; the vineyard sources vary accordingly. The wine is always structured for long life. It almost invariably is satisfying. But it's a winemaker's wine, rather than an expression of place.

Of the Chardonnays, they are both classic Carneros in their leaness and purity. The Los Carneros Vineyard bottling is the better, and more distinctive, of the two. But really, in the end, you want Phelps for its stellar Cabernets. Insignia is the popular favorite, but the greater particularity of the Backus Vineyard bottling makes it a personal favorite of this taster.

Pillar Rock—A little-known new producer with twenty-two acres of vines in Stags Leap District opposite Silverado Cellars. Very promising, intense, lush wines from the 2001 and 2002 vintages. Pillar Rock has every possibility of becoming a new star in Stags Leap District.

Piña Cellars—A tiny producer issuing an exceptionally good Howell Mountain Cabernet from Buckeye Vineyard, which reveals the dusty intensity of Howell Mountain Cabernet with exceptional mid-palate density. A label worth looking for.

Pine Ridge Winery—Founded in 1978, former owners Gary and Nancy Andrus unrelentingly pursued an expression of place in their Cabernets, which is the house specialty and the majority of production. Pine Ridge is located in the Stags Leap District and, not surprisingly, there is a Cabernet designated as Stags Leap Vineyard. It almost always is one of the best examples from the area. The Rutherford Cuvée is a less outspoken (about place) bottling, but still impressive.

Separate bottlings of a Howell Mountain Cabernet and a Diamond Mountain Cabernet under the Andrus Reserve label demonstrate all anybody will ever need to know about the somewhereness of these two places. The winemaking style (supple, accessible, and a bit too oaky) is present in both, but two Cabernets couldn't be more different in character. A massive Carneros-grown Merlot from Crimson Creek Vineyard is also part of the portfolio. It, too, shows lovely, glossy fruit with an awful lot of new French oak present to (unnecessarily) tart it up.

Plumpjack Winery—When billionaire Gordon Getty announced that he was going to open a companion winery to his San Francisco Plumpjack Café and wine retail shop, many folks rolled their eyes. They imagined yet another glossy, high-end, rich man's Napa winery that was—to modify a famous Texas line—all label and no grapes.

Yes, it *is* true that Plumpjack is a high-end winery. And, yes, there is a lot of *bella figura*, as the Italians put it—beautiful style—at least in terms of packaging. Plumpjack made a splash by offering its $150 Cabernet with a screwcap—a good idea that took guts and made headlines. (Sure, Getty can afford to lose money more easily than most, but so can others in Napa Valley who didn't dare to try to change people's minds about screwcaps, even though they know they're better than corks.)

What Getty did was lease vineyard land in Oakville on the eastern side of the valley floor from the McWilliams family. Insiders long knew that the McWilliamses owned a choice parcel. Getty built a modest, utilitarian winery nearby—nothing flashy, as one might have expected—and issues an Oakville Cabernet Sauvignon that has gotten consistently better with each vintage. The 2001 Plumpjack Cabernet will really put the winery at the pinnacle, as that vintage is Plumpjack's best ever. Look especially for the tiny quantity of (ultra-expensive) Reserve Cabernet, which accounts for just 5 percent of Plumpjack's already small estate production.

Pride Mountain Vineyards—One of the most dramatically sited vineyards in Napa Valley, Pride sits atop Spring Mountain, right at the Mayacamas Mountain ridge line which separates Napa County from Sonoma County. Indeed, a portion of its vineyards lie in Sonoma County.

Like everyone else on Spring Mountain, Pride's best wines are its Cabernet and Merlot. Spring Mountain creates intrinsically big, dense, rich wines and Pride's winemaking style emphasizes these qualities. For some tasters the wines are just *too* big. They are, to be sure, massive. That acknowledged, there's just enough restraint in the winemaking to allow the sheer characterfulness of Pride's fruit to shine through. Frankly, were it not for the intensity of distinctive flavor in these wines the style would indeed be excessive. This taster is an agnostic about the style but a devout believer of the grapes.

Quintessa—While Agustin Huneeus, Sr. was still co-owner and CEO of Franciscan Estates, he dreamed of a private winery devoted to creating a profound Cabernet Sauvignon. After considerable research and not little perseverance, Huneeus and his wife, Valeria, secured the last large undeveloped tract of land on the valley floor in Oakville. It was previously a cattle ranch, as were so many other spots in Napa Valley before the wine boom began anew in the 1970s.

The former owner was an elderly woman who had had many previous offers for her land. She knew that grapevines were inevitable, but was looking not just for a deep pocket, but one with the right sensibility. Eventually, it was really Valeria Huneeus, a Columbia University-trained Ph.D. in microbiology (she also has a degree in agronomy) who convinced her that she and her husband would be respectful caretakers.

With 240 acres of vines, Quintessa is one of Napa Valley's most signifi-

cant single vineyards. Planted entirely to Cabernet Sauvignon and its blending cohorts, Quintessa is being carefully plotted to discover just the right sites
for each variety. Unlike most valley floor locations, Quintessa is surprisingly
hilly. This means multiple nooks, crannies, and exposures, which is both a
challenge and an opportunity.

Already, one-quarter of the vineyard is farmed biodynamically, the better
for the wine to remain true to its place. Very likely, the entire vineyard will
one day be cultivated in this ultra-organic fashion.

In 2003 a new underground winery was inaugurated, just in time for that
year's harvest. Many of the grapes from Quintessa's vineyard are sold to others, the better to select what Huneeus and his staff consider the best lots for
the Quintessa label, which is the sole wine issued so far.

And how is the wine? "Luxurious" might be the best descriptor. It's lush,
full-bodied, decidedly Oakville/Rutherford in its equilibrium and powerful
gentility. One senses also that it's still early days. With a vineyard this large,
with so many different exposures, it will take time. But the odds are good
that, in time and with the requisite rigor, Quintessa will emerge as one of
Napa Valley's "First Growths."

Quixote—Carl Doumani has always owned exceptional vineyards and
buildings. With his newly created Quixote, started in the late 1990s, he has
done it again. Doumani first achieved fame with his Stags' Leap Winery, a
historic manor house and vineyard that dates to the 1880s. His Cabernet
Sauvignon from that estate was always exceptional, although it was overshadowed by neighbor and archrival Stag's Leap Wine Cellars.

Doumani is a Napa Valley original, a charming, artistic soul who has lit-
tle interest in, or capacity for, the hail-fellow-well-met clubbiness of Napa
Valley. (Really, he should have been in the more idiosyncratic Santa Cruz
Mountains.)

When Doumani sold Stags' Leap Winery in 1997 (for a reported $17 mil-
lion) to what is now Beringer Blass, he retained about 150 acres of adjoining
land, which now holds twenty-seven acres of vines, mostly his beloved Petite
Sirah and Cabernet Sauvignon, along with other Bordeaux-type vines for
blending purposes. Two wines are issued, both proprietary-named: Quixote,
which is a blend of Petite Sirah and Cabernet, and Panza, a less expensive
Cabernet Sauvignon. The first wines appeared in the 1999 vintage.

So far, both wines are very well made and promising. Since it's still early days, it's not quite fair to render judgment on them yet, except to say that the wines are rewarding drinking.

Any discussion of Quixote winery is not complete without mention of Doumani's extraordinary winery facility, a phantasmagoric structure created by the late Friedensreich Hundertwasser, featuring a gold-leaf onion dome and a swirl of fractured tiles both inside and out. It is, without question, the most original winery in Napa Valley and its most delightful, too. Would that more winery owners shared Doumani's simultaneous irreverence and seriousness of purpose.

Raymond Vineyard and Cellar—Why the Japanese brewery Kirin was willing to pay a reported $26 million for Raymond in 1988 is the sort of event for which the word "mystifying" was invented. The Raymond family, which owned Beringer Vineyards until 1971, owned only eighty acres of vineyard in Napa Valley, although the brand itself at the time was bigger—90,000 cases of Chardonnay alone at the time—thanks to purchased grapes. The wines and Raymond reputation were honorable and still are. But there was little about Raymond wines, then or now, that explained that kind of money, especially since most other big-buck expenditures have been for either huge brands or large-scale vineyard holdings.

Since that purchase (which occurred before Japan's "bubble economy" burst), Raymond has settled into a large-scale, lucrative complacency. It's a commercial brand that trades on its Napa Valley origins, but little more than that.

Regusci Winery—For years, one of the best-kept secrets of Stags Leap District was that a good piece of it was owned by the Regusci family, which has lived there since 1932. They farmed their own land and sold the grapes, as well as managed neighboring vineyards. Finally, in 1996, Regusci issued Stags Leap District Cabernet under its own label. Like so many growers turned winemakers, the early bottlings needed work. Too often, the wines were dilute. (Growers tend to overcrop—it's how they make money, after all. Ambitious wineries strive for low yields and make their money by selling their wines at high prices, which growers can't do.) Happily, the Regusci wines appear to be arriving at a better, higher standard. Worth watching.

Reverie Vineyard—Norman Kiken, a former New Yorker, was one of the "back East" partners who co-owned Pine Ridge Winery with Gary and Nancy Andrus. Visiting Pine Ridge over the years gave Kiken a taste for Napa Valley living. You know what happened next. Kiken bought an unplanted piece of land on Diamond Mountain in what has turned out to be a kind of golden enclave with von Strasser, Diamond Creek, and Dyer all within literal shouting distance of each other.

Unusually, Reverie Vineyard is planted to grape varieties previously untested on Diamond Mountain, such as Roussanne, Grenache, Barbera, and Tempranillo in addition to the expected Cabernet Sauvignon and Cabernet Franc. The 2001 Roussanne (just thirty-five cases) was stunning, with its yellow/gold hue with a greenish cast, lanolin scent, and lemon/pineapple taste. Tempranillo is less impressive, although the Barbera has possibilities.

As you might expect, Cabernet Sauvignon shines, although the winemaking style makes the Cabernets taste a bit too blurry and unfocused for really top quality. This is a winery still seeking its focus, but the prospects are good and the adventurousness admirable.

Rombauer Vineyards—Few Napa Valley wineries have a more loyal, far-flung, and devoted following than Rombauer Vineyards. (Silver Oak Wine Cellars comes immediately to mind as another example.) Frankly, it's hard to fathom the reasons why. Rombauer wines, virtually without exception, are overtly commercial, almost industrial, manipulated-tasting versions of their types, the kind of wines a Top 40 radio station would make if they turned to wine instead of the airwaves.

Rombauer's Chardonnay, a popular favorite, is oaky, somewhat sweet, and simple. Yet it sells in sizable quantity at far from giveaway prices. The Cabernet is little better nor is the Merlot much of anything. Perhaps it's the Rombauer name (Irma and Marion Rombauer were the original authors of *Joy of Cooking*). And, in fairness, some critics have given the wines better reviews that this observer cares to. Fair enough. Certainly, assiduous marketing over many years has helped. Whatever the reasons for Rombauer's success, it works. So why should they change?

Rubissow-Sargeant Vineyards—A long-time Mount Veeder winery that marches, like so many folks on funky, individualistic Mount Veeder, to its own beat. Cabernet Sauvignon and Merlot, along with a blend of Cabernet Franc and Merlot called Trompettes, are the tickets here. The wines are variable and show the leanness that reveals just how cool Mount Veeder can be for Cabernet. One wishes for more depth and mid-palate density. Look for the genuinely fine Reserve Cabernet. Also, an experimental unfiltered and unfined bottling of Trompettes showed a much greater richness, which couldn't help but make a taster wonder whether a lighter hand with the filter might resupply the wines with richness that they might well have had—and lost.

Saddleback Cellars—See *Venge*.

St. Clement Vineyards—Now owned by Beringer Blass, St. Clement was formerly owned by the Japanese company Sapporo. Frankly, this is a winery in need of not merely work, but resuscitation. Not a single wine tasted was anything other than mediocre, at best. Even the oddly named Meritage bottling called Oroppas (which is Sapporo spelled backwards) was banal.

Saint-Supéry—The "luck of the Irish" might be better described as the "luck of the French" when it comes to Saint-Supéry. Owned by the French Skalli family, their good fortune (a reported $18.5 million of which was originally invested in Saint-Supéry) was to have their 1,500-acre Dollarhide Ranch in the Pope Valley entitled to the AVA designation Napa Valley.

Where is Pope Valley, you ask? The answer is: far away from anything either a timid BATF bureaucrat or anyone without a vested interest would reasonably imagine as "Napa Valley." Geographically, Pope Valley is about ten air miles from the Calistoga end of Napa Valley. For a bird to get to there, it would have to fly over the Howell Mountain part of the Vaca Range. Only after it left the Vaca Range would it reach the isolated Pope Valley.

Economically, however, Pope Valley has close ties to Napa Valley. Along with neighboring way-over-the hills Chiles Valley and Wooden Valley, Pope Valley is connected to influential Napa Valley interests, notably the Louis Martini Winery, which owns 929 acres in Chiles Valley and about 350 acres in Pope Valley. When the original Napa Valley AVA was proposed, these three outlying areas were excluded. You needn't be a wine genius to figure out what happened next. The revised Napa Valley AVA proposal, approved by the BATF, included all three areas as part of Napa Valley.

Saint-Supéry knows full well where the rest of the world thinks Napa Valley is found: Its winery is located on Highway 29, nestled between the heartland hamlets of Oakville and Rutherford. It offers, by the way, one of the most intelligent and informative tours you will find anywhere.

As for the wines, nearly all from the Pope Valley property, Saint-Supéry has made great strides. The early releases were bland and uninstructive as to place. New vintages have shown greater flavor resonance and polish. The best wine in the extensive lineup is the Meritage bottling, a Bordeaux-type blend of good refinement. That said, even at its improved level, Saint-Supéry's (pleasing) wines have yet to make a case that Pope Valley is the equal of the "real" Napa Valley. But they've got the Napa name on the label and that's what really counts in the marketplace. The Saint-Supéry name, by the way, is that of the former owner of the winery site. It was used because it sounded conveniently French.

Saintsbury—Located in the Carneros district, Saintsbury singlehandedly demolishes the old assertion that California cannot create Pinot Noirs of a Burgundian standard of delicacy and finesse. It is not alone in this, but Saintsbury was one of the first to lay claim to a new era of California possibilities for Pinot Noir at a time when a lot of folks said it couldn't be done.

After an unpromising start in the early 1980s, Saintsbury's reach equaled its grasp in the mid-1980s. By the 1990s, Saintsbury became a bulwark of first-rate Pinot Noirs. In both its early-release, lower-priced Garnet bottling and its flagship Saintsbury Pinot Noir, you can find the kind of berryish fruit intensity and firm acidity for which Carneros is fast becoming recognized. Oak is becoming ever less intrusive; taste transparency is becoming increasingly prominent. No winery has been more methodical in its investigation and pursuit of newly available Pinot Noir clones than Saintsbury, which surely explains its steady improvement over the years.

The Chardonnays are always well made, with the Reserve bottling being one of the best renditions of Carneros Chardonnay in almost any recent vintage. But really, it's Pinot Noir that puts Saintsbury on the map.

Schweiger Vineyards—A Spring Mountain District winery that, like so many others on that zone, delivers its best wines through the vehicles of Merlot and Cabernet Sauvignon. Both wines are rich and intense, although there's a bit more vintage variation than one might like. A less-persuasive Spring Mountain-grown Chardonnay is offered, which has lovely density and thick texture, but seems a bit one-dimensional. Also offered is an interesting, 100 percent Cabernet Sauvignon port-style wine, also Spring Mountain-grown.

Screaming Eagle Winery and Vineyards—One of Napa Valley's "cult Cabernets," Screaming Eagle (frequently contracted on Internet wine chat boards to "Screagle") has been the recipient of lavish praise. Usually it's easy to see why the so-called cult Cabernets receive such raves. They are almost uniformly lush, rich, intense Cabernets. Yet that's not how this taster would describe Screaming Eagle, which is comparatively more austere, restrained, even buttoned-down compared to its similarly high-flying brethren.

Is it all that compelling a Cabernet? For this taster, no. It's certainly an excellent wine, displaying classic characteristics of its Oakville site, with a good, solid meatiness and nice detail. But I cannot say that I have ever found it to be that much of a sit-up-and-take-notice Cabernet. Of course, if someone else is paying . . .

Sherwin Vineyard—Located on Spring Mountain next to Barnett Vineyards, Sherwin is one of those not-yet-released wineries that, by virtue of its vineyard location and the known achievements of its neighbors, is worth watching.

Shafer Vineyards—If pressed to single out one winery in Stags Leap District that exemplifies what the area is all about, I would point today to Shafer Vineyards. Its Cabernets now deliver the flavor resonance and texture that make Stags Leap District Cabernets so identifiable in blind tastings. Other wineries in the area deliver the goods, too. Shafer just seems to do it a touch more dramatically. Two Cabernets are offered, a regular Stags Leap District and a Hillside Select bottling. The Hillside Select is the richer of the two, but both wines provide the succulence that sets Stags Leap District apart.

Showket Vineyard—One of the backbone vineyards and wineries of "Oakville East." Located higher up on the rocky slope of the Vaca Range just above Dalla Valle, the Showket family is creating simply superb Cabernets, filled with the textural richness and flavor density that sets this zone apart from any other in Napa Valley. They are, foremost, serious growers who only later decided to hang out a winery shingle. This has all the makings of being one of Napa Valley's star wineries in the near future.

Signorello—A winery with a mixed bag of offerings, some decent while others downright exciting. An overly oaky white Bordeaux-type blend of Sémillon (60 percent) and Sauvignon Blanc (40 percent) has admirable richness and intensity but the oak mars its purity. An estate-grown Chardonnay is pleasant but lacks real character. There's a lot of "winemaking" going on with the Chardonnay.

More rewarding is the Las Amigas Vineyard Pinot Noir from Carneros, which delivers good, dense, chocolately Pinot Noir fruit. The estate-grown Cabernet Sauvignon varies with the vintage, as the site can taste "cool" for Cabernet, exhibiting a certain lightness and, sometimes, vegetal notes. More successful vintages, such as 2001, have created absolutely exciting wine, filled with ripe flavors and superb finesse. A special bottling of Cabernet Sauvignon (250 cases) called Padrone is noticeably, even dramatically, more intense and dense with an impressive mineral note.

Silver Oak Wine Cellars—No winery is more aptly named than Silver Oak. Actually, it would be even more descriptive if was called Golden Oak: No high-priced California winery has a more devoted following. If Liberace made wine, it would be Silver Oak Cabernet. The wines are always soft, showy, and gaudy with oak. Yet somewhere underneath all that is some real ability, too.

The mainstay bottling comes from Sonoma's Alexander Valley, which delivers just the sort of suppleness that has come to be identified with Silver Oak wines. Stripped of the excess oak, it is a characteristic Alexander Valley Cabernet. That said, the fruit lacks sufficient character to support the oak. The Bonny's Vineyard Cabernet comes from a 3.68-acre single vineyard in Oakville/Rutherford. Although texturally a bit thin, the scent is pure Oakville/Rutherford in its mintiness and cedar—once past the oak. The regular "Napa Valley" bottling is the least of the three. If the dime-store cologne of heavily vanilla-scented American oak were removed, some pretty good wine could be found underneath. But then, à la Liberace, the winery probably wouldn't be on quite such friendly terms with the bank.

Silverado Vineyards—Another top-drawer Cabernet producer in Stags Leap District. The winery is owned by the heirs of Walt Disney, and it has, virtually from its first vintage in 1981, issued pluperfect examples of Stags Leap District Cabernets. As in all good examples from the area, Silverado delivers opulence of flavor and texture.

The Chardonnays are less impressive. Here, the grapes come from vineyards in Stags Leap, Yountville, Coombsville, and Carneros. A regular and a Reserve Chardonnay are offered. As is usually the case, the Reserve is noticeably better. Yet in both versions all one gets is well-made Chardonnay of no real distinguishing character. The same is true for the Sauvignon Blanc. Really, it's the Cabernet that's the ticket.

Sky Vineyards—Just when you think that Napa Valley has become an exclusive preserve of the rich, the market-minded and the chichi, you come across Sky Vineyards. Actually, one doesn't quite come across Sky Vineyards. You have to seek it out, and, it must be said, owner-winemaker Lore Olds isn't especially interested in receiving visitors.

Sky Vineyards is aptly named: It's at the very top of Mount Veeder, right on the ridge line at 2,100 feet, separating Napa County from Sonoma County. When you reach Sky, not only have you reached the end of the line, as it were, but you're also transported into another time dimension. Founded in 1973, Sky Vineyards has really never left the late 1960s and has no intention (and no reason) to do so. Olds used to work at neighboring Mayacamas Vineyards, which is also timeless in its own fashion—more Jane Austen's genteel eighteenth century than Sky's more hippie-ish aura.

Sky makes just one wine: Zinfandel. All fourteen acres of Zinfandel vines are head-trained, including newly planted vines. (There is an experimental row of more conventionally trained vines dedicated for research on behalf of UC Davis; they, too, find a purity to the place, it seems.) Everything here is hand-done, including the extraordinary labels, which change every vintage and are the work of Olds. His artwork, arrayed throughout his funky wood cottage, is good enough to make you think that Olds is an artist who owns a vineyard, rather than a winemaker who dabbles in art on the side.

And how is the wine? In two words: burly and lovely. Sky Zinfandels are dense, characterful, authentic wines that taste like they come from the earth, rather than a marketing person's vision of what will sell. They also age beautifully. To taste Sky Zinfandel is really to taste California itself.

Smith-Madrone Vineyards and Winery—Brothers Stu and Charles Smith, owners and winemakers of Smith-Madrone, have kept the faith longer than most in Napa Valley. Located high atop Spring Mountain, their vineyard dates to 1971. To taste an array of Chardonnay, Cabernet, and Riesling vintages at Smith-Madrone is equivalent to a wine version of an archeological dig.

You can taste all the winemaking changes that California went through from the mid-1970s to today. For example, the Chardonnays did not, in the

1980s, undergo malolactic fermentation, an old California white wine approach that is, in fact, enjoying a revival today. Yet other vintages, from the mid-1980s to the early 1990s, had the Chardonnay fermented with their skins, an approached now generally recognized as undesirable for long-term aging.

Today, Smith-Madrone Chardonnay has arrived at an admirable aesthetic, exhibiting a lemon-butter scent and Chablis-like restraint.

The Cabernets too have rung the winemaking changes, and it's fair to say that they have never been better than they are today. These are great Spring Mountain Cabs, filled with a blackish fruit plumped with earthy intensity, a green olive scent, and supple tannins. Earlier vintages, it must be said, tasted a bit "over-brewed," with bitter, harsh tannins. Those deficiencies are now gone.

Worth noting are the exceptional dry Rieslings made at Smith-Madrone. Their six-acre Riesling vineyard, planted in 1972, has issued a string of superb, earthy, sappy dry Rieslings that reveal just how appropriate Riesling is to Spring Mountain—and doubtless other hillside sites in California. Here, an archeological wine dig of seventeen vintages reveals nothing but jewels. Rieslings dating as far back as 1977 not only were immensely drinkable and fresh-tasting but beautifully made. If California ever creates a "cult Riesling," then Smith-Madrone is a sure contender. This is a wine worth buying and aging, as it rewards decades of cellaring, like great Rieslings everywhere in the world.

Spottswoode Vineyard and Winery—One of Napa Valley's most sought-after wines and rightly so. Located in Saint Helena, the thirty-eight-acre vineyard planted to Cabernet Sauvignon, Cabernet Franc, and Merlot is located at the base of the Mayacamas Mountains. From the first vintage in 1982, an unspectacular year from which Spottswoode released a simply spectacular wine, the winery has remained one of Napa Valley's finest estates. And it has never stopped.

Should anyone doubt the primacy of source in fine wine, all they need do is look at Spottswoode. The vineyard, along with good winemaking, to be sure, delivers consistent, reliable greatness. It also delivers a consistency of character, in this case a certain gentle restraint. Although the winemaking emphasizes polish and refinement, the same techniques applied to, say, Mount Veeder or Diamond Mountain grapes would result is a different tasting wine. Here, there is spice, mint, and dimension—served up with almost Southern gentility. A Sauvignon Blanc also is made, but it offers little compared to the stellar Cabernet.

Spring Mountain Vineyard—If asked to identify what might be considered the single greatest wine property in California today, I'd have to say the 845-acre Spring Mountain Vineyard. Mind you, the wines themselves do not yet equal the property itself. But someday they very likely will.

The story here involves ultra-secretive Swiss banking billionaire Jacqui Safra. (He was also the money behind Woody Allen's movies, as well as the object of a lawsuit by Allen. Safra's companion, Jean Doumanian, was Allen's longtime producer.)

Safra has a reported passion for wine and decided to purchase property in Napa Valley. First, he bought the historic Tiburcio Parrott estate, originally created in the 1890s, that was revived by Michael Robbins as Spring Mountain Winery. Robbins went bankrupt and Safra bought the property. (Tiburcio Parrott's grand Victorian manor house became visually famous as part of the opening shot of the TV soap opera, *Falcon Crest*.) It is a magnificent old structure, a jewel in its own right, to say nothing of its 257 acres of land.

But Safra did not stop there. He subsequently cobbled together three more (previously separate) estates: the 120-acre former Château Chevalier (owned by the late Gil Nickel of Far Niente), Streblow Vineyard with 33 acres of land, and the 435-acre Draper Vineyard, owned since the 1940s by wine importer Jerry Draper and his sister.

With these estates amalgamated into one, Safra created an unprecedented hillside estate with 226 acres of vines in 130 different vineyard blocks. He immediately set about planting, or replanting, vines throughout the difficult, steep slopes of Spring Mountain. Moreover, he chose to replant with the dense spacing, sometimes as close as meter-by-meter, used in Bordeaux and Burgundy. It is an expensive approach and rarely seen in hillside properties. Of course, the winery facilities have been completely refurbished, including newly dug tunnels.

Relatively few visitors have seen Spring Mountain Vineyard, as Safra is secretive to the point of paranoia. He'd just as soon nobody saw it, but his staff (rightly) insist that it's hard to sell wine unless visitors are welcomed. Only recently has the winery accepted visitors, by appointment only, at a cost of $25 per person (the fee is applied, however, to any wine purchase you might make, which is fair).

And how are the wines? Works in progress might be the best phrase. Everything is estate-grown and many of the new plantings are only just reaching bearing age. The vast complication of exposures and soils on the property has winemaker Tom Ferrell keeping all 130 vineyard blocks separate.

The Sauvignon Blanc is one of California's finest: rich, redolent, and infused with a taste of the soil rarely found in most Sauvignon Blancs anywhere. It's the only white wine produced at Spring Mountain Vineyard.

Reds are Cabernet Sauvignon (along with the usual blending cohorts such as Cabernet Franc and Merlot) and Syrah. Both are intense, burly specimens, sometimes too much so. Spring Mountain District reds are big boys, and wines from this estate are no different. Indeed, the challenge is to tame the tannins and tease out the subtleties that this area's red wines are known to possess.

No estate in California has more potential for greatness than Spring Mountain Vineyard. Time will tell whether its abundant promise is fulfilled.

Stag's Leap Wine Cellars—Owner Warren Winiarski was rocketed to fame by his 1973 Cabernet Sauvignon placing first in the now-legendary 1976 Paris wine tasting. In it a group of famous French wine tasters compared California Cabernets and Chardonnays in a blind (labels unseen) tasting against famous red Bordeaux and white Burgundies.

At the time there was no Stags Leap District and it was difficult, if not impossible, to establish whether Stag's Leap Wine Cellars was a one-off or part of some larger expression of place. Today we know, of course, that it's the latter.

That said, there's no denying Winiarski's efforts in creating some of Stags Leap District's finest and most representative Cabernets. The winery eschews the AVA designation not because Winiarski doesn't think that it exists in the wines. Instead, he disagrees with the entire AVA process, which, unlike European appellations, has no restrictions or requirements concerning which grapes can be grown or how the vines are tended or the wines made.

Consequently, Stag's Leap Wine Cellars issues one wine designated SLV (Stag's Leap Vineyard), which is always a rewarding bottling. But the two most famous, and best, Cabernets issued by the winery are its signature Cask

23 bottling (a blend of the best barrels) and the single-vineyard Fay Vineyard. Both are in Stags Leap District. In some vintages, it can be a real horse race as to which is the better wine, although Cask 23 has the cachet, as well as the higher price. Both are outstanding and superb examples of the luxuriant suppleness only Stags Leap District Cabernets can deliver.

Stags' Leap Winery—Former owner Carl Doumani sold Stags' Leap Winery in 1997 for a reported $17 million to what is now called Beringer Blass. Under Doumani, the winery performed fitfully, as he was reluctant to make the necessary investments to allow this vineyard to realize its full potential. Longtime winemaker Robert Brittan, who almost heroically worked to improve the vineyard and winemaking, has now been given the resources (and capital) to finish the job he started under Doumani.

Keep in mind that Stags' Leap Winery, one of the historic properties of Napa Valley, occupies what may well be the epicenter of Stags Leap District. The vineyard is at the very heart of that part of Stags Leap District east of the Silverado Trail bounded by Shafer on one side and archrival Stag's Leap Wine Cellars on the other.

Today, although the portfolio has expanded under Beringer Blass to include a rather dull Chardonnay (from purchased grapes), as well as a surprisingly fine Viognier (from a Beringer-owned vineyard on the east side of the valley north of Napa), the *raison d'être* of Stags' Leap Winery is its Cabernet Sauvignon. Two versions are offered, the better one by far is that designated "Estate," as here you get only the fruit grown in the winery's own vineyard. It is rich, lush, dense, classic Stags Leap District Cabernet in its gentility yet offered in a more austere style than others in the neighborhood. It's a wine where you can say with certainty, "This couldn't have come from just anywhere."

Worth noting is the Petite Syrah (sic), which is about 60 percent estategrown and has a devoted following. It's a strong, rich wine but a bit monolithic.

A new offering, "Ne Cede Malis" ("Don't give in to misfortune"), named for the credo of the property's original nineteenth-century owner, Horace Chase, is blend of Petite Sirah, Carignane, Syrah, Peloursin, and Mourvèdre. It's dense, rich, and almost liquorous in texture—a big mouthful of wine.

Staglin Family Vineyard—Good Cabernets from a winery that has, fairly or not, been criticized for its *nouveau riche* affectations. (For one brief moment, the winery insisted that you had to commit to purchasing a case of wine in order to be allowed to visit by appointment. That policy was quickly discontinued after a spasm of complaints.)

The extraneous social commentary aside, Staglin is now issuing a steady stream of solid, rewarding Cabernets from their fifty-acre vineyard in Rutherford. Although not especially original-tasting, Staglin does represent a very high standard in valley floor-grown Cabernet.

Steltzner Vineyards—Another Stags Leap District winery, but with a twist: The Steltzners like to late-harvest their Cabernet grapes, with the result that their wines are noticeably ripe-tasting. For some, they may well be overripe, but I cannot say that they seem so to me. If anything, it's simply an amplification of what Stags Leap District already delivers. It is to Steltzner's credit that their Cabernets don't cross the line from opulence to excess.

Sterling Vineyards—Sterling is a winery that seems to have lost its way, somehow marooned in a corporate fog. It's now owned by Diageo, which bought Seagram Château and Estates, the previous owner. At one time Sterling had ambitions to create some of Napa Valley's best wines, including some striking Cabernet and Chardonnay from nearby Diamond Mountain. Today, it seems more content to offer competent, adequate wines but no more than that.

The once ballyhooed Winery Lake Vineyard Pinot Noir has long since been overshadowed by other, better, Carneros-grown Pinot Noirs. The best wine, as has long been the case, is the Sterling Reserve Cabernet, which does indeed have real quality. Overall, though, Sterling Vineyards seems to be a winery that lost—or misplaced—its original resolve to stand out from the pack.

Stony Hill Vineyard—One of the stalwarts of Napa Valley. Stony Hill is located at the base of Spring Mountain and is indeed within the Spring Mountain District AVA. But in many ways, it is its own entity. Started in the early 1950s by Fred and Eleanor McCrea, Stony Hill became legendary for its Chardonnay made—as it still is today—without any malolactic fermentation. That was the old California way and it served, and continues to serve, Stony Hill's Chardonnay very well indeed.

Inevitably, Stony Hill lost some of its original luster as new wineries appeared. For too long a time it was overlooked, if only because the necessary marketing was absent as Eleanor McCrea became elderly. The winery had its longtime mailing list of customers and that was enough.

Finally—and happily—in the late 1990s Stony Hill was "rediscovered." Nothing really had changed, including the tiny, woodsy winery, but California wine lovers had begun to realize what a jewel this old vineyard really is. Stony Hill Chardonnay is the essence of what California Chardonnay can be: pure, free of oakiness, filled with savor, and yet somehow unpretentious. It is rewarding, even exciting drinking—if you can find it.

A small amount of (good) Gewürztraminer is also made, which has its own following.

Von Strasser—Rudy von Strasser is one of the most active producers on Diamond Mountain and was very involved in helping establish the AVA designation. Located in the "golden enclave" next to Diamond Creek, Reverie, and Dyer, von Strasser's vineyard production is augmented by grape purchases from other growers. This is not easy, as von Strasser points out, because there are only about 500 of vines in the entire appellation.

Von Strasser offers a rare Diamond Mountain-grown Chardonnay, but for this taster it seems too "worked-on," plumped with a lot of oak, lees-contact, barrel-aging, etc. The underlying material seems lovely, but there's too much makeup.

The reds are better, including a lovely Diamond Mountain Zinfandel from Monhoff Vineyard, as well as a pleasing "Red Wine" from the (Piedmontese-inspired) Sori Bricco Vineyard, also on Diamond Mountain. The best of the reds is von Strasser's own estate-grown Cabernet Sauvignon, which exhibits the classic Diamond Mountain characteristics of soft tannins and strong whiffs and tastes of cocoa and dark chocolate.

Summit Lake Vineyards—A small family vineyard high on Howell Mountain that remains devoted to Zinfandel, which was Howell Mountain's original wine vocation. Summit Lake's Zins are beautiful wines, brimming with the fine detail that distinguishes Howell Mountain Zinfandels from any others in Napa Valley or, for that matter, anywhere else. So far, the (newer) Cabernets are less good, but have some promise. Worth noting is an exceptional Zinfandel Port called Clair Riley's Private Reserve. It's one of the best Zinfandel Ports I can recall tasting.

Swanson Vineyards—A well-established Oakville winery that lost some luster in the 1990s and is seeking to restore it. Different levels of wines, of very different qualities, makes it hard to generalize about Swanson. The best bets are the Salon Wine Selection Merlot, which comes entirely from the Schmidt Vineyard that is enviably located in Oakville west of Highway 29 up against the Mayacamas Mountains.

This same vineyard is also the source of the proprietary-named Alexis, which is a blend of Cabernet Sauvignon, Merlot, Cabernet Franc, (about 65 percent combined), and Syrah (about 35 percent). It's a good, glossy, supple red wine with some minerality. A new Petite Sirah, grafted over from Sangiovese vines, shows promise. Worth noting is the Angelica dessert wine made entirely from Mission grapes grown on Deaver Ranch in Amador County. It's a very pretty, sweet dessert wine with the strong licorice scent that characterizes Angelicas, with excellent acidity.

Terra Valentine—A winery that's been "recalled to life" (to borrow from Charles Dickens) under a new name. Terra Valentine occupies the strange winery structure on Spring Mountain that was previously called Yverdon. Entirely hand-built and designed by original owner Fred Aves, that winery somehow petered out over time. When Aves died, the winery was willed to a charity, which had no interest in reviving it. Eventually, Angus and Margaret Wurtele, from Minnesota, bought the property and renamed it Terra Valentine. They also purchased vineyard land elsewhere on Spring Mountain to create the thirty-five-acre Wurtele Vineyard. An additional thirty acres of vines were planted in 2002, also on Spring Mountain. The first wines appeared in the late 1990s, all Cabernets.

Quality is impressively high for such a new effort. This is yet another Spring Mountain District winery that has every possibility of making a mark in the coming decade. To watch closely.

Philip Togni—Perhaps the most famous producer on Spring Mountain, longtime winemaker Philip Togni (originally with Cuvaison) has issued a series of Cabernets from his small family vineyard that have received rave reviews. The original vineyard dates to 1883, but Togni's vines were planted in 1981.

Togni is a self-professed Bordeaux lover and makes his Cabernet with the express intent of creating wines that will age with the grace and detail that characterize the famous Bordeaux châteaux. The wines are made with uncommon austerity and really need a minimum of a decade's aging. Not every vintage, one regrets to say, has turned out as successfully as this winery's many admirers might have hoped. Some bottlings, such as 1993, can display vegetal notes. Togni's vineyard, like other spots on Spring Mountain, has some spots with less than ideal exposure, which can create grapes of less than perfect ripeness. That noted, when Togni's wines are good, they are spectacularly so. Both the 1990 and 1991 Cabernets are outstanding today and a still-too-young 1996 shows great promise.

Trefethen Vineyards Winery—Trefethen was catapulted to fame when its 1976 Chardonnay placed first in the widely reported Gault-Millau *Grand Marathon des Vins du Monde* tasting in 1979. Since then, Trefethen has come to be (rightly) associated with Chardonnay, which indeed does well in Trefethen's Oak Knoll vineyard, which lies midway between the city of Napa and the town of Yountville. The Trefethen holdings are an impressive 550 acres. A good part of their production is sold to Domaine Chandon, which has been associated with Trefethen from the sparkling winery's inception in the early 1970s.

Trefethen is less well known for its Cabernets, in part because they have not been as consistently successful as the Chardonnays. Here, the relative coolness of the Oak Knoll area becomes genuinely cool for Cabernet—but not inevitably so. The lean, supple character of what is essentially Yountville-area Cabernet Sauvignon is displayed in Trefethen Cabernets as well. In the best years, the Cabernets can ally real depth with a restrained grace; in the lesser vintages, they can be downright vegetal. Starting in 1985 a Reserve Cabernet has been offered, which is significantly better than the regular Cabernet. They are now among Napa Valley's most original—and rewarding—Cabernets and have, if anything, been too long overlooked.

A word should be said about Trefethen's dry White Riesling. The winery has doggedly refused to give up on this wine and there's no (qualitative) reason why it should. Rieslings of almost any kind, let alone dry versions, fetch derisory prices these days. Trefethen's is one of California's best. Like all truly good dry Rieslings, the Trefethen Riesling ages wonderfully well. It has long been, and still is, perhaps the best deal for dry white wine in Napa Valley.

Truchard Vineyards—This Carneros vineyard and winery came to fame with its Merlot, and rightly so. It was a revelation in the late 1980s when

Carneros was discovered to be suitable not only for Chardonnay and Pinot Noir, which at the time was considered its sole destiny, but also for such red grapes as Merlot and Syrah. It was Truchard's Merlot that changed people's minds and continues to do so. This is lush, succulent, cool-climate Merlot that, despite far more competition, still stands out as one of the best from Carneros.

Turley Wine Cellars—It's hard to even pretend to be objective about Turley wines. Simply put, you either love 'em or push them away. I'm afraid that I am in the latter group. Larry Turley, you see, likes big, bold, high-alcohol wines that he sincerely believes delivers a resonance of flavors absent from wines that are not allowed to get quite so ripe.

In fairness, a winemaker with less integrity would pursue such overripe (to my taste) grapes and then surreptitiously run the wine through a spinning cone to remove the excess alcohol—which in Turley wines can reach as high at 17 percent. Turley, to his credit, does no such thing. His wines emerge as they really are: huge, intense, ultra-ripe, and high alcohol because of that ripeness. I sincerely admire this integrity, much as I personally don't care for the aesthetic itself.

The best Turley wines, for this taster, are the Zinfandels, although the Petite Sirahs have turned in noteworthy performances over the years. Turley wines are the sort you really have to try for yourself. If you like this style, then you'll be in heaven, as nobody does it better.

Venge/Saddleback Cellars—Owner-winemaker Nils Venge is a longtime Napa Valley winemaker who now works as a consultant to various estates such as Keenan. He wisely bought some land for himself in Oakville. All of his Oakville estate wines are labeled Venge; the Saddleback Cellars label is used for any wines where purchased grape are included, even though certain bottlings can be as much as 95 percent estate-grown. Venge is exacting in his integrity.

The best wine is, not surprisingly, the Venge Cabernet Sauvignon, which is produced only in tiny quantity, typically about 300 cases a year. It displays the classic Oakville valley-floor tastes of black cherry and cassis with a scent of green olives.

Sometimes, though, the wines can seem a littled "pinched" by excessive woodiness from the two and one-half years this wine spends in barrel.

"Woodiness" is different, by the way, from "oakiness" in that there are no sweet vanilla flavors. Rather, it's a matter of fruit drying out. One could wish for a bit more mid-palate density too, presumably from lower vineyard yields.

Those caveats voiced, Venge's Cabernets are nevertheless lovely wines made in a style that has genuine integrity. Venge Merlots are pleasant, but not especially distinctive—a common theme of Oakville Merlots.

The Saddleback Cellars bottlings, all Cabernets, are very fine and often display a hint of mint. Typically, they are sourced entirely from Oakville, often with Venge's own vineyard providing the majority of the fruit.

Viader Vineyard—Delia Viader (pronounced Vee-ah-DURR) has garnered considerable attention for herself and her wines, as she is certainly a Napa Valley original. Her steep hillside on Howell Mountain, below the 1,400-foot boundary where the AVA begins, is easily sighted and was the focus of a spirited debate about the environmental effects of hillside planning.

Viader's most promient wine is a proprietary bottling simply named Viader. It's an estate-grown red wine that's typically about two-thirds Cabernet Sauvignon and one-third Cabernet Franc. It has been well-reviewed by others, but the appeal escapes me. A generous vertical tasted at Viader failed to persuade me of the distinction of Viader wines. Too often they seemed muddy and lacking in clarity of flavor. One gets the impression that too much Cabernet Franc is employed, which too often imparts a vegetal note as well as magnifies that sense of muddiness.

Delia Viader insists that these are wines that truly need a decade's worth of aging. In fairness, a 1995 did show beautifully, as did a lean but still attractive 1993. A 1991, however, was less persuasive. A secondary bottling, labeled "V" is also offered, made mostly from Petit Verdot and Cabernet Sauvignon.

Villa Mt. Eden/Conn Creek—Now owned by Stimson Lane (the owner of Washington State's Château Ste. Michelle), the two labels of Villa Mt. Eden and Conn Creek have knocked around Napa Valley for years. At one time Villa Mt. Eden made some pretty good wine. (They sourced some of their grapes from the McWilliams property now leased by Plumpjack Winery.) Conn Creek once had a reputation as the source of good Cabernet.

Today, these two brands are frankly commercial, with little that's noteworthy. Many of the wines are sourced from outside Napa Valley, such as Chardonnay and Pinot Noir from Bien Nacido Vineyard in Santa Barbara

County, Zinfandel from Sierra Foothills, and Pinot Noir from Russian River Valley. The top-of-the-line Napa Valley Cabernet has the proprietary name Anthology. It's an ordinary wine with no distinguishing qualities.

Vinoce Vineyards—Located at the northernmost extreme of the Mount Veeder AVA (which is to say, upvalley away from San Pablo Bay), Vinoce has received some attention because the vineyard is located on the estate of comedian Robin Williams. The vineyard is actually owned by the caretakers of Williams' estate, Brian and Lori Nuss, who were allowed to carve off a piece of property of their own on which they planted a twenty-five-acre hillside vineyard with a spectacular view. (Most of their grapes are sold to others, including Robert Craig Wine Cellars and Cuvaison, among others.)

The estate Vinoce wine is a red simply called Vinoce. It's a varying blend of mostly Cabernet Franc with a balance of Merlot and Cabernet Sauvignon. Several vintages reveal it to be a pleasing wine with a violet Cabernet Franc scent but an indeterminate muddiness or lack of focused flavor. This is clearly a vineyard still searching for just the right mix, but the odds are good that its dedicated owners will achieve their vision. Worth watching closely.

Wing Canyon Vineyard—A small family winery on Mount Veeder, Wing Canyon Vineyard creates lovely, delicate, pure Mount Veeder Cabernet with uncommon finesse and mineral notes. Not much wine is made, so this is a producer you have to seek out. But it's worth the effort. Wing Canyon is the source of some of Mount Veeder's finest Cabernets, along with those of Mayacamas Vineyards higher up on the mountain.

York Creek Winery—Few great wine estates have "flown under the radar" quite as stealthily as York Creek Winery in Spring Mountain District. The reasons have something to do with the fact that this vineyard only recently decided to make its own wines after decades of selling its grapes to others. (It was Ridge Vineyards that gave the York Creek name whatever fame it has, courtesy of Ridge's series of York Creek-designated Petite Sirahs.)

But mostly it has to do with York Creek's owner, Fritz Maytag, who is far better known as the owner of San Francisco's Anchor Steam brewery. Maytag, the grandson of the famous appliance manufacturer (the family long ago sold that business), is a man who prefers to live a discreet life. And although he has owned York Creek for decades, he is virtually unknown and unseen in Napa Valley's often frenetic social life.

However, York Creek Winery is one of Napa Valley's great vineyard estates, with 125 acres of vines spread across a much larger property. Few people have actually visited the vineyard, as Maytag prefers it to remain as private as possible. You drive past some of York Creek's vines on Langtry Road as you head toward neighboring Cain Vineyards, which lies at the end of the road. It is an idyllic spot, where you can truly get a sense of rural Napa Valley as it was in less-frenzied times.

York Creek's wines are only just appearing now. And they are classic Spring Mountain reds in their power, pungency, and earthy grandeur, as well as tannic sturdiness. These are not slight wines. They are built to last, with the stuffing to do so. Look for a superb Cabernet Sauvignon, excellent Petite Sirah, and a very impressive port-style wine made from traditional Portuguese grape varieties. Maytag has fashioned an array of wines (made in a separate section of his brewery in the Potrero Hill section of San Francisco), as he produces small lots of wines and only later decides how (and whether) to blend. Only a small fraction of his vineyard production, no more than one-fifth, is sold under the York Creek Vineyards label. Most of his grapes continue to be sold to other wineries, such as Cain, Barnett, and Ridge, among others.

SONOMA COUNTY

A mystery that magnifies the earth but does not lie.
What is Pure Land to that?
　　　　　　　—Jack Gilbert, *Monolithos: Poems 1962 and 1982*

G ood poetry somehow answers unasked questions. As it happens, Jack
　　Gilbert did not inquire, "What is fine wine?" Yet his is the most elegantly simple answer: *A mystery that magnifies the earth but does not lie.* The
stature of such an accomplishment is revealed by what the poet asks instead:
What is Pure Land to that?

Nowhere in California has there been more "pure land" for fine wine than
in the sprawl of Sonoma County. Yet no wine area in California has waited
longer to transform. Sonoma's longtime crops of melons and bulk wine
grapes, among many others, offered little magnification of the earth, or much
telling of its truth. That Sonoma lent itself to winegrowing was apparent
from the start: It was Sonoma County, not Napa Valley, that sparked some of
the earliest wine interest in California settlers.

The nineteenth-century California humorist George Horatio Derby,
writing under the pen name Squibob in what was once California's largest
daily newspaper, *Alta California*, usually delighted in skewering what even
then was California's pretension toward proclaiming itself heaven on earth.
Yet even he felt compelled to acknowledge, in 1850, that "Sonoma *is* a nice
place . . . enjoying an unvaryingly salubrious climate, neither too warm nor
too cold. With little wind, few fleas, and a sky of that peculiarly blue description that Fremont terms *the Italian*, it may well be called . . . the Garden of
California." He also noted that "The most luscious grapes [are] to be found
there." (The fleas still are few.)

Just why Sonoma County took so long to transform from "pure land" to
something more articulate is puzzling. Some of the explanations are straight-

forward, such as its ability to support enormous grape yields thanks to easy irrigation and a high water table along the Russian River Valley. The restraint required for fine wine was no match against the ready market for high-yield bulk wines.

But part of Sonoma's slow crawl toward transformation is due to something less provable, but perhaps no less forceful. Why, for example, has neighboring Napa Valley, not Sonoma County, long been the place where wealthy newcomers to wine built their winemaking pleasure palaces?

After all, Sonoma County was where the northern California wine rush began. The town of Sonoma was the site of the last, and northernmost, Spanish Mission: the Mission San Francisco, founded in 1823. Only one year later, a vineyard of more than one thousand grapevines was successfully installed. It was this vineyard that supplied grapevines to George Yount in 1838 when he established Napa Valley's first vineyard in what is now Yountville.

By that time, what has since come to be called the Sonoma Mission was the private property of the army officer who originally secularized the Spanish-owned church holdings, then-lieutenant (later general) Mariano Guadalupe Vallejo. It was Vallejo who laid out the town of Sonoma. And it was Vallejo who established his own vineyard outside of Sonoma, which he named Lachryma Montis, or "Tears of the Mountain." The name referred to a mountain spring he used to irrigate his vineyard, making it one of California's earliest vineyard irrigation efforts.

After Vallejo came Agoston Haraszthy, who started the still-extant Buena Vista winery in 1856 with the purchase of 560 acres of land northeast of the town of Sonoma. Six years later, in 1862, Haraszthy had 300 acres of bearing vineyard. He also built himself a grand, Roman-style villa that no longer exists. Chinese laborers dug extensive tunnels, which do remain. (Making the picture neater yet, Haraszthy's son, Atilla, married Vallejo's daughter and started his own vineyard next to Vallejo's Lachryma Montis vineyard.)

Sonoma County was attracting attention, as well as investors of considerable worth. Jacob Gundlach started his Rhinefarm next to Buena Vista. Charles Kohler, who first brought California wine (grown in the then-larger Los Angeles vineyards) to a national market, created a grand winery and vineyard in the town of Glen Ellen. Grandest of all was Issac de Turk in Santa Rosa. By the 1880s, his was the largest business in Santa Rosa, as well as the largest winery in Sonoma County.

Yet despite this significant history, as well as no fewer than 118 wineries by 1891, Sonoma County never managed to rival Napa Valley in high-society esteem or architectural lavishness. It was to Napa Valley that wealthy San Franciscans came both to play and establish vineyards. More than Sonoma County, Napa Valley was home to winegrowers of showy ambition, be they American-born or immigrant.

It was Napa Valley where Frederick Beringer built his imposing stone and timber mansion, where Gustave Niebaum erected his substantial brick winery for his Inglenook estate, and where San Francisco investor William Bourn built the enormous stone winery called Greystone. All three structures, among others, are still in use.

Then as now, Napa Valley was where wealthy owners built show-off wineries. Sonoma County, in contrast, was where people went to farm. Why was this so? And why did this pattern repeat itself in the 1970s, when winegrowing again became fashionable among wealthy Californians? Napa Valley boosters like to point to themselves as "keepers of the flame," noting such wineries as Beaulieu (founded in 1900) and Inglenook (founded in 1879), both of which managed to get through the thirteen devastating years of Prohibition. Yet Sonoma County had its own survivors: Korbel (founded in 1862), Simi (founded in 1876), and Sebastiani (founded in 1904).

Nothing about the quality of the land distinguishes Napa Valley from Sonoma County. But something about the lay of the land does: The sheer sprawl of Sonoma County flavored its fate. No one has captured this better than the novelist Lawrence Durrell in his essay, "Landscape With Literary Figures":

> 'You write,' says a friendly critic in Ohio, 'as if the landscape were more important than the character.' If not exactly true, this is near enough the mark, for I have evolved a private notion about the importance of landscape, and I willingly admit to seeing characters almost as functions of a landscape . . . You begin to realize that the important determinant of any culture is after all the spirit of place.[7]

[7] *The New York Times Book Review*, June 12, 1960

Perhaps more than any other element, it is Sonoma's "spirit of place" that best explains why it evolved so very differently from Napa Valley. The most obvious feature is size. Sonoma County is more than twice as large as Napa County: 1,604 square miles compared to Napa's 744 square miles.

But size alone is not the cause of Sonoma's strikingly different spirit of place. Instead, it is the shape and feel of the landscape. In Napa Valley one has a feeling of being on display. Its narrow configuration is inherently public. Far from a detraction, it is this publicity that attracts—or at least lends itself to—a certain sort of ostentation. The configuration of Napa Valley allows one literally to be "in society." It is this delicious confinement of landscape that was then, and still is today, the appeal of Napa Valley for wealthy outsiders. After all, why build a show-off winery (or house), if no one can see it? And wealthy newcomers to Napa Valley in the 1880s, or in the 1980s, had no intention of going unnoticed.

In comparison, Sonoma County lends itself to an assured privacy—almost to fugitiveness. You can get lost in Sonoma County, in every sense. In the Russian River Valley, the river twists on the ground like a landed fish. Each bend of the river is its own world, isolated in sight and sound from the landfall of a neighboring bend. The result is a remove of the sort found in the mountain hamlets of Appalachia. (It should be noted that in the late 1800s some wealthy San Francisco families sought this privacy as well as the Russian River Valley's cool summer climate. But winegrowing was not their goal.)

The many landscape isolations of Sonoma County help explain why it— never Napa Valley—was the place of choice for winemaking communes. By their nature, they seek refuge from prying eyes. The most notorious was Fountain Grove, which was established outside of Santa Rosa in 1875. That year, Thomas Lake Harris, the English founder of a communal religious sect called the Brotherhood of the New Life, bought 400 acres of land north of Santa Rosa.

By 1883 the commune was devoted entirely to winegrowing; by 1888 the property expanded to 2,000 acres (400 of which were vineyard) and production reached 200,000 gallons of wine annually. It even published what was surely California's first winery newsletter, the *Fountain Grove WinePress*. (I am indebted to Thomas Pinney's *A History of Wine in America: From the Beginnings to Prohibition* for these and other details.)

Harris propounded some delightfully wacky religious ideas. According to Thomas Pinney, "Harris taught that God is bisexual, and that everyone, man and woman, has a celestial counterpart with whom to seek eternal marriage. Unluckily, the counterpart is elusive: it may move from one body to another, and in any case it is hard to know for sure where it dwells, and when." Perhaps the choicest bit was that Harris, according to Pinney, wrote about how "the world is filled with tiny fairies who live in the bosoms of women and sing heavenly harmonies inaudible to worldly ears." He was run out of town in 1892 and never returned.

Despite that, Fountain Grove remained and continued to produce wine under the guidance of a Japanese convert to the Brotherhood of the New Life, Kanaye Nagasawa. He owned the winery and vineyards until his death in 1934. Everything eventually died by 1951, although the Fountain Grove label still exists.

Farther north was another sect of sorts, the Icaria Speranza commune. Inspired by the utopian communism of Frenchman Étienne Cabet's book *Voyage en Icarie*, the adherents eventually arrived in California, purchasing 885 acres along the Russian River near Cloverdale in 1881. The Icarians believed in what they called True Christianity, taught universal brotherhood, and—thanks to its original French members—required that all Icarians read and speak French as a prerequisite for membership. By 1887 the commune dissolved due to debt.

The most famous communal—really, cooperative—effort was the Italian Swiss Colony. Here the impulse was not religious, but idealistic social philanthropy. It was founded by a successful banker, Andrea Sbarboro, a native of Genoa. He figured that a way to help his fellow Italians was to create a grape-growing business modeled on the principles of the savings and loan societies where he made his fortune. Using payroll deductions, the workers could own shares in the company.

In 1881, Sbarboro bought 1,500 acres of land in Asti, a tiny town virtually within shouting distance of the Icarian commune in Cloverdale. Workers got $30 to $40 a month, plus room, board, and free wine. Despite the name, the community was virtually all Italians. However, they wanted no part of Sbarboro's scheme to deduct $5 a month from the wages to pay for shares in the company. They smelled a (nonexistent) rat. Not a single worker participated.

Eventually, the company became like any other, although still exceptionally paternalistic. It also went into winemaking, not Sbarboro's original intention, which was only to grow grapes. By 1900, it had become the largest single winery in California and by 1910 owned 5,000 acres of vineyard, much of it far afield from Sonoma County. Although a financial success, by 1913 it was absorbed into the California Wine Association cartel.

The fugitive, even furtive quality of the tucked-away terrain of Sonoma County is further demonstrated by its being the home of the Bohemian Grove. Located near Guerneville on the Russian River, the 2,700-acre Bohemian Grove is the site of a famously private retreat of San Francisco's Bohemian Club.

Every July approximately 1,500 men from around the country assemble at Bohemian Grove for two weeks (some stay only for one week or come only on the weekends) to enjoy each other's company, participate in elaborate theatrical productions, and listen to "lakeside talks" from distinguished speakers.

This is no ordinary club. And its speakers and entertainers are no ordinary performers. Bohemian Grove is perhaps the most exclusive assemblage of American corporate leaders, high-ranking political figures, top-level entertainers, and prestigious academics—at least those who are male, anyway. It also is famously secretive, indeed genuinely furtive. For example, when then-President Richard Nixon was invited to give a strictly off-the-record "lakeside talk," the press was outraged and insisted on covering the event. The president was disinvited.

That Bohemian Grove was created in 1880, and that the chosen site was the dense, secretive redwoods of Sonoma's Russian River Valley, speaks volumes. The publicness of Napa Valley was unthinkable. Even in 1880, when the Bohemian Grove was first established, Sonoma County felt right. Surely, Napa Valley was considered, as it was the playground of choice for rich and powerful San Franciscans. Yet even in those unpopulated times, Napa's publicity of place felt wrong. Sonoma's spirit of place is a sense of real or imagined isolation.

The force of the Sonoma landscape has also created a sense of place different from what is publicly perceived. In the public mind, there exists something called the Napa/Sonoma wine country, as if the two were one. Why is this so? Partly it's proximity. But mostly it's public relations, fueled by economics. It comes down to this: Sonoma County grapes fetch a price that can be as much as one-third less per ton, 17 percent less per ton than the same grape variety grown in Napa Valley. Such is the cash-on-the-barrel difference that a famous name can command for an otherwise anonymous bunch of grapes.

Like a local politician jostling for position next to a visiting national luminary at a public reception, Sonoma County finds it useful to be publicly associated with Napa Valley. Its growers want parity. And they are savvy enough to know Napa Valley grapes command a premium due to a perceived, rather than actual, difference in quality. If the public sees the two counties as equal, all the better for Sonoma County.

Yet Sonoma County really sees itself linked with Mendocino County. Witness the willingness of Sonoma wineries to use Mendocino County grapes. In comparison, Napa wineries do so infrequently. This is longstanding; it is a function of landscape.

It's landscape that makes Sonoma and Mendocino, if not blood relations, then kissing cousins. That both counties have always been largely rural environments devoted to farming adds to a sense of commonality. But landscape binds them. The Russian River runs south from Mendocino into Sonoma, where it eventually empties into the Pacific Ocean after meandering through the Alexander and Russian River Valleys.

Identical in effect, and in much of its path, is Highway 101. Along its Mendocino/Sonoma segment, Highway 101 is a fellow traveler with the Russian River for more than fifty miles from Ukiah to Healdsburg. Far from quarreling with the landscape, it falls in with it and in the process, becomes a natural feature.

In comparison, no ease of movement exists between Sonoma and Napa. The Mayacamas Mountains are a formidable wall. To this day, crossing the Mayacamas is not a carefree drive. The roads that span it are narrow, few, and twisting. Even with modern transportation and communications, a sense of identification and connection, real or imagined, between Sonoma and Napa still is effectively discouraged. Such is the persistence of place upon the spirit.

The Complication of Sonoma County AVAs

No wine area in California offers more of a jumble of viticultural areas than Sonoma County. At last count, there were thirteen AVAs in Sonoma County.

Sorting through them is a challenge, if only because they reflect two opposing perspectives, one taking the broadest possible view and the other almost claustrophobically focused. What results is a multiplicity of AVAs that crowd upon each other and frequently overlap.

The broad view creates AVAs of intentionally outsize scale, as the North Coast and Sonoma Coast AVAs. Producers seeking this sort of AVA are those who want to buy from as many sources as possible, yet sell the resulting blend under an attractive, seemingly specific geographic name. It is the wine labeling equivalent of what military strategists call carpetbombing.

The supreme example of this is the North Coast AVA. It incorporates all of Napa, Sonoma, Mendocino, Lake, Marin, and Solano counties. At about 4,687 square miles of land, the North Coast AVA is three times larger than the Central Coast AVA (1,562 square miles), its closest rival in geographical meaninglessness.

Northern Sonoma AVA

Compared to the North Coast AVA, the designation Northern Sonoma AVA passes for precision bombing, even though it manages to strike seven of Sonoma County's eleven AVAs. It holds 544 square miles. The Northern Sonoma AVA is everything in Sonoma County north of Santa Rosa.

The obvious question is why is there a Northern Sonoma AVA? Viticulturally it is meaningless, incorporating as it does such wildly different climates as those of warm Knights Valley, cool Green Valley, and every gradation of heat, fog, and sunshine in between.

The answer is found the Federal Register citation 27 CFR 4.26 ¶ 21336B: the definition of "estate bottled." You would think that "estate bottled" would be available to any winery making wine exclusively from grapes grown on its own property. But the regulations say differently. Just making wine exclusively from your own grapes is not enough. Instead, the winery facility itself must be located in the same legally defined grapegrowing area where the grapes are grown. So, if you own or lease a vineyard in the Alexander Valley AVA and your winery is in the Dry Creek Valley AVA, you're out of luck.

It so happens that E. & J. Gallo do own a winery in Dry Creek Valley, along with 600 acres of vineyard there. And Gallo also owns 500 acres of land in the Alexander Valley, as well as 400 acres in the Russian River Valley. Without a Northern Sonoma AVA, it would be impossible for them—or any other winery in a similar situation—to use the sought after phrase "estate bottled" on their label. This is why there is a Northern Sonoma AVA.

Sonoma Coast AVA

Sonoma Coast AVA is yet another of the macroscopic views of Sonoma County. It takes in 750 square miles, making it the largest AVA in Sonoma County. Sonoma Coast AVA is configured on coolness. Like an isobar on a weather map that shows areas sharing a common temperature, the boundaries of Sonoma Coast zig, zag, and undulate in response to the season-long warmth of the land. It is designed to signal those parts of Sonoma County with no more than 2,800 degree-days of heat during the growing season, which puts the warmest spots at what growers call "high Region II." By California standards, this is well within what is considered "cool." Because Sonoma Coast is shaped only according to coolness, it overlaps five other, smaller AVAs: the Sonoma part of Carneros, a sliver of Sonoma Valley, the western portion of Chalk Hill, all of Green Valley, and most of Russian River Valley.

But most of the Sonoma Coast AVA actually is a large chunk of western Sonoma land that was previously undesignated. If nothing else, the Sonoma Coast AVA illustrates how Sonoma County really comprises two realms: the mostly warm eastern, or inland, portion of the county and the mostly cool, ocean-influenced western section. Inland AVAs such as Dry Creek, Alexander Valley, Knights Valley, Sonoma Mountain, and much of Sonoma Valley share a comparable heat. Numerous distinctions exist among them, but viticulturally they are a planetary system held together by a common sun that shines upon them more often than it does the cool, fog-shrouded nooks of the Russian River Valley.

Like the Northern Sonoma AVA, Sonoma Coast exists partly as a convenience for wineries wishing to blend far-flung holdings and still be entitled to say "estate bottled." (Sonoma-Cutrer is one such winery.) Not least, it tidied things up. With the creation of the Sonoma Coast AVA in 1987, roughly 85 percent of Sonoma County's land area found itself entitled to at least one AVA designation.

The Western AVAs of Sonoma County: The Ocean Influence

As mentioned previously, two realms are found in Sonoma County. They are distinguished simply by their susceptibility to the influence of the Pacific Ocean. Since the entire western border of Sonoma County *is* the Pacific Ocean, it doesn't take much imagination to recognize that those areas open to its cool breezes and moist air are going to be dramatically different than cloistered inland areas.

The progression from cool to warm is fairly straightforward: As you go from west to east you go from cooler to warmer, wetter to drier. Excluding the all-encompassing Sonoma Coast AVA, the western, ocean-influenced AVAs are three: the Russian River Valley and its two subsets, the Green Valley AVA and the Chalk Hill AVA. In addition, there's what this observer likes to call the "real" Sonoma Coast, what might be called "Sonoma Coast West."

Sonoma Coast West

There is no such AVA called Sonoma Coast West. But while it's missing on any official map, Sonoma Coast West most definitely exists in the glass. This is the "real" Sonoma Coast. It might be imagined as that area closest to the Pacific Ocean from, say, Jenner in the south, where the Russian River empties into the Pacific, to somewhere around the village of Annapolis in the north, embracing an area perhaps six miles inland (east) from the Pacific Ocean. Someday it is sure to be its own AVA.

Sonoma Coast West is mountainous terrain, not easily cultivated and sparsely populated. Logging has long been its daily bread, although that occupation is dying out. Like parts of Mendocino, which it resembles, Sonoma Coast West has a certain cantakerousness about it. Many residents moved there precisely to get away from others and rather resent its "discovery" by deep-pocketed vineyard developers who want to plant its best slopes. No new vineyard in Sonoma Coast West is created without a long, bruising battle not just with the locals, but also with environmentalists intent on preserving the hillsides from development.

Despite a relative paucity of vineyards, those that are present, such as Flowers Camp Meeting Ridge, Hirsch Vineyard, Marcassin, among others, are not merely good. They are profound. What's more, it's already clear that this zone has a vocation of place for Pinot Noir and, to a lesser degree, Chardonnay, like few others anywhere in California.

Even by California standards, where bizarre climates shaped by fog and elevation are the norm, Sonoma Coast West stands out. The coastal mountains create ridgelines running parallel to the ocean, anywhere from roughly 900 to 2,000 feet in elevation. Yet nearly all of the vineyard in Sonoma Coast West are just one to five miles inland from the ocean as the gull flies. Since the fog rises only to the 900-foot level, everyone's vineyards are sited above that critical demarcation. The unobstructed sunshine offsets what might otherwise be crippling coolness from the cool breezes of the Pacific Ocean so nearby.

What results, especially as interpreted by the Pinot Noir grape, is an unrivaled intensity of flavor buoyed by surprisingly high acidity. Berry size tends to be small verging on minute. At Flowers Camp Meeting Ridge Vineyard, for example, both the berry and cluster size of their Pinot Noir are so small that you can hold twenty fully ripe clusters in the cupped palms of your two hands, like holding a family of baby gerbils. Flavor intensity is magnified by the disproportionate ratio of skin to juice (the flavor is in the skins). Tannins, however, are also consequently magnified as well.

Chardonnay, so far, does not seem to this taster to be quite so receptive to the peculiarities of Sonoma Coast West as Pinot Noir. It's certainly good and often better than that. But so far, perhaps because of soil (largely sedimentary rock, sandy clay, and clay loam), the Chardonnays have seemed a bit heavy and bulky. Then again, it may be more a matter of suitable clones and appropriate winemaking techniques than anything else. One would be a fool to count out Chardonnay in this environment at so early a stage.

One thing is already clear: Sonoma Coast West is an extraordinary location for Pinot Noir. Sonoma Coast West has the capacity—although not yet the achievement—of someday creating America's *grand cru* Pinot Noirs. To be a true *grand cru*, a Pinot Noir—whether in America or Burgundy—has to deliver profound originality and complexity of flavor in a wine that's bigger than most, yet has such finesse that its proportions seem ideal and effortless.

Russian River Valley AVA

No two wine areas in California are more alike than Mendocino's Anderson Valley and Sonoma's Russian River Valley. Both are subject to profound ocean influence, thanks to rivers making their way to sea. In the Anderson Valley it's the Navarro River; in the Russian River Valley it's the namesake Russian River. They look the same: moist, dark, densely forested, and isolated. More to the point, they both succeed with the same grapes, notably Gewürztraminer and, oddly enough, Zinfandel. Some of California's greatest Zinfandels are grown in these two seemingly unlikely—given Zinfandel's reputation for liking warmth—locales.

Of course, there are differences. Foremost among them is the size of the Russian River Valley AVA. It occupies 150 square miles, boasts 9,000 acres of vineyard, and has about forty-five wineries. The Anderson Valley, in comparison, has little more than 2,000 acres of vines and fewer than two dozen wineries, tops. Moreover, where the Russian River Valley has its hills, it also has broad, flat stretches. The Anderson Valley, in comparison, is a narrow slash between steep mountains. Still, the similarities of place, as revealed through the wines, are striking.

Both districts face a challenge from Chardonnay and Pinot Noir. So far, Russian River Valley has met with greater success with Chardonnay and, especially, Pinot Noir. Partly this is due to its sheer size. Russian River Valley has numerous, and sufficiently different, sites where these delicate varieties can excel. It is for just this reason that the Russian River Valley has become one of the most accomplished places for Pinot Noir in California.

What the Russian River Valley has, which is missing in both the Carneros district or the Santa Maria Valley, is the opportunity to locate sites with both a suitably cool microclimate *and* distinctive soils. Carneros has the climate, but not the soil variations. Santa Maria Valley has some soil differences, but its Pinot Noirs have been marred by vegetal flavors due to inappropriate clones. This is changing, however.

Russian River Valley producers have put down a vineyard here and there, persistently feeling about the landscape, like a contact lens wearer on hands and knees searching for a missing lens. The opportunities will come, as they have in Burgundy's Côte d'Or, when some lucky soul manages to find a nexus where a just-right microclimate hovers over a just-so soil. Probably along the gravelly banks of the Russian River itself is where such opportunities will be most rewarding.

Chardonnay is successful, in part because it is such an accommodating grape, both to vineyard and winemaking. For a long time Russian River Valley Chardonnays did not fully reflect some of the unusual particularities of place present there. The problem was the same shared by Anderson Valley and Oregon's northern Willamette Valley: inappropriate clones.

Remember that when Professor Harold Olmo of UC Davis embarked on his Chardonnay clonal selection program, which produced stellar results, the "ideal" Chardonnay clone was one that responded to sites significantly warmer than those of the western portion of the Russian River Valley, Anderson Valley, or Willamette Valley. All three cool districts wrestle with Chardonnay clones inappropriate to them. Only now are the new cool-climate Dijon clones in place. It's still too soon to "call" the game, but what is emerging is already purer and finer than many earlier Chardonnays.

Although the Russian River Valley AVA extends as far west as Guerneville (pronounced Gurn-ville), where the dense redwood domain of Bohemian Grove is found, the vineyard action really begins around Forestville, a few miles farther inland from Guerneville. Guerneville is about eight miles from the ocean and very cool.

At Forestville, the vineyard plantings splay in four directions: north, south, east, and northeast. North of Forestville, following the course of the Russian River on both sides, is a constellation of vineyard sites. South of the Russian River at the Forestville point is one of the subset AVAs: the Green Valley AVA (q.v.). East of Forestville is the third cluster of vineyards. On either side of River Road, which is the main drag, are found yet more vineyards. Farthest inland—northeast of Forestville—is the other subset AVA: the Chalk Hill AVA. It is planted mostly to Chardonnay.

Despite this diversity, the Russian River Valley is cohesive only to this extent: All of its wines reveal a delicacy that derives from a cool climate. That said, the degree of this delicacy, both in taste and texture, can vary significantly. Green Valley wines are noticeably more austere and delicate than the wines grown in Chalk Hill. Nevertheless, delicacy is the hallmark.

Proof of this is found in Gewürztraminer—if you can still find any. Chardonnay has all but eradicated it. Only Mendocino's Anderson Valley delivers comparable textural delicacy and clear-cut definition of flavors. Gewürztraminer is a trickier grape to grow than generally recognized. The intensity and opulence of its spiciness makes it susceptible to excess, unless grown in sites where it is suitably throttled. This was repeatedly achieved in Russian River Valley, and one can only hope that a small, but loyal, market can ensure its continued availability.

Chardonnay offers another sort of proof. One need only compare a Russian River Chardonnay with one from neighboring Alexander Valley. The Russian River version generally is leaner, a bit more tart, and is structured differently: delicacy again. Chardonnay is not as good an example as Gewürztraminer, if only because it lends itself so easily to cosmetics. But coolness will win out, and in places such as Green Valley it certainly does.

A word should be put in for Zinfandel, which is far better associated with the inland Sonoma districts of Dry Creek Valley, Alexander Valley, and Sonoma Valley. Appropriate as it is to those places, it also shines—with a different luminosity of flavor—in the Russian River Valley. Although Zinfandel has long been grown in Russian River Valley—after all, it *is* an old winegrowing area—it is not typically cited as the source of anything extraordinary. Perhaps this is due to a preference among Zinfandel fanciers for the chewier, denser style of Zinfandel exemplified by Dry Creek Valley. Fair enough. But Zinfandel also lends itself to a more supple style, something more akin to Pinot Noir than Cabernet Sauvignon. This is where the Russian River stands out.

A few wines are so extraordinary that Zinfandel's suitability to the cooler Russian River Valley cannot be doubted. Here again, the similarity to Anderson Valley is noticeable. Both places grow Zinfandel to Pinot Noir perfection. Both are working with old vines, as the new plantings in both districts are devoted to market-driven wines such as Chardonnay. Yet the old-timers were on to something. Martinelli Vineyard's Jackass Hill Zinfandel comes from a very steep old vineyard located in one of the coolest sites of all: the westernmost part the Green Valley AVA.

In the 1990 vintage, De Loach decided to issue three named-vineyard Zinfandels, all from old plantings. All were exceptional and they excited interest in Russian River Zinfandel. The same effect occurred with the early recognition of the unusual and exceptional goodness of Limerick Lane Zinfandel, from the nearly century-old vines of neighboring Collins Vineyard.

Sonoma County–Green Valley AVA

As previously noted, Green Valley is a sub-appellation of Russian River Valley AVA. It is the coolest section of the area, which is why it seceded, as it were, from Russian River Valley. In essence, it is the Russian River Valley magnified: more ocean influence, cooler temperatures, crisper wines. Iron Horse is the signature winery and appears to be a sensitive vehicle for Green Valley's particularity of place.

Because of its coolness, Green Valley is the place of choice for sparkling wine producers. Iron Horse makes its sparkling wine from Green Valley–grown grapes. It also is a major source of Château St. Jean's sparkling wine. In fact, its sparkling wine facility is located in the area. Chardonnay is Green Valley's strong suit, nowhere better proved than in Kistler's Dutton Ranch bottling. Pinot Noir is less convincing, although promising. Dehlinger uses Pinot Noir from the appellation as, of course, does Iron Horse. The all-important delicacy is present. What's missing is a little more depth. The odds, however, are in favor of the Green Valley AVA emerging as a choice source of Pinot Noir in the years to come.

The proper name of the AVA is Sonoma County–Green Valley because there also exists a Green Valley AVA in Solano County. It, too, has the county name appended.

Chalk Hill AVA

A subset of the Russian River Valley AVA, Chalk Hill is noticeably warmer and hillier than most of the other areas. The hills are thought to deflect the invasion of ocean air. Also, Chalk Hill is in the easternmost portion of the Russian River Valley AVA, which further contributes to its relative warmth. It is something of a transitional zone between the "true" Russian River Valley and the eastern, mountain-influenced Sonoma County AVAs.

In its application to become a separate AVA, a distinction of soil was noted: a whitish soil that, the Chalk Hill name notwithstanding, is actually volcanic ash. Chalk Hill Winery is the major winery in the AVA; Rodney

Strong Vineyards makes a point of issuing a Chalk Hill-designated Chardonnay. One cannot find any apparent distinction in the wines, which are mostly Chardonnays. So far, the Chalk Hill AVA can be found only on a map.

The Eastern AVAs of Sonoma County: The Mountain Influence

The influence of mountains—or their absence—upon Sonoma County's wine districts comes down to this: Either the ocean influence invades or is repelled. The degree to which it is kept out determines, to a great extent, the warmth of the site. The one mitigating factor is elevation: The higher you go, the lower the temperature. This is known as the Normal Lapse Rate. But if you're on the valley floor, unless that valley is in Tibet, this isn't going to be of much help. This, in a nutshell, is the story of the Dry Creek Valley, Alexander Valley, Knights Valley Sonoma Valley, and Sonoma Mountain AVAs. All are tucked between mountains in the eastern half of Sonoma County, well away from the Pacific Ocean and its cool air and fog.

Such a geographical situation can be enormously beneficial. The trick, as always, is to grow those grapes that respond favorably. Not for nothing is Dry Creek Valley renowned for Zinfandel. It's no coincidence that parts of Sonoma Valley and all of Sonoma Mountain are unusually rewarding for Cabernet Sauvignon. And as the vintages and wines mount up, it is becoming apparent that the twenty-four-mile long Alexander Valley is no more climatically cohesive than is thirty-two-mile long Napa Valley. What grows well at one end of Alexander Valley does not perform quite so admirably at the other end. Here again, mountains make the difference.

Dry Creek Valley AVA

Nowhere is the mountain influence so evident to eye and skin than in Dry Creek Valley. As the map shows, it is exactly parallel to neighboring Alexander Valley. But where Alexander Valley is broad and receptive to a tickle of ocean influence at its southern end, the narrow Dry Creek Valley is pocketed between mountains like a watch in a waistcoat.

Nowhere in Sonoma County, which abounds in areas of remove, is the sense of being out of harm's way greater than in Dry Creek Valley. A tributary of the Russian River, the valley of Dry Creek is almost what Westerners call a box canyon. You enter into it, following the creek's course, only to discover that the land seems to be closing in on you, narrowing the deeper you go. And then, all of a sudden, the road comes to an abrupt end. You feel almost that you have to back out, like a horse that can't turn around.

Dry Creek Valley is not entirely insulated from ocean influence: It gets quite a lot of rain considering its otherwise cloistered circumstance. But it sees no breeze. As a result, it's also warm. But even there, it shares a similarity with its parallel universe neighbor, Alexander Valley. In both districts, the southern ends of the appellations are cooler than the northern. (Really, it's northeastern and southeastern, but we'll let that go for clarity's sake.) The town of Healdsburg is a portal for the southern ends of both districts. Whatever is left of the ocean influence slips through Healdsburg and trickles into both Dry Creek Valley and Alexander Valley. In neither case does it get very far. But some effect is felt.

What results in Dry Creek Valley has been a gradual sorting-out of grape varieties to site: Chardonnay and Riesling at the cooler southern end; Zinfandel and Cabernet Sauvignon at the northern end, as well as in the middle. This is far from decisive. Rather, it is just a community's slowing emerging sense of what is appropriate. As everywhere else, plenty of dissenters beg to differ. As a result, Dry Creek Valley shelters remarkably diverse plantings for so small and narrow a location. One would be hard-pressed to think of another fifteeen-mile-long and perhaps two-mile-wide valley where you can find such an assortment of grapes cheek by jowl as Zinfandel, Pinot Noir, Chardonnay, Riesling, Sauvignon Blanc, Barbera, Muscat Canelli, Syrah, Cabernet Sauvignon, Nebbiolo, Viognier, Sémillon, Cabernet Franc, Malbec, Chenin Blanc, Petite Sirah, Merlot, Gewürztraminer, and Gamay Beaujolais, among others.

Even by California standards, that is a boggling assortment of grape varieties for so small a place. The intensity of this cultivation is revealed by the fact that Dry Creek Valley has 6,000 acres of vineyard. This is only one-third less than in all of the much-larger Russian River Valley. However, it is less than half of the far more spacious Alexander Valley, which has 15,000 acres of vines.

Still, one grape variety is acknowledged by all to be supreme: Zinfandel.

For many Zinfandel aficionados, Dry Creek Valley is their Elysian Field, a place of perfect Zinfandel happiness. Let's put it this way: It offers one *kind* of Zinfandel bliss. Those most delighted with Dry Creek Valley Zinfandels always are respectful, even appreciative, of the berryish cooler-climate Zinfandels such as those from Russian River Valley or the softer, more supple Zinfandels of Alexander Valley. But they find no release from worldly care in them.

That Zinfandel speaks in Dry Creek Valley is incontestable. Proof is found in an almost uncanny consistency across vintages, vineyards, and wineries. It is a creature even a first-year student in Zinfandel taxonomy can readily anatomize. When classically made, they are dense, slightly metallic, and more than hinting of tar. The best versions offer a degree of detail frequently lacking in Zinfandels grown elsewhere. This is thanks in part to texture. The denseness of flavor is delivered with a certain dexterity, like a big man handling a small baby.

Dry Creek Valley Zinfandels tend not to have the exuberant wild berry flavors or Pinot Noir-like texture found in Russian River Valley Zinfandels. Perhaps because of this, one (rather odd) term that keeps cropping up in my notes is "solemn." They somehow remind me of an unbending church elder of strongly held conviction. They do last. But they seem not to transform, only soften with age. That said, they are among California's most distinctive wine expressions and proof—if any is needed—of the pedigree of Zinfandel.

Among the many other wines issuing from Dry Creek Valley, Sauvignon Blanc certainly is noteworthy. Here again, one finds a richness and depth. The consistency is nowhere near that of Zinfandel, though. Too often, grassiness can intrude. Chardonnay wanders all over the taste map. (Where does it not these days?) No singular Dry Creek Valley quality leaps to mind. Various Rhône varieties show exceptional promise, notably Syrah and Viognier. Also, a Barbera made by Preston Vineyards gives one reason to think that this long-overlooked grape might find a new respect in the reddish soils of Dry Creek Valley.

Rockpile AVA

In the northwestern corner of Sonoma County is one of Sonoma County's most recent AVAs, memorably named Rockpile, created in 2002. Effectively, it is an extension of Dry Creek Valley AVA, the boundaries of which reach high into the uninhabited, rugged hills above the valley floor. About 18 percent of Rockpile actually overlaps with the Dry Creek AVA.

Rockpile is aptly named, as the land—a collection of bare-rock ridgelines at an 800-foot elevation overlooking manmade Lake Sonoma—is hardly inviting. The name derives from an old 29,000-acre cattle and sheep spread called Rockpile Ranch owned in the mid-1800s by a corrupt local sherriff named Tennessee Bishop, who supposedly (and very likely) put county prisoners to work building roads on his ranch. Reportedly the prisoners dubbed it Rockpile.

Red wines such as Zinfandel are grown here. It's one of the warmest Sonoma County AVAs, as its 800- to 2,000-foot elevation puts it above the fog line. No wineries are located in Rockpile, and there are just 200 acres of vines. As with so many new appellations, its distinction has yet to be established in the bottle, as vineyards there date only to the 1990s. Rosenblum, Kenwood, Seghesio, Paradise Ridge, and St. Francis are among the wineries currently sourcing from Rockpile. Bold, strong Zinfandels are the ticket here, although Syrah, Petite Sirah, Cabernet Sauvignon, and other Bordeaux varietals are planted as well.

Alexander Valley AVA

When the Russian River heads south from Mendocino County, it rolls past Hopland and plunges into a narrow, mountainous chasm. About a dozen or so rough miles farther south, it arrives in the peaceable precincts of Cloverdale, which is the northernmost point of the Alexander Valley. From here on, the Russian River has an easy time of it, meandering down the twenty-four-mile length of a gradually broadening valley.

The easygoing, almost somnolent quality of the Russian River as it makes its way through the Alexander Valley somehow is emblematic of the valley itself. It is an expansive place: flat, filled with sky, and plumped with thick topsoil. It can grow anything. Cloverdale, for example, likes to point out that it is the northernmost point in America where orange trees grow—probably palm trees, too. That tells you something about how warm it gets in the northern Alexander Valley.

Ease of production also has made the Alexander Valley something of a cash cow for wineries located elsewhere. Alexander Valley appears to have a disproportionate number of absentee landlords: The grapes are hauled off to wineries located elsewhere. Sometimes the resulting wine is designated as Alexander Valley, such as Château Montelena's Alexander Valley Chardonnay or Château St. Jean's Robert Young Vineyards Chardonnay. Sometimes the wine is lost in an anonymous blend.

The significance of Alexander Valley lacking resident wineries—which is only now changing—is twofold. Resident wineries mean drumbanging. It is vital for establishing a public identity. Wineries tend to tout the area in which they are found. When drumbangers are present, the effect can be dramatic: Witness what Jordan Vineyard did for Alexander Valley's public image when it arrived in the mid-1970s.

Second is the tendency—always heatedly denied—of some absentee landlords to pursue quantity over quality, especially if the grapes are intended for blending. This is certainly not always so, but anyone who has lived in a rented house knows that the owner tends not to take quite as devoted and expensive an interest as in his own house.

Even the wines themselves are easy. Nowhere in California can be found such consistently supple Cabernets and Zinfandels as in Alexander Valley. Where other districts wrestle with the hard tannins of these two famously tough grapes, in Alexander Valley they are as tame as house cats, yet no less a member of the breed for that.

The challenge for Alexander Valley winegrowers is to deliver wines of rigor. This has been best achieved, ironically, by the red wines. It is ironic because they once were derided (rightly) as being overly vegetal. The problem was just what you'd expect when dealing with rich, bottomland soil: Cabernet and Merlot grew luxuriantly in the gravelly loam that pads the valley floor, especially the part nearest the river banks. Not surprisingly, the vines responded with massive crops and fabulous foliage. Rigor, in the form of severe pruning and leaf-thinning, soon put a little spine into the wines. What emerged then was an unrivaled combination of depth and suppleness.

This same easygoingness is the undoing—or at least the challenge—of Alexander Valley Chardonnay. Almost invariably, the Chardonnays emerge as ripe, plump, soft, and pretty—a wine version of nineteenth-century feminine beauty. Regrettably, the nineteenth century also liked its women docile and vacuous and here, too, the analogy applies.

Although Alexander Valley has scored some real successes with Chardonnay, it seems to this observer that the Chardonnays do not deliver much distinction of place. Usually they are pleasant and almost never offensive. But only rarely is an Alexander Valley Chardonnay the sort of wine that can make you sit up and say, "This wine couldn't have come from just anywhere." Quite the opposite. Many Alexander Valley Chardonnays taste as if they could have come from a half-dozen places. The best ones are succulent, if a little blowsy. The same is largely true of Sauvignon Blanc as well.

Zinfandel and Cabernet Sauvignon are another story. Here the litmus test— "Could this have come from just anywhere?"—shows a different result. Nowhere else in California are there Cabernets and Zinfandels of such inherent suppleness. Alexander Valley consistently creates California's most texturally distinctive red wines. This seems particularly so in the southern, somewhat cooler half of the valley, but that may well be a function simply of its having more vineyards and wineries to explore.

Discovering this distinctive suppleness is easily achieved. Taste a Jordan Cabernet Sauvignon side by side with a Sausal Zinfandel. The grape varieties obviously are different, as are the age of the vines. Jordan's is a relatively young vineyard; Sausal's Zinfandel vines are nearly a century old. The winemaking facilities certainly differ. Yet if Jordan made a Zinfandel it would taste—and above all, *feel*—pretty much like Sausal's.

The Zinfandels do become somewhat more rasping, and a bit less supple, when grown north of Geyserville. The northern half of the valley, between Cloverdale and Geyserville, is warmer. It rewards Zinfandel almost equally well, but differently. The resulting wine tends not to be as polished or supple. Instead, it is slightly coarser, more assertive. Ridge Vineyards has made a specialty of what it calls "Geyserville Zinfandel," and it is superb. To see the textural difference between an Alexander Valley-grown Zinfandel and one from outside its borders—albeit quite close by—try Ridge's Geyserville Zin side by side with its Lytton Springs bottling from the Dry Creek Valley.

What is true for Zinfandel also applies to Cabernet Sauvignon. Here again, the texture is unusually prominent. Going back to an earlier example, Sausal's Cabernet Sauvignon is more like Jordan's than not, nowhere more so than in an identical textural silkiness. That it is not mere winemaking is proved by the fact that many other Alexander Valley Cabernets deliver this same easy-down-the-gullet quality.

More than most California Cabernets, those from the Alexander Valley are unusually rewarding drinking when still very young. This is no fault. Instead, it is a blessing. The best Alexander Valley Cabernets deliver as much depth, distinction, and detail as many of the delayed gratification renditions grown elsewhere. Slow maturation is no guarantee of quality and Alexander Valley Cabernets prove it.

Merlot is perhaps Alexander Valley's calling-card red wine. A grape variety that is intrinsically soft, it too emerges from the Alexander Valley with the signature suppleness. Rarely does it achieve much flavor distinction. Then again, rarely does Merlot do that anywhere. Nevertheless, Alexander Valley Merlots typically are pleasing, indeterminate wines: the sort of red wine that goes with everything—and nothing.

Knights Valley AVA

Despite the absence of an apostrophe, Knights Valley was named after Thomas Knight, a former Maine farmer who had to take up his old occupation after a powder keg explosion destroyed his wagon and belongings. And despite the fact that Knights Valley is a Sonoma County AVA, it really is more an extension of Napa Valley. The geography is pure California in its incomprehensibility.

Essentially, Knights Valley is an extension of the Calistoga end of Napa Valley. Many visitors to Napa Valley reach Calistoga on Highway 29 and figure that they've hit the end of the line. If you turn left, you go over the Mayacamas Mountains, winding up in Santa Rosa. If you turn right, you go through the town and are on the winding, mountainous road heading to Clear Lake.

However, if you go straight, on Highway 128, you will soon arrive in Knights Valley. And when you come out of the enclosed bowl of Knights Valley—*voilà!*—you are dumped onto the doorstep of the Alexander Valley.

Because of its being cupped in the mountains, well away and protected from the ocean influence, Knights Valley is one of the warmest locations in

Sonoma County. It is virtually a fiefdom of Napa's Beringer Winery, which owns the majority of the 1,000 acres of vineyard planted there. Beringer issues a Knights Valley-designated Cabernet Sauvignon and a Sauvignon Blanc. Neither wine delivers much distinction of place.

Smaller quantities of wines have been made from Knights Valley grapes by Whitehall Lane and Peter Michael Winery, the latter being one of only two actually located in Knights Valley.

Sonoma Valley AVA

It is impossible not to compare Sonoma Valley with Napa Valley. And why not? Except in size—Napa Valley is wider and longer—they are twins. They share a common appellation in the Carneros AVA at their southern ends, where both begin at the shore of San Pablo Bay. They are divided by a common mountain range, the Mayacamas. They even curve in the same northeasterly fashion. Their soils are largely alike, their gradations of temperature altering in the same fashion: cool by San Pablo Bay and growing increasingly warmer the deeper into the valleys you go.

Both districts are venerable winegrowing areas, although here Sonoma Valley can lord it over Napa Valley. It started growing grapes earlier (in the 1820s) and was acclaimed sooner. Yet by the turn of the century, Napa Valley was the cynosure and Sonoma Valley was a near-backwater.

Why was this so? Why should Sonoma Valley have faltered when Napa Valley went from strength to strength? The answer is unclear, and not necessarily logical. Partly it has to do with the availability of land. Napa Valley simply has more arable land than Sonoma Valley. To this day, a dramatic disparity exists in vineyard acreage: Napa Valley has about 33,000 acres of vines, while Sonoma Valley reports just 13,500 acres.

Fashion plays a role, as has been discussed previously. Napa Valley became the place of choice for wealthy investors. Perhaps had Haraszthy's Buena Vista Winery—which by 1862 was the largest vineyard in America—enjoyed long-term success, the attractiveness of Sonoma Valley to the fashion-following wealthy might have been different. As it was, the Buena Vista Winery, founded in 1857, began to decline less than a decade later.

In 1868, Haraszthy left California for Nicaragua a bitter and publicly abused man. He is thought to have either drowned in Nicaragua or been eaten by an alligator—or both. One way or the other, he never returned. Buena Vista eventually failed altogether in 1876. As Ruth Teiser and Catherine Harroun report in *Winemaking in California* (1983), "When Frank Bartholomew bought what was left of Buena Vista's old stone buildings in 1941, he had difficulty finding out who had built them." This is a telling point. Nobody in Napa Valley ever had difficulty discovering who built any significant structure or cellar there.

Scale also plays another role. While Napa Valley saw a good number of large wineries based there, after Sonoma Valley's early rush to fame and long, lingering eclipse, it had just one really large winery: Sebastiani Vineyards, founded in 1904. To this day it remains one of the few large wineries in Sonoma Valley, with the newly revitalized Buena Vista (owned by the Racke family of Germany) a distant second in size. The rest of Sonoma Valley's approximately forty-two wineries (Napa Valley reports 280 wineries) are young and comparatively small. For all the patina of its heritage, Sonoma Valley has only recently been revitalized.

The length of Sonoma Valley (about twenty-four miles) inevitably means that it harbors cooler and warmer districts. Sonoma County's part of Carneros is actually the southern end of Sonoma Valley. Sonoma's part of Carneros is subject to the same influences, and delivers the same wine results as Napa's section. This is why the Carneros AVA can stand alone on a wine label. Neither the Napa Valley part of Carneros nor the Sonoma Valley part need say anything more than "Carneros AVA." (See Carneros in the Napa Valley chapter for more information on the AVA.)

Once past the Carneros AVA boundary, Sonoma Valley remains relatively cool. Sonoma-Cutrer's famed Les Pierres Vineyard, planted to Chardonnay, is found just across the Carneros boundary line in Sonoma Valley. The Durrell Vineyard, whose Chardonnay is bottled by Kistler and Kendall-Jackson, among others, is adjacent to Les Pierres. In fact, two of its parcels face each other, one inside the Carneros boundary and the other on the Sonoma Valley side.

The terrain only begins to heat up at the mid-valley point, roughly at the southern tip of Sonoma Mountain AVA. Fog from San Pablo Bay can reach quite far into the valley, ameliorating some of the warmth. From around Glen

Ellen north to Kenwood its effects are negligible. Sonoma Valley grows progressively warmer the farther north (inland) you go.

Because of these gradations of warmth, as well as the penetration of fog, Sonoma Valley—like Napa Valley—is still sorting out what it can grow best and where. Clearly, the southern end is conducive to cool-climate grapes, notably Chardonnay and Pinot Noir. This, in fact, is where growers are steering. Also, Gewürztraminer is widely planted, with encouraging results. They are different, however, from Gewürztraminers grown in the Russian River Valley: more intense and slightly less delicate, but no less good for that. There's some fiddling with Merlot—Buena Vista winery takes the bow. The results are so far unconvincing, but not unpromising.

Once past clear-cut cool, which grapes do best is problematic. Elevation can play havoc with tidy theories. Some of Sonoma Valley's best vineyards can be found on the slope of the Mayacamas Mountains, such as Hanzell, Carmenet, and Louis Martini's Monte Rosso, among others. At these higher elevations, upward of 2,000 feet, they are above the fog line and subject to an entirely different set of conditions. Cabernet Sauvignon certainly performs splendidly there, but one taste of Hanzell's Chardonnay reminds you that Chardonnay cannot be excluded from consideration.

On the valley floor and at lower elevations, mid- and northern-Sonoma Valley is indisputably red wine country—Cabernet Sauvignon and Zinfandel to be specific. Sonoma Valley Cabernets are invariably meaty. You can taste a warm, pleasing heat in them, along with a smack of iron-red earth. A Sonoma Valley Cabernet typically is a formidable wine: luxuriantly fruity, moderately tannic, but above all, forceful in flavor. What saves them is that they are not bullying. Instead, they simply are big, but filled with grace.

One would think that Sonoma Valley Zinfandel would fit, in its flavor fashion, a similar description. Of course, they can be made that way. But the Zinfandels seem surprisingly gentle. At first they are reminiscent of Dry Creek Valley Zinfandels, but at least one feature sets them apart: a greater berryishness. Where Dry Creek Valley delivers a bone-deep strength of flavor, Sonoma Valley offers up the berry qualities so often missing in Dry Creek Valley versions. On the other hand, tar isn't a common flavor note, as it is in Dry Creek Valley. Still, Sonoma Valley Zinfandels are large-scale. Simply taste a Sonoma Valley Zinfandel, such as one from Haywood, side by side with a Russian River Valley Zinfandel, such as one from De Loach, to see the difference in "bone structure."

Sonoma Mountain AVA

Of all of Sonoma County's multiple AVAs, none is more baffling than Sonoma Mountain. The bafflement comes from the niggling, gnawing sense that *something* is different about Sonoma Mountain Cabernets. But putting a finger on that difference, let alone identifying its source, continues to be elusive.

Sonoma Mountain is a subset AVA of Sonoma Valley. The Sonoma Mountain range is a sort of freestanding mountain range that starts gently enough almost from San Pablo Bay and extends, arches sharply upward midway up the valley at around Glen Ellen, and then gradually descends into oblivion right at Santa Rosa. It is a geographical bell-shaped curve set on end in what would otherwise be a very wide valley. It is the Sonoma Mountains that make Sonoma Valley so narrow.

Not much wine is produced from the Sonoma Mountain AVA; at least not that much is so labeled. Laurel Glen and Benziger of Glen Ellen wineries are the torchbearers. And their Cabernets alone doublehandedly make a case for the distinctiveness of Sonoma Mountain. Kenwood makes an absolutely classic Sonoma Mountain Cabernet Sauvignon from the 110-acre Jack London Ranch. In it you can find the massiveness and tight focus that sets this district apart.

The Zinfandels seem less distinctive than the Cabernets, but the samples are relatively few. The standout bottling surely is Kenwood's Jack London Ranch Zinfandel, which, like the Cabernet Sauvignon, is identified as coming from Sonoma Valley. Still, the Jack London bottling is impressive, resonant Zinfandel.

In theory, all of these wines, and others, should taste the same, or nearly so, as those from the vineyards on the Mayacamas Mountain. The two mountain ranges face each other. The soils are about the same. The vineyards can be at similar elevations. Yet something is different. The only obvious difference is exposure: Most of the Sonoma Mountain vineyards face east. All of the Mayacamas-flank vineyards face west. Is that enough? Good question. It does get the morning sun and it cools sooner in the afternoon, thanks to its not getting the afternoon sun. Also, it's slightly breezier in the afternoons.

What Sonoma Mountain Cabernets offer is a pungency and tightness, as well as sheer massiveness. Granted, the same can be said of the Mayacamas-flank Cabernets. But Sonoma Mountain seems to have more of these, delivered in greater focus. The vineyards are uniformly warmer day to night than those on the valley floor, thanks to being above the fog line. Yet, so too are the higher-elevation Mayacamas vineyards. Whatever the cause, one impression remains: No appellation in Sonoma County offers more tantalizing promise for Cabernet Sauvignon than Sonoma Mountain.

Bennett Valley AVA

Bennett Valley is the newest of Sonoma County's thirteen AVAs, created in December 2003. It's really a quite small appellation scooped out of three already-existing AVAs: Sonoma Valley, Sonoma Mountain, and Sonoma Coast. Located just south of the city of Santa Rosa, the Bennett Valley AVA takes its name from, and parallels, the eponymous valley created by Matanzas Creek, which runs through it. Indeed, it was Matanzas Creek Winery (now owned by Kendall-Jackson Wine Estates) that pushed for the new appellation, which is five and one-half miles long and just over three miles wide.

Relative to Sonoma Valley directly to the west and Sonoma Mountain on its southern border, Bennett Valley is cooler and foggier, although nowhere near as much as, say, Carneros or Russian River Valley. But growers there (650 acres of vines are present) insist that it really is different. We shall see.

Sonoma County Producers Worth
Seeking Out (And Some Not)

Adler Fels Winery—Located in Sonoma Valley, Adler specializes in white wines, notably Sauvignon Blanc (labeled Fumé Blanc) and Chardonnay, as well as Gewürztraminer. Good wines but well below the top rank in Sonoma County.

Alexander Valley Vineyards—Although Alexander Valley Vineyards, sited in the eponymous valley, issues an array of wines, only one consistently shines: Cabernet Sauvignon. Vintage after vintage, the Cabernet demonstrates the somewhereness of Alexander Valley. It is a shining, utterly reliable example of the intrinsic Alexander Valley style with this grape: supple and soft, yet detailed. The other wines, such as Chardonnay and Merlot, are merely pleasant.

Arrowood Winery and Vineyards—The former winemaker of Château St. Jean, Dick Arrowood inaugurated his namesake winery in 1984. The former, founding winemaker of Château St. Jean, Arrowood has always extended his winemaking talents across a wide range of wines, as many as fifteen or twenty wines across a range of almost a dozen different grape varieties. Few of Arrowood's wines come from vineyards owned by the winery, which inevitably leads to changes from one vintage to the next. Still, Arrowood's Cabernet and Chardonnay are almost invariably rewarding—particularly the Réserve Spéciale bottlings. Look also for two good single-vineyard Syrahs, one from Russian River (Saralee's Vineyard) and the other from Sonoma Valley (Kuljian Vineyard).

In 2000, Arrowood signed a rather complicated $45 million deal with Robert Mondavi Winery. Arrowood now leases the winery back from Mondavi, but it's really part of the Mondavi portfolio, if still technically separate.

Bannister Wines—A small winery owned by Marty Bannister, who is a partner in the Sonoma County wine anlaysis company called Vinquiry. Bannister specializes in small lots of vineyard-designated Chardonnays, Pinot Noirs, and Zinfandels. The wines vary somewhat with the vintage in terms of sourcing. Look for a pretty Pinot Noir from Floodgate Vineyard in Anderson Valley, as well as a lovely, elegant Chardonnay blended from Rochioli and Allen Vineyards in Russian River Valley, as well as good Chardonnay from Porter-Bass Vineyard in Russian River Valley.

Benziger Family Winery—When the Benziger family sold its wildly successful low-end winery called Glen Ellen for a reported $40 million dollars in 1993, the family decided (astutely) to move upmarket. After all, they retained 85 acres of vines in Sonoma County and a golden list of vineyard connections from which to purchase grapes. Actually, Benziger Family Winery was initiated in 1988, well before the sale, but it received only scant attention, which is understandable if you're running an operation selling four million cases. After the sale it became, like the last remaining child of a once-large family, the object of unremitting attention—all for the good.

It's all a bit complicated, if only because Benziger still issues plenty of wines. What's more, there's a separate Imagery series that specializes in small lots (typically just a few hundred cases) of single-vineyard designated wines from various grapes and locales.

In the end, the wines to look for are those identified as "Sonoma Mountain." They are identified as Grown, Produced, and Bottled and therefore come from Benziger's own vineyards. These are their "Estate" wines: Cabernet Sauvignon, Cabernet Franc, Zinfandel, and Sauvignon Blanc. Look for these and you won't go wrong. They are all unmistakably wines of place, especially the two Cabernets and the Zinfandel: taut, substantial, and beautifully defined.

Besides the estate wines, the next good bet are the various single-vineyard bottlings. Look for a lovely, rich Merlot from Blue Rock Vineyard in Alexander Valley, as well as Carreras Vineyard Zinfandel from Dry Creek Valley.

In its estate and vineyard-specific wines—especially the reds—Benziger is one of California's most rewarding producers.

Buena Vista Winery—When the Racke family of West Germany acquired Buena Vista in 1979 from its previous owner, Young's Market in Los Angeles, it undertook a revitalization program of a scope and ambition outsized even by California standards. The vineyard now totals around 1,000 acres, all in the Carneros AVA. Three labels are seen: Classics for the least expensive wines; Carneros Estate, and Carneros Grand Reserve.

So far, the ambition exceeds the achievement. Buena Vista is dedicated to Carneros-grown wine and in that respect, its wines are undeniable expressions of place. That said, these expressions have not yet proved as convincing as some others. Chardonnay is clean, pure, and varietal, but little else. The style has become better defined in recent vintages, veering toward a lemony austerity that better serves Carneros fruit.

Almost alone among Carneros producers, Buena Vista is pursuing Cabernet Sauvignon. Here again, the reach exceeds the grasp. Too often the Cabernets can be weedy. At their best, however, they are reminiscent of Loire Valley Cabernets Francs in their delicacy and berry notes. But that accomplishment has yet to be consistent. A Special Selection Cabernet Sauvignon is also issued. Here, the consistency is greater, with more depth and stronger fruit. It demonstrates the potential of Carneros, as well as the challenge.

So far, despite considerable resources, Buena Vista has not evolved into anything other than a good, if unexceptional, commercial winery. Its wines do not make a strong case for the Carneros appellation, which is a pity when one thinks of the wines from such Carneros sources as Hyde Vineyard, Hudson Vineyard, Saintsbury, and Truchard, among others. See also *Haywood Winery*.

Davis Bynum Winery—Having expanded greatly since its origins in Berkeley, the Davis Bynum Winery is only slowly emerging as a winery of note. But it is, finally, happening. The vehicle is Bynum's array of vineyard-designated wines, notably an excellent Russian River Valley Chardonnay from the Allen and McIlroy vineyards, as well as a superb Pinot Noir from Rochioli Vineyard called Le Pinot, among other Pinot Noirs.

Look also for a zippy Fumé Blanc (Sauvignon Blanc) from Shone Far Vineyard in Russian River Valley.

Less impressive are the more generic varietal bottlings, which bring the usual changes from Chardonnay to Pinot Noir to Sauvignon Blanc. They're pleasant enough, but far from noteworthy. The red wines are made in a soft, plush style with noticeable oakiness.

Carmenet Vineyard—One of the wineries of publicly owned Chalone, Inc. (along with the namesake Chalone, Acacia, and Edna Valley Vineyards wineries). The name is taken from the old Bordeaux term for Cabernet and it is apt. Located at a high elevation in the Mayacamas Mountains not far from Hanzell Vineyards and Louis Martini's Monte Rosso Vineyard, Carmenet used to issue distinctive Mayacamas Mountain Cabernet. Today, the label has degenerated into a brand name for wines blended from various sources around the state, few of which are anything more than commercial. Best bets are the Moon Mountain Cabernet Sauvignon Reserve and a Zinfandel from Evangelho Vineyard in Contra Costa County.

Chalk Hill Winery—The lead winery for the Chalk Hill AVA, it is surprisingly large (about 75,000 cases annually from 310 acres of vineyard) and still has yet to become anything really distinguished. True, the winery has improved considerably, especially in its Chardonnays. Everything is admirably 100 percent estate-bottled. But the Chalk Hill AVA remains, at least to this taster, relatively mute, creating pleasant wines, but nothing that makes you sit up and say "This could not have come from just anywhere."

Château St. Jean— No winery achieved more acclaim in the late 1970s and early 1980s than Château St. Jean. Founded by several wealthy Central Valley grape growers in 1973, Château St. Jean made its fame and fortune with several named-vineyard, ripe-tasting Chardonnays. (It is pronounced, American-style, like blue jeans, as it was named after the wife of one of the owners.) Foremost among them were Robert Young Vineyard and Belle Terre Vineyard, both in Alexander Valley.

It is ironic that Château St. Jean, located in Sonoma Valley, really is an Alexander Valley winery—at least if one goes by the source of its finest wines. Acclaim also was achieved with a Sauvignon Blanc from the Petite Étoile Vineyard, which created rather intense, forceful Sauvignon Blanc and an intense Cabernet Sauvignon from the Wildwood Vineyard in the Sonoma Mountain AVA.

Château St. Jean was purchased in 1984 by the Japanese liquor giant Suntory Ltd., which, according to *Wine Spectator*, had invested $40 million in Château St. Jean.

During the late 1980s and through part of the 1990s, Château St. Jean actively concentrated on creating ever-better red wines. In truth, it always made fine red wines, but it never made its reputation on them. Indeed, it had all but given up on red wines by 1980, concentrating almost exclusively on whites.

Château St. Jean still issues lovely white wines, none better than its forty-four-acre, estate-owned La Petite Étoile Vineyard near Windsor in the Russian River Valley. It has consistently created one of California's finest Sauvignon Blancs.

And its stalwart single-vineyard Chardonnays, which have been in the portfolio for decades, are still superb: Robert Young Vineyard Chardonnay and Belle Terre Vineyard, both in Alexander Valley. If you're seeking a rich, creamy, luxuriant Chardonnay, these are the two wines that are always at their pinnacle.

That acknowledged, Château St. Jean today is better known for its reds. Its Cinq Cepages bottling, composed as the name suggests from the five classic Bordeaux varieties (it's three-quarters Cabernet Sauvignon) is a lush, rich, opulent Cabernet from Sonoma Valley. It rocketed to fame when the 1996 vintage was annointed Wine of the Year by *Wine Spectator* in 1999. It's fine wine, if a bit oaky.

Overall, this is a winery that has made tremendous strides in creating rewarding red wines, while staying a beautiful course with its standard-bearer white wines.

Château Souverain—Few California wineries have a more checkered past—and have lived to tell about it. In outline, Château Souverain was founded in 1973 by Pillsbury, during the first phase of the Gold Rush years in California winegrowing. (The second occurred in the early 1980s.) It was named Souverain of Alexander Valley, to distinguish it from the original Souverain Winery founded by J. Leland Stewart in Napa Valley. Pillsbury dumped both operations in 1976. The Sonoma winery was bought by a consortium of grape growers. (The Napa facility became Rutherford Hill Winery.)

In 1986, after a spectacular lack of success, the renamed Souverain Cellars was again sold, this time to the Swiss-owned Nestlé corporation. Unlike Pillsbury, Nestlé was more serious. It rebaptized the winery as Château Souverain, modernized it, and severely contracted the production, limiting it exclusively to Sonoma County grapes. In fact, it's mostly Alexander Valley.

Owned today by Beringer Blass, Château Souverain has gone from strength to strength, and is a reliable, consistent source of archetypal Alexander Valley Merlot, Syrah, Sauvignon Blanc, and especially Cabernet Sauvignon. It wisely transferred its Chardonnay emphasis to Russian River Valley grapes, especially for its Winemaker's Reserve bottling. When you've tasted these three, you've tasted Alexander Valley at some of its very best. Look especially for the Winemaker's Reserve bottlings. Not least, Château Souverain provides good value. In short, it has finally become not just a survivor, but a major winner against some stiff competition.

Christopher Creek Winery—A small winery issuing intriguing, if a bit oaky, estate-grown Syrah and Petite Sirah from the Russian River Valley, as well as Zinfandel from Dry Creek Valley where the owners, the Wasserman family, also have property. Worth watching.

Cline Cellars—Some wineries seem designed to drive wine writers nuttier than they already are. One such is Cline Cellars (another is Rosenblum Cellars). No sooner do you taste one interesting—or better than that—wine, than you stumble over another bottling. This is because Cline Cellars specializes in sourcing its wines from all sorts of vineyards and, often, bottling them in separate vineyard-designated lots or under a proprietary name.

I can think of at least six different Zinfandels, for example, a Cline specialty. Then there are such Rhône varieties as Roussanne, Marsanne, and Viognier, in addition to the great red grape called Mourvèdre. This in addition to blends, red and white, called Côtes d'Oakley, named after the town of Oakley in Contra Costa County where some of its grapes come from.

Cline Cellars itself is located in Carneros. The top pick for this taster is the Small Berry Vineyard Mourvèdre, from Contra Costa County, followed closely by Cline's Carneros-grown Syrah. The Zinfandel array boggles. Frankly, they're all good, and I've never been able to choose among them. All Cline Zins are big bruisers, with abundant fruitiness and lip-smacking intensity.

Clos du Bois Winery—The worth of the Alexander Valley, in every sense, has never been made more apparent than with Clos du Bois Winery. After an initial purchase of land in neighboring Dry Creek Valley, former owner Frank Woods began buying hundreds of acres of vineyard land in Alexander Valley, with the total eventually topping 600 acres of vines.

With such vineyard resources, Clos du Bois began issuing a series of ever-better wines, all of them exemplars of Alexander Valley: Sauvignon Blanc, Chardonnay, Cabernet Sauvignon, Gewürztraminer, and above all, Merlot.

What Clos du Bois delivered then, and still does today, is a ripe fruitiness heralded by full-blown oakiness. It is a combination destined for commercial success, which Clos du Bois achieved when it was sold for a reported $40 million to Hiram Walker, Inc., a major distiller. Today it is owned by Allied Domecq.

The wines have continued in the successful formula, spearheaded by two named-vineyard Chardonnays (Calcaire in Alexander Valley and Flintwood in Dry Creek Valley) and two named-vineyard Cabernet Sauvignons (Marlstone, a Bordeaux blend, and the 100 percent Cabernet Briarcrest, both from Alexander Valley).

The best bets are the two Alexander Valley Cabernets, the Bordeaux-blend Marlstone Vineyard and the pure Cabernet Briarcrest Vineyard. Both display the classic Alexander Valley softness and suppleness. The Winemaker's Reserve bottlings are of excellent quality, in a big, lush, rich fashion. The Chardonnays at first flatter the palate and then bore it. Clos du Bois Merlot, practically its hallmark wine, is predictably ripe-tasting and lush, as well as oaky. Overall, Clos du Bois is reliable (and reliably oaky, too), but rarely exciting.

David Coffaro Estate Winery—One of the most original producers in Sonoma County, David Coffaro is something of a scourge among California wine producers who insist that they just *have* to get $50 a bottle just to break even. Coffaro, whose vineyard is located in Dry Creek Valley and who also buys from neighboring growers, typically sells his wines for less than $15 on futures. And since he never makes a bad wine, frankly, you'd be crazy not to sign up to buy Coffaro's futures offerings. I have friends who routinely order six or eight cases of various Coffaro futures offerings.

The odd thing is that you never know quite what the wine will taste like, except that it will be red, full of fruit, and almost always blended among various grape varieties. Coffaro loves to blend, and he tells you in precise percentages just what's in each bottling. So it's no secret or anything.

In recent vintages, Coffaro has relented and issued a number of 100 percent varietals, including Zinfandel, Carignan, and Cabernet Sauvignon. They're all lovely: intense, free of intrusive oakiness, and purely made. To those who say you can't find superb California wines at reasonable prices, I always have just two words to say: David Coffaro.

Copain Wine Cellars—Wells Guthrie, whom I never met, is the former tasting coordinator for *Wine Spectator*. He got the bug bad: He started his own winery. Copain specializes in purchasing fruit, typically from organically grown vineyards, in Sonoma and Mendocino counties. An array of wines are offered: Pinot Noir, Zinfandel, Syrah, and Viognier. The winemaking style emphasizes intense, rich, very ripe fruit with some noticeable oakiness. That noted, they are frequently very rewarding wines that are worth pursuing. Production is small, with each single-vineyard offering typically running to just a couple of hundred cases each, if that.

La Crema—Specializing in Chardonnay and Pinot Noir, La Crema also specializes in a blowsy, oaky style of winemaking that emphasizes a lot of winemaking cosmetics at the expense of the underlying fruit. Not my style of wine.

De Loach Vineyards—Founded in 1975 by former San Francisco fireman Cecil De Loach, this winery started small and remained so for years. The turning point was probably the 1990 vintage, from which Cecil De

Loach launched three named-vineyard Zinfandels, in addition to its regular blended version.

All three Zinfandels—Barbieri Ranch, Papera Ranch, and Pelleti Ranch—were impressive and helped make the De Loach name, as it was only in the 1990s that Russian River Zin began to get any respect. Reminiscent of the wincing knowledge that, during the Depression, producers in Burgundy made sparkling wine out of Chambertin is the fact that some of these grapes previously were used to make white Zinfandel. Such was the Zinfandel Depression of the 1980s.

Since then, the De Loach Zinfandels began to get ever more gargantuan, eventually becoming almost obese with glossy fruit and reaching alcohol levels of nearly 16 percent. The winery also expanded its production girth as well. In the go-go years of the 1990s, De Loach brought its vineyard portfolio to 600 acres of vines and production ballooned to 250,000 cases a year of as many as thirty different wines. In 2003, saddled with $30 million in debts, De Loach filed for Chapter 11 bankruptcy protection.

There seems little doubt that the winery will continue in a slimmer version. And it will bear watching what, if anything, this reduction in size will do for wine quality, which has become rather slack. To watch.

Dehlinger Winery—Dehlinger is a winery that has utterly transformed itself from rather straightforward, almost hard-edged wines in the 1980s to the creator of superb Pinot Noirs and Chardonnays from its Russian River Valley vineyard.

The reason is easily traced. Owner-winemaker Tom Dehlinger is obsessive about plotting and identifying the soils and microclimates—and the resulting attributes in the wines—of the numerous subplots in his fifty-acre vineyard.

Prior to the stylistic change, Dehlinger frequently purchased grapes from various sources in Sonoma County. But today, the wines are exclusively estate-bottled, with much of the holding located near the Green Valley AVA in Forestville, where the winery is located.

Dehlinger's Pinot Noirs and Chardonnays are exemplars of the sort of finesse and nuance achieved in the best Russian River Valley vineyards. Various subplot names are employed for his best bottlings such as Goldridge (referring to a soil type) and Octagon (a site near an octagon-shaped structure).

Not to be forgotten is Dehlinger's stunning Syrah, also grown in the same site. (Russian River Valley has *capacity*.) Like the Pinot Noir, it's lush, intense, and beautifully defined. Indeed, it's one of California's finest Syrahs.

Today, Dehlinger wines are hard to obtain, as most are sold off the winery mailing list. But if you can find one, grab it. Dehlinger wines represent an impeccable standard regardless of the vintage.

Dutton-Goldfield—A new winery launched in 1998 by Steve Dutton and Dan Goldfield. Dutton's is a famous name in Russian River Valley by virtue of the acclaimed creation of Dutton Ranch Chardonnay, which was first brought to popular attention by Kistler winery.

Dutton Ranch has since been cited by many wineries in the area, and you could be forgiven for thinking that it's a single vineyard. It isn't. Instead, Dutton Ranch is actually a brand name. It's an amalgamation of forty-nine different, noncontiguous vineyards spread across the wide expanse of Russian River Valley, mostly west of Sebastopol. Warren Dutton (Steve is his son) owns about 400 acres of vines and leases another 375 acres of vines, most of which is Chardonnay. All are identified as Dutton Ranch. Really, there is no such place. It's just a business name.

All of that said, Dutton-Goldfield is making lovely wines. Indeed, their Dutton Ranch Chardonnay is an exemplar of its type. So, too, is the Dutton Ranch Pinot Noir. Other Chardonnays and Pinot Noirs from other vineyards are also offered, such as Rued Vineyard Chardonnay (Green Valley AVA), Maurice Galante Vineyard Pinot Noir (Green Valley AVA), and an unusual Pinot Noir sourced from Marin County from Devil's Gulch Ranch. A promising winery with a deft winemaking touch.

Dry Creek Vineyard—One of the longtime (1972) wineries of the Dry Creek Valley, the wines of Dry Creek Vineyard are a mixed lot. Most of the winery's fame derives from this winery's signature Fumé Blanc (Sauvignon Blanc). Cabernet Sauvignon and Chardonnay are fairly straightforward, neither being especially distinctive. But the Zinfandels—there's an Old Vines, a Heritage Clone, and a Reserve—are well worth seeking out, as they reflect the goodness and depth of Dry Creek Valley AVA Zins.

Owner David Stare is one of the handful of California producers (Chappellet and Casa Nuestra wineries in Napa Valley are two others) committed to Chenin Blanc. Happily, the Dry Creek Vineyard version (the grapes come mostly from the Sacramento area) is one of California's better renditions:

deliberately austere and long-lived. Still, nobody in France's Loire Valley has much to worry about. That said, the Dry Creek version is worth seeking out, especially if you spot one with some bottle age on it.

Estancia Vineyards—Owned by Franciscan Vineyards in Napa Valley, the Estancia label was created by former Franciscan co-owner Agustin Huneeus, Sr. as the vehicle for Franciscan's 240 acres in Alexander Valley. (Franciscan/Estancia was sold to Constellation.)

Huneeus believed that California wine suffers from an excess of hype, nowhere better expressed than in its wine pricing. At the time, as Huneeus freely admitted, Franciscan couldn't sell all of its wine from both its Napa Valley and Alexander Valley properties. So creating a lower-priced wine was a necessity as well as a pleasure. From this marriage of business and belief came Estancia.

From the first, Estancia was recognized by consumers and critics as a deal. Originally, the Alexander Valley property grew Chardonnay, Sauvignon Blanc, and Cabernet Sauvignon. All three were released under the Estancia label, at a relatively low price. All were well made and occasionally exceptionally fine, especially for the money.

But Alexander Valley vineyards are worth too much to be confined to the low end. So, since 1988, the Chardonnay came from Franciscan's vineyard in Monterey County called Pinnacles. Then came Pinot Noir from the Monterey property, as well as a Merlot under the Estancia label blended from several sources. All of these wines are ho-hum.

The only Estancia wine worth investigating is, not so ironically, the Estancia wine that sports an Alexander Valley designation: Estancia Meritage, a Bordeaux-type blend. It's a genuinely good, if oaky, Cabernet blend with Alexander Valley's characteristic softness and lush quality. Everything else from Estancia is straightforwardly commercial.

Fanucchi Vineyard—Lovely old-vine Russian River Valley Zinfandel from this small producer (pronounced fah-NEW-key). Also, a rarely seen old California white wine called Trousseau Gris, which used to be called Gray Riesling. It's not at all related to Riesling, but is a white mutation of a red grape called Trousseau, grown in the Jura region of eastern France. Another name for this variety is Chauche Gris. Fanucchi's version is appetizing.

Ferrari-Carano Vineyards and Winery—Tasting Ferrari-Carano wines brings to mind the e.e. cummings observation that "A world of made is not a world of born." Nothing about Ferrari-Carano's Fumé Blanc or Chardonnay evokes much of a sense of place. Quite the opposite. Both are polished to a high gleam. The Chardonnay is buffed with new oak and plenty of it. There is much hoopla to Ferrari-Carano, the reasons for which escape me. Cabernet Sauvignon and Merlot, both served up as blended wines, are similarly lustrous and equally anonymous.

Field Stone Winery and Vineyard—Field Stone has not distinguished itself despite its relatively long-term (1977) presence in the Alexander Valley. Its signature wine is Cabernet Sauvignon, offered in several versions: a straight Alexander Valley designation, Turkey Hill Vineyard, and a Staten Family Reserve. The Petite Sirah from very old vines better displays the Alexander Valley origins, which is impressive given the notorious toughness of this grape variety. Field Stone wines have always been adequate but rarely more than that. The State Family Reserve Cabernet is the best bet here, followed by the Petite Sirah. Field Stone's Chardonnay makes little impression.

Fisher Vineyards—Although located on the Mayacamas Mountains in Sonoma Valley, where twenty-five acres of vines are planted, Fisher also owns vineyards in Napa Valley, not far from Calistoga (Lamb Vineyard).

The wine to look for from Fisher Vineyards (the family name—and the money—derive from "Body by Fisher" automobile manufacturing) is the Cabernet Sauvignon "Coach Insignia." It comes exclusively from Fisher's Sonoma vineyard and its origin shows. It is dense, tannic, and plumped with flavor (as well as oak). The Coach Insignia Chardonnay is less good, although the Whitney's Vineyard Chardonnay has some genuine character, if a bit too much oak.

Look also for the Cabernet Sauvignon from Lamb Vineyard (not to be confused with Herb Lamb Vineyard) in Napa Valley, which is a winner.

Flowers Vineyard and Winery—One of California's heroic wineries. Walt and Joan Flowers, who own a major nursery in Pennsylvania, became enthralled with California winegrowing. Originally, they started to look for property in Napa Valley (briefly considering the former Eisele Vineyard subsequently purchased by the Araujos). But the Flowers decided that, really, their heart was in Pinot Noir, not Cabernet. And besides, they say they wanted to pioneer something rather than assume custodianship of an already known quantity such as Eisele Vineyard.

Pioneer they did. The Flowerses created the first winery (although not the first vineyard) sited in the Camp Meeting Ridge zone of what I call "Sonoma Coast West." Indeed, they called their vineyard Camp Meeting Ridge.

To see Flowers Vineyard and Winery is to realize just how exceptional an area Sonoma Coast West really is. You're just a mile or two from the Pacific Ocean as the seagull flies. Yet the elevation puts you way above the fog line. You're surrounded by forests. Almost like monasteries in the Middle Ages, you can see only a few other outposts of civilization in the form of vineyards. From Flowers you can see Hirsch Vineyard (the first vineyard planting, I believe, in the zone), as well as Marcassin's vineyard. Jason Pahlmeyer of the eponymous winery in Napa Valley is installing a vineyard nearby. The sense of isolation is genuine and strongly felt.

But the wines justify everything. Walt and Joan Flowers have been methodical in attempting to identify just what clones of Pinot Noir and Chardonnay work best in their site, as well as which vine density works best. (They've discovered that the classic meter-by-meter density is not advisable.)

Pinot Noir from their Camp Meeting Ridge vineyard is the signature wine. Simply put, it's magnificent—one of America's greatest Pinot Noirs. Tannin levels in these wines can be unusually high for Pinot Noir, thanks to the tiny berry size where the ratio of tannin- (and flavor-) laden skins is disproportionately high compared to the quantity of juice in the berry. They've worked in the winery to ameliorate this. The resulting Pinot Noir is filled with layers of flavor and an unmistakable soil dimension.

For this taster, the Chardonnay from Camp Meeting Ridge is less persuasive. It's very fine, but not as thrilling as the Pinot Noir.

A new vineyard has recently been installed that will increase the production of estate-grown wines and provide further opportunities for investigating subplots. Flowers also purchases fruit from other vineyards, such as Chardonnay from Porter-Bass Vineyard and Pinot Noir from Van der Kamp Vineyard at a high elevation on Sonoma Mountain, among others.

But really, it's the Camp Meeting Ridge Vineyard that makes Flowers such a stellar winery. And it's the wine you should vigorously seek out.

Foppiano Vineyards—An old-line Russian River Valley producer, founded in 1896 by Giovanni Foppiano, an immigrant from Genoa, Italy.

Foppiano has always offered good, solid wines at fair prices and continues to do just that today. The best Foppiano wine, by pretty much universal acclamation, is their Petite Sirah, a classic of its type, with rich, frank goodness. The Foppiano wine lineup is now quite extensive, reaching down to Paso Robles for an excellent Syrah, as well as ringing the usual Chardonnay/Merlot/Cabernet changes required of every large winery. Reds seem to be better than whites at Foppiano. They just have a better feeling for it, I guess. Go for the Petite Sirah, then investigate the appealing Cabernet Sauvignon.

Frei Brothers Winery—One of several "sub-labels" employed by Gallo of Sonoma. The wines are all made at the Gallo of Sonoma facility, using grapes from their many Sonoma County vineyards. The wine that really stands out under the Frei Brothers label is the Merlot, which is superb for the money, exhibiting the characteristic (when good) scent and taste of dark chocolate. See also *Rancho Zabaco*.

J. Fritz Cellars—Chardonnay is the J. Fritz specialty, with three bottlings, all from the Dutton Ranch (or rather, ranches): a regular Dutton Ranch bottling, Ruxton Vineyard-Dutton Ranch, and Shop Block-Dutton Ranch. All three are admirable Russian River Valley Chardonnays, with the two named-vineyard designations being noticeably more dimensional and flavorful.

Red wines are increasingly fine at J. Fritz. There's a strong, good Cabernet from the Rockpile AVA, as well as several Zinfandels from the Dry Creek AVA. Look especially for the Old Vine bottling.

Overall, J. Fritz is a winery that in the past decade has evolved into a performer with real strength, emphasizing single vineyards and making wine with admirable clarity of flavor.

Gallo of Sonoma—It will probably take another generation of wine drinkers before the perceived bulk-wine stigma of the Gallo name is finally erased, but there's no doubt the the reason this will occur is Gallo of Sonoma. Simply put, no winery in California today offers better quality for the money. The reason—as always—is vineyards. If you can control your grapes you can ensure your quality.

When Gallo finally (and belatedly) decided that the future lay in fine wines rather than bulk bottles—although they still make plenty of that, too—they turned their sights to Sonoma County. Not only did it have more potential vineyard land than Napa Valley, but its farming orientation is much more to the Gallo liking. Not least, the Gallos have long had ties to the area, buying a considerable tonnage of grapes from Sonoma over the years. In 1978 they bought the former Frei Brothers winery, from which they had long bought grapes and wine.

Starting in the 1980s, they began buying large tracts of land suitable for vineyards or that were already planted: 800 acres in Dry Creek Valley where the winery is located, 400 acres in Russian River Valley, 200 acres in Alexander Valley. Their total ownership in Sonoma County will eventually reach 2,000 acres, if it hasn't already.

Equally important, the Gallo of Sonoma operation is a separate winemaking facility from the mother ship in Modesto. And although they still answer to the check-writers in Modesto, winemaker Gina Gallo and vineyard director Matt Gallo really do run the show in Sonoma. The Gallos may have employed Gina as their "poster girl" in their ubiquitous advertising, but the reality is that Gina really is the winemaker in fact as well as name. Of course, as in any large winery, there are plenty of other winemakers, but she's the real thing.

Three levels of wines are offered: wines designated simply as Sonoma County; five different single-vineyard bottlings; and two "Estate" bottlings. The basic Gallo of Sonoma wines, made from purchased grapes and wines as well as estate-grown are, as you might expect, straightforward. Rarely do they leap out as exceptional, although the Merlot and, surprisingly, the Pinot Noir are exceptional values.

Really, the best wines are the single-vineyard bottlings. Look especially for the Frei Ranch Cabernet and Zinfandel, as well as the Stefani Vineyard Cabernet Sauvignon. Among the whites, there's excellent Chardonnay from Laguna Ranch (just across the road from Dehlinger Vineyards), as well as a very promising, quite austere Chardonnay from Two Rock Vineyard in Petaluma, an extremely—almost radically—cool site. It's still a work in progress, as the fruit is unlike anything else in the Gallo portfolio.

The Estate wines, intended to be the ultimate wines, have not proved so, at least for this taster. Both the Cabernet and the Chardonnay are fine wines, especially the Cabernet. But they seem more "made" than "born." Go for the single-vineyards and you won't go wrong. See also *Frei Brothers Winery and Rancho Zabaco.*

Geyser Peak Winery—If Napa Valley's Franciscan Vineyards isn't the comeback champion of California, then Geyser Peak surely is. A century-old Sonoma County winery, until the 1990s Geyser Peak made wines that could charitably be described as banal. Then the Australians arrived in the form of Penfolds Winery. They brought with them winemaker Darryl Groom.

The ownership saga is a complicated one, the gist of it being that in 1989 Penfolds bought half the winery from owner Henry Trione, who had only purchased it seven years earlier, in 1982. But only two years later Penfolds had financial difficulties and sold its half-share back to Trione. Then, in 1992, Trione—who was just about to sell the winery again—accepted an offer to sell 25 percent of the winery to former Sebastiani Vineyards president Dennis Pasquini. Wisely, Pasquini kept Groom, even giving him a 5 percent equity share. Good investment.

Trione and Pasquini added new capital to the winery, building a new facility for Groom. In the meantime, Pasquini—who knows how to market a bottle of wine, or rather, millions of bottles—set about reforming Geyser Peak's woeful image. Groom, for his part, kept improving what was in those bottles.

Today, Geyser Peak is a huge success. None of its wines are ever likely to be counted among California's very finest. But nearly all of them are easily counted among some of California's best values. Groom has a particular knack with Sauvignon Blanc. Numerous tasters, myself included, have been surprised by the flavor purity of Groom's citrusy, non-oaked Sauvignon Blanc.

Cabernet Sauvignon has also proved unusually fine, notably the Reserve bottling, which really is an exceptional expression of Alexander Valley-grown Cabernet Sauvignon.

Glen Ellen Winery—Glen Ellen is the 1980s version of a successful bulk winery. The Benziger family created the brand and then sold it to Hueblein in 1993 for $40 million. Heublein, in turn, sold it to the current owner, The Wine Group, which bought it from Diageo. Glen Ellen managed to strike a nerve in the marketplace by offering attractively low-priced wines through canny buying and blending. Almost everything offered was labeled by grape variety. Shortly after the winery's founding in 1980, Glen Ellen rocketed to success, growing exponentially larger every year. They now sell several million cases annually. The wines are, as you might expect, commercial and unremarkable.

Gundlach-Bundschu Winery—Dating to 1858, this is one of California's oldest wineries, and Gundlach-Bundschu remains one of the most deter-mined wineries in the state. Located in Sonoma Valley, the centerpiece of Gundlach-Bundschu's 375 acres of vineyard is their 125-acre Rhinefarm Vineyard, which was founded by Jacob Gundlach in 1858 right next to Haraszthy's Buena Vista Winery. The Rhinefarm vineyard still remains in the same spot, which is just across the line from the Carneros AVA. Technically, it is Sonoma Valley AVA.

In the 1980s Gundlach-Bundschu began its slow, steady crawl toward top quality. Where once its wines were rustic and coarse, by the late 1980s they showed considerable polish and subtlety. Almost all of the wines now are identified as "Grown, Produced and Bottled." Wines designated Rhinefarm Vineyard are the top picks.

Really, it's the red wines that truly excel, all Rhinefarm-designated. Look for a supple and very pure-tasting Merlot, as well as a pleasant but far-from-exceptional Cabernet Sauvignon. White wines are pleasant, but little more than that. Gundlach-Bundschu is a winery that, by virtue of its vineyard holdings, seems tantalizingly capable of grabbing the proverbial brass ring, but has yet to do so.

Hanna Winery—One of Alexander Valley's latest stars, Hanna Winery went from a mere twelve acres of vines when it began in 1985 to 250 acres of vines today. Started by Dr. Elias Hanna, a San Francisco cardiac surgeon, the winery remains family-owned, with daughter Christine Hanna as general manager.

Hanna has long had a deft touch with white wines and it still does, issu-ing a tart, citrusy Russian River Valley-grown Sauvignon Blanc. Chardonnays are attractive but not compelling. Much better is the Alexander Valley-grown Cabernet Sauvignon which—typical of the area—is soft, lush, and polished.

Considering the growth of this winery, it has retained an impressive sense of purpose and control over its winemaking. Indeed, Hanna wines are better today than ever before, no doubt because of its ownership of its own vineyards.

Hanzell Vineyards—Founded in 1956 by James Zellerbach, the winery and its vineyards are located high in the Mayacamas Mountains looking down on Sonoma Valley. Aesthetically, Hanzell is one of the most elegant wineries in the state. After Zellerbach died in 1963, his wife, Hana (hence Hanzell), sold the winery and never visited again.

It subsequently was sold to Douglas and Mary Day who, in 1975, sold it to a wealthy Australian, Barbara de Brye. Upon her death in 1991, it technically was passed into the hands of the trustees of the de Brye estate, as her son Alexander, the sole heir, was then sixteen years old. Today, in his late twenties, he is actively involved in running the estate, where he lives part of the year, dividing his time between California and the family home in London.

The Hanzell wines—Chardonnay and Pinot Noir—were made for years by winemaker and general manager Bob Sessions, who retired in 2001. Today, his son, Ben, is the winemaker. Sessions struggled with the Pinot Noir, which was erratic for years. Starting with the 1985 vintage and improving steadily after that, the Hanzell Pinot Noirs have emphasized a greater berry quality, while still retaining an extraordinary earthiness, an authentic and admirable *goût de terroir*.

But this flavor of site is at its most pronounced in the Chardonnay, which is dense and profound when allowed to mature for ten years in the bottle. Few California Chardonnays deserve longer aging than Hanzell's. (Other nominees include Mayacamas Chardonnay, Ridge Monte Bello Chardonnay, and Mount Eden Estate Chardonnay.)

It is difficult to over-praise Hanzell, as it has stood the test of making great wines continuously for decades. Few California wineries have so lustrous a track record and fewer still deserve to be called a true *grand cru*. But that's what Hanzell really is, California's first authentic and proven *grand cru*.

Haywood Winery—Located in Sonoma Valley, Haywood has issued a series of lovely Zinfandels and Cabernet Sauvignons from its ninety-acre Los Chamizal Vineyard just outside of the town of Sonoma. Today, the winery is owned by Allied Domecq. (It also owns or co-owns Atlas Peak, Brancott, Buena Vista, Callaway, Clos du Bois, Mumm Napa Valley, and William Hill wineries.) The Los Chamizal Vineyard, however, was retained by founder Peter Haywood, who sells the grapes to his former winery.

Although Haywood now issues the usual array of standard, lookalike California Chardonnay, Merlot, and Cabernet Sauvignon, it's the Los Chamizal bottlings that you want. Although always too oaky—and continuing that unfortunate tradition—the Los Chamizal Cabernet and Zinfandel are truly exceptional in their dusty, blackberry, black cherry fruit. There's a real "smack of the earth" in Los Chamizal that even all that oakiness can't obscure.

Paul Hobbs Winery—The story of Paul Hobbs might be characterized as "inside every commercial winemaker oppressed by a corporate owner, there's an artisan producer crying to get out." Hobbs got out. Formerly a vice president/winemaker for Simi Winery—whose wines were and continue to be banal—he started Paul Hobbs Winery in 1991. The idea then and now was to concentrate on vineyard-designated wines.

Originally, all the grapes were purchased, but in 1998 Hobbs bought nineteen acres in Russian River Valley and planted most of it to Pinot Noir. He intends to locate his own winery on that site in the future. (Currently the wines are made in a facility shared by other wine producers, a common California method of reducing overhead.)

Hobbs' wines inevitably vary with each vineyard, but there's no mistaking the overall high quality. There's real rigor here. Best known for issuing lush, intense, full-throated Chardonnays—look especially for the Walker Station Vineyard in Russian River Valley and the Richard Dinner Vineyard in Sonoma Mountain—it would be a mistake to overlook Hobbs' Cabernet Sauvignon from Hyde Vineyard in Carneros. All of these wines, and others, are polished to a lapidary gleam without losing their individual distinctiveness. Hobbs has demonstrated that he is one of today's preeminent winemakers in California—no small achievement considering the competition.

By the way, Hobbs drolly explains his winery name by noting, "I come from a family of thirteen: two parents, two girls, and nine boys. I'm telling you in case you wonder why I put my first as well as my last name on my labels."

Imagery Estate—See *Benziger Family Winery*.

Iron Horse Vineyards—Iron Horse was originally a pure expression of the cool Green Valley AVA; it has since expanded into Alexander Valley with its T-bar-T Ranch. Today the combined estates total 244 acres of producing vines, which constitute the Iron Horse Estates, the Thomas Road Vineyard, and T-bar-T Ranch. Ninety-nine acres of Chardonnay and eighty-five acres of Pinot Noir are in the Green Valley AVA, while sixty acres of Cabernet Sauvignon, Cabernet Franc, Sangiovese, Merlot, Viognier, and Sauvignon Blanc are in Sonoma's Alexander Valley.

Add to all that the fact that both still and sparkling wines are produced and you've got quite a mixture of wines. For this taster the best Iron Horse wines are, surprisingly, its sparkling wines. It's surprising simply because so few wineries perform better with sparkling wine than with more easily made still wines. Yet the Pinot Noir and Chardonnay from their Green Valley vineyard clearly lend themselves to bubbly. Indeed, the still Pinot Noir is decidedly lesser, although the Chardonnay is good in its lean fashion.

The Alexander Valley bottlings are good but unexceptional. The best bet is the Cabernet Sauvignon followed by the Merlot. These are designated T-bar-T on the label. Really, it's the sparkling wine you should seek out, none better than the LD (late-disgorged) bottling, which is easily one of California's best. Also the Brut Rosé is excellent, with unmistakable Pinot Noir berryishness. The sparkling wines, along with the Chardonnay are lean, crisp, and very true to their Green Valley AVA origin.

J Vineyards and Winery—A spinoff from Jordan Vineyard and Winery, this producer was originally solely dedicated to creating sparkling wine. It still does. And its packaging, with a bold yellow, swoopy "J" painted on the bottle is both unmistakable as well as masterfully designed. It remains one of the world's best wine bottle designs, to this viewer's eye, anyway. Also the bubbly inside ain't half bad, although it's not in the same league as Roederer Estate or Iron Horse.

In recent years, J Vineyards and Winery has expanded its production to still wines, including four different Pinot Noirs. The best of them is the Nicole's Vineyard bottling, from an estate-owned property in Russian River Valley. Look also for a promising Russian River Valley Pinot Gris.

Although sparkling wine continues to be the flagship with this winery, there's some clear promise in its still wine program. This is a winery that will likely come fully into its own in the next few years.

Jordan Vineyard and Winery—No Sonoma County winery arrived with more hoopla than Jordan Vineyard and Winery when it set up its château-like shop in the Alexander Valley, just north of Healdsburg. Tom Jordan, originally from Denver, made his bundle in oil and gas exploration. After briefly considering purchasing a property in Bordeaux, he decided to create a Bordeaux-type château in the Alexander Valley instead. Jordan, more than any other winery, put Alexander Valley on the map.

From the first wine, the 1976 vintage, Jordan Cabernet epitomized Alexander Valley. At the time, some tasters concluded that Jordan Cabernet's suppleness was merely a matter of winemaking. The winery did nothing to disabuse such a notion. In fact, it is much more a matter of place. That said, the winery certainly seeks to emphasize this intrinsic feature of place, and it does this admirably well.

Jordan Cabernet has come in for criticism for not aging well. This is a misapprehension. To the extent that it does not transform dramatically, the criticism probably is justified. But it does endure, thanks to good balance. In this it shares a common fate with many other Alexander Valley Cabernets: They are good out of the starting gate and only occasionally transform into something other than what they were at the outset. So what? The challenge in fine wine is to be distinctive, not just long-lived. Jordan Cabernet is distinctively Alexander Valley. That said, it is not necessarily much superior, if at all, to a dozen other renditions.

Jordan Chardonnay used to be a rather boring affair, but since the transition to Russian River Valley fruit (the early Chardonnays came from Alexander Valley), the newer Jordan Chardonnays have some zip and purity. That said, Jordan is best for its Cabernet, which remains as rewarding as ever.

Kenwood Vineyards—Kenwood is one of the success stories of Sonoma Valley. Started in 1970, its wines have evolved over the years from fairly coarse, rustic renditions to some of Sonoma's most polished and profound wines, especially the reds in their Jack London Vineyard bottlings and their Artist Series Cabernet.

Although the labels read Sonoma Valley, Kenwood's finest wines actually come from a single vineyard located in the Sonoma Mountain AVA: the 110-acre Jack London Ranch. From this vineyard, Kenwood (which has exclusivity for the vineyard, but does not own it) makes a superb Cabernet and an equally fine Zinfandel. The label does not read "Sonoma Mountain" because the winery feels a loyalty to the Sonoma Valley designation, to which the wine also is entitled. The Jack London Ranch Pinot Noir remains the least successful of the three wines from this site.

Kenwood's other notable wine—indeed, its most sought-after bottling—is its Artist Series Cabernet, so named because of the changing artwork on the label. Blended from various sources in Sonoma Valley, the Artist Series comes mostly, if not entirely (it depends on the vintage) from the Lindholm and Montecillo vineyard on the Sonoma side of the 1,400-foot level of the Mayacamas Mountains.

As the winery has grown (it now sells about 300,000 cases and is now owned by Gary Heck, who also owns Korbel Champagne Cellars), Kenwood inevitably issues a fair amount of commercial-grade wine of the usual suspects such as Chardonnay and Merlot. They are acceptable, but not soul-stirring. Look instead to the Jack London Vineyard wines, as well as the famed Artist Series, and you will be well served by Kenwood.

Kistler Vineyards—Few small wineries are as dedicated to vineyard-designated wines as Kistler, located high in the Mayacamas Mountains above Sonoma Valley. Founded in 1978, Kistler has in the past decade emerged as one of California's most impressive sources for Chardonnay and, more recently, Pinot Noir.

Choosing among the Kistler Chardonnay offerings is difficult on several levels. First, finding them is a challenge, as the word long ago got out, and the wines are snapped up and squirreled away by the winery's ardent fans, many of whom await word of the latest offerings via a winery mailing list.

Even the generic "Sonoma County" Chardonnay surpasses most offerings. It actually is a blend made from batches from all of the vineyards used in Kistler's vineyard-designated Chardonnays.

Probably Kistler's most famous Chardonnay is its Dutton Ranch, which put that brand name (it's not all one vineyard, but a brand name for forty-five separate, noncontiguous sites in Russian River Valley) in lights. Everyone's Dutton Ranch Chardonnay is different, and you can bet that no one's is better than Kistler's in its taut yet honeyed scent and taste.

Carneros Chardonnays arrive through separate bottlings of Hyde Vineyard and Hudson Vineyard. Both are about as good as Carneros Chardonnay gets, conveying both the leanness that is the hallmark of Carneros allied to the richness that Kistler always manages to tease out.

McCrea Vineyard is richer and more full-bodied than any of these. You can feel the great sunshine in the wine, thanks to its Sonoma Mountain AVA location. Not least is Kistler Estate Vineyard, high in the Mayacamas Mountains. It, too, bears a resemblance to another Mayacamas Mountain Chardonnay, namely that from Hanzell. Here again, the winemaking is different, but the underlying structure and delivery of the fruit shares a commonality. It is perhaps the richest and most concentrated of the Kistler Chardonnays.

Yet both Chardonnays jostle for attention and praise: the rich, succulent

Kistler Estate Vineyard, Durrell Vineyard, and Vine Hill Vineyard, to name but three. There's also a new (to me) bottling called Les Noisetiers.

Worth noting are Kistler's Pinot Noirs, which have become increasingly more focused and less intrusively oaky in recent years. Kistler is privileged to get fruit from Flowers' Camp Meeting Ridge Vineyard and sometimes creates a better Pinot Noir from it than Flowers itself.

In recent years, Kistler has turned in a virtually flawless performance. This is acknowledged, indeed embraced, by its legion of fans. Finding a Kistler wine is almost as challenging as the wines themselves, but Kistler deserves the effort. At the moment, it is probably the source of more Chardonnays of the highest caliber than any other California winery.

Kunde Estate Winery and Vineyards—The Kunde family (rhymes with Dundee) has grown grapes in Sonoma Valley since 1879, making them one of the oldest—if not *the* oldest—grape-growing family in Sonoma County. Yet until the 1990 vintage, the family never issued wines under its own name, preferring to sell its grapes to others.

Since then Kunde has demonstrated that there's nothing like owning your own grapes. Sauvignon Blanc is the premier wine here, always a rich yet tart affair. Look especially for the Magnolia Lane bottling, an effective blend of roughly 85 percent Sauvignon Blanc with the balance composed of Sémillon and a splash of Viognier.

Chardonnay is the other Kunde trademark and although to this taster it is not quite as satisfying as the Sauvignon Blanc, it's a wine by which you can't go wrong with either. It's pure, clean, and plumped with a satisfying—if not especially layered—fruit. The single-vineyard Wildwood bottling is demonstrably richer, if a bit heavy.

A Sonoma Valley-grown Cabernet Sauvignon from the six-acre Drummond Vineyard is a taut, somewhat oaky wine of good underlying quality. Numerous other wines are offered, including Sangiovese, Barbera, Cabernet Franc, Gewürztraminer, and even a Zinfandel Port. But really, Kunde is at its best with Sauvignon Blanc and Chardonnay.

Laurel Glen Vineyard—This is the signature winery, and the driving force, of the Sonoma Mountain AVA. It is Laurel Glen's Cabernets, the only wine it makes, that drive home the impression that Sonoma Mountain delivers a distinguishing difference that sets it apart. Laurel Glen Cabernet Sauvignon is almost invariably massive, tight, and dense. Yet equally invariably the wines retain a near-gyroscopic balance. They emerge brimming with grace. A second label, called Terra Rosa, employs purchased grapes. It usually is very fine, but the Laurel Glen bottling stands by itself.

Lambert Bridge Winery—Based in Dry Creek Valley, Lambert Bridge issues a large array of wines from what is, by California standards, a relatively small winery of some 25,000 cases. The winery specializes in creating blends, although a few single-vineyard bottlings are offered as well. This works well enough, in that it does ensure an attractive consistency, but there are few high points. Zinfandel is a certain winner here. Look also for the few single-vineyard bottlings offered, as Lambert Bridge does know where the grape goodies are buried, especially in its native Dry Creek Valley AVA.

Landmark Vineyards—Pinot Noir and, especially, Chardonnay are the tickets here. Landmark became, well, something of a landmark thanks to the acumen and rigor of winemaking consultant Helen Turley who was brought in back in 1993, before her name (and her fees) became golden. She was just the sort of medicine the doctor ordered. Under her tutelage, Landmark focused on Chardonnay and Pinot Noir and upgraded its standards.

Today, Landmark creates very fine, if slightly uneven, wines. It is hampered by not owning any of its own vineyards, always a detriment to an ambitious producer—especially with Pinot Noir. Still, Van der Kamp Vineyard Pinot Noir from Sonoma Mountain called Grand Detour is a rewarding wine, as is the Lorenzo Vineyard Chardonnay from Russian River Valley, which is Landmark's best Chardonnay.

Other Chardonnays, with proprietary names such as Damaris and Overlook are blended from grapes from Monterey and Sonoma counties. They are pleasing enough, but lack real character.

Ledson Winery and Vineyards—With its first vintage in 1993, Ledson Winery and Vineyards has tried to position itself as an ultra-premium winery. It built a gaudy, McMansion type "castle" in Sonoma Valley, put its wines in ultra-heavy bottles, and did all the usual posturing expected of pretenders to the ultra-premium throne. However, the wines aren't good enough. Oh, they are adequate to be sure, with a pleasant Merlot and conventional Chardonnay. But there's a lot more packaging and posturing at Ledson than there is delivery of the real wine goods.

Limerick Lane Cellars—One of Russian River Valley's supreme producers. If you want to taste Zinfandel at its most Pinot Noir-like pristine—the sort of Zin only the Russian River Valley can create—then it's Limerick Lane you should seek out. The wine comes entirely from the century-old Collins Vineyard, owned by the winery. Also, there's a rich, deep, supple, memorable Syrah from Collins Vineyard as well. This is a winery that has no need to put on airs (and doesn't). It quietly creates unusually consistent Zinfandel and Syrah and has a loyal following to applaud its effort. Count me among them.

Lytton Springs Winery—See *Ridge Lytton Springs*.

MacRostie Winery and Vineyards—It's all about Carneros at MacRostie, especially Chardonnay. The wines are classic Carneros in their lean structure and hints of melons and limes. A new vineyard, called Wildcat Mountain in the interior hills of the Carneros appellation, planted to Pinot Noir, Chardonnay, and Syrah, was installed in 1997. These vines may well vault MacRostie to another level of quality different from the many Carneros Chardonnay competitors. To watch.

Marcassin—Created by winemaking/winery consulting couple Helen Turley and John Wetlaufer as their own personal vineyard, Marcassin is testimony to the significance of "Sonoma Coast West." Located near Flowers Camp Meeting Ridge, Hirsch Vineyard, and Martinelli Winery's Blue Slide Vineyard, Marcassin makes two wines: Pinot Noir and Chardonnay.

It's the Pinot Noir that truly tells the tale of greatness in this area; the Chardonnay (as at Flowers) is unpersuasive to this taster. Chardonnay, as always, shows the hand of the maker with almost innocent transparency. If you like all that toasty, lees-stirring kind of Chardonnay winemaking, then you'll love the Marcassin Chardonnay. The Turley/Wetlaufer winemaking style is fully in evidence. You *know* a winemaker has been there when you taste their wines. It's full-throttle winemaking where you can easily see the hand of the maker.

Happily, the quality of the Pinot Noir grapes at Marcassin is more than characterful enough to take it on, delivering not just Pinot Noir's usual berry flavors but a dimension that can only be attributed to soil combined with the oddly cool yet intensely sunny microclimate of Sonoma Coast West. The Pinot Noir is flat-out profound.

The problem with Marcassin Pinot Noir is simply finding it. The estate vinyard is just six and one-half densely planted acres. But if you can, don't miss it. There are other named-vineyard bottlings under the Marcassin label from nearby vineyards, such as Blue Slide Ridge, as well as Three Sisters and Bondi Home Ranch.

Mark West Estate Winery—A winery that has decided to specialize in Pinot Noir and Chardonnay after wandering all over the grape variety map. So far, however, the results are ho-hum, with blended "Sonoma County" bottlings of both, along with Pinot Noir sourced from Edna Valley.

Martinelli Winery—Martinelli's wines are the sort you either love or leave. Frankly, they're not for me. It's a lush, swoopy, high-intensity winemaking approach (the consultant is Helen Turley of Marcassin) that emphasizes a lot of oak and plush fruit.

That said, there's no denying that Martinelli's wines *are* interesting, style aside. The "Sonoma Coast West" Blue Slide Ridge Vineyard is compelling Pinot Noir. And the Jackass Hill Zinfandel (first made famous by Burt Williams of Williams Selyem) is sensational. Also noteworthy is the increasingly rarely seen Gewürtzraminer, which used to be a Russian River Valley specialty. Martinelli continues the tradition and does a lovely job of it.

Chardonnays are ripe, quite oaky, and not for those who prefer a more austere approach to this grape. Still, the underlying quality is present.

If all this sounds a bit conflicted, it is. The fruit at Martinelli is admirable. The winemaking style is, given the delicacy of Russian River Valley-grown fruit, a bit too intrusive for this taster's palate.

Matanzas Creek Winery—Sold to Jess Jackson of Kendall-Jackson Estates in 2000, Matanzas Creek is undergoing the latest in a series of transformations over the years. Perhaps best know for its Chardonnays, there are now some inviting Cabernets and Merlots to consider. A new AVA, spearheaded by the winery, called Bennett Valley (through which Matazas Creek runs) was approved in December 2003. Time will tell about the long-term influence (and vineyard opportunities) provided by the new ownership. To watch.

Mayo Family Winery—Based in Russian River Valley, Mayo Family Winery first came to some measure of fame with its opulent, compelling Russian River Valley Zinfandel from Ricci Vineyard. Since then, it has branched out to numerous vineyard-designated bottlings, many of them worthy of equal attention. For example, there's a Cabernet Sauvignon from Los

Chamizal Vineyard (see Haywood) that demonstrates just how distinctive a site Los Chamizal is.

Not everything is sourced from Sonoma County. There's a new Sauvignon Blanc from Emma's Vineyard in Napa Valley, along with an intriguing and powerful Syrah from Page-Nord vineyard near the Stags Leap District.

All of these new offerings make Mayo Family Vineyard difficult to assess at present. If they can handle these various lots with deftness, then this will be a winery to seek out for more than just an outstanding Zinfandel. To watch closely.

McIlroy Cellars—A small family winery with its own vineyard (Aquarias Ranch) in Russian River Valley. Pristine, detailed winemaking allows these wines to shine with clarity. Look especially for one of the better Chardonnays grown anywhere in Russian River Valley, as well as a nicely detailed Pinot Noir. Worth special attention is a terrific Zinfandel from Porter-Bass Vineyard near Guerneville from eighty-year-old vines grown in one of the coolest sites of any Zinfandel vineyard I can think of. McIlroy is one of Sonoma County's best-kept secrets.

Merry Edwards—A flurry of fat, lush, rather soft Pinot Noirs has emerged from Merry Edwards in recent vintages, several of them vineyard-designated. There's clearly a push toward higher quality here, and it's certainly in the right direction. The "Méthode Ancienne" Klopp Vineyard Pinot Noir is certainly tasty, as is the Olivet Lane Vineyard Pinot Noir. But one can't help wishing for a little more restraint and detail in the winemaking style. Still, this is a winery heading somewhere good.

Murphy-Goode Estate Winery—One of the larger estates in Alexander Valley, the 300-acre Murphy-Goode vineyard has long issued reliable wines. It issues the usual Alexander Valley suspects: Chardonnay, Sauvignon Blanc, Merlot, and Cabernet Sauvignon. Typical of so many other Alexander Valley producers, its Cabernet Sauvignon is the standout, especially the Brenda Block label. The Merlot also is a fine rendition, again in the soft, rather blurry style characteristic of Alexander Valley Merlots. Depending upon the vintage, a varying amount of Merlot is blended into the Cabernet. The Chardonnay and the Sauvignon Blanc (labeled Fumé Blanc) both are well made. Indeed, Murphy-Goode acquired its original reputation from its Sauvignon Blanc. But the whites, typical of Alexander Valley, are not as compelling as the reds.

Nalle Winery—For many fans of Dry Creek Valley Zinfandel, those made by Doug Nalle (rhymes with pal) represent a pinnacle of Dry Creek Valley perfection. Indeed, the Nalle Zinfandels are definitive renditions, offering the strong tar scent and chewy density that sets apart Dry Creek Valley Zinfandels from other versions. They are beautifully made wines from purchased grapes yet impressively consistent over the vintages. Worth celebrating is Nalle's dry Riesling, sourced from Mendocino County. Few wineries today create a *new* Riesling, but Nalle is a believer. Worth pursuing.

J. Pedroncelli Winery—It is hard not to feel warm toward this longtime (founded 1904), family-owned winery located in Dry Creek Valley. The Pedroncelli family is classic Sonoma County in its devotion to farming, it understated approach, and its insistent modesty in pricing and presentation. That said, these same virtues have kept Pedroncelli from achieving what others, using the same raw material, have accomplished.

Pedroncelli has never been a winery in the forefront, but with its single-vineyard and Special Vineyard Selection bottlings it seems to have awakened to the fact that California wine buyers thirst for something special. They are attempting now to answer that thirst, but it's too soon to judge the results. This has always been an honest, stand-up family winery that never put on airs. So it's hard not to root for them to succeed in this newfound ambition. To watch closely.

Pezzi King Vineyards—Rich, intense red wines from this relatively new (1993) Dry Creek Valley winery. Zinfandel is, forgive the expression, king here. After all, that's Dry Creek Valley's specialty. Several different bottlings, all good, are offered. Look especially for the Maple Vineyard Zinfandel, which delivers the sort of wild berry intensity that sets Zinfandel apart from the more "serious" Cabernet Sauvignon. Not far behind is Pezzi King's estate-bottled Zin, as well as an "Old Vines" bottling. All are beautifully made and shine with pure Zinfandel flavors of berries and dust.

Other wines, such as Sauvignon Blanc and a Sonoma County Chardonnay, are blended from various sources and labeled "North Coast." These are meat-and-potato wines of no great distinction.

Preston of Dry Creek Winery and Vineyards—Located deep into the Dry Creek Valley, Preston is one of the most innovative and adventurous of the Dry Creek Valley wineries. Where everyone in California seems to be ramping up to becoming bigger wineries, buying fruit from anywhere and everywhere, Lou and Susan Preston have taken the opposite approach. Starting in 2001, they downsized to just 8,000 cases from an all-time high ten years earlier of 30,000 cases.

Today, the wines come only from the estate vineyard in Dry Creek. The new focus has resulted in lovely wines. Truth be told, Preston always made some of Dry Creek's most honest-tasting wines, free of the oaky flourishes and stylistic tricks employed by winemakers chasing high scores. Today, though, the quality of Preston's wines is more apparent, courtesy of the new focus on their organically grown and certified estate fruit.

Among the whites there's a superb, austere-style Sauvignon Blanc popping with grapefruit flavors. An opulent, tropical Viognier is also appealing.

It's red wines that have always been Preston's specialty. Petite Sirah, Mouvèdre, Carignane, and Zinfandel are the standouts, all handled in a pure, unintrusive winemaking style. This is a winery worth seeking out for its purity and utter lack of what might be called "taste pretension."

Quivira Vineyards—One of the most reliable labels in Sonoma County is Quivira Vineyards (pronounced kee-VEER-ah). For once, the specialties are easy to pinpoint and almost embarrassingly easy to praise: Zinfandel above all and Sauvignon Blanc. Fully seventy-three acres of their ninety-acre vineyard in Dry Creek Valley are planted to these two varieties, plus Cabernet Sauvignon. All come from the Dry Creek Valley and are convincing examples of their respective breeds. Former winemaker Doug Nalle (see *Nalle Winery*) helped establish the style and standards for Quivira. These remain firmly in place.

Quivira also offers an array of named-vineyard Zins from neighboring growers such as Dieden Vineyard, Standley Ranch, and Anderson Ranch, as well as a subplot on Quivira's own property called Wine Creek Ranch. All of these are unusually fine Zinfandels. Really, Quivira just doesn't miss.

A. Rafanelli Winery—The strength of Dry Creek Valley as a source of distinctive Zinfandels and Cabernets is nowhere better demonstrated than at A. Rafanelli Winery. (The "A" stands for Dave Rafanelli's father, Americo.) Here you'll find the restrained intensity and richness of flavor that help set apart Dry Creek Valley Zinfandels from other versions made elsewhere. The same is true for Rafanelli's Cabernet Sauvignon. There's no winemaking razzmatazz here, just an authenticity of place illuminated by deferential wine-making. Rafanelli is one of the stars of Dry Creek Valley.

Rancho Zabaco—Another "sub-label" of Gallo of Sonoma. Rancho Zabaco is something of a specialist label for various Zinfandels grown in Gallo's Sonoma County vineyards, as well as for an impressively good Pinot Gris and an appealing Syrah. But really, it's the Zinfandel that stands out. Five different Zins are offered and—no surprise—the best ones come from named vineyards, notably Chiotti Vineyard and Stefani Vineyard. All are made in a lush, plush, can't-miss-the-fruit style, but why not? It works. Zinfandel, after all, should be all about fruit.

Ravenswood Winery—Few wineries are more publicly and closely associated with Zinfandel than Ravenswood in Sonoma Valley. (Ridge is, of course, the first name that springs to mind.) Like Ridge, the fans of Ravenswood Zinfandels are numerous, ardent, and vocal. And like Ridge, Ravenswood also issues a top-drawer Cabernet Sauvignon. The comparison extends in one other respect: Like Ridge, Ravenswood reaches out to various vineyards in far-flung locations to secure its Zinfandel grapes.

Ravenswood pulled off the neat trick of having a cult-like following for its wines while at the same time expanding to what—compared to its boutique image—can only be called mind-boggling proportions. It now sells 450,000 cases a year. That was irresistible to Constellation, which paid a whopping $148 million in 2001 to buy Ravenswood, which had already gone public before the sale. (The stock was trading at about $12 a share; Constellation offered $29.50 a share.)

The cash cow, then and now, was the Vintner's Blend bottlings of Zinfandel, Merlot, and Chardonnay, which made up the bulk, in every sense, of the production. Ignore it.

Instead leap up to what Ravenswood has always excelled at, namely its vineyard-designated wines, which now number at least one dozen. Most famous among them, and a personal favorite, is the Dickerson Vineyard Zinfandel from Napa Valley. Most famous, perhaps, is the Pickberry Vineyard in the Sonoma Mountain AVA, which creates a Bordeaux-type blend of Cabernet Sauvignon, Merlot, and Cabernet Franc.

These, and all the other vineyard-designated reds, are made in Ravenswood's signature (and trademarked) "No Wimpy Wines" approach.

For lesser fruit this style is merely bullying. But for the really fine grapes, the style truly amplifies the voice of the land.

So far, Ravenswood's new owner seems content to let Ravenswood be Ravenswood. And why not? It's been a brilliant success—lightning in a wine bottle.

Ridge Lytton Springs—The Lytton Springs name can cause some confusion. The confusion arises because it first became prominent among Zinfandel fanciers when Ridge Vineyards issued a series of Ridge Zinfandels identified as "Lytton Springs" in the early and mid-1970s. It took its name from a hamlet called Lytton, which lies just barely inside the Dry Creek Valley AVA, adjacent to the Alexander Valley AVA border.

Then the owner of the vineyard that supplied the grapes to Ridge (whose vineyard was named Valley Vista Vineyard), decided to establish his own winery called—you guessed it—Lytton Springs Winery. Ridge's grape source dried up. Making matters even more complicated is the fact that, starting in 1984, Ridge secured Zinfandel grapes from a vineyard close to the original Valley Vista Vineyard and began reissuing a series of Zinfandels labeled Ridge Lytton Springs. Got all this?

Finally, in 1991, the owner of Lytton Springs Winery decided to sell the winery, as well as the fifty-acre Valley Vista Vineyard. This time Ridge took no chances: It purchased the winery and its vineyard for a reported $1.5 million—a steal, in retrospect. Ridge has since constructed an ambitious, environmentally sensitive straw-bale winery made with rice straw.

After all this, how are the wines, you ask? They're swell. After all, it's Ridge making them and if any winery knows how to create superb Zinfandels, it's Ridge. Besides, the old-vine fruit from the estate vineyard is hardly new to Ridge. Now they own it though, which gives Ridge total control.

J. Rochioli Vineyards—You could make a case—not airtight, mind you, but good—that Rochioli Vineyards is the most significant Pinot Noir vineyard in all of Russian River Valley. It's quite a story, in a way, because the Rochioli family itself was really just a farming family. But they did know how to farm. And they had the luck (and vice versa) to have Burt Williams of nearby Williams Selyem Winery make named-vineyard Pinot Noirs from Rochioli Vineyards. They were spectacular. And they awakened everybody to the prospect that, really, it was Russian River Valley rather than the then-ballyhooed Carneros district, that was *the* source for more-than-plausible California Pinot Noir.

Keep in mind that when all this was occurring in the early 1980s, a lot of observers were skeptical about California ever producing a Pinot Noir you could confuse with a good red Burgundy. It was Williams Selyem Rochioli Vineyard bottling that changed people's minds in a single sip. (That wine is today Rochioli's West Block bottling.)

Not surprisingly, Rochioli decided to hang out their own winery shingle, as there's far more money to be made in grape processing than grape growing. After a shaky start, Rochioli has made the transition to become a star winery.

Of course the Pinot Noirs are superb, none better than the impossible-to-find West Block bottling. The regular Russian River Valley bottling is pretty fine in its own right.

Chardonnay is classic Russian River Valley in its pear flavors and supple elegance. More controversial is the Sauvignon Blanc, which changed style from something ripe to something more edgy and citrusy. Personally, I think it's superb, a stylistic change for the better. However, opinions are divided. If you see it, try it. As a friend of mine likes to say, "You'll agree for yourself."

The Rochioli name is widespread in Sonoma County because the family still sells its Pinot Noir grapes to others, all of whom are delighted (and probably required) to cite the Rochioli name on the label. Truly, you can't go wrong with almost anything from Rochioli.

Rutz Cellars—Creating Burgundy-style Pinot Noir and Chardonnay has become a dream, if not an obession, for numerous California winemakers. And a disproportionate number of them are based in Sonoma County. Count Rutz among them. A variety of named-vineyard Pinot Noirs and Chardonnays are offered. Quality, unfortunately, has proved variable with an overemphasis on oak. This is a small producer still finding its way, it seems. To watch.

St. Francis Vineyards and Winery—A Sonoma Valley winery located in Kenwood, St. Francis seems to have had a mixed track record. "Soft" seems to be the tasting term that springs to mind when thinking about the various St. Francis offerings. The pleasant Gewürztraminer is round and soft; ditto for the various Chardonnays. Merlot is rich and rewarding, especially the Reserve version, but like so many other Merlots, it too is easygoing. Only the intense Cabernet Sauvignon seems to have backbone. Overall, these are good wines, but somehow unconvincing. The Cabernet is the pick of the (generally handsome) litter.

Sausal Winery—Every wine taster has his or her secret admiration. Mine is for the Zinfandel of Sausal Winery in Alexander Valley, especially the Reserve bottling. It is pure Alexander Valley in structure and gentility, yet the depth of flavor and character make it extraordinary. The vineyards are old: The regular Zinfandel comes from fifty- to seventy-five-year-old vines. The Reserve Zinfandel is from a 100-year-old vineyard.

Upon tasting Sausal's Zinfandels, one cannot help but conclude that they could not have come from just anywhere. The Cabernet Sauvignon is similarly reflective of (Alexander Valley) place. The wines now seem a bit rustic compared to what is made elsewhere in Alexander Valley today. Perhaps one's palate gets recalibrated, but a bit more polish might be inviting in these otherwise characterful wines.

Sebastiani Vineyards—One of Sonoma County's largest wineries (it's hard to keep count any more of who's biggest this week), Sebastiani tries to be all things to all drinkers. At the low end, it issues jug-type wines of acceptable but otherwise uninteresting quality. But then, that's what jug wine is about.

At the high end, Sebastiani offers a series of vineyard-designated and estate-grown wines of rarely less than good, but rarely outstanding, quality. Cabernet Sauvignon, especially the Cherryblock bottling, is the pick of the offerings, along with a Russian River Valley Chardonnay from Dutton Ranch. (Is there anybody in Sonoma County who *doesn't* make a Dutton Ranch Chardonnay?)

For a while, it seemed as if Sebastiani was really going to take on the heavy-hitters. But it seems to have settled back into, if not complaceny, then a comfortable marketing slot. After all, Sebastiani has been in the marketplace for decades and still has a strong and reliable following for its moderately priced wines. The genuine high-end has never been its forte—and still isn't.

Seghesio Family Vineyards—Zinfandel is the ticket at Seghesio, plain and not so simple. Multiple bottlings are offered, all of them quite wonderful. Look for a powerful Sonoma County Old Vines bottling, as well as the San Lorezo Vineyard Zin from Alexander Valley. Then there's Cortina Vineyard from Dry Creek Valley, which is packed with Dry Creek's dusty quality.

Seghesio offers all sorts of other wines, notably an array of Italian varietals such as the rarely seen white grape Arneis, as well as Sangiovese, and a quite good Barbera. A Cabernet Sauvignon (60 percent) and Sangiovese (40 percent) blend is issued under the name Omaggio (homage). It's all right.

Truly, it's the Zinfandels that make Seghesio a standout Sonoma County winery.

Schug Carneros Estate Winery—A mixed bag from this Carneros property. Chardonnay is, of course, its livelihood, as it is for nearly everyone in the Carneros district. And the Schug version, especially its Heritage Reserve bottling, is an admirable effort. But these days it's mighty hard to create a Carneros Chardonnay that's all *that* much different from everyone else's. More original is Schug's Heritage Reserve Cabernet Sauvignon from Sonoma Valley, which tends to be oaky, but does have good, dense flavors with a note of currants.

Siduri Wines—Adam and Dianna Lee, the owners/winemakers of Siduri, are a modern California success story. Arriving in the early 1990s from Texas, this young (twentysomething at the time) couple were practically inflamed with a passion for creating Pinot Noir. So far, so normal in California in the 1990s—except maybe for their extreme youth at the time.

But they had—and continue to have—*something* that touched a nerve. Where others failed, the Lees managed to convince some of California's most sought after Pinot Noir vineyard owners, such as David Hirsch of Hirsch Vineyard in Sonoma Coast West, to sell them a small quantity of grapes. Hirsch had probably by then turned down several dozen similar supplicants, he recalls. Ditto for Pisoni Vineyard in Santa Lucia Highlands.

File it under "the world loves a lover." And their passion is real. And their work, in a small, utilitarian warehouse winery in Santa Rosa, has been unremitting.

Siduri issues multiple Pinot Noirs—and only Pinot Noir—from what seems to be a hit parade of great American Pinot Noir vineyards: Pisoni and Gary's vineyards in Santa Lucia Highlands, Clos Pepe in Santa Rita Hills, Hirsch in Sonoma Coast West, Van der Kamp on Sonoma Mountain, and Archery Summit in Oregon's Willamette Valley.

All of these are issued as vineyard designates. And they're all beautifully made in a rich, somewhat extracted style that relies perhaps a touch too heavily on cold maceration. That noted, these are luscious wines made with exquisite care and concern. To drink Siduri is to drink some of the best Pinot Noirs made in America today.

Simi Winery—Perhaps it's a tasting blind spot, but I have never cared for Simi wines. It's been decades of tasting now, and still, if ever there was a winery that has played it safe, it's Simi. The wines are always well crafted, reasonably true to type, but mostly boring. The noteworthy exception to this is the Reserve Cabernet Sauvignon from Alexander Valley, which is a soft, lush, pretty wine. Most everything else is played right down the middle. Simi does a decent job overall, but hardly anything special.

Sonoma-Cutrer Vineyards—Chardonnay is the *raison d'être* of Sonoma-Cutrer, and few wineries have made a better case for the potential of this grape variety in California. So much so, in fact, that Sonoma-Cutrer and 1,000 acres of vines were sold to drinks giant Brown-Forman in 1999 for $125 million.

The finest wine is still the Les Pierres Vineyard, which lies just on the other side of the Carneros AVA in the Sonoma Valley AVA. It is one of California's most gratifyingly austere Chardonnays. The Russian River Ranches Chardonnay reflects the origin of its name. The Cutrer is the fullest of the three, but it lacks the finesse of Les Pierres. All of the Sonoma-Cutrer Chardonnays are made in a lean, taut style.

All Sonoma-Cutrer Chardonnays used to be identified as simply coming from Sonoma Coast, whose appellation this winery was active in creating. That's now changed, reflecting the current emphasis on smaller AVAs for high-end wines. Les Pierres now says Sonoma Valley AVA and the Cutrer reads Russian River Valley.

Although the sheer glamour of the winery has now faded, which was inevitable, the fact remains that it still is one of the leading Russian River Valley Chardonnay producers. But what once seemed unique—as Sonoma-Cutrer was most tasters' introduction to Russian River Valley Chardonnay—now seems almost quotidian.

Rodney Strong Vineyards—Previously known as Sonoma Vineyards, this winery has knocked from pillar to post in search of an identity. First it began as Tiburon Vintners. Then it became Windsor Vineyards. Then it emerged anew as Sonoma Vineyards. Finally, after being taken over by a large national importer, it emerged yet again, in 1984, as Rodney Strong Vineyards. In the meantime, although the name has remained the same, Rodney Strong Vineyards changed owners two more times since 1984. Rodney Strong, the winemaker and founder of this multiply reincarnated operation, has somehow always lived to tell the tale.

The tale being told isn't anything spellbinding. Several named-vineyard wines are issued, in addition to the usual blends. The Chardonnay Chalk Hill Vineyard in the Chalk Hill AVA is an empty experience. The Zinfandel Old Vines River West Vineyard in the Russian River AVA reveals some of the finesse and delicacy that this area can impart, but it is swamped by the taste of American oak. The Cabernet Sauvignon Alexander's Crown Vineyard from the Alexander Valley AVA is the best of the bunch. Too often these are pleasant but rather boring wines that keep a close look-out on the popular taste of the moment.

F. Teldeschi Winery—A Dry Creek Valley Zinfandel producer that makes classic, dense, slightly old-fashioned Zinfandels from—where else?—Dry Creek Valley. This is a producer that harks to what Dry Creek Valley Zins used to taste like before some of them got tarted up with a lot of new French oak—and prices to match. A good, solid performer.

Topolos at Russian River Vineyards—A winery that has issued some pretty odd-tasting wines in its (long) day. But the Zinfandels are always worth looking into, as they're the winery's main draw. The winery's estate vineyard is now farmed biodynamically, as are some of the vineyards from which grapes are purchased. There seems little continuity to what's consistently good here, but then, perhaps I have not tasted assiduously enough to find the pattern. Zins are easily the best bet, though.

Trentadue Winery—The Trentadue family used to own what is now the Montebello vineyard of Ridge Vineyards. The family moved from Santa Clara County to Sonoma County and now farms about 200 acres of vines, in addition to running their own winery. Ridge still remains connected to the Trentadues, having signed a thirty-year contract for a Trentadue-owned Zinfandel vineyard near Geyserville in the Alexander Valley.

Trentadue's wines have improved over the years, although the winery still occupies a middle ground of quality. There's a good, sound Merlot from Alexander Valley. Look also for Old Patch Red, a mixture of various red wine grapes from a roughly four-acre patch of very old vines. Carignan is also a winner, and it too comes from some very old vines.

Viansa—This is the winery created in 1989 by Sam Sebastiani after he was booted from the Sebastiani family winery. Located in the Carneros district, Viansa has found its identity as a kind of immovable feast of all things Cal-Ital. It's as much a tourist destination for buying Italianate knick-knacks as it is a winery (gift baskets, olive oils, wine jewelry). Still, there's a pleasant, if unexceptional, Barbera. Ditto for Sangiovese. An Arneis is acceptable, but that's a very tricky grape variety for everyone. Viansa reflects the California-winery-as-tourist-attraction more than it does a California winery as, well, a winery.

Williams Selyem Winery—A lot of fans of Williams Selyem held their breath (and maybe their noses) when the sale of the winery to New York City multimillionaire John Dyson was announced in 1998. Dyson had done nothing wrong. Quite the opposite. He paid a good chunk of change (a reported $9.5 million) for a winery that owned no vineyards, had a facility little bigger than a McMansion's garage, and had barely any inventory. He bought a brand.

The fear among Williams Selyem's devoted following was that the vineyard-designated Pinot Noirs they had come to cherish would somehow be mangled in a new corporate maw or lost altogether. They were wrong.

The (tasting) reality is that Williams Selyem is as good as it ever was, maybe even better. The new winemaker, Bob Cabral, replaced the beloved Burt Williams, who had a certain intuitive genius with Pinot Noir. Cabral had the sense (and the intrinsic modesty) to effectively say, "If I can do it as well as Burt, I'm a happy man." He *is* doing it as well as Burt, maybe even a bit better if only because he has more vineyard sources from which to create even more single-vineyard Pinot Noirs, as well as Zinfandels. (Williams' favorite wine was not, as it happens, his Pinot Noirs but the Jackass Hill Zinfandel he made from grapes bought from the Martinelli family vineyard. After Burt left, the Martinellis wised up and kept the grapes all for themselves.)

Today, there's practically a spew of vineyard-designated wines emerging from Williams Selyem, many from previously unknown (or at least unrecognized) vineyards. Chardonnay production has increased considerably, nearly all of it sourced from Russian River Valley, where the winery itself is sited.

The "big" productions (about 1,500 cases) are such wines as Russian River

Valley Pinot Noir, which is consistently fine. Almost inevitably better—or at least more distinctive—are such single vineyards as Hirsch, Coastlands, and Precious Mountain Vineyards, all on Sonoma Coast West. There's Ferrington Vineyard in Anderson Valley and, just down the road, Weir Vineyard in the little-known Yorkville Heights AVA, both producing interesting, original Pinot Noirs.

The list continues. But the important feature is simply this: Williams Selyem wines have never been better or more worthwhile than they are today. Considering what Burt Williams and Ed Selyem did in their own day, that's no small achievement.

Robert Young Estate Winery—A classic example of a grower of considerable acclaim, in Alexander Valley, deciding to hang out their own winery shingle. Robert Young Vineyard first came to fame (and presumably some fortune) courtesy of a named-vineyard Chardonnay from their grapes originally issued by Château St. Jean in 1975.

To say that it was a success doesn't begin to capture the galvanizing effect that wine had on the burgeoning audience for California wines at the time. Its honeyed ripeness was like no other Chardonnay and the Robert Young name was made. Château St. Jean still makes the wine and it is, in fact, still a world-beater. It was one of California's earliest vineyard-designated Chardonnays.

In the meantime, the vineyard sold grapes to others and Robert Young's children eventually assumed command of the 300-acre vineyard. Everything was replanted in the 1990s due to phylloxera. In 1997 the Young family decided that they, too, should process at least some of their own fruit. The wheel coming full circle (or rather, it was never broken), they asked Dick Arrowood, the original winemaker at Château St. Jean who made the Robert Young wine famous, to return to the fold as their winemaking consultant.

Not surprisingly, the wines from this estate are far better than what usually emerge from a brand-new winery. The Chardonnay is, natch, all it ever was, if not better: lush, honeyed, yet somehow beautifully balanced. There's also a Bordeaux-type Cabernet Sauvignon (with Merlot and Cabernet Franc) called Scion that is plump, succulent, and seductive. To the extent you can say this about so new a winery, Robert Young Estate Winery is as reliable a fine winery as any in Sonoma County.

MENDOCINO COUNTY

*There are two kinds of taste, the taste for emotions of surprise
and the taste for emotions of recognition.*
                              —Henry James, *Partial Portraits* (1888)

The usual view of wine regions is geographic: hills over here, valleys over there. Boundaries inevitably are drawn with pencils sharpened by politics. This is certainly the case in California and, for that matter, everywhere else in the world.

But perhaps a better way—or at least an equally useful way—would be to view wine districts from a Jamesian perspective: Which areas create wines of surprise? Which issue the recognizable, the familiar? A taste for the familiar in wine, what James called a "taste for emotions of recognition," drives the market. Witness the domination of Chardonnay and Cabernet Sauvignon.

The finest wines trigger a "taste for emotions of surprise." Almost always, they are wines of place; they display somewhereness. The emotion of surprise occurs precisely because this sensation of somewhereness is unpredictable—indeed, unknowable, until the very moment of tasting the wine.

Mendocino County, more than most areas of California, can be broadly divided using Henry James' insight. It comes down to this: The narrow, supremely cool Anderson Valley creates wines of surprise. Almost everywhere else in Mendocino the wines are boringly recognizable. Of course there are exceptions, but they are just that.

Technically, Mendocino County contains eight AVAs, with another two in the offing. Most frequently seen is the Mendocino AVA, which embraces the entire county. The other major name is Anderson Valley AVA. The remaining AVAs are also-rans. Two are "one-man-band" appellations: McDowell Valley AVA (the sole user of which is McDowell Valley Vineyard) and Cole Ranch AVA (effectively a defunct AVA created by Fetzer back in the 1980s). Equally obscure is Potter Valley AVA, which is rarely cited on a label. Still rarely seen are the Yorkville Highlands, Redwood Valley, and Mendocino Ridge AVAs.

Growers are now considering two more possible AVAs: Sanel Valley (a small zone which that sense, because there's a "there there") and Ukiah Valley. (Because of its large size and variety of flatland and hillside exposures, it promises to be an overly broad, meaningless appellation.)

Anderson Valley AVA

Anderson Valley is one of the tidiest appellations in California. It is about twenty miles long—by air—and little more than one mile wide. The valley is a gash in the Coast Range Mountains, through which runs the Navarro River. The key is that both the Navarro River and, more importantly, the Anderson Valley itself, reach the Pacific Ocean. The Navarro empties out; the Anderson Valley lets the sea air pour in.

Nowhere is the effect of ocean air more obvious to the naked eye (and uncovered skin) than Anderson Valley. The northern boundary of the AVA starts about nine miles from the Pacific. At that point, the fog practically raids the valley. As might be expected, its force diminishes as it penetrates deeper inland. Three towns provide convenient markers: The hamlet of Navarro at the northern end is the first. The midpoint is Philo (rhymes with high-low), midway along the length of the valley. Farthest inland is Boonville, which marks the most inland boundary of the AVA.

The difference in temperature is both easily imagined and quantified. Boonville, farthest inland, regularly is eight degrees Fahrenheit warmer than mid-point Philo. They are eight miles apart. Every mile that separates them results in a temperature difference of one degree Fahrenheit. In terms of the UC Davis degree-days measurement, Philo has roughly 1,900 degree-days, where Boonville has 2,300 degree-days.

The marine air and fog influence are felt at around two or three P.M. Where a typical midday temperature in July might reach eighty degrees, the nighttime temperature hovers in the high forties. One extreme example occurred on July 5, 1989: The temperature was only five degrees above freezing, at thirty-seven degrees Fahrenheit.

The vineyard development of the Anderson Valley is still adolescent. Only 2,000 acres of vines are found, with a good chunk of that planted by the sparkling wine producer Roederer Estate. New plantings of Pinot Noir, taking advantage of the cool-climate Dijon clones so necessary for Anderson Valley, promise a potentially impressive blossoming of the appellation as one of California's most desirable Pinot Noir locales. The results, however, are not yet in, so this remains (optimistic) speculation.

Because of the cool location, the typical Anderson Valley grape varieties are the predictable cool-climate suspects: Riesling, Chardonnay, Pinot Noir, and Gewürztraminer. So far, the results lend themselves to a distinctive commonality. Anderson Valley has a clear vocation of place for Gewürztraminer and late-harvest Riesling. Almost nowhere else in California can you find, from winery after winery, such a strong familial resemblance despite stylistic winemaking differences. Only Sonoma's Russian River Valley can rival the delicacy and finesse of Anderson Valley's exquisite Gewürztraminers (and they are rapidly disappearing in Sonoma). The same can be said of the late-harvest Rieslings, which manage to retain Mosel-like delicacy while imparting the honeyed scents of ripe Riesling affected by botrytis or noble rot.

Both Pinot Noir and Chardonnay so far have been much less impressive. For this observer, it seems all but certain that this underachievement with Pinot Noir and Chardonnay is directly related to clonal selection. When most of Anderson Valley's vineyards were installed, in the 1980s, the cool-climate Dijon clones for both Pinot Noir and Chardonnay were commercially unavailable. Certainly, there were good Pinot Noir clones already suitable for Anderson Valley. And indeed some good Pinot Noirs have surfaced from time to time. But suitable Chardonnay clones were fewer.

As previously mentioned, the odds are very much in Anderson Valley's favor that its new Pinot Noir and Chardonnay vineyards, with these newly available clones, will transform the area. Inevitably, it will take time—especially with Pinot Noir—but it's hard to imagine how it cannot occur, given the Anderson Valley's climatic aptitude for these varieties.

Mendocino Ridge AVA

Anderson Valley is more complicated yet. Everything so far described applies to what might be called Anderson Valley *bas*. There's also an Anderson Valley *haut*, which happily has become a separate AVA called Mendocino Ridge. This new (1997) AVA is one of the most unusual, in that it is the only noncontiguous AVA anywhere in America. Originally, the vineyards of Mendocino Ridge were in the Anderson Valley AVA. But they were always their own world: more sun, no fog, yet subject to the cooling temperatures that come with higher elevation.

Mendocino Ridge is really a reflection of a continuing—if only tenuously so—tradition that dates back more than a century. In the 1890s, Italian immigrants planted vineyards in logged-out patches above the fog line, which starts at about 1,400 feet.

Families with names such as Frati, Tovani, Giusti, and Giovanetti selected a section known as Greenwood Ridge for their homesteads. They did so for two reasons, the more important one being access: Greenwood Ridge was intersected by a twisting mountain road of some eighteen miles that connected the coastal town of Elk (then called Greenwood) with the interior Anderson Valley. The other reason is one frequently mentioned in connection to Italian immigrant winegrowers: The hillsides reminded them of home. In Italy, as elsewhere in Europe, grapes were found to perform better on hillsides than on valley floors.

Considering their grapes of choice—Zinfandel, Alicante Bouschet, Carignane, Muscat, Palomino, and Malvasia—they were right. None of these sun-loving varieties could have prospered in the cool, frost-prone Anderson Valley floor. But once above the fog, the sunshine was uninterrupted. The ridge sites rarely saw spring frosts.

The presence of these Italian immigrants in Anderson Valley was reflected in the curious local dialect that developed in isolated Anderson Valley in the 1890s. Extensive, localized vocabularies are rare in the United States and largely confined to isolated mountain regions of longstanding habitation, such as Appalachia or the bayous of Louisiana. That a dialect, however limited, could have emerged as late as 1890, in a state as recently settled as California, reveals just how isolated was the Anderson Valley.

The local dialect is called Boontling, a contraction of Boonville and lingo. No longer spoken, it lives on as a cultural artifact, with modern-day locals sprinkling their conversation with an occasional Boontling term for colorful effect. (A city person is a "brightlighter," for example.) But at the turn of the century, Boontling was commonly used and in it we can see the Italian presence duly noted. For example, Greenwood Ridge was, in Boontling, "Iteland"; wine grapes were known as "Frati shams," referring to the Frati family.

Anyway, there weren't many of these "ridge vineyards" but, as Spencer Tracy said in *Pat and Mike*, "What's there is *cherce*." Equally as important, they survived, eventually concentrating only on Zinfandel. Such "ridge vineyards" as Ciapusci Vineyard, Mariah Vineyard, Zeni Vineyard, and DuPratt Vineyard create some of the greatest Zinfandels in California. All are found between 1,400 feet and 2,400 feet elevation. Jed Steele, when he was winemaker for Kendall-Jackson in the 1980s, sought out these grapes and demanded an audience for them. Kendall-Jackson continues to issue named-vineyard Zinfandels under their Edmeades label from several of these vineyards, all of them stunning.

The distinction of place was so strong and obvious that it made true wine sense to create a separate appellation. It is noncontiguous because the minimum elevation requirement of 1,200 feet applies to a wide swath of mountainous terrain sandwiched between the Pacific Ocean and the Anderson Valley floor. The AVA-eligible sites are best envisioned as mountain tops poking through the fog. (Some folks call the ridge vineyards "islands in the sky.")

Even though the entire AVA encompasses a huge 410 square miles, less than one-third of that area—87,466 acres—lies above 1,200 feet. And of that, it's estimated that only 1,500 to 2,000 acres are appropriate for vineyard cultivation. Today there are just seventy-five acres of vineyards, all historic Zinfandel plantations. Perhaps someday there will be more vineyards than these scant seventy-five acres, but given the current climate of environmental activism, where such hilltop plantings now generate fierce resistance, one would be well advised not to be overly hopeful about expansion.

Potter Valley AVA

Apart from Anderson Valley, everything else in Mendocino County can be considered "inland." Potter Valley is one such place. Located twelve miles northeast of Ukiah, it contains about 1,000 acres of vines growing in a higher-elevation valley, about 1,000 feet above sea level. Because of its inland site, the days are hot. The elevation does, however, deliver cool nighttime temperatures. So far, nothing distinctive has emerged from Potter Valley, perhaps because the grapes often are used in blends. One rarely sees a label citing Potter Valley AVA. Sauvignon Blanc is thought to be its strong suit. No winery is located in Potter Valley.

McDowell Valley AVA

A "one-man-band" appellation, McDowell Valley is pretty much the domain of McDowell Valley Vineyards (q.v.). All told, about 750 acres of vines are planted, most of it owned by or under contract to McDowell Valley Vineyards. It, too, is a warm, inland-Mendocino climate that is making a mark with Syrah.

Cole Ranch AVA

Why this sixty-acre vineyard is entitled to its own appellation continues to escape me. A specialty of Fetzer Vineyards, which has issued a string of Cabernets from the site, this tiny, mountainside AVA in the hills southwest of Ukiah has consistently failed to impress, thanks to persistent bell pepper and vegetal notes. Fetzer left off using the Cole Ranch designation since the 1983 vintage. Since then, the Cole Ranch grapes have been employed in the Cabernet "Reserve" label.

Redwood Valley AVA

Redwood Valley became an AVA in 1996 for one powerful reason: Fetzer Vineyards. It's where Fetzer has substantial vineyard plantings. Redwood Valley lies north of Ukiah, adjacent to, and west of, the Potter Valley AVA. Although the Russian River is much better associated with Sonoma County, it also flows through Mendocino County. Redwood Valley is a north/south stretch of land that begins just south of Ukiah around Talmage and extends north of Ukiah. It is roughly fifteen miles long and parallels the Russian River. Along its length are several well-known Mendocino County wineries such as Parducci, Weibel, Cresta Blanca (now Mendocino Estates), Fife, and Frey. It was in the Redwood Valley that Fetzer Vineyard first began with a 110-acre vineyard. Today, its Redwood Valley vineyard is designated Home Ranch.

The town of Hopland in Redwood Valley is where Fetzer has its (several) million-dollar hospitality facility and its Valley Oak Ranch Vineyard. It is where Fetzer's Sundial Vineyard is located. Jepson and Milano wineries are also located near Hopland, but it's Fetzer that brought the Hopland name to public attention. The McDowell Valley AVA lies directly east of Hopland, about five miles away.

Sanel Valley

The tiny Sanel Valley also lies along the Russian River, south of Talmage and north of Hopland. Depending upon who is doing the defining, the Sanel Valley is about five miles long. So far, it is an unheralded name, yet Sanel Valley seems to be a promising location, especially for Sauvignon Blanc. Jepson makes its exceptional Sauvignon Blanc from its Sanel Valley vineyard. Husch, over the mountains in Anderson Valley, has its La Ribera Vineyard in the Sanel Valley, from which it creates yet another fine Sauvignon Blanc, as well as promising Cabernet Sauvignon. Milano Winery actually vineyard-designates its wines as "Sanel Valley Vineyard." It is an area to watch, particularly for Sauvignon Blanc. Likely it will become an AVA—and deserves to.

Mendocino County Producers Worth
Seeking Out (And Some Not)

Ceago—A label created by former Fetzer co-owner Jim Fetzer. Originally based on his biodynamic Ceago Vineyard north of Ukiah, Fetzer subsequently sold that vineyard to Brown-Forman for Fetzer Winery's Bonterra line of organic wines. Jim Fetzer then bought land in Lake County where he is developing a new seventy-acre biodynamic vineyard as well as installed a multi-million dollar visitor center called Ceago del Lago to promote biodynamic agriculture.

The wine specialty will be Cabernet Sauvignon, according to the winery, although a Merlot appears from the original Ceago Vineyard in Ukiah, as well as a Sauvignon Blanc from the family vineyards in Redwood Valley. To watch closely.

Fetzer Vineyard—Fetzer is one of the great (commercial) success stories of California wine. Started in 1968 by the late Barney Fetzer, a former lumber industry executive, the phrase "explosive growth" perhaps best describes the winery's expansion. Considering that its first vintage in 1968 was just 2,500 cases and that Fetzer is now one of the five largest wineries in California, this is a winery that has enjoyed phenomenal success. The Fetzer family sold the winery to Brown-Forman in 1992 for a reported $82 million. The Fetzer family retained about 1,000 acres of vines in Mendocino, most of the grapes from which are sold to Brown-Forman. However, several Fetzer family members—founder Barney Fetzer had six children—are starting their wineries using fruit from the family vineyard. See *Ceago, Jeriko, and Saracina wineries.*

This growth was—and still is—fueled by sales of broad appeal wines such as white Zinfandel and price-sensitive Chardonnay, both of which Fetzer issues in sizable quantities. The winery now reaches not only to numerous wine districts in California that lie well beyond Mendocino, but also to the vineyards of Washington State.

In the past decade, Fetzer has shown an extraordinary commitment to organic cultivation. Its Hopland tasting room has a large public garden that explains and proclaims the virtues of organic cultivation. The winery has made this feature one of its advertising and public relations selling points.

Fetzer's best wines are released under their Reserve designation. Reds, especially Cabernet and Zinfandel, are the best bet. The style of Fetzer's winemaking, like so many other California wineries, has evolved over the years. Now, considerable emphasis is placed on polish allied with a too-noticeable amount of new oak, often strongly vanilla-scented thanks to the use of American oak barrels. The Ricetti Vineyard Zinfandel is one of the better efforts, while the winery still is wrestling with the optimum style for its Cabernet Reserve. Until the 1983 vintage, the wine was labeled "Cole Ranch," which still is the vineyard source for the Cabernet Reserve. It has yet to deliver anything special. Most of the Fetzer offerings are well made, but rarely exceptional.

Fife Vineyard—Dennis Fife lives in Napa Valley (where he has a small vineyard on Spring Mountain) but his ties to Mendocino are strong. Indeed, some of Fife's best wines emerge from Redwood Valley. (Fife purchased the old Konrad winery.) Look for Fife's Redhead Zinfandel, which effectively captures the burly, not-quite-rustic-but-not-quite-refined quality of Redwood Valley Zinfandels.

Frey Vineyard—Located at the northern tip of Redwood Valley, Frey's claim to anybody's attention is that the wines are organically grown and sulfite-free, i.e. having fewer than ten parts per million of sulfites. That's about it, though. The wines themselves are variable, with an occasional Cabernet or Zinfandel showing some distinction. But mostly, Frey is a winery more committed to being sulfite-free and organically grown than it is to creating distinguished wines. Politics before palate, you might say.

Gabrielli Winery—A small Redwood Valley producer specializing in strapping, no-holds-barred red wines. Look for strong yet graceful Zinfandel from Goforth Vineyard in Redwood Valley, as well as Syrah from Gabrielli's estate vineyard. Multiple wines are offered each year, most from Mendocino, although there's a fine Zinfandel from old vines from Luvisi Vineyard in Napa Valley. Zinfandel is best here overall, with Syrah coming on strong.

Germain-Robin—Laurels to the finest brandy made in California go to this Mendocino distillery located high in the hills above Ukiah. Its location is so far off the beaten track that its having obtained a government license to operate a still (an old alambic still imported from the Cognac region) was practically a courtesy on the distillery's part. On the other hand, there are some advantages: Germain-Robin brandy is served at the White House.

The distillation is performed by Hubert Germain-Robin, a native of France's Cognac region (the family Cognac company is Jules Robin, founded in 1783). He joined forces with co-owner Ansley J. Coale, Jr., who attends to the business side. Germain-Robin brandies are composed of several grape varieties, the proportions of which are kept secret. But the owners do concede that Colombard is a significant addition. In fact, they fear for its disappearance. Mendocino County is home to ancient Colombard vines, some being eighty years old. Because the price achieved by Colombard is so low, the vineyards are fast being rooted up. The other grapes employed are Chenin Blanc, Palomino, and, unusually (by Cognac standards), two red wine grapes: Pinot Noir and Gamay.

Germain-Robin is issuing exceptional brandies, good enough to rival all but the best Cognacs from France. What it lacks, and what the finest Cognacs have, is access to old stocks for blending. After all, the first release—100 cases designated Lot # 1—first appeared only in 1987. Numerous special lots are now issued, all of them exceptionally good and always intriguing. If America has a better brandy-maker than Germain-Robin, I haven't tasted it—although competition is emerging.

Goldeneye—An odd name for a wine until you realize that a goldeneye is a type of duck and the owner of this new (1996) vineyard and label is Napa Valley's Duckhorn winery. In pursuit of a place where Pinot Noir can prosper, Duckhorn bought land in Anderson Valley and planted Dijon clones of Pinot Noir. Too few vintages are available for judgment, but Goldeneye is extremely promising.

Greenwood Ridge Vineyard—Based in Anderson Valley, Greenwood Ridge is a winery that has yet to define itself. It makes wines from multiple sources, reaching into Sonoma County, as well as elsewhere in Mendocino County. The Anderson Valley-grown Sauvignon Blanc is noteworthy, but most promising in the long run is Greenwood Ridge's own vineyard in what is now the Mendocino Ridge AVA: a ridge vineyard at the 1,200-foot level close to Dupratt Vineyard. The twelve-acre vineyard is planted equally to Cabernet Sauvignon, Merlot, and Riesling.

Handley Cellars—An Anderson Valley winery that shows especially well with Anderson Valley-grown Gewürztraminer. Sparkling wine, also from Anderson Valley, is less appealing, being on the citric side. Look also for an excellent dry rosé made from a blend of Pinot Noir and Pinot Meunier. An Anderson Valley-grown Pinot Noir shows well what can be done in this area, as it displays just the sort of finesse so lacking in some other California renditions. There's also some good, but not exceptional, Chardonnay and Sauvignon Blanc from Sonoma County's Dry Creek Valley, where the Handley family owns a vineyard.

Husch Vineyards—A longtime winery (founded 1971), Husch displays what Aristotle, in his *Poetics*, found most objectionable: to be inconsistently inconsistent. Ever since I can remember, Husch has made bizarre wines cheek by jowl with some surprisingly good ones. Yet no pattern of inconsistency seems to have emerged. Considering that this small winery offers fourteen different wines, this is perhaps not so surprising. The best bets at Husch are the wines from their La Ribera Vineyard over the mountains from Anderson Valley in the tiny Sanel Valley. Here, an excellent Sauvignon Blanc emerges as well as an (occasionally) impressive Cabernet Sauvignon. Also, there's a pleasant Pinot Noir and a pleasing Muscat Canelli.

Jeriko Estate—The third Fetzer brother—Dan Fetzer—to start his own label. Jeriko Estate is located next to John Fetzer's Saracina vineyard. Also devoted to organic agriculture, various wines are planned including Chardonnay, Pinot Noir, Syrah, and Merlot, most of which will appear in 2004.

Jepson Vineyards—Located in the Sanel Valley near Hopland, Jepson is an ambitious winery specializing in Chardonnay and Sauvignon Blanc. The various Chardonnays veer strongly to the buttery end of the spectrum. Pleasant, but nothing special. The Sauvignon Blanc, however, is superb. Some of the most refined, detailed Sauvignon Blanc that I've tasted in California has come from Jepson. Some *méthode champenoise* Blanc de Blanc sparkling wine is made. So far, it lacks distinction. Also, a good, oaky brandy is produced exclusively from Colombard grapes, using a classic alambic pot still.

Kendall-Jackson Wine Estates—Located in Lake County, which is directly east of Mendocino County, Kendall-Jackson has become a huge wine empire selling four million cases a year, making it the one of the largest wineries in America. Kendall-Jackson owns a whopping 11,000 vineyard acres in California. At least a half-dozen different winery labels are involved, including Edmeades, Pepi, La Crema, and Cambria, among others.

In 1988, Jess Jackson purchased two-thirds of the 1,000-acre Tepesquet Vineyard in Santa Barbara County, along with creating a new winery (Cambria) to handle some of the grapes. Kendall-Jackson gets these grapes as well. In 1988, the vineyard of the former Edmeades Winery in Anderson Valley was purchased. That same year, Jackson purchased the vineyard and winery of Zellerbach Vineyards in Sonoma County, renaming it Stonestreet Winery. (The Zellerbach name is owned by someone else, who continues to use it as a brand for blended wines.)

But the Kendall-Jackson brand remains the flagship operation. The winery itself is utilitarian and is crammed with thousands of small oak barrels, American and French. Indeed, a prominent taste of oak is one of the hallmarks of the Kendall-Jackson style. As long as winemaker Jed Steele was in command (he departed in 1991), no wine of stature escaped from Kendall-Jackson without first being branded with oak. This feature continues to this day.

In a winery this large, there are levels within levels. For the Kendall-Jackson label there are, effectively, two levels: the everyday Vintner's Reserve and the superior Grand Reserve. It was the Vintner's Reserve Chardonnay that catapulted Kendall-Jackson into a power winery.

Not only was the original Vintner's Reserve Chardonnay wine unmistakably oaky (it still is), it was also quite sweet. Turns out that Americans loved a sweetish Chardonnay. Today, though, as the American palate has matured, the sweetness of Kendall-Jackson's Vintner's Reserve Chardonnay has been modulated. Where before it was close to 1 percent residual sugar, the latest version is only half that. (Most tasters' threshold for perceiving sweetness is about 0.3 percent residual sugar.)

Oakiness notwithstanding, Kendall-Jackson can create some striking wines. After all, they've got the grapes. The best bets are Zinfandels, Cabernets, and Merlots. Look for anything vineyard-designated. The range is now enormous and varies with the vintage, as Kendall-Jackson is constantly tinkering with their marketing in an attempt to go up-market and command higher prices. So, for example, they dream up categories with names like "Stature." These come and go. Look for vineyard designations and the odds will be in your favor.

Lazy Creek Vineyards—Another Anderson Valley winery that adds luster to the valley's reputation as the source of some of California's finest Gewürztraminer. Along with that Navarro Vineyards, the Gerwüztraminer from Lazy Creek is one of the finest, redolent with the floral spiciness and delicacy that characterizes the best Anderson Valley Gewürztraminers—or those from anywhere else, for that matter.

McDowell Valley Vineyards—McDowell Valley Vineyards is the McDowell Valley AVA. And it has chosen to specialize in Rhône grape varieties, especially Syrah. In any lineup of California Syrah contenders it would be a mistake not to include McDowell Valley Vineyards. Look also for a good Grenache as well as a newly reissued Petite Sirah.

Navarro Vineyards—More than any other Anderson Valley winery, Navarro Vineyards has enjoyed both a consistency of quality and a devoted following. So devoted is its following that Navarro is one of the most privileged wineries in California: It sells at least one-third of its wines directly to clients by mail. Then there are the winery visitors. Not only does this mean pocketing retail prices for its production, it also means a practically guaranteed audience for its efforts. Because of this, one only rarely sees Navarro Vineyards on retail shelves, although the wines do appear on restaurant lists.

Navarro's claim to fame originally rested with its Gewürztraminer, which is still one of best in America. Anderson Valley is a wellspring of beautifully delicate Gewürztraminer, none better than that from Navarro. Late-harvest Riesling, another Anderson Valley strong suit, is also one of Navarro's specialties. Chardonnay, so far, seems less successful. This, too, is so far reflective of Anderson Valley. Pinot Noir, a variety the winery has long been struggling with, has achieved a new level of accomplishment, adding structure and flavor depth that was previously lacking. Overall, for table wines (as opposed to sparkling wine) Navarro is today the single best winery in Anderson Valley.

Obester Winery—Previously located in Half Moon Bay, between San Francisco and Santa Cruz, Obester moved to the Anderson Valley in 1989. Ten acres of Anderson Valley vineyard were planted in 1990. Its wines, therefore, are from purchased grapes. Some come from Anderson Valley, some from elsewhere in Mendocino County, and some from Ventana Vineyards in Monterey.

Pacific Echo—Formerly Scharffenberger Cellars, which specialized in sparkling wine, this Anderson Valley winery was renamed Pacific Echo shortly after it was purchased by LVMH Moët Hennessy Louis Vuitton. Despite that luxury goods giant's deep pockets (and its experience with its flagship Domaine Chandon in Napa Valley), the sparkling wines of Pacific Echo are—forgive me—mere echoes of what's created just down the road in Anderson Valley at Roederer Estate. It's the one to beat and Pacific Echo hasn't. Good but far from exceptional sparkling wines.

Parducci Wine Cellars—No winery is more devoted to Mendocino County than Parducci, which has operated out of Ukiah since 1932. At one time, when John Parducci was running the show, the wines represented a genuine standard, as well as offered exceptional quality for the money.

Today Parducci wines are struggling to return to form, with occasional success. The winery was purchased in 1996 by venture fund owner Carl

Thoma (sic) (Thoma/Cressey Equity Partners).

The 150,000 case winery was sold in April 2004 to the Mendocino Wine Group, which is a partnership between former Fetzer Vineyards president Paul Dolan and members of the Thornhill family, who own La Ribera Vineyards (See Vineyard Registry).

Best bets are a good Sauvignon Blanc from Lake County, as well as solid Petite Sirah and Zinfandel. The winery owns vineyards in Talmage and Hopland, both just south of Ukiah. Prices are always reasonable; quality is unvaryingly adequate, but only rarely more than that.

The new owners will surely change Parducci wines, very likely for the better, as the winery has a (valuable) permit to produce as much as 400,000 cases of wine.

Roederer Estate—The California outpost of the great French Champagne house Louis Roederer, this was one of just two French Champagne houses that elected to locate outside of Napa or Sonoma counties when the French decided California was the place to set up shop. (The other was Maison Deutz in the Arroyo Grande section of San Luis Obispo County, which failed and is now Laetitia winery.)

After extensive investigation, Roederer decided that the cool climate of Anderson Valley was ideal and in 1981 put down roots. It is the largest landowner in Anderson Valley, with more than 350 acres of vineyard. Its sparkling wine, a blend of Chardonnay and Pinot Noir, is one of the most distinctive—and rewarding—in California. More than any other California sparkling wine producer, Roederer Estate is as much an expression of source as it is of blending expertise and winemaking prowess. Founding winemaker Michel Salgues recently retired, but he established the template for handling Anderson Valley grapes (and trained the current winemaker), so the future is secure. Given a string of ever-better bottlings, it's now easy to flatly say that Roederer Estate creates America's finest sparkling wines, bar none.

The basic Roederer Estate bubbly is still California's benchmark bottling. It clearly tastes different from anything sourced from the Carneros district in Napa and Sonoma, which is where most of California's other high-end bubbly comes from. But in order to get the necessary acidity, growers in Carneros have to pick their grapes for sparkling wine in August—a month or more before grapes for still wines from Carneros get picked.

Anderson Valley, in comparison, is so intrinsically cool that Roederer can arrive at the necessary acidity only in mid-September, which means that the grapes have achieved more mature flavors, all the while retaining the requisite high acidity. That the difference is tasteable is proved by the fact that when various California sparkling wine producers were duking it out in the 1990s, everyone's retail price saw considerable discounting—except Roederer's. Partly this was due to Roederer's small size, but also it was its demonstrably different quality. People tasted the difference and were willing to pay the premium. They still are. Roederer continues to demand, and get, a premium, even for its basic Brut bottling.

The top of the line, in every sense, is Roederer's L'Hermitage bottling, which is a paragon of flavor dimension allied with finesse. It would easily vanquish many, if not most, French Champagnes in a blind tasting—although the finest French Champagnes do have savor from chalky soil absent in L'Hermitage. Look also for an exceptional rosé sparkling wine, which is perhaps Roederer's best-kept secret, as little is produced.

Saracina—This is the new label of yet another Fetzer brother (John Fetzer) using grapes from his 160-acre organic vineyard near Hopland. The winery reports that it will specialize in Zinfandel, Syrah, and Sauvignon Blanc. It's too early to judge quality.

Steele Wines—Former Kendall-Jackson winemaker Jed Steele left his employer in 1991 (trailing behind him a lawsuit involving whether the techniques by which Kendall-Jackson's best-selling sweetish Chardonnay was made were proprietary or not). He created his own label and winery and, in 1996, purchased the former Konocti Winery in Lake County, which is where Steele wines are made today.

Steele was always a tinkerer and loves issuing an array of wines, many of which are as over-oaked as they were when he worked at Kendall-Jackson. Hardly a shy flower, Steele believes in the preeminence of the winemaker and frankly declares, "I have come to realize that the ultimate creation can only be achieved if one goes *beyond the terroir.*" (Emphasis his.) Beyond the terroir lies—well, the winemaker.

That noted, Steele does issue some fine wines, none better than his longstanding passion, DuPratt Vineyard Zinfandel from the Mendocino Ridge AVA. Steele championed these forgotten Zinfandel vineyards high above the

Anderson Valley floor, and he cannot be congratulated too much for rescuing them from obscurity.

Much of the Steele production is devoted to admirable but not exceptional "California" Chardonnay, Pinot Noir, and Pinot Blanc. Look for good, if oaky, Zinfandel from Pacicini Vineyard in Napa Valley. Also, there's a string of small production lots that are vineyard-designated. These are the Steele wines worthy of closer investigation.

Steele also offers a second label called Shooting Star, which cost less and can often be good value. Like the Steele label, there are typically about two dozen wines to choose from. Keeping up with Steele/Shooting Star isn't easy, but Jedediah Tecumseh Steele has always been an ambitious winemaker willing to put his mark on many wines—indeed to go beyond the terroir.

Christine Woods Vineyards—Named after one of the pioneers of Anderson Valley, this small winery is the source of unusually good Cabernet Sauvignon grown in the Anderson Valley at higher elevations. What consistently emerges is a gentle Cabernet with a lovely, perfumey scent, a far cry from the more brutish, muscular sorts grown in warmer districts.

MONTEREY COUNTY

For decades, California wine has been discussed county by county. This is fine for, say, Napa or Sonoma where county and wine are largely one, as their county-wide ambitions are singularly focused on the fine-wine ambition.

This is not so with Monterey County. Instead, you have two separate and very unequal entities. You can divide these two unequal worlds into "mega-Monterey" and "micro-Monterey." Monterey County wine boosters would prefer that you gloss over this, for reasons to be explained momentarily.

First, you have the Monterey County of vast, corporate vineyards dedicated to the economical production of bulk wines. These wines are labeled "Monterey," if they're labeled at all. (Most wind up in anonymous bulk blends.)

The majority of Monterey County's vineyards are entitled only to this "Monterey" appellation, with no other sub-appellation available to them. And, even if a sub-appellation *does* exist, such as the San Lucas or Hames Valley AVAs, it doesn't necessarily signify superior quality, at least so far.

Then there's the Monterey County of small producers and vineyards creating place-specific wines from pockets of exceptional goodness. These wines come not from "Monterey" but from a handful of meaningful sub-appellations such as Santa Lucia Highlands AVA, Carmel Valley AVA, Chalone AVA, and others.

Recognizing this extreme division of wine ambition makes it easier to understand Monterey County's particular brand of boosterism. Every California wine area has, of course, its drum-banging. (Napa Valley is unrivaled.) But Monterey County's version is different. Monterey County's version is a kind of corporate have-your-cake-and-eat-it-too.

In the San Joaquin Valley—the bulk wine capital of California—no one ever tried to proclaim, while gushing out grapes and wines in industrial quantity at industrial prices that their wines are genuinely fine and deserving of a premium. This is the trick that Monterey County's boosters are trying to pull off.

Many of California's largest wine corporations (Diageo, Brown-Forman, Gallo, Mondavi, Beringer, Kendall-Jackson, and Constellation, among many others) have a powerful interest is associating the name "Monterey" with high quality while, at the same time, pursuing and benefiting from industrial bulk-wine farming practices. All of these corporations, among others, own thousands of acres of vineyards in Salinas Valley and buy yet more grapes or wine from independent growers.

Their mega-Monterey wines can indeed be pleasant. But they're not *that* good. Yes, mega-Monterey wines are superior to those from the hot San Joaquin Valley. They're clean and fruity with noteworthy crispness. They are better-quality bulk wine. That's the extent of the achievement.

However, if wineries sourcing from Monterey County can grow (or buy) grapes cheaply and yet still command a premium because of the public's perception that "Monterey" has cachet, well then, they're golden. So it's in the big corporate winery and grower interest to have "Monterey" perceived as something finer and less industrial than it really is.

To get to Monterey County's real quality threshold you have to instead focus on micro-Monterey: Santa Lucia Highlands, Carmel Valley, or perhaps another, as-yet-unproven small appellation of genuine distinction where growers strive for—and achieve—a greater extreme of quality.

Mega-Monterey

Conventionally, when Monterey County winegrowing is discussed, what is really being referred to is the Salinas Valley. But there is no Salinas Valley AVA. Anything grown there goes by the AVA name "Monterey," which is wrongly (if understandably) thought to be anything in Monterey County itself. Actually, most of political Monterey County lies outside of the Monterey AVA. Instead, the Monterey AVA is pretty much all of the Salinas Valley, while sidestepping the Carmel Valley and Chalone AVAs.

More to the point, most of the grapes grown in "Monterey" don't even get identified at all. The vast majority of Monterey County's 40,367 acres of vines is found on its eighty-five-mile-long valley floor, the great majority of which is entitled only to the Monterey AVA designation.

An estimated 80 percent of these grapes disappear into bottlings with names such as "Coastal," "Central Coast," or just "California."

Of course, some of these wines could be sold under a more specific place name such as one of Monterey County's four Salinas Valley sub-appellations: Arroyo Seco, Santa Lucia Highlands, San Lucas, and Hames Valley. Monterey County's other two AVAs, Chalone and Carmel Valley, are not in the Salinas Valley and not entitled to the "Monterey" AVA designation.

Winegrowing in Salinas Valley began with a "best of both worlds" optimism. The reference was the pennies-to-the-gallon, cheap bulk wine world of the San Joaquin Valley, which parallels Salinas Valley eighty miles to the east.

Prior to the original fine-wine boom of the 1970s, it was the hot San Joaquin Valley that served as the supplier of choice for bulk wine producers and, for that matter, many smaller wineries looking to save a few pennies. The machine in the mind fiddled endlessly with grape hybrids that could retain acidity in the baking heat of the San Joaquin. There was little impulse—or reason—to pull up stakes and plant vines where good levels of acidity could be achieved effortlessly, i.e., a cool climate.

Salinas Valley is the cool-climate version of the hot San Joaquin Valley. Of course, this isn't how its growers would like to be seen, but it's so. In both places the machine in the mind is supreme. In both places, huge vineyard tracts owned by absentee corporations grow grapes on contract for absentee wineries located elsewhere.

Salinas Valley emerged as a cool-climate rival to the San Joaquin Valley. No longer would the grapes from California's hot interior valleys suffice. Still, size was necessary. California's traditional "North Coast" districts—Napa and Sonoma—had neither the scale nor the psychology of absolute control previously supplied by the San Joaquin Valley. If only they could get that valley cooler! No way. And there was no way that the UC Davis grape hybrids so painstakingly engineered to overcome this deficiency would be accepted by Americans newly entranced by European-pedigree grapes such as Chardonnay, Cabernet Sauvignon, and Riesling.

So, in the 1970s, the sandy, alluvial soil of Salinas Valley saw vineyard building on a vast scale. It was as if Egyptian pharaohs took to wine. Instead of life in the hereafter, the machine in the mind promised modern-day corporate pharaohs something preferable: absolute control in the here and now. No other cool-climate area could even pretend to offer grapes grown with engineering precision on such a scale.

The monumental scale was irresistible. For example, the Prudential Insurance Company of New Jersey planted a single contiguous vineyard eleven miles long and five miles wide, probably the largest single vineyard in the world. The vineyard still is there; Prudential is gone. Revealingly, the San Bernabe Vineyard south of King City was purchased in 1988 by Delicato Vineyards, a large jug wine producer based in the San Joaquin Valley. It currently has 7,636 acres of vines. In 2003 Delicato applied to the BATF for its own San Bernabe AVA. No ruling was made at this writing.

Prudential's vineyard was just one, admittedly outsize, example. But it had rivals, the most prominent being The Monterey Vineyard. In 1973, a consortium of partnerships founded The Monterey Vineyard, planting 9,600 acres of vines. A 600,000-case winery was built. By 1977 most of the partnerships dissolved, the vineyards having been sold off or abandoned to other crops. The winery was sold to the Coca-Cola Company of Atlanta, which had its own grandiose plan: to beat Gallo at its own game.

Here again, the rivalry (and similarity) of Monterey County and the San Joaquin Valley surfaces. But Coca-Cola couldn't, or wouldn't, cut it. The wines were good, but the profits—and the control—weren't anywhere near as exhilarating as with soda pop. They sold The Monterey Vineyard in 1984 to yet another corporate pharaoh, Joseph E. Seagram & Sons.

In buying into the illusion of absolute control, various corporate owners stumbled into a quagmire of growing the wrong grapes in the wrong places. The San Martin Winery, for example, once had contracts to 13,000 acres of vines. After the winery was sold in the late 1970s, many of the grapes were without a buyer. The vines were uprooted and the land returned traditional Monterey crops such as broccoli, strawberries, and asparagus.

The most famous blunder involved Cabernet Sauvignon. Vineyards north of King City, for example, mostly were too cool for Cabernet. But in the 1970s, Cabernet (and to a lesser extent, Zinfandel) was the grape of choice. Corporate chieftains in Rahway, New Jersey, or some such place looked at the trend reports. They decreed that they, too, must plant Cabernet in their newly acquired Salinas Valley vineyard land. And so in it went. What came out were harrowing taste experiences: wines of near-corrosive acidity and a penetrating smell of asparagus or bell pepper. These became infamous as the Monterey County "veggies."

Over the years, growers insisted that the problem was not climate, but simply the timing of the irrigation. Yet to this day, even though the veggies have been modulated somewhat, no one would point to much of the Salinas Valley as a source for distinctive Cabernet Sauvignon or Zinfandel. It's too cool, at least in the northern half, although the southernmost reaches such as San Lucas and Hames Valley AVAs have some prospects.

Still, the demand for Cabernet is such that, in 2002, there was 46 percent more Cabernet planted in Monterey than there was ten years earlier—5,525 acres to be precise. Much of the pre-1990 Cabernet vines were either grafted over or uprooted. The new plantings are now found south of King City, where it is warmer, and a scant few hundred acres in the Carmel Valley AVA, also a more Cabernet-conducive site.

Like the San Joaquin Valley, the Salinas Valley is arid, with just eight to eleven inches of rainfall annually. But this is no problem. If anything, it is an opportunity. Flowing underneath is a gargantuan aquifer fed by what is believed to be the largest underground river in North America. Best of all, the soil is sandy—ideal for irrigation. The quick-draining alluvial sands allow a grower to know to the last droplet how much water is absorbed and how much more is needed.

The land is eye-achingly flat. Machines rumble across vineyards that stretch for thousands of acres in a single piece. Vines are pruned by an odd amalgam of men attached to machines: Mexican laborers six rows abreast scissoring off canes using powered secateurs, each of which dangle from a hydraulic hose attached to a twin-armed tractor straddling the rows. During harvest, huge grape-picking combines snuffle across the flats, working day and night.

As is common in so many parts of western California, the climate is marine-influenced—to an extreme. And this influence extends surprisingly far inland. This is because the Salinas Valley, nestled between the Santa Lucia Range on the west and Diablo and Gavilan ranges on the east, is virtually a chute for cold, wind-driven ocean air from Monterey Bay at the northern end of the valley. The ocean air has nowhere else to go but inland. During the summer, this inevitably results in afternoon fogs that do not dissipate until the next morning, driven off by intense sunshine. This is why the Salinas Valley also grows tens of thousands of acres of strawberries, artichokes, garlic, and broccoli, among other produce aisle items. The evening and morning coolness treats these crops tenderly.

Much of the Salinas Valley—at least half of it, anyway—is subject to what the locals call "howlers" and what the rest of us call pretty impressive winds. If a land mass can have small craft warnings, it would be the northern end of the Salinas Valley. In the early years of grape-growing, vineyards were sometimes stripped of their leaves by these "howlers." Eventually, growers started planting wind breaks and trellising the vines differently.

As you might expect, the valley also grows warmer the farther from Monterey Bay you get. King City, which at fifty miles from the bay is the midpoint of the valley, is considered the demarcation point of cooler to warmer. That said, even there the climate still is affected by the ocean influence. It is only when you're within hailing distance of Paso Robles does the climate go from cool maritime to warm continental—with a vengeance.

The difference in summer temperatures between Salinas, only twelve miles from the bay, and Paso Robles at the opposite end of the Salinas Valley 100 miles away, reveals the phenomenal effects of ocean exposure. In August, for example, the average *maximum* temperature in Salinas is just 71 degrees. In Paso Robles it's 93 degrees. Little wonder that Paso Robles has its own AVA. Elevation plays a minor role. The valley floor gradually increases in elevation as it goes south (really, southeast). The city of Salinas is just seventy-four feet above sea level; Paso Robles is at 740 feet.

As for the character of wines grown in the vast tracts of flat Salinas Valley vineyards, you can look at it in two ways. One perspective is that, for industrial winegrowing, the quality of the wines is impressively high. Indeed, seemingly all of the white wines emerging from Salinas Valley vineyards are fruity, clean tasting, and appetizingly tart. The red wines are less consistently successful, but even here, the same clean, fruity attributes apply. San Joaquin Valley can't do anywhere near as well.

A different perspective finds only a limited quantity of characterful wines. Once past pleasant, sometimes even dramatic fruitiness, and good acidity, one would be hard-pressed to think of many Salinas Valley wines that linger in the mind as wines of character. Those that do, such as Santa Lucia Highlands, are not Salinas Valley wines. They rightfully have their own appellations. It's fair to say that if the label reads "Monterey," the wine is a Salinas Valley issue.

Arroyo Seco AVA

Lying between Soledad and King City on the Salinas Valley floor is the Arroyo Seco AVA, which straddles both the east and west sides of Highway 101. With 8,500 acres of vines it is by far the largest AVA apart from that of "Monterey" itself. Numerous wineries around the state use Arroyo Seco grapes, although the name only occasionally is invoked, either because the grapes are blended with others from elsewhere or because producers prefer the better-known designations of Monterey or Central Coast.

Whether Arroyo Seco really is much different, if at all, from other sections of the Salinas Valley is open to question. Its growers point to the softball-size rocks embedded in the soil called "Greenfield potatoes," a legacy of an ancient riverbed.

Certainly, the Arroyo Seco wines deliver undeniable flavor intensity, but so do other sections of the Salinas Valley. One thing is certain: Arroyo Seco is one of Salinas Valley's choicer spots.

The pioneers of Arroyo Seco are Mirassou and Wente wineries, both of which planted vineyards in this flat, quintessentially Salinas Valley area in the early 1960s. Both still retain sizable vineyards. Wente, in particular, helped establish some identity for Arroyo Seco with a series of well-received late-harvest Rieslings, all of which cited Arroyo Seco on the label as the vineyard source. These wines, perhaps more than any other, brought Arroyo Seco to its original public attention.

Subsequently, both Ventana and Jekel carried the banner. Ventana, in particular, has carried it farthest, in large part because it sells grapes from its 400-acre vineyard to numerous wineries, some of which cite "Ventana Vineyard" (but not necessarily Arroyo Seco) on their labels.

Carmel Valley AVA

The Carmel Valley AVA was created largely due to the efforts of William Durney of the eponymous winery, who established his vineyard in 1968. He died in 1989 and his winery was sold in 1994 and renamed Heller Estate.

Carmel Valley has little if anything to do with Monterey County as it is commonly envisioned, as it's utterly removed from the flatland of Salinas Valley. Located in the hills southeast of coastal Carmel, its higher elevation sees less fog than either the coast or the Salinas Valley, resulting in a warmer microclimate and more sunshine. Also, it is significantly more rainy, with between sixteen and twenty-two inches of rain annually, compared to the Salinas Valley's eight to eleven inches of rain.

Although Carmel Valley proponents point to a warmer climate, "warm" is relative. Compared to Salinas Valley, it's warm. But too often, Cabernets from Carmel Valley can display herbaceous or vegetal flavors. This suggests that, in certain spots, Carmel Valley isn't all that warm. Still, the zone has prospects, which will probably become more apparent with appropriate viticultural techniques.

Bernardus winery is now the area's major drumbeater. It's still small: The entire AVA has fewer than 300 acres of vines, most of them Bordeaux-type varieties. Producers there still seem to be wrestling with extracting the particular qualities of this site. Bordeaux-type red wine blends are more distinctive than the whites. More time is needed, but something original is clearly present.

Chalone AVA

The original petition for AVA status for this area high in the hills of the Gavilan Range above Soledad had it as "The Pinnacles," after the nearby Pinnacles National Monument. But the Paul Masson winery owned a vineyard on the valley floor called Pinnacles. In the early 1980s, Seagram owned Paul Masson, and it strenuously objected to the use of the name. (Seagram subsequently sold Paul Masson. Today, the 1,200-acre Pinnacles vineyard is owned by wine giant Constellation Brands, which acquired it as part of its purchase of Napa Valley's Franciscan Winery in 1987.)

A certain poetic justice is found in the AVA having the same name as the sole winery in the AVA. (Technically, the Chalone name comes from two peaks, the North Chalone Peak and South Chalone Peak, which themselves are named after a local Indian tribe.) After all, if Chalone Vineyards didn't exist, there wouldn't be any need for an AVA at all. The Chalone AVA is one of the relative few that cross county lines. Most of it is in Monterey County; a portion crosses the ridgeline of the San Benito Mountains into San Benito County.

The distinction of this AVA, expressed through the extraordinary wines of Chalone Vineyards, lies in its elevation (a mean of 1,650 feet above sea level) and its soil (heavy deposits of limestone). Few AVAs anywhere occupy a more distinctive—or removed—location than the Chalone AVA. To see just how different it is, one need only compare a Chalone Vineyards Chardonnay with any good Chardonnay from the Arroyo Seco AVA. The two AVAs are fewer than six miles apart. Yet the wines are indisputably foreign to each other due to extreme differences in elevation and soil.

Santa Lucia Highlands AVA

Santa Lucia Highlands is the star of the Monterey County wine show. It demonstrates, if nothing else, the worth of genuine wine appellations.

Santa Lucia Highlands is part of the Salinas Valley, lying north and west of Arroyo Seco. It's subject to the same strong, cool winds as other parts of the northern Salinas Valley. And for generations, it has grown the same row crops, such as head lettuce. Many of the farmers in Santa Lucia Highlands, as elsewhere in Salinas Valley, are of Italian descent with names like Pisoni and Franscioni. (This is John Steinbeck country, after all.)

Just what sets Santa Lucia Highlands apart is at once obvious and yet still a bit mysterious. The obvious part is location. The Highlands are alluvial fan terraces that rub right up against the Sierra de Salinas mountain range. (Carmel Valley lies on the other side of the Sierra de Salinas.)

Santa Lucia Highlands is not especially high in elevation itself, with many of the vineyards at about 400 to 600 feet above sea level, with some vineyards as high as 1,200 feet in elevation. The terraces are nearly all facing southeast, which is ideal for catching the morning sun. Soils are a farmer's dream: rich, black dirt with gravel underneath for good drainage. Gravelly loam is a good general descriptor.

Climatically, there really isn't much difference between Santa Lucia Highlands and the parallel stretch of the Salinas Valley floor below it between

Gonzales and Soledad. They both get the afternoon breezes and fog. They both receive intense sunshine in the morning and early afternoon.

Yet there's no disputing that *something* is different about Santa Lucia Highlands. The wines themselves tell us that. They are richer, more intense, and more characterful than what's grown along the same length on the Salinas Valley floor. Chardonnays are luscious and intensely fruity yet underlain with a mineral/gravel note. Pinot Noirs are inky-dark, massively fruity yet improbably well balanced. More than with the Chardonnay, Santa Lucia Highlands creates a singular Pinot Noir like no other grown anywhere. It may not be everyone's idea of Pinot Noir—finesse is not its strong suit—but it has originality, with massive black cherry and blackberry flavors. And despite its Syrah-like appearance, it's definitely Pinot Noir in taste.

Surely soil is part of the reason for such distinction—allied, of course to the cool climate and intense sunshine. Keep in mind that the growing season in Salinas Valley in general is unusually long. Those "howlers" shut down the grapevines in the afternoons, the vines protecting themselves from moisture loss from transpiration by closing their stomata, the minute breathing pores of the leaves. So the vines only "grow" during the morning and early afternoon. As a result, fruit maturation (the fruit doesn't mature if the plant isn't supplying itself with water and nutrients) takes longer than is common elsewhere. Happily, the climate is so moderate that the growing season extends well into November.

Not to be ignored is the outsize fine-wine ambition of several of Santa Lucia Highland's best growers. (The appellation has few resident wineries headquartered there.) Santa Lucia Highlands has Monterey County's most ambitious grape growers, in large part thanks to the (profitable) examples of Pisoni Vineyard and Robert Talbott Vineyard's Sleepy Hollow Vineyard.

Both create exceptional wines (Pisoni specializes in Pinot Noir; Sleepy Hollow grows both grapes, but it excels with Chardonnay). Both command exceptional prices from wineries fortunate enough to be able to buy their grapes. Other growers have taken note and followed their lucrative examples.

For example, Napa Valley's Caymus Vineyard established its Mer et Soleil Vineyard in Santa Lucia Highlands. Gallo has invested as well, as have Mondavi and Jekel.

Over time, Santa Lucia Highlands may well subdivide into northern and southern sections, with the cooler northern part specializing in Pinot Noir and Chardonnay and the warmer southern end (abutting Arroyo Seco) pursuing Chardonnay as well as red varieties such as Merlot and Syrah. Much remains to be explored, if only because the multiple terraces that make up this thirty-mile-long-by-four-mile wide appellation create numerous microclimates of exposure and soil. At present, Chardonnay comprises roughly half of Santa Lucia Highlands' 2,300 vineyard acres.

San Lucas AVA and Hames Valley AVA

Located in the southern end of the Salinas Valley, close to where the Monterey County border meets San Luis Obispo County, San Lucas and Hames Valley AVAs are the warmest zones in the Salinas Valley. Hames Valley is the southernmost AVA in Monterey County, skirting the San Luis Obispo County border. San Lucas is just north of Hames Valley. The Monterey Vineyards' Paris Valley Ranch (1,100 acres of vines) is located in the San Lucas AVA, as is Lockwood Vineyard's 1,850-acre vineyard.

Historically, this was cattle-grazing country until vines first began being planted in the 1970s. Today both areas are dedicated to modest, inexpensive bottlings from more than 8,000 acres of vines of numerous varieties, both red and white. So far, neither AVA has distinguished itself with fine wines.

Monterey County Producers Worth Seeking Out (And Some Not)

Bernardus Vineyards and Winery—The leading producer in the Carmel Valley AVA, Bernardus—owned by Dutch-born Bernardus "Ben" Pon—is slowly evolving into creating wines of greater polish and refinement. Not everything under the Bernardus label comes from Carmel Valley. The Sauvignon Blanc, an intensely fruity, bright-acid bottling, is sourced mostly from Arroyo Seco in the Salinas Valley. The ripe, textbook Chardonnay is designated "Monterey County" and is blended from as many as seven different vineyards, including Sleepy Hollow in Santa Lucia Highlands and Ventana in Arroyo Seco.

Really, the Bernardus wine that sets the estate apart is their Bordeaux blend called Marinus. Designated Carmel Valley AVA, it comes from their thirty-six-acre Marinus vineyard, planted in 1990, mostly to Cabernet Sauvignon (twenty-five acres) and Merlot (nine acres), with an acre each of Cabernet Franc and Petit Verdot. It's Marinus that matters: beautifully delineated, supple, and well balanced with an herbal component that, in lesser years, can turn a bit too vegetal. It resembles, in the best sense, classic Bordeaux from the 1960s, 1970s, and early 1980s.

Chalone Vineyard—Few vineyard locations are more remote than Chalone's. To get to it you drive high in the brown, parched hills above Soledad, seemingly to no apparent end and certainly to nothing that could possibly be green. Finally, you veer onto a private road, eventually to come upon a luscious swale of verdant vineyard. One is reminded that eyes, too, can thirst—for green-ness. The equally remote vineyards of Calera, which are also in the San Benito Range, evoke a similar response. But Chalone's is the more dramatic: The surrounding landscape is more brutally bare rock and lizard-dry.

That someone, a Frenchman, could have first found Chalone's remote location and established a vineyard there at the turn of the century continues to leave me in awe. He must have been a Burgundian, crazed by the heat and urged on ever higher into the mountains, propelled by an atavistic French urge for limestone. That's my explanation, anyway.

Today, Chalone has 174 acres of vineyard, 110 of them planted to Chardonnay, the balance mostly to Pinot Noir and a little Pinot Blanc and Chenin Blanc.

Whatever the truth, the result today is a series of exceptional—but by no means consistent—Chardonnays and, to a lesser degree, Pinot Noirs. At their best, Chalone Chardonnays are magnificently dense with a powerful flavor of the soil: The limestone speaks. At their worst, they can have off flavors or excessive oxidation through winemaking mismanagement. The Pinot Noir also has this wonderful savor of the site, but too often lacks delicacy. After all, the site sees a lot of sun and warmth, located as it is high above the fogs of the Salinas Valley floor.

The best Chardonnay is designated Reserve, but it is reserved in every sense, namely, only for the shareholders of Chalone Inc., the publicly held company that owns Chalone Vineyards, along with Carmenet, Acacia, and

Edna Valley Vineyards wineries. Still, the regular, publicly available Chardonnay—designated as the Estate Chardonnay—is more than admirable. It is always worth seeking out. If there's a drawback, it's that the wines can be a bit too oaky for some tastes. The Pinot Noir is always interesting, but too often a bit raisiny in taste, thanks to the warmth. Nevertheless, it cannot—and should not—be ignored.

Château Julien Wine Estate—An estate seemingly still in search of itself. The estate vineyard is located in Carmel Valley AVA, which creates the ho-hum Private Reserve and Estate Vineyard bottlings of Chardonnay, Cabernet Sauvignon, and Merlot. Pleasant wines, but no more than that.

Estancia—Originally created by Agustin Huneeus, Sr., the former co-owner of Franciscan Vineyards, as a vehicle for Franciscan's Alexander Valley grapes, Estancia has mushroomed in size and reach. Because it offered unusually good value, the Estancia label quickly caught on. Huneeus then purchased the 1,200-acre Pinnacles ranch in the Salinas Valley as the primary source for the burgeoning Estancia brand. It, too, was a success, especially the ripe, fruity Chardonnay.

Now owned by Constellation Brands (which bought Franciscan), Estancia also developed 700 acres of vines in Paso Robles (Paso East), to further supply the popular brand. The Monterey-sourced Chardonnay from the Pinnacles vineyard is good value; the Pinnacles-sourced Pinot Noir is unimpressive.

Hahn Estates/Smith & Hook—Owned by the Hahn family, Smith & Hook was the prime mover in creating the Santa Lucia Highlands AVA, where the original 500-acre Smith horse ranch was located near the southern end of the appellation near Arroyo Seco. The Hahns also own more vineyards in Salinas Valley, for a total of 1,400 acres of vines. The Hahn Estates label runs the gamut from everyday wines with a "Monterey" designation to more ambitious offerings from Santa Lucia Highlands AVA. Quality is attractive, but not yet stellar. To watch.

Heller Estate—The former Durney Vineyard, which pioneered and helped create the Carmel Valley AVA, was purchased in 1994 by a group of European investors. The 120-acre estate vineyard in Carmel Valley is certified organic. Wines are variable, with the Chardonnay being the best bet.

The Hess Collection Winery—Napa Valley-based Donald Hess owns a 350-acre vineyard in the Salinas Valley that is the source of much of the lesser-priced Hess Select line. Like so much else from Salinas Valley, the wines are fruity and simple with little pretense to offering anything more.

J. Lohr—Jerry Lohr was one of the earliest proselytizers of the Arroyo Seco AVA, planting vineyards near Greenfield in the early 1970s. He now owns 904 acres of vines in Arroyo Seco, 810 of which are Chardonnay. Most of these grapes go into the J. Lohr Estate brand, the best-known wine of which has the brand name Riverstone for the popular Arroyo Seco-sourced Chardonnay. (The label reads "California" though.) Lohr's equally well-known Seven Oaks Cabernet—again, a proprietary name—comes from Lohr's 1,000-acre estate in Paso Robles (Paso East). The Riverstone Chardonnay is typical Salinas Valley issue: fruity, simple, and pleasant.

Jekel Vineyards—Bill Jekel and his identical twin brother, Gus, were early big believers in the promise of Arroyo Seco as a place apart and planted their vineyard in the 1970s. The winery came later, in 1978. The wines, however, were always less convincing than Jekel's oratory. Although the Riesling that emerged back then was noteworthy, the reds were harrowing. Arroyo Seco is simply too cool for Cabernet and the notorious Monterey County "veggies" tarnished the winery's image. The brothers eventually sold the winery and vineyards, only to buy it back later and then, finally, sell it to Brown-Forman, which also owns Fetzer, Korbel, and Sonoma-Cutrer wineries, among others. Best bets are Chardonnay and Riesling.

Joullian Vineyards—A Carmel Valley AVA winery that so far has not issued any red wines that persuade one to think that Carmel Valley is a place apart.

Lockwood Vineyard—One of the better big-scale Salinas Valley wineries, Lockwood (like J. Lohr) is dedicated to creating wines from grapes they grow themselves. Lockwood's wines come from a 1,850-acre vineyard in the San Lucas AVA at the southern end of the Salinas Valley. In warmer vintages Lockwood's Cabernets are fully ripe and pleasing; cooler vintages see the flavors shading a bit toward the herbaceous. Overall, a good value brand. Other labels in Lockwood's portfolio include Shale Ridge, Lawson Ranch, and Hidden Mesa.

Mer Soleil Winery—Planted in the northern end of the Santa Lucia Highlands in 1988, the 320-acre Mer Soleil (Sea & Sun) vineyard is the creation of Charlie Wagner, owner of Caymus Vineyards in Napa Valley. The first Chardonnay appeared in 1993 and since then, Mer Soleil Chardonnays have received rapturous reviews for their opulence and intensity. Indeed, the Mer Soleil Chardonnay is the over-the-top essence of Monterey County Chardonnay. For this palate, it's too much of a good thing: too fruity, too intense, and too oaky.

Michaud Vineyard—The only other vineyard in the Chalone AVA, owner-winemaker Michael Michaud worked for Chalone Vineyard for nineteen years, sixteen of them as winemaker and general manager. (He left Chalone in 1997, the same year as his inaugural vintage with his own label.)

Michaud purchased land near Chalone's vineyard and, in 1986, planted thirteen acres of Chardonnay from Chalone's 1946 planting. Since then, Michaud's holding expanded to 262 vineyard acres. Michaud sells these grapes—Chardonnay and Pinot Noir—to others, as well as producing about 7,000 cases in a custom-crush arrangement with Testarossa Winery.

As with Chalone Vineyard, the Chardonnay is the standout wine, made (not surprisingly) in the full-throttle Burgundian style that Michaud practiced when he was winemaker there. This is a winery to watch very closely.

Mirassou Vineyards—One of the pioneers (along with Wente) in Monterey County, planting its first vineyards in 1961 and 1962. Today, this sixth-generation California winegrowing family owns 1,100 acres in the Arroyo Seco AVA, close to Soledad. Mirassou's array of wines, including sparkling wines, are always "correct": clean, well-made, but without much character. In an attempt to go up-market, the winery has issued a variety of special labels. But so far, none have stood out as really distinctive. Chardonnay is the best bet.

In September 2002, the Mirassou brand (although not their vineyards) was purchased by Gallo. The Mirassou family will continue to run the winery, according to early reports.

The Monterey Vineyard—After an almost soap opera history, The Monterey Vineyard settled into mediocrity after its purchase by Seagram in 1984. (Seagram, in turn, was bought by international drinks giant, Diageo, in December 2000.) In 1988, the 1,100-acre Paris Valley ranch south of King City was purchased, which now is the major—but not the only—source for The Monterey Vineyard wines. The usual array of commercial wines is offered. Almost without exception they are dull.

Morgan Winery—One of the drum-beaters for the Santa Lucia Highlands, where owner-winemaker Dan Lee owns sixty-five acres (and buys grapes from neighboring vineyards). Morgan makes a wide array of wines of varying quality. But there's no question that Morgan's best bottlings are his single-vineyard designated Pinot Noirs from Santa Lucia Highlands, such as Rosella's Vineyard (owned by Gary Franscioni), Garys' Vineyard (co-owned by Gary Franscioni and Gary Pisoni), and Morgan's own densely planted Double-L Vineyard. All three are within a few miles of each other.

A Santa Lucia Highlands Pinot Gris is a bit too acidic for this palate. Chardonnay, however, is right on target, with roughly 80 percent of the "Monterey"-designated wine actually sourced from Santa Lucia Highlands. It's Morgan's cash cow and a handsome creature it is too: lush, ripe, and consistently rewarding.

But look first for the single-vineyard Pinot Noirs, which are a kind of annual report on the work-in-progress state of Pinot Noir grape-growing and winemaking in Santa Lucia Highlands.

Paraiso Vineyards—A sizable Santa Lucia Highlands vineyard (211 acres) Paraiso is perhaps the southernmost vineyard in the Santa Lucia Highlands appellation. Grapes are purchased by various wineries, and Paraiso issues promising Chardonnay, Pinot Noir, Syrah, and Riesling. A winery to watch.

Pisoni Vineyards and Winery—Perhaps the most famous vineyard name in Monterey County. Gary Pisoni is the son of traditional Salinas Valley farmers (Ed and Jane) who grew—and still grow—the usual row crops of the region. But somehow, their son Gary, a wild spirit if ever California nurtured one, became entranced with wine—Pinot Noir in particular. Gary Pisoni forayed to Burgundy, became enthralled like so many others before him, and decided that the family farm in the northern end of the Santa Lucia Highlands was ideal.

Here, the story gets a little murky. Supposedly, Pisoni returned to California with a "suitcase clone" of cuttings from Burgundy's fabled La Tâche vineyard, smuggled in his underwear. Yet others say that he really got his material from a neighbor who got it from the Domaine de la Romanée-Conti (DRC), the owner of La Tâche, and other vineyards. DRC, for its part, has asked Pisoni, on pain of lawsuit, to stop invoking the DRC name. Today, Pisoni has forty acres of Pinot Noir planted in 1988 to what is now called the

"Pisoni clone," whatever that may be.

All this makes for entertaining public relations. The reality is that, however important clones are with Pinot Noir (and they are), no one would ever confuse a Pisoni Pinot Noir with a La Tâche, anymore than you might confuse a sumo wrestler with a ballet dancer.

Pisoni, for his part, is uncommonly dedicated. Unlike so many other Salinas Valley growers, Gary Pisoni is obsessive about low yields. His vineyard management is meticulous, bordering on fanatical. He has the courage to sell his grapes for some of California's highest prices, often selling them not by the ton, but by the acre. Buyers can then prune their own vines for even lower yields, if they like—which they often do.

The result has been a string of Pisoni-designated Pinot Noirs from producers such as Ojai, Siduri, Arcadian, Testarossa, Miner, and others. Gary Pisoni has his own small label as well, called Pisoni Estate. But most of his grapes go to others. Nearly all have excited comment, as the wines are massively rich and opulent. See also *Roar*.

Roar—It is impossible to separate Pisoni Vineyard from Roar winery for the simple reason that Gary Franscioni (owner of Roar) and Gary Pisoni are themselves inseparable. Both are the sons of traditional Italian-American farmers in Santa Lucia Highlands, both went to grade school together in Gonzales, and then both went to college at Cal Poly in San Luis Obispo.

When Gary Pisoni returned from Burgundy fired with the Pinot Noir ambition in the late 1980s, his childhood (and adult) buddy Gary Franscioni was amused but interested. Pisoni is a visionary madman type; Franscioni is more level-headed. They understand each other.

Finally, in 1995 Franscioni realized that a) his pal may be "nuts," but he's making a lot of money from his new cash crop, and b) he loved the taste of Pisoni's Pinot Noir. So Franscioni took part of his family's 200 acres in Santa Lucia Highlands and created two vineyards.

First was a joint venture with his friend Pisoni called Garys' Vineyard, a fifty-acre Pinot Noir plot planted entirely to the so-called Pisoni clone. Then, in 1996, Franscioni planted another fifty-acre Pinot Noir vineyard called Rosella's Vineyard, after his wife. It's planted entirely to the Dijon clone 777. These grapes are sold to several different wineries, including neighbors such as Morgan, among others.

Starting in 2001, Gary Franscioni created his own label, called Roar after the "howlers" that come roaring in every afternoon from Monterey Bay sixteen miles away. Roar wines are made by Adam and Dianna Lee of Siduri winery, who also buy grapes from Pisono and Franscioni for their own wines.

Roar issues separate Garys' Vineyard, Rosella's Vineyard, and Pisoni Vineyard bottlings, as well as a more generic Santa Lucia Highlands Pinot Noir. All are intense, lush, massive wines typical of the zone. Clearly, this is a label to watch closely.

Robert Talbott Vineyards—Perhaps more than any other Monterey County winery, Robert Talbott Vineyards has gone from strength to strength thanks to astute vineyard developments. The original Talbott vineyard is their Diamond T Vineyard in Carmel Valley AVA, which is twenty-four acres of Chardonnay planted in 1982 at a 1,200-foot elevation eight miles from Carmel Bay.

Then, in 1989, the family bought a 125-acre ranch in Santa Lucia Highlands, where they constructed a winery and installed their 110-acre River Road Vineyard. In 1994, they purchased the 450-acre Sleepy Hollow Vineyard in Santa Lucia Highlands, from which they had previously purchased grapes. Subsequently, the Talbott family bought the 224-acre Del Mar Vineyard in Arroyo Seco, which is devoted exclusively to Chardonnay.

Clearly, with a total of 808 vineyard acres, almost three-quarters of which are in Santa Lucia Highlands, the Talbotts are major grape growers. They also own genuinely significant vineyards, never mind the scale. This explains why Talbott wines, especially the Chardonnays, have steadily improved every vintage. And the odds are good that they'll keep improving, as their ambition is substantial and focused. Various cuvées are offered, named after the Talbott children. The Pinot Noirs are less successful than the Chardonnays, but they will likely become finer in short order. Talbott is one of Monterey County's best producers, using their scale to excel, rather than merely to profit.

Siduri—Although based in a warehouse winery in Santa Rosa in Sonoma County, thirtysomething owners/winemakers Adam and Dianna Lee are intimately tied to Santa Lucia Highlands by virtue of buying grapes from Pisoni Vineyard. Their ties only grew with their custom production of Roar, the brand created by Gary Franscioni.

Siduri wines are always deeply colored (from cold-soak macerations), silky, and beautifully made in a modern, ebulliently fruity style. They do not own any vineyards themselves, but by virtue of tremendously hard work, passion, and no little charm, they have managed to secure Pinot Noir grapes from some of California's most sought after vineyards, as well as grapes from Oregon.

Testarossa—An ambitious producer that buys Pinot Noir and Chardonnay grapes from all the right vineyards in Santa Lucia Highlands: Pisoni, Garys', Sleepy Hollow, and the Michaud Vineyard adjacent to Chalone Vineyards in the Chalone AVA. Multiple single-vineyard Chardonnays and Pinot Noirs are offered, all of them striking in their respective individuality. Drinking Testarossa wines is like taking a short course in Santa Lucia Highlands terroir.

Ventana Vineyards/Meador Estate—No one has proclaimed the glories of Monterey County in general and the Arroyo Seco AVA in particular more than Ventana owner Doug Meador. Perhaps more than any other owner-winemaker in California, Meador has personally tinkered with all sorts of innovative grape-growing techniques in pursuit of the Holy Grail of high yields *and* high quality.

His theories are well founded, but you can't beat terroir in the end. And that end has Ventana issuing yet more Salinas Valley wines with admirable fruitiness, crisp acidity, and not much in the way of profundity. After a series of viticultural and financial exigencies since the winery's founding in the 1980s, Ventana's wines have become consistent. Best bets are the Gewürztraminer and Riesling, along with a pleasant Chardonnay.

Wente Brothers—With 700 acres in Arroyo Seco planted in the early 1960s, Wente has been a linchpin winery for Monterey County grapes. As mentioned previously, it was Wente's late-harvest or spätlese Rieslings from the late 1960s and early 1970s that first drew huzzahs for the potential of Monterey County in general and Arroyo Seco in particular.

Since those dazzling debut wines, Wente had faltered for a while and, happily, is now on the comeback trail thanks to their Vineyard Reserve series. Look for an excellent Chardonnay designated Riva Ranch, as well as a Riva Ranch late-harvest Riesling. A Pinot Noir, designated Reliz Creek (also in Arroyo Seco), is less convincing, but has promise. Interestingly, all of these Vineyard Reserve bottlings are identified as "Monterey" rather than Arroyo Seco.

SAN BENITO COUNTY

I f ever California had a "work in progress" wine region it's San Benito County. It's a good bet that even Californians couldn't find it on a map. The easiest way is to think of it as due east of Monterey County, over the mountains.

Much of San Benito County occupies a parallel if much narrower and more broken-up set of valleys nestled between the Gavilan Range and the Diablo Range to the east. Unlike the easily cultivated Salinas Valley, San Benito County is hilly or mountainous.

Hollister lies at the northern end of the county (where Calera Wine Company is located). Paicines is at roughly the midpoint (where Almaden had its vineyards). And Chalone is toward the southern end of the county, high up in the mountains in the Gavilan Range on the west side of the county.

For decades, San Benito County was the fiefdom of Almaden, which owned 3,500 acres of vines extending from Hollister to Paicines. Almaden single-handedly created both the Paicines and Cienega Valley AVAs.

Although at one time Almaden was a true California powerhouse, it lost its way decades ago. (It was Almaden, advised by consultant Frank Schoonmaker back in the 1950s, that pioneered varietal labeling.)

In 1987 Almaden was sold to Heublein, which decided that the brand was good for little more than cheap bulk wine. For that, you can't beat Central Valley, which is precisely where Heublein decamped, virtually abandoning its vineyards in San Benito County.

Like the collapse of the old Soviet Union, with the departure of monolithic Almaden, viticultural San Benito slowly reconfigured itself into smaller states.

For example, you've got the ambitious Pietra Santa winery near Hollister, which arose in 1989 from a 455-acre former Almaden parcel purchased by Joseph Gemelli. (His brother, Ken, bought another parcel nearby and is setting up his own winery.)

Then you have DeRose Vineyards, just down the road from Pietra Santa. The DeRose and Cedolinio families bought old Almaden acreage as well as Almaden's vast underground wine cellar, renowned in its day as the world's largest underground wine storage facility, covering some four acres. DeRose has about 100 acres of vines, forty acres of which date to 1900 or earlier, which had been literally abandoned decades earlier by Almaden. Most notable are some 115-year-old Negrette vines, once known as Pinot St. George.

In 1991, New York investor John Dyson (who also owns Willams Selyem winery in Sonoma County) purchased a 640-acre chunk of Almaden's old vineyard holding in Paicines, which he redeveloped into a 550-acre vineyard called Vista Verde. Although mostly devoted to Chardonnay, Cabernet Sauvignon, and Merlot, the vineyard also has smaller plantings of such varieties as Pinot Noir, Arneis, Tocai Friulano, and Viognier.

Most of the grapes are sold to corporate operations such as Beringer and Kendall-Jackson, as well as supplying Dyson's New York State winery called Millbrook. Vista Verde Pinot Noir has also appeared under the Williams Selyem label, under the Central Coast designation.

A big chunk of Almaden's vineyards, renamed Blossom Hill, was passed along like a foster child through a series of unwelcoming corporate homes. Blossom Hill now is owned by the drinks giant Diageo, which sources grapes for the brand from—you guessed it—Central Valley. The grapes from the old Blossom Hill vineyards now wind up mostly in Sterling Vineyards Vintners Collection and Coastal brands, also owned by Diageo.

Mount Harlan AVA (San Benito County)

Calera Wine Company—A "one-man-band" AVA, the sole vineyard and winery using Mount Harlan AVA, is the Calera Wine Company. Calera lies about twenty air miles from Chalone, with which it shares at least a few outward similarities. Both are located in the San Benito Range. Calera is on the eastern flank, though, in the valley near the town of Hollister, and Chalone is on the other side of the ridge, on the western flank above the Salinas Valley near Soledad.

Calera's vineyards are located several miles away from the winery itself, high in the hills. Like Chalone's, it is a thrilling journey, the remoteness of the site a testament to the tenacity and risk-taking of its originator, in this case the thoroughly late twentieth-century American owner of Calera, Josh Jensen. But he, too, had something in common with the Frenchman who earlier founded the Chalone vineyard: Both were looking for limestone. Both found it.

Calera's claim to (considerable) fame is its four vineyard-designated Pinot Noirs: Jensen, Mills, Reed, and Selleck. All are named after significant people in owner Josh Jensen's life. The 13.8-acre (Stephen Fairchild) Jensen vineyard is named after his father; the 14.4-acre (John Everett) Mills vineyard is for a former winery neighbor and friend; the 4.4-acre (William Garrard) Reed vineyard is for one of Calera's original partners and investors; and the 4.8-acre (George A.) Selleck vineyard is named for a friend of Jensen's father, a California wine competition judge in the 1940s and 1950s and one of the founders of the San Francisco Wine and Food Society.

It has taken me a long time to appreciate Calera Pinot Noirs. Originally, I found them too meaty and sun-drenched. To a degree, they still strike me that way. It's a warm site for Pinot Noir. Whether because my palate has changed or Josh Jensen's winemaking and grape-growing has evolved—probably some of both—I find myself more receptive to the originality and goodness of Calera's Pinot Noirs.

The savor of site is still most apparent in the Mount Harlan-designated Chardonnay, the first vintage of which was 1986 from three-year-old vines. Also worth noting is the Viognier, which is intensely floral and spicy. Calera was a pioneer of Viognier in California and, happily, its version remains one of California's best, despite all the new competition.

Calera is one of California's most important wineries thanks to Jensen's purity of vision and the rigor of his grape-growing and winemaking. You cannot find such genuinely fine wines like these anywhere else. And isn't that what real wine greatness is all about?

Cienega Valley AVA (San Benito County)

DeRose Vineyards—Rich, strong red wines made in a slightly rustic fashion. Best bets so far are the rare, rustic yet tasty Negrette, a red variety that has almost disappeared from California. Viognier from 100-year-old vines (which must be the oldest Viognier vines in California) is strong, but pleasing. Also, good Zinfandel. Like so much else in San Benito County, DeRose Vineyards is still (understandably) a work in progress.

Flint Vineyards—A new garagiste winery created by former Calera cellarmaster Scott Flint. Early wines were sourced from Monterey and Santa Clara Counties. Newer wines are coming from San Benito County fruit. Small, but promising.

Pietra Santa Vineyards—Easily the most ambitious (in terms of winery investment) operation in San Benito County, Pietra Santa is an Italian-American's dream of the Old Country moved to California. Born in 1958, owner Joseph Gimelli is a second-generation Italian-American raised in San Jose. Having made his bundle in waste management and recycling businesses, Gimelli built a Tuscan-style winery on a former Almaden parcel of 455 acres, most of which required replanting as the old vines were overgrown and ravaged by wild boars. Today, the winery has 150 acres of vines, notably such Italian varieties as Dolcetto and Sangiovese, as well as the expected Cabernet Sauvignon, Chardonnay, and Merlot, among others.

Wine quality is quite good, but not yet soul-stirring or eye-opening. As for nearly everyone in San Benito County (except longtime Calera Wine Company) it's still early days. It would be wrong-headed (or worse) to expect wineries in this area to emerge as full-fledged contenders for the fine-wine crown overnight. Still, the potential is there, and Pietra Santa ("sacred stone") is unquestionably a winery to watch.

PASO ROBLES

To read about California wine is to hear two words endlessly repeated: Napa and Sonoma. Considering that California has more than 1,100 wineries, this mantra-like drone of "Napa/Sonoma" demonstrates, if nothing else, the power of brands.

For many folks, their mental map of California consists of San Francisco and Los Angeles, with not much in between. Paso Robles is almost equidistant between them, with San Francisco 180 miles to the north and Los Angeles 166 miles to the south—at least by the car.

The full name of the city is El Paso de Robles ("the pass of oaks"). It's an old Spanish settlement, effectively founded in 1797 with the creation of Mission San Miguel. Paso Robles has a charming town square around which many of the town's restaurants and shops are clustered.

But the biggest wine landmark is actually a freeway, Highway 101. This is because there are two wine realms in Paso Robles: One is east of Highway 101 and the other is west of 101. I call them Paso East and Paso West. The differences are temperature and soils, as well as topography.

Paso East is flattish, and its vineyards are large-scale and high-volume. Paso West is hilly, and its wineries are small. One is decidedly hot (Paso East), while the other is warm but certainly cooler (Paso West).

Soils are different, too. Paso West has an impressive amount of calcareous soil such as limestone and chalk. Paso East has some of this calcareous material, but it's mostly sandy loams and the like.

Is Highway 101 an accurate boundary? Of course not. It's just the most obvious marker. You could point instead to a more natural boundary, the Salinas River (Highway 101 parallels it), which even the Paso Robles Vintners and Growers Association acknowledges in their detailed discussion of Paso Robles soils:

"Soils west of the Salinas River [Paso West] are mainly derived from sedimentary rocks of the Miocene Age Monterey Formation. These rocks are both calcareous (carbonate-rich) and siliceous (silica-rich). . . . Soils east of the Salinas River [Paso East] are derived from variable parent materials. Soils adjacent to the major creek and river systems are mainly derived from weathered alluvial sediments. . . ."

Nobody denies that there *are* differences between these two realms. It's just that nobody wants to be on what might be perceived as the "wrong side of the tracks." Where Paso East is big-scale, commercial, and in service to bulk wines and big brands, Paso West has the panache of small artisanal wineries and is dedicated to high-polish wines selling for premium prices.

There's no mistaking the cordite whiff of a class war in the works. For example, the Paso West crowd has grown sufficiently large and formed separate associations to distinguish themselves (and their fledgling reputations) from the Paso East crowd. You have the Paso Robles Westside Grand Crew with nine members and The Far Out Wineries of Paso Robles with another dozen members. The line in the chalky soil has unmistakably been drawn.

Yet no one in Paso Robles wants to define boundaries, let alone codify them in a new AVA. No matter. It will happen anyway. As Paso Robles wines gain more attention, the wines themselves will drive the process. The existing Paso Robles AVA boundary—which throws a fraternal arm around both Paso East and Paso West—is almost useless and certainly out of date.

Yet despite the very real differences between Paso East and Paso West there's also a commonality to many Paso Robles wines, especially the reds. You can pick up just about any Paso Robles red, whether Cabernet Sauvignon, Syrah, Zinfandel, Merlot, or Pinot Noir, and you will find the following:
- Soft, sometimes seemingly nonexistent, tannins
- Intense, deep color verging on the opaque
- An unmistakable scent and taste of dark chocolate
- A soft lushness with a velvety "mouth feel"
- Above all, a rich, opulent, voluptuous fruitiness, often with a whiff of violets

Reading such a list of attributes, any reasonable person will ask: What's not to like? Good point. It's amazing, really, that Paso Robles reds have not seen more acclaim, as these are the very qualities that most wine drinkers clamor for.

The white wines are less distinctive and impressive. Exceptions exist (especially with white Rhône varieties such as Marsanne, Roussanne, and Grenache Blanc), but many parts of both Paso West *and* Paso East seem a bit warm for white wine greatness. Still, the jury is out on white wine potential, especially for the cooler parts of Paso West.

Is Paso West incontrovertibly superior to Paso East? Yes and no. Now that the wine boom is over, Paso East growers are, for the first time, lowering yields and striving for quality. The results are encouraging and some of the latest wines from Paso East are mighty fine.

Paso West, in fairness, has the edge. It has more of that desirable limestone soil and many sites cooler than anywhere in Paso East. At their best, the finest Paso West wines will beat the finest Paso East wines, not just because of artisanal ambition but because of the classic delineators of wine quality everywhere in the world: soil and temperature.

Paso East

The same Santa Lucia Range that separates Monterey County's Salinas Valley from the Pacific Ocean continues performing that trick as it heads south for Paso East. The climate of interior Paso Robles is continental, despite being just thirty air miles from the ocean's edge.

A laser beam aimed west from the city of Paso Robles would reach the Pacific Ocean thirty miles away at Point Piedras Blancas—and probably disrupt its lighthouse. It would, by the way, also slice through William Randolph Hearst's castle at San Simeon, which lies only a few miles away. (It would also have passed through tiny York Mountain AVA, about seven miles west of Paso Robles.) But it would have to be shot from up high, as the 3,000-foot-high Santa Lucia Range would otherwise block the beam, just as it keeps ocean breezes from reaching Paso East.

Just how hermetically the Santa Lucia Range seals off Paso East from any significant ocean influence is revealed by temperature. In June, July, August, and September, the average maximum temperature at Point Piedras Blancas is sixty-one degrees Fahrenheit. In the city of Paso Robles, it's 90.5 degrees Fahrenheit. During the winter months, November through April, the city of Paso Robles has an average minimum temperature of thirty-six degrees Fahrenheit. Little wonder that Paso East's growing season numbers 205 days compared to the near year-round 356-day growing season at Point Piedras Blancas.

What saves Paso East from being just another hot inland area growing baked and raisined grapes is elevation, as well as the effects of the final sigh of cool ocean air from the west. Keep in mind the "normal lapse rate": For every 1,000 feet in elevation, the temperature drops three and one-half degrees. The city of Paso Robles is 740 feet above sea level.

Paso East vineyards typically are between 600 feet and 1,000 feet in elevation. It's hot during the day. You do get some afternoon breezes—siroccos, really—that help disrupt what would otherwise be an oppressive inversion, or blanket of immobile hot air.

But nowhere does the California rallying cry of "warm days and cool nights" apply more than to Paso East (and Paso West, too). In July and August, the two hottest months of the year, the average maximum is ninety-three degrees Fahrenheit (you can count on the thermometer topping 100 degrees Fahrenheit at some point during the day). But the average nighttime temperature is just fifty-two degrees. That's quite a drop—a daily difference of forty-one degrees Fahrenheit.

Paso Robles growers insist that theirs is the most extreme daily diurnal temperature swing of any winegrowing area in America, but they're wrong. Washington State's Yakima Valley is more extreme yet. But that's just bragging rights. Paso Robles' diurnal temperature range in the summer is assuredly extreme.

How the grapes respond is what counts. Cabernet Sauvignon and, to a lesser degree, Zinfandel are the red wine grapes of choice in Paso East. Chardonnay, inevitably, is widely planted, although not with a comparable degree of success. It's too warm.

The Cabernets, though, are of real interest. They exhibit an expected ripe fullness of fruit. Unexpectedly, the wines are relatively soft and devoid of harsh tannins. They're round and early maturing. And while they're not necessarily "flabby," they cannot be said to have piercing acidity either. Paso Robles Cabernets are comforting. They feel wonderfully smooth in the mouth, a sensation abetted by a distinctively strong chocolate note.

The Zinfandels are similarly strong yet gentle. Here again, one would expect tough, long-lasting wines. Yet more often than not, the Paso Robles Zinfandels come on strong, yet veer off from harshness just when you're bracing for the impact. Of course, the wines can be made that way, but that requires an almost brewed-tea extraction that throws everything else out of whack as well.

More than with Cabernet, the Paso Robles area has an unusually long history of growing Zinfandel, dating as far back as the 1850s and continuing almost uninterrupted to this day.

Probably the most promising grape on the scene is Syrah. Paso East Syrah is classic warm-climate Syrah, with whiffs of black pepper and leather. But like all the other reds, Syrah also conveys the signature dark chocolate note, as well as relatively soft tannins and good, although not exceptional, acidity. In time, there's a good chance that Paso East will be as known for its success with Syrah as it is today for creating good, solid commercial Cabernets. Numerous other grapes are grown in Paso East, such as Cabernet Franc and Merlot, with varying degrees of success.

The greatest challenge for Paso East is cultural. It's the province of huge corporate-owned vineyards that (anonymously) supply wineries throughout California. Such big brands as Meridian (owned by Beringer Blass), Fetzer, and J. Lohr own thousands of acres of vines in Paso East.

Although there's real quality in Paso East vineyards, it's dominated by frank commercialism. During the wine-boom years of the 1990s, growers in Paso East cranked up the vineyard yields to supply the demand. Since many of the grapes were destined for big, bulk low-end blends (the Paso Robles reds supplying fruit intensity and color), growers had no commitment to quality. It was all about scale and volume. It's estimated that only about 40 percent of Paso Robles wines end up in wines so designated.

After the wine boom ended, many growers found themselves with grapes that nobody wanted even at giveaway prices. The bulk wine business bottomed out and, truth be told, the quality of the overcropped Paso East grapes simply wasn't very good.

So today, there's a new interest in better quality, which means lower yields. Still, Paso East remains consecrated to large-scale winegrowing. Theirs isn't a culture that lends itself to the kind of achievement-at-any-cost that characterizes California's finest wine precincts. Consequently, Paso East's wine culture is inherently different from that of Paso West, which is focused on the artisanal nuances of small-scale winegrowing.

Paso West

Paso West is by no means a new wine area. Quite the opposite. You can still find vestiges of old Zinfandel plantings that date from the 1890s. The old-timers, all European and mostly Italian, knew they were on to something. Also, in those pre-drip irrigation days, certain hillsides intercepted more rain than others, making grape growing more plausible in Paso West than in arid Paso East. (Rainfall varies wildly, with as much as sixty inches a year on the slopes near the Pacific Ocean to just eight inches annually in parts of Paso East.)

But after Prohibition, grape growing anywhere in Paso Robles (which until the 1970s meant Paso West) was subsistence farming at best. It wasn't until the 1960s that winegrowing was revived in Paso West, notably by Dr. Stanley Hoffman whose Hoffman Mountain Ranch created a brief stir in the 1970s with Pinot Noir and Cabernet Sauvignon. His vineyard is now reverently nurtured by its current owner, Adelaida Cellars.

As previously noted, Paso West is a world apart from Paso East. Its most extraordinary feature is soil. I've never seen, in California anyway, a wider swath of white calcareous soil than in Paso West. Growers blithely report finding petrified whale bones in their vineyards. You find some of this soil just across the Salinas River in Paso East as well.

The other significant feature to Paso West is a topographical formation that makes a huge temperature difference: the Templeton Gap. It's just what the name suggests: a big opening through the Santa Lucia Mountains. Recall that little more than thirty miles of mountainous terrain separates the city of Paso Robles from the Pacific Ocean.

Although the cool ocean air does trickle through the hills of Paso West, it sails right through the Templeton Gap. As you might expect, vineyards closest to this gap in Paso West are cooler than those tucked into hillsides farther away.

This combination of soil and the cooling effects of ocean air create exceptional wine opportunities that growers in Paso West are only just starting to sort through. Ocean air or no, Paso West is still warm during the day, although vineyards closest to the Templeton Gap are considered plausibly cool enough to grow Pinot Noir. The Santa Lucia Mountains effectively prevent fog from invading, so the skies of Paso West are improbably blue and clear in the summer when the fog is dense at the ocean's edge.

At this moment, it seems to this observer that Syrah is the ticket for Paso West. What emerges is a cool-climate Syrah taste, characterized by blueberries and boysenberries. When coupled with a mineral inflection from the limestone soil, the best Paso West Syrahs are simply world-beaters. Much depends, as it always does, on the particulars of site. There's still a lot of groping around left to do.

But the evidence is already such that, several decades from now, generations of wine lovers will wonder why it took Californians so long to rediscover such an extraordinary location.

Paso Robles Producers Worth Seeking Out (And Some Not)

Adelaida Cellars—A work in progress. Adelaida Cellars has meandered along a hit-and-miss path, but the current owners, the Van Steenwyk family, are now investing both the money and the commitment to doing things right. New vineyards have been planted and a promising new winemaking team installed. To judge from the location of the vines, Adelaida Cellars has the potential to be one of the stars of Paso West. Time will tell.

L'Aventure—A Paso West winery that has received considerable attention. Frenchman Stephan Asseo (from Bordeaux) bought a 127-acre ranch in 1997 in Paso West near the Templeton Gap and proceeded to install a variety of grapes including Syrah, Cabernet Sauvignon, Petit Verdot, Grenache, Chardonnay, Mourvèdre, Roussanne, and Viognier. A Cabernet, Syrah, and Zinfandel blend is issued under the proprietary name of Optimus.

L'Aventure's winemaking style emphasizes substantial fruitiness allied to equally substantial oakiness. While this certainly has its admirers, I cannot count myself among them. Not everything, by the way, is estate-grown. The best bet is the Estate Cuvée Syrah, although it too displays a heavy hand with quite toasty oak.

Austin Hope/Treana Winery—The Hope family has three labels: Treana, Austin Hope, and Liberty School. Quality varies considerably. Liberty School is the most commercial of the three and the quality is acceptable, but nothing special. The real ticket is the Austin Hope Syrah, followed (at a distance) by the better-known Treana red, which is a blend of Cabernet Sauvignon, Merlot, and Syrah.

Carmody-McKnight Estate Wines—Former actor Gary Conway (né Carmody) makes compelling Cabernet Franc, as well as persuasive Cabernet Sauvignon and Chardonnay from his Paso West vineyard, adjacent to Justin Vineyards. Carmody-McKnight, as much as any winery, makes the case for the distinctiveness of Paso West wines. It's an outstanding producer.

Castoro Cellars—A larger (25,000 cases) winery sourcing grapes from both Paso East and Paso West. Look for very fine Cabernet Sauvignon (from mostly Paso West vineyards) and a superb Syrah Reserve (half of which comes from Paso East vineyards).

Château Margene—This tiny producer shows just what rigor and ambition can achieve in Paso East. Little known right now, but a comer. Excellent Cabernet Sauvignon Reserve (from Paso West grapes) and a superb Cabernet Franc from their estate vineyard in Paso East.

Le Cuvier—Former owner of Adelaida Cellars, John Munch, sold that property to pursue a jewel-box sort of winery. He named his venture Le Cuvier, the little cellar room. Grapes are purchased entirely from Paso West growers. He's a firm believer in using wild yeasts, as evidenced by this whimsical declaration:

"There is firm empirical evidence to the effect that wild yeast and other varied wine pathogens die of boredom unless given an interesting environment within which to practice their art. Thus we dedicate ourselves to making life interesting for the wild beasties who seem content to do all the work."

Munch is an invitingly idiosyncratic sort, the kind whose wines either wow or make you wonder—or both. For example, he makes a Chardonnay that spends four years (!) on its lees or sediment, in barrel, before bottling. The result is a white wine of a deep yellow/gold hue (but still healthy-looking) with a decidedly "leesy" scent and some mineraliness. It tastes the way white Burgundies were made a century ago. I liked it, quite a lot in fact. But it was also like no other California Chardonnay in my experience. California needs more such free-thinkers.

Dark Star Cellars—Owner-winemaker Norm Benson is one of those admirable California purists who strives to make wine as naturally as possible, using non-interventionist techniques. Cabernet-Merlot blends are the specialty at this 4,000-case winery, most notably a proprietary label called Ricordati. Lovely wines, brimming with flavor and intensity.

Dunning Vineyards—Tiny (1,500 cases) west side winery issuing lovely, minerally Zinfandel and Cabernet Sauvignon, as well as a very fine, oak-free Chardonnay made from Paso West grapes.

Eberle Winery—Perhaps the best-known name in Paso Robles, Gary Eberle (a former football player) has been a key figure in the development of the area. Eberle started as the founding winemaker in 1973 for the now-defunct Estrella River Winery in Paso East. (Most of the Paso East vineyards are located on what's called the Estrella Plain.) In 1982 he started his own label.

Eberle is one of the earliest Syrah supporters and was instrumental in introducing the variety to California. To this day, growers refer to the Estrella clone of Syrah, which Eberle introduced via the UC Davis experimental vineyard (which in turn sourced it from Australia's Barossa Valley).

In 1996 Eberle opened an underground wine cellar in Paso East which produces about 25,000 cases a year, nearly all from Paso East grapes. A variety of wines are offered including Chardonnay, Viognier, Zinfandel, Barbera, Syrah, and Cabernet Sauvignon. One regrets to say that they are uniformly uninspired.

EOS Estate Winery—A label of Arciero Vineyards in Paso East. Visitors to the area can't miss EOS Estate Winery as it's surely the most extravagantly large winery (78,000 square feet) in Paso East—probably in all of Paso Robles. The owners report that it is modeled after a monastery in Monte Cassino, Italy.

Wines sold under the EOS label include the full Paso East array: Chardonnay, Zinfandel, Cabernet Sauvignon, Merlot, Petite Sirah, and a late-harvest Muscat. Wines are fairly heavily oaked; quality is adequate but decidedly commercial.

Garretson Wine Company—Owner-winemaker Mat Garretson is one of

California's most enthusiastic boosters of Rhône grape varieties, especially Viognier and Syrah. A former wine retailer in Atlanta, Garretson became a brand manager for Wild Horse Winery and, in 2001, established his own label making wines from purchased grapes.

Garretson does not confine himself to Paso Robles. He has Viognier from Vogelzang Vineyard in Santa Ynez Valley's Happy Canyon, as well as a Roussanne blended from Stolpman and Westerly Vineyards, also in Santa Ynez Valley.

Various proprietary-named bottlings, some with unpronounceable names such as The Celeidh, are issued. For a 3,000-case winery, the array of offerings is extensive. It's hard to generalize, especially since the grape sourcing can (and surely will) change every vintage. Still, Garretson is striving for high quality. Occasionally he achieves it. But because there's no estate vineyard to guarantee continuity, every vintage is inevitably a bit of a new bet. Red wines tend to be very dark and rich, as Garretson clearly likes big wines.

J. Lohr—Jerry Lohr is one of California's most ambitious wine producers. If he were in Napa or Sonoma, he'd be world-famous. Instead, he located himself first in Monterey County (mostly for white wines) and later in Paso Robles (for the reds). At present, Lohr has 1,250 acres of bearing vines in Paso East. J. Lohr reds reveal just what Paso East can do on a large scale. They are textbook reds: intense, deeply color, richly fruity, and filled with that chocolate scent and taste. You can't beat 'em for the money. The top wine is Lohr's Hilltop Vineyard Cabernet Sauvignon, sourced from a single plot in his Paso East vineyards. Look also for Syrah, as well as Lohr's workhorse Seven Oaks Cabernet, which is a nice mouthful of wine for very little money.

Justin Vineyards and Winery—Paso Robles' showcase winery, Justin is all about the west side. A stunning winery is just completed, replete with a separate three-room inn and seven-day-a-week restaurant (open to the public). Owner Justin Baldwin is determined to put Paso West on the wine map. And he does not flinch from making a case that Paso West is a world apart from Paso East, either.

Numerous bottlings are offered, such as the signature wine called Isosceles, a Bordeaux-type blend of Cabernet Sauvignon and Cabernet Franc. Quality is good, but so far, Justin still seems to be groping to find a level of wine quality equal to its architecture.

Martin & Weyrich—An ambitious Paso East producer formerly known as Martin Brothers that recently purchased one of Paso Robles' oldest west side vineyards and wineries, York Mountain Winery. There's excellent Pinot Grigio, as well as a fine Roussanne from York Mountain. Also look for a lovely sweet white Muscat (similar to Moscato d'Asti) brand-named Allegro.

Meridian Vineyards—Owned by Beringer Blass, which is itself owned by the Australian beer and wine giant Foster's, Meridian is one of the linchpin producers in Paso East.

Very little is designated as "Paso Robles" on Meridian labels. Most of the 1.5 million cases produced are blended from various vineyards owned or leased by Beringer Blass throughout the Central Coast, as well as from bulk purchases. A Paso Robles-designated Cabernet Sauvignon is good, typical Paso Cab: soft, chocolatey, and supple. Meridian wines are commercial at best. For this level, one would be far better served by J. Lohr winery.

Midnight Cellars—A Paso West winery created in 1995 from a former barley farm, Midnight Cellars is on track to become one of the better-known small producers in Paso West. Chardonnay, Merlot, Zinfandel, and a Bordeaux-type blend brand-named Mare Nectaris are produced. The estate-grown Zinfandel is a stunner, as is a Zin/Syrah blended labeled Gemini. The Mare Nectaris bottling is promising.

Nadeau Family Vintners—A small (1,600-case) Paso West family winery using mostly purchased grapes, in addition to a small estate vineyard planted primarily to Zinfandel. Specializing in Zinfandel, the winemaking emphasizes powerful fruit made in a straightforward, non-oaky style. Pleasant wines, especially the vineyard-designated Zins.

Opolo Vineyards—Rudyard Kipling had obviously never been to Opolo Vineyards when he famously wrote "East is East, and West is West, and never the twain shall meet." Partners Rick Quinn and Dave Nichols own 200 acres of vines in Paso East and eighty acres of vines in Paso West, where the winery is located in an old barn. (Quinn is of Yugoslavian descent and the name Opolo refers to a rosé-style wine made along the Dalmation Coast; the partners liked the sound of it.)

Most of the fruit from Opolo's vineyards is sold to others throughout California. All wines under the Opolo label are estate-grown, although the labels do not indicate whether the fruit is Paso East or Paso West. The partners, however, will freely tell you the sourcing for each wine, so tasting there is a fascinating exercise in the differences between Paso East and Paso West with most of the grape growing and winemaking variables removed. Some wines are blends of both.

And the results? A Paso East Cabernet is very fine, as is a proprietary label called Rhapsody, which is 40 percent Cabernet Franc. Generally, this taster preferred the Paso West-grown bottlings, but there's no denying the inherent quality of Paso East for Cabernet and Merlot. Worth watching.

Peachy Canyon—Fine, pure Zinfandels from the Paso West winery. The Zins come from west side grapes and the mineraliness shows. Peachy Canyon is an exemplary Zinfandel producer striving for purity too rarely seen these days. Worth noting is the excellent value offered, as pricing (at this writing) is most reasonable.

Robert Hall Winery—One of the signature wineries of Paso East, owner Robert Hall built a showcase winery to process the grapes from his 300 acres of vines. Various reds are issued, notably a good but not great Syrah, a pleasant Merlot, and a very good rosé blended from Syrah, Grenache, and Mourvèdre called Rosé de Robles. The standout wine for this taster, interestingly enough, is a superb Vintage Port made from traditional Portuguese port varieties grown in several Central Coast locations.

Saxum—Here's a real sleeper: Saxum Bone Rock Syrah. Located on the west side and owned by the Smith family, Saxum mostly grows grapes for others in their sixty-five-acre James Berry Vineyard. But they have reserved a 1.5-acre terraced site called Bone Rock planted entirely to Syrah for their own label called Saxum (Latin for stone). Just 300 cases are produced. This is flat-out great Syrah: intense, supple, made like a Pinot Noir, and revealing a similar berry scent allied with strong minerality. Also, there's a Broken Stones labeling (400 cases) which is mostly but not entirely from the estate James Berry Vineyard, with the balance coming from two nearby Paso West vineyards. It is similar to but not quite as characterful as the Bone Rock bottling. Saxum is an extraordinary winery and likely to be one of California's Syrah stars.

Tablas Creek—The winery that put Paso West on the map thanks to the fact that the co-owners of Tablas Creek are the Perrin family of France. They own Château Beaucastel, one of the most famous wineries in Châteauneuf-du-Pâpe in France's Rhône Valley. The other owner is Robert Haas, who is their American importer. It was the soil that convinced them that Paso West was the place for them.

And how are the wines? Very good. But given the pedigree, expectations run high. Look for the Côtes de Tablas Blanc, an impressive white wine blend of Viognier and Marsanne. Also, check out the white Esprit de Beaucastel, which is mostly Roussanne and wonderfully minerally. The reds are dense, strong, powerful, and clearly built for long aging, but so far, are not as persuasive as others in the zone. The Tablas Creek site seems warmer than some and one suspects that the owners are still trying to calibrate their viticulture.

Tobin James Cellars—A Paso East winery that never met a grape variety that co-owner Tobin "Toby" James didn't want to bottle separately. As a result, there's a vast array of Tobin James offerings that ring the changes from ordinary to exceptional. And you never know whether that same offering will be repeated the next vintage, either.

All of this "chaos" is conveyed to the winery's loyal followers with an infectious joyousness. Their James Gang wine club has a strong following. Best bets are various Zinfandels, as well as an excellent (and rare) Primitivo. Look also for the Ranchita Canyon Vineyard Petite Sirah from a thirty-five-year-old Paso East vineyard that grows some of California's finest Petite Sirah. (David Bruce Winery also buys its grapes.)

Turley Wine Cellars—Napa Valley-based Larry Turley bought the old Pesenti Winery in Paso West in 2000, mostly for its eighty-year-old Zinfandel vineyard. A newly installed winery now issues a Pesenti Vineyard Zinfandel, starting with the 2000 vintage. The style is pure Turley: massive, a bit oaky, and emphatic. It's pure in its way—if you like that style.

Wild Horse Winery—Ken Volk, the former owner (and still director of winemaking) of Wild Horse Winery, has probably been the most active drum-beater for Paso Robles. In 2003, Volk sold his winery for $48 million to Peak Wines International, the Australian company that owns Geyser Peak and Canyon Road wineries.

Volk is also one of the most vocal proponents of the worth of Paso East, contending that the differences between Paso East and Paso West are overstated. His winery and forty-eight-acre vineyard are, not surprisingly, east of Highway 101.

Volk is not necessarily wrong in his assessments. He's very knowledgeable about geology and rightly points out that some of the same characteristics that typically define Paso West, such as cooler temperatures and calcareous soils, can also be found in certain sections (such as his vineyard) in Paso East.

Wild Horse wines run quite a gamut, as Volk is adventurous in bottling offbeat grape varieties such as Verdelho, grown in the estate vineyard in Paso Robles. (It's quite good.) Generally, though, Wild Horse wines adhere to an attractive commercial standard, but rarely rise above that.

Windward Vineyard—Owners Marc Goldberg and Maggie D'Ambrosia (who are married) planted their fifteen-acre Pinot Noir vineyard in one of the cool zones in Paso West, in the Templeton Gap. Devoted to red Burgundies, they are committed (as Dr. Stanley Hoffman was before them) to the belief that the calcareous soil of Paso West allied with selecting just the right cool location can create one of America's most profound Pinot Noirs.

Have they achieved that? Not yet. But I, for one, wouldn't care to say that it's not possible. What Windward has already accomplished is creating pure, elegant Pinot Noirs that certainly have a distinction of place. Tannins are a bit hard, though. And one wishes for a greater dimensionality of fruit flavor.

Since so much with Pinot Noir depends upon a broad clonal mix in the vineyard and particular techniques in the winery, the odds are excellent that Windward Pinot Noirs will continue to evolve. Every follower of American Pinot Noir should keep tabs on this small, ambitious estate.

York Mountain Winery—Proof of Paso West's winegrowing heritage is found in this oddball estate. York Mountain Winery was purchased in 2001 by David and Mary Weyrich, owners of Martin & Weyrich Winery in Paso East. They are only the third owners since the original York Mountain Winery was created in 1882 in a remote nook in the Santa Lucia Mountains seven miles west of Highway 101.

Its founder, Andrew York, christened it Ascension Winery and planted Zinfandel, Alicante Bouschet, and Mission grapes. The wine was shipped by horse-drawn wagon to the San Joaquin Valley and also by boat to San Francisco. Somehow (surely by bootlegging), it survived Prohibition.

York Mountain has its own AVA, based on what has long been acknowledged as the peculiarities—and not least, the history—of the site. The Weyrich family intends to expand the vineyards already there, as well as turn the winery into a prettily removed bed and breakfast. At present, the York Mountain Winery label is used for grapes grown elsewhere than just the estate vineyard.

EDNA VALLEY AVA

In many respects the Edna Valley AVA is a miniature version of the much larger Santa Maria Valley just to the south of it. Where Santa Maria Valley has more than 5,000 acres of vines, Edna Valley has just 800 acres. But its conditions, and their causes, are virtually identical. Only the lay of the land varies: Where Santa Maria Valley is a broad plain, Edna Valley is narrow and elongated. Nearly all grapes grow on the valley floor, as if in a cup.

Edna Valley lies nine miles inland from the Pacific Ocean directly between the towns of San Luis Obispo on the north and Arroyo Grande on the south. The cool ocean air is ushered inland through portals formed by the Santa Lucia Range on the north and the Irish Hills on the south. No sooner do the breezes push through Edna Valley than they arrive in the town (and AVA) of Arroyo Grande, which is just two miles south of Edna Valley's southern border.

One other similarity to nearby Santa Maria Valley is also present: Edna Valley creates intense, lush Chardonnay in the same coconut-scented fashion. Frankly, I'm not sure that Chardonnays from these two areas are easily distinguishable. Pinot Noir has proved less noteworthy, again not unlike the Santa Maria Valley experience.

That said, there's a strong push toward improving the Pinot Noirs from Edna Valley. Unlike Santa Maria Valley, which has been reluctant to replant its Pinot Noir vineyards, Edna Valley has seen significant new Pinot Noir acreage, with emphasis on the new clones. Overall, the Edna Valley Pinot Noirs deliver good, solid, "true" Pinot Noir fruit, but without much distinguishable character. In a term rarely used for Pinot Noir, they are "reliable."

Arroyo Grande AVA

Although it has its own AVA, not much distinguishes Arroyo Grande from Edna Valley. There are only two distinguishing features that affect parts of

Arroyo Grande: Certain sections of it (the eastern part) are warmer than the rest of Arroyo Grande and all of Edna Valley. Second, some parts of Arroyo Grande are hilly, although—again like neighboring Edna Valley—most of it is pretty flat.

At the moment, Arroyo Grande wines are pretty much indistinguishable in taste from Edna Valley. Perhaps, decades from now, a more nuanced set of boundaries will emerge that captures whatever differences present themselves from the inland, eastern sections of Arroyo Grande and the hills of southernmost Edna Valley.

Effectively, Arroyo Grande AVA currently means a cool, ocean-inflected, flat vineyard area sandwiched between its equally cool and flat Chardonnay- and Pinot Noir-dominated neighbors, Edna Valley and Santa Maria Valley.

Edna Valley and Arroyo Grande Producers Worth Seeking Out (And Some Not)

Alban Vineyards—If ever there was a case in California for the rewards of independent thinking and sheer courage of one's convictions, it's Alban Vineyards. Owner-winemaker John Alban located his sixty-five acres of vines in the hills of what is technically the southernmost tip of Edna Valley AVA. It abuts the northernmost boundary of Arroyo Grande AVA. The truth is that Alban Vineyards is probably entitled to its own appellation.

The key element to the site is that it's hilly, where everyone else's vines are pretty flat. Also, John Alban consecrated his vineyard exclusively to Rhône varieties. That was back in 1989, long before the Rhône Rangers galloped into view. Everyone in Edna Valley thought he was nuts. Everyone in Edna Valley was wrong. In fairness, everyone is now suitably contrite, as Alban's wines are spectacularly good.

Look especially for lovely Syrah, a knockout Roussanne, and an improbably good late-harvest Viognier, among others. Alban Vineyards is one of California's greatest wineries, as well as an example of courage and conviction rewarded.

Baileyana—This winery is inextricably tied to Paragon Vineyard, and both are owned by the Niven family, which pioneered winegrowing in Edna Valley in the early 1970s. The short history of Baileyana is that Catherine

Niven, wife of Paragon founder Jack Niven, decided that she wanted a winery of her own, which she originally named Tiffany Hill. It was renamed Baileyana—originally a vineyard name—in the early 1990s.

Paragon Vineyard, with 1,000 acres of vines, was more than large enough to supply what was conceived of as a small brand. By 1998, the brand exceeded 10,000 cases and Baileyana was handed to the Nivens' children.

They, in turn, brought in Burgundy-born Christian Roguenant, a Frenchman who gives the lie to the misconception of the French as haughty know-it-alls. The original winemaker for the defunct Maison Deutz (now Laetitia), Roguenant was lured to Baileyana with an offer to construct a winery to his specifications, as well as the prospect of working with grapes from the Nivens' new Firepeak Vineyard, planted to the latest Dijon clones for Chardonnay and Pinot Noir. The new winery is enormous (150,000 case capacity, with room to grow to 250,000 cases) and is used mostly as a custom-crush facility for producers buying Paragon grapes.

Baileyana's Firepeak Vineyard, located on the valley floor at the base of 781-foot-high Islay Hill, has 190 acres of vines in one of the cooler sections of Edna Valley, only a few miles from the ocean. Early examples of both the Chardonnay and Pinot Noir from this vineyard are very promising, especially the Chardonnay, which is lighter and crisper than the more floral, rich style commonly offered from Edna Valley. This is because of the new, cool-climate clones.

Firepeak Vineyard Pinot Noir is also composed of new Dijon clones and is austere, detailed, and likely to emerge as a front-runner among Edna Valley Pinot Noirs. Look also for a Firepeak Vineyard Syrah, which is promising, especially for so cool a site. It shows Syrah's characteristic cool-climate blueberry scent. This is a winery to watch, especially for their estate-grown wines.

Claiborne & Churchill—A small family winery in Edna Valley with a mixed bag of offerings. Pleasant Pinot Noir, but far from noteworthy. Ditto for Monterey County-sourced Riesling.

Corbett Canyon Vineyards—A large winery owned by The Wine Group (which also owns giant bulk producer Franzia, as well as several other bulk wineries). Although Corbett Canyon's vineyards are certainly capable, based on location, of excelling, little of note has emerged from this unambitious brand.

Domaine Alfred—An ambitious Edna Valley producer committed to bio-dynamic agriculture. So far, the wines (Pinot Noir, Chardonnay, Pinot Gris) are one-dimensional and, in the case of the Pinot Noir, heavy-handed. Perhaps experience will provide the dimensionality and finesse currently missing.

Edna Valley Vineyard—This brand was created in 1980 as a partnership between Chalone Wine Group and the Niven family (owners of Paragon Vineyard) as a way for Paragon to process some of its own grapes and make money as a winery. Because Paragon was—and still is—the largest grape grower in Edna Valley, it was inevitable that Edna Valley Vineyard, in turn, became the powerhouse Edna Valley Winery.

Today, Edna Valley Vineyard is a national brand with a deservedly loyal following for its ripe, rich, always reliable Chardonnay. There's a new push to create Pinot Noir superior to anything offered previously, thanks to access to Firepeak Vineyard (see *Baileyana*). Quality is good; prospects are better yet. To watch.

Kynsi Vineyards—Small, underachieving winery using purchased grapes. Nothing special, with underwhelming Pinot Noirs from Paragon Vineyard and Cambria's Julia's Vineyard. Better Chardonnay from Edna Ranch Vineyard.

Laetitia Vineyard and Winery—A large and potentially fine winery in search of itself, Laetitia fairly can be called a work in progress. Located in Arroyo Grande within sight of the ocean, this cool site was originally Maison Deutz, built by the eponymous French Champagne house in pursuit of the once-hot California sparkling wine market. Deutz planted 185 acres of Chardonnay, Pinot Noir, and Pinot Blanc. The winery failed.

In 1997 Maison Deutz was purchased and renamed Laetitia, in honor of the new owner's daughter. It virtually abandoned sparkling wine (a little is still made) and concentrated on Pinot Noir and Chardonnay.

In 1998 the winery became a partnership, and then finally, in 2001, one of the partners, former banker-turned-retailer-turned-energy entrepreneur Selim Zilkha, bought the winery outright. He is the current owner.

By the time Zilkha assumed sole ownership, the partnership had expanded Laetitia's vineyard to 611 acres, 75 percent of which are Pinot Noir. With 456 acres of Pinot Noir, Laetitia likely has the largest single Pinot Noir vineyard in America.

At present, the winery is groping to find its identity. Clearly, it lies with Pinot Noir. The latest versions are well made and true to type. But they are not yet outstanding or even especially distinctive. In fairness, they are good and fairly priced. At minimum, Laetitia has the capacity, in every sense, to supply America with a fine Pinot Noir at a fair price. At best, it might some-day deliver much more than that.

Ortman Family Vineyards—The new, small venture of longtime wine-maker Chuck Ortman. Ortman began as winemaker for Napa Valley's Spring Mountain winery in the 1970s. He consulted to numerous Napa Valley wineries before starting Charles Ortman Winery, which became Meridian Vineyards. It was sold to Beringer, with Ortman remaining as winemaker for a vastly expanded operation. In 1999, with his son Matt, he founded yet another winery using purchased grapes from Napa Valley, Edna Valley, and Santa Barbara County to create Cabernet Sauvignon, Pinot Noir, Chardon-nay, and Syrah. The scale is small and the winery too new to judge.

Paragon Vineyard Company—The core vineyard business created by Jack Niven. With 1,000 acres of vines in Edna Valley, it dominates the AVA. Paragon sells its grapes to numerous buyers and processes some of them in Paragon's winery ventures, Baileyana and Edna Valley Vineyard.

Piedra Creek Winery—Tiny (twenty-five barrels or 625 cases) winery specializing in Zinfandel and Italian grape varieties. A proprietary label called Florianus is a blend of Lagrein and Teroldego. Nothing special so far.

Rancho Arroyo Grande Winery and Vineyards—A brand-new project of entrepreneur Gary Verboon, this stunning 4,000-acre ranch has 200 acres of vines tucked in the hills and valleys of easternmost Arroyo Grande. A show-case winery is under construction at this writing. A warmer site than proba-bly anywhere else in Arroyo Grande, it still is fairly cool and subject to extreme diurnal temperature swings, varying as much as forty degrees in tem-perature from day to night.

Verboon is betting the proverbial ranch on Rhône varieties and Zinfandel. So far, a 2001 Syrah is quite cool and definitely cool-climate in its blue-berry/boysenberry taste and silky texture. Zinfandel is excellent: intense, con-centrated, and beautifully balanced. A Rhône blend of Syrah, Mourvèdre, Grenache, and Counoise labeled Thereza Cuvée (after Verboon's wife) is a pleasing, cohesive blend.

Much remains to be done at this property, but it has the potential to become one of California's grandest estates *if* the necessary rigor is applied and sustained. To watch closely.

Saucelito Canyon—Located next door to Rancho Arroyo Grande (or vice-versa) Saucelito Canyon is literally surrounded by its far bigger, better-funded neighbor. Zinfandel has been grown on this property since the 1880s. In fact, when owners Bill and Nancy Greenough bought the property in 1974, three acres of the original 1880 Zinfandel vines remained buried under deep undergrowth. The roots were still alive. So Greenough grafted new Zinfandel shoots to those original roots, as well as planting an additional seven acres of Zinfandel, plus an experimental acre of Merlot, Cabernet Franc, and Malbec. The vines see no drip irrigation, a rarity these days in California.

Happily, this profound labor of love in a remote location pays off in superb Zinfandel, although not much of it. Total production never exceeds 2,500 cases and some vintages see half that. Saucelito Canyon Zinfandel is intense, concentrated wine with soft tannins and, in some years, a slight, classic Zinfandel raisin note. This is one of California's great Zins, bar none.

Stephen Ross Wine Cellars—The confusingly named Stephen Ross Wine Cellars is the creation of owner-winemaker Stephen Ross Dooley. "Somehow, I didn't think Dooley Cellars sounded quite right," he laughs. Grapes are purchased from various Edna Valley and Arroyo Grande vineyards, although Ross—er, Dooley—recently planted a Pinot Noir Vineyard called Stone Corral Vineyard in Edna Valley in partnership with the Talley family. The winemaking here is quite accomplished, with well-made Pinot Noirs of varying character depending upon the source of the grapes. Also, there's a good Zinfandel from the Dante Dusi Vineyard in Paso Robles, among other wines. The wines are made at the Tolosa facility in San Luis Obispo (q.v.).

Talley Vineyards—Easily the most famous name in Arroyo Grande, Talley Vineyards is a classic example of how professional farmers in a traditional flatland farming area saw a good cash crop in this newfangled wine business everybody's talking about.

Founder Oliver Talley started growing crops in the cool, flat Arroyo Grande Valley in 1948. He was a good farmer and successful. His son, Oliver, watched the new vineyards being installed in nearby Edna and Santa Maria

Valleys and saw some possibilities, especially on the hillsides (worthless to traditional farming) abutting their valley-floor farmland. So he planted an experimental vineyard in 1982. It eventually expanded to 130 acres.

Three vineyards now exist, two in Arroyo Grande (Rosemary's and Rincon) and one in Edna Valley (Oliver's). Rincon is the original property, founded in 1983, with ninety acres of vines, half of which is Chardonnay and one-third of which is Pinot Noir.

Rosemary's Vineyard is Talley's claim to (justified) fame. Located on a slope surrounding Don and Rosemary Talley's home, the original eight-acre vineyard was planted in 1987, equally divided between Chardonnay and Pinot Noir. An additional fifteen acres was planted in 2001 and 2002, entirely of Pinot Noir.

Oliver's Vineyards is seventeen acres of just Chardonnay in Edna Valley.

Talley wines adhere to a generally high standard for both Chardonnay and Pinot Noir. However, there is no question that Rosemary's Vineyard is the standout wine, with a strikingly perfumey scent and a distinct minerality. (This minerality shows through particularly in the Chardonnay.) Just why Rosemary's Vineyard is so clearly superior to nearly everyone who tastes the Talley lineup side by side is one of those mysteries for which the word "terroir" is invoked.

Climatically it's little different, if at all, from nearby Rincon Vineyard just down the road. The winemaking is identical, as are the grape-growing practices. Soil likely explains it (a fair amount of limestone) coupled with the particularities of its exposure. But really, it's not anything obvious. Yet it's there in the wine. The new fifteen acres of Pinot Noir will likely modify the taste, as new clones and rootstocks are present. It should be even better yet, but that remains to be seen—and tasted.

Tolosa—A very large winery that is as much in the business of custom-crushing for other labels as for anything else. Tolosa's partners own the 510-acre Edna Ranch Vineyard in Edna Valley. Most of the grapes are sold to others, with some processed in Tolosa's modern, utilitarian winery across the road from the San Luis Obispo airport.

Tolosa also has yet another winery in the northern part of San Luis Obispo County in San Miguel, designed to received Paso Robles grapes. It's twice the size of the Edna Valley facility.

Tolosa is a proper wine label producing about 4,000 cases. The wines are quite good. Tolosa's winemaker, Ed Filice, is deft in handling small lots while at the same time juggling vast quantities of grapes and wines for Tolosa's bread-and-butter business of custom-crushing. Look for a good, if rather chunky, Pinot Noir Edna Ranch from mostly new clones, as well as a striking Edna Ranch Syrah that provides yet more evidence of the real potential of cool-climate Syrah in California.

Wedell Cellars—A small, passionately committed winery that's the life's dream of fortysomething Maurice Wedell and his wife, Susan. An accountant by trade (let it never be said that accountants lack life's juices), Wedell is enthralled by Burgundy and frankly admits that his desire is to create a wine as close to a great Burgundy as possible.

Has he done it? Not yet. But you've got to applaud the rigor.

Encouraged by John Alban, the couple planted five acres of Chardonnay and one acre of Pinot Noir in the hills of southernmost Edna Valley, near Alban Vineyards. Vines are densely planted and crops kept to extremely low tonnages, typically with just one cluster per shoot.

To this palate, the Chardonnay is a little too "leesy," where the sediment in the barrel is stirred to extract more flavor. You can do more or less of this; Wedell prefers more. Also, there's quite a lot of oak, too much for me. Still, the underlying material is lovely. The Chardonnay reminds one of a very pretty girl wearing too much (unnecessary) makeup. Ditto for the oaky, yet potentially fine Pinot Noir.

Wolff Vineyards—Still largely unknown under its current name, Wolff Vineyards is instantly recognizable by its former name, MacGregor Vineyards. One of Edna Valley's best-known Chardonnay vineyards, MacGregor grapes are used by several wineries, most famously Mount Eden Vineyards.

A 125-acre vineyard started in the mid-1970s by Andy MacGregor, it was sold to Jean-Pierre and Elke Wolff in 1999. Born in Belgium, Jean-Pierre Wolff is an electrical engineer who helped found an electrical testing company and teaches at the university level. The Wolffs are committed environmentalists and the vineyard is becoming a model of ecologically sensitive management.

Although famous for its Chardonnay (fifty-five acres), there's also Pinot Noir (thirty-seven acres) and a newly installed plot of Teroldego, Syrah, and

Petite Sirah. The majority of these grapes continue to be sold to others, with the MacGregor name being slowly phased out over a period of years.

Wolff's own production is limited to just a few thousand cases, made by Jean-Pierre and his son, Andrea. The Chardonnay is, as might be expected, very fine with typical Edna Valley richness; the Pinot Noir, from new clones, is ripe and a bit stemmy-tasting, as Wolff likes to include stems during the fermentation.

SANTA BARBARA COUNTY

Test every concept by the question,
"What sensible difference to anybody
will its truth make?"

—William James,
Some Problems of Philosophy (1911)

T he "sensible difference" of Santa Barbara County wines derives from the peculiarity of its terrain. More than most places in California—which is famous for baffling local climates—Santa Barbara County is strange. Few fine-wine areas in California are farther south. Few are sunnier. Fewer still are cooler. Like a Baked Alaska, it makes no sense until you bite into it. In the same way, until a warm Southern California summer day suddenly turns wintry, the unlikely coolness of Santa Barbara County makes no sense. Even then, it leaves you wondering why.

The usual explanation is "sea breezes." That's true, but no more enlightening than the ubiquitous phrase "warm days and cool nights" found on seemingly every label of California wine. William James' rigor is needed: What accounts for one of California's most southerly wine areas having one of its coolest climates? More importantly, does its "truth" make a consistently sensible difference in the wines?

Santa Barbara County is a sprawling area subdivided officially, and more or less accurately, into three viticultural appellations: Santa Maria Valley, Santa Ynez Valley, and the newest AVA, Santa Rita Hills. Of the three, Santa Maria Valley is unrelentingly cool, while Santa Ynez Valley is warmer. Santa Rita Hills, which lies west of Santa Ynez Valley across Highway 101, is closer to the ocean and is as cool as Santa Maria Valley. But its soils are different, about which more in a moment.

Santa Maria Valley AVA

Santa Maria Valley is the location of one of the most dramatic—and success-ful—standoffs of maritime cool against interior heat anywhere in California. Keep in mind that without the intrusion of ocean influence, Santa Barbara County would be formidably warm: Beyond the mountains that seal off Santa Barbara County lies one of the hottest places in America, the Mojave Desert.

It may as well be on the other side of the world. This is because of the beneficent bent, literally, of a set of mountains along the coast. Everywhere else in California the numerous coastal ranges run north/south, in Santa Barbara County the mountains swivel at the same point where the coastline of California suddenly curves inward. On a state map it looks as if something unimaginably huge took a bite out of the nether end of California.

Just this once, the north/south axis is turned east/west, hence its name: the Transverse Range. It is the only place along the length of West Coast of the United States (excluding Alaska) where such a landform phenomenon occurs. It doesn't last, though. South of the city of Santa Barbara, the coastal Santa Monica Mountains pick up the north/south pattern and carry it to Los Angeles.

The Transverse Range is as significant for wine in Santa Barbara County as the gap of the Golden Gate is for wine in Napa and Sonoma. With the Golden Gate, the ocean itself is allowed to invade the interior; with the Transverse Range, it's an ocean of maritime air. Either way, it brings a degree of heat relief that would otherwise be absent. In the Santa Maria Valley, the funneling of ocean air is so strong that from the perspective of a grapevine, it wouldn't matter if the ocean itself invaded, rather than just its cool air.

The fact that the ocean air in Santa Barbara County is cool might not seem at first glance to be so unusual. Yet it is. It is the most southerly point along the California coast affected by the summer fogs that afflict the Men-docino County coastline (650 miles north of Santa Barbara) and San Fran-cisco (375 miles to the north).

The cause is unusually cold water "squeezed" up toward the coastline from deep within the ocean. Just how cold is revealed by the fact that the summer temperature of the water *at the surface* off the San Francisco coast is fifty-six degrees Fahrenheit, which is colder than the waters off Cape Flattery, the northernmost point on the Washington State coastline. This phenomenon starts in northern California in late spring and gradually extends south, reaching its fullest length—around Santa Barbara—in August. The wide band of this deep ocean upwelling typically is found just off the coast, surprisingly close to the shoreline.

When ocean winds blow across this cold water, the effect is the same as when a block of ice is placed in front of a fan. When the resulting chilled, moist breeze meets warm inland air, the result is haze or fog. For example, the city of Santa Maria—about eighteen miles inland—experiences eighty-seven days of heavy fog (visibility of one-quarter mile or less), most of it in the late summer, which is just when the cold water zone is at its most southerly extension. In comparison, the city of Santa Barbara, right on the water, has just nineteen days of heavy fog. This is because the southernmost extension of the cold water zone stops at Point Concepcion, which is north of Santa Barbara and just where the California coastline takes a sharp turn almost due east. It is the beginning of the "bite" into the southern California coast.

The "mouth" of the Transverse Range opens widest right at the coast, roughly fourteen miles across, between the towns of Grover City and Guadalupe. The offshore winds blow directly inland, hurrying across the broad alluvial apron formed by the Santa Maria River as if instructed by a traffic cop. Indeed, once ashore, the wind is no longer its own master. It has no option but to follow the course of the Transverse Range in the same way that water keeps to a streambed.

Eighteen miles inland, just past the city of Santa Maria, the course begins to narrow. It also curves: What was once a straight shot due east becomes an increasingly narrow path heading southeast. After another dozen or so miles deeper inland, the wind finds itself boxed in—and played out—as it arrives at a pinch point. This is the end of the Santa Maria Valley. It also is the dividing line between ocean cool and inland hot. Not coincidentally, it also marks the beginning of the Santa Ynez Valley. There, the vegetation is different and the warmth noticeable.

Aesthetically, the Santa Maria Valley is one of the least attractive wine-growing regions of California—at least to an eye lulled by dreamy traditional wine landscapes. Much of the Santa Maria Valley is raw, naked, rounded hills scoured clean of vegetation. What vegetation is present—grapevines—seems almost manmade. To a degree that's so. Mile after mile of otherwise empty hills are detailed with ramrod-straight ranks of irrigated vines kept upright by glistening aluminum trellises. These fixtures catch the sun, giving the land a sheen like metallic sweat.

Nowhere else in California, except for a few spots just up the coast from Santa Maria Valley such as nearby Arroyo Grande, is there a confluence of forces—sunshine and cold air—of such intensity. Usually, one or the other prevails. Not so in Santa Maria Valley. There, it's more Sisyphean: No sooner does the fog roll in than it is burned off by the dazzling sunshine. Yet the effect of the sunshine is modulated by the shunted cold ocean air. And so it goes, back and forth, resulting in an improbable equilibrium revealed by the wines.

The soil seemingly offers little influence: Spots of the Santa Maria Valley can be almost pure sand, while most places are sandy loam. Some clayey loam can be found as well. The minimal rainfall—just fifteen to twenty inches in a non-drought year—means that all vineyards are irrigated.

From this unlikely locale emerges what may well be some of California's most distinguishable wines. Chardonnay is the vehicle of choice. Perhaps more than any other white wine in California, Santa Maria Valley Chardonnay is so consistently a wine of place that it can be readily identified in a blind tasting. And if your guess is wrong, you probably won't be off by much, perhaps mistaking it for nearby Edna Valley or another Central Coast area such as Monterey County.

At its best, Santa Maria Valley issues California's most opulent Chardonnays, wines bulked with luxuriant fruit flavors yet given "cut" or definition by a superb acidity. The massive fruit is teased out by the dazzling sunlight; the discipline of acidity is installed by the commanding ocean coolness. Amid all the gilded luxuriance of fruit in Santa Maria Chardonnays is a pronounced yet curiously pleasing note of coconut. The giveaway, though, is an underlying hint of lime.

Not quite as consistently successful—when is it ever?—is Pinot Noir. At this writing, Santa Maria Valley Pinot Noir is in the throes of transition—and competition. Where Chardonnay was seemingly an instant success, Pinot Noir has been a struggle. For years, the birthmark of Santa Maria Valley Pinot Noir was an intrusive scent of camphor or sometimes a vegetalness or weediness. (Call it herbaceous, if you wish to be more flattering.) Or it was a whiff of tomato.

But despite this there was always real Pinot Noir potential. The wines had lovely acidity and flavor definition. Occasionally, some pristine flavor purity would emerge, reminding even the most severe critics that Santa Maria Valley is a place where Pinot Noir must be taken seriously.

Winemakers were, understandably, defensive. "It's a matter of irrigation timing," they once said. "Once we get that fine-tuned, you'll see, these flavors will disappear." They didn't. Then, it was suggested that "canopy management" was the problem. "When we reduce the excessive foliage," they said, "you'll see a big change." That, too, was only episodically effective.

In fairness, over the years, the trademark camphor/vegetal/tomato notes *did* diminish. But they never completely went away for all wines all the time. The problem all along was clonal. They had (in the aggregate) the wrong Pinot Noir clones for the right climate. One such clone is the so-called Martini clone, a strain of Pinot Noir first used by the late Louis P. Martini in his vineyard in Napa Valley's Carneros district. It's one of the sources of the vegetalness. Also, there's the Wadenswil clone (also known as clone 2A), which tends to create overly delicate fruitiness.

Now, however, the newly available Dijon clones—such as clones 113, 114, 115, 667, and 777—are slowly being installed in Santa Maria Valley vineyards and, *voilà!*, all the former birthmarks are gone. It's like seeing a previously murky painting wiped clean of disfiguring varnish. What emerges are vibrant colors and details you never previously saw.

The problem, at this writing, is that Santa Maria Valley has been slow to replant. Recall that, despite the fact that most of Santa Maria Valley vineyards are grown on vinifera rootstocks (and thus extremely susceptible to phylloxera), the area has been mercifully spared any infestation. So, unlike almost everywhere else in California (except Monterey County), there was no pressing necessity to replant.

Add to that the concentrated ownership structure of Santa Maria Valley vineyards, similar to Scottish fiefdoms. Vast vineyard tracts are held by just a few landlords, several of them headquartered far off in the Bay Area. Of the 8,043 acres of vines in Santa Maria Valley, 85 percent is owned by just five owners:

Cambria (Kendall Jackson): 1,506 acres
Dierberg Santa Maria Valley Vineyard (family owned): 160 acres

Loma Verde Vineyard (family owned): 218 acres

North Canyon Vineyard (Beringer): 948 acres

Flood Vineyard (Jim Flood): 300 acres

Riverbench Vineyard (Mark Fahey): 311 acres

Sierra Madre Vineyard (Robert La Vine): 567 acres

White Hills Vineyard (Dale Hampton): 2,948 acres

Garey Vineyard (Premier V Partners): 378 acres

Robert Mondavi: 485 acres

Bien Nacido: 900 acres

Because Santa Maria Valley is carved up into prohibitively expensive large parcels, it is extremely difficult for small wineries to purchase land for their own vineyards. Consequently, they are dependent, à la Blanche DuBois, on the kindness of the "lairds" for their grapes. These small winemakers are not, in effect, masters of their vinous fate. While grape contracts are let for specific rows or blocks within a vineyard, which clones are planted and how they are trained is the vineyard owner's prerogative.

Until now, there was little (business) reason for these owners to replant. After all, it is expensive, not only in new vines, but lost income for three years until the new vines bear fruit. In fact, it's five or six years before vines deliver a full crop.

Some replanting to the new Pinot Noir "Dijon clones" has already occurred. But there's been no rush to change—and until now, little competitive pressure to do so. With the advent of Pinot Noirs from Santa Rita Hills— which are almost entirely from new clones and rootstocks grown in a similarly cool climate to Santa Maria's—that's changed. Competition has arrived. What's more, nearly all of these new Santa Rita Hills vineyards are winery-owned, which means that their Pinot Noirs will be aggressively marketed.

Santa Ynez Valley AVA

Santa Ynez Valley is less easily characterized than neighboring Santa Maria Valley. This is because, unlike its neighbor, Santa Ynez Valley contains both cool and relatively warm sites. Viticulturally, the Santa Ynez Valley is best envisioned as a sort of enclave, with cool air attempting to reach it from two sides: from the west through Lompoc and from the northwest through Santa Maria. In both cases, only limited supplies get through, with more at the edges.

For those with an eye for a well-turned piece of countryside, the interior portion of Santa Ynez Valley—the area around the towns of Los Olivos and Santa Ynez—is one of the most beautiful landscapes in California wine country. It is almost a shock to see it after voyaging through the wind-scoured, almost glaciated bareness of Santa Maria Valley. You emerge into a rolling, folded landscape with centuries-old live oaks that are situated, catlike, on what always seems to be just the right spot for maximum aesthetic effect. If the English countryside were transformed into an American Western landscape, it would look like Santa Ynez Valley: open, rolling hills that beg to be ridden across. Cattle dot the hillsides, yet the farmyard utilities are tucked away from sight. The just-so geometry of the grapevines only adds to the illusion of rural perfection.

When *Making Sense of California Wine* was published in 1992, Santa Ynez Valley was struggling for identity. Because of its interior placement, Santa Ynez displays gradations of warmth, with the cooler spots located at the fringes near Highway 101. Unlike cool Santa Maria Valley, its wine destiny was not self-evident. A climatic uniformity is absent, making for both difficulties and opportunities.

Today, however, the tentative groping and fine-tuning of the past twenty years has given way to a new confidence. Although the results are still mixed, it's already clear that Cabernet Sauvignon, Merlot, Grenache, and Sauvignon Blanc are surely part of Santa Ynez Valley's destiny.

Happy Canyon and Ballard Canyon

A new group of vineyards, employing the latest trellising techniques, rootstocks, and clones, is already making itself felt. The once-frustrating complication of temperature gradations with the zone is now seen as an opportunity. Two of the newest sub-districts are informally known as Happy Canyon and Ballard Canyon. Neither has official standing, which will be a long time coming. No matter.

Happy Canyon is the easternmost section of Santa Ynez Valley and is consequently also the warmest part of the AVA. No ocean influence reaches it. It's about ten degrees warmer on an average growing season day than, say, Los Olivos, the epicenter of Santa Ynez Valley. An embryonic zone, it already has at least four newly established wineries or vineyards (Westerly, Vogelzang, Grossini, and Barrack) with a collective 250 vineyard acres. Early returns show that Viognier performs exceptionally well in Happy Canyon, with good promise for other Rhône varieties as well.

Ballard Canyon, which follows the eponymous road south from Los Olivos to Solvang, used to be mere grazing land, like so much else in Santa Ynez Valley. But in the late 1990s the area saw considerable investment and grape-growing ambition. It's still unclear whether there is a cohesive distinction of place to the Ballard Canyon area, as soils and elevations are mixed. Some soils are calcareous, while others are sandy or sandy loam.

Ballard Canyon runs parallel to Highway 101, and when you stand on its hilltops you can easily feel the ocean influence. Certain sites, such as Beckmen and Stolpman vineyards, share the calcareous soil and at least some of the ocean-influenced climate of Santa Rita Hills west of Highway 101. Significant new plantings from Rusack and Lemille Vineyards add to Ballard Canyon's possibilities.

Los Alamos Valley

If you doubt the desirability of a formal appellation or AVA, the saga of Los Alamos Valley shows what happens when a winegrowing zone lacks identity.

The town of Los Alamos lies midway along Highway 101 between Los Olivos to the south and Santa Maria to the north. All those vineyards you see on either side of Highway 101 as you drive north of Los Olivos for several miles are in Los Alamos Valley.

Los Alamos Valley is a surprisingly large winegrowing area that straddles Highway 101, although most of the vineyards are east of Highway 101 in the lovely rolling hills of Cat and Howard Canyons. The best way to envision Los Alamos is to see it occupying the hills and valleys between Foxen Canyon Road and Highway 101. That's hardly exact, but it's about right.

Curiously, Los Alamos Valley does not exist on any official wine maps, despite having 5,600 acres of vines—which is as much, or more, than in Santa Maria Valley. Yet it has no AVA of its own. And few wineries ballyhoo it. Los

Alamos Valley has as much right to wine legitimacy as Santa Maria Valley and Santa Rita Hills, which it resembles in its comparable coolness. Like those two AVAs, Los Alamos Valley also grows thousands of acres of Chardonnay and Pinot Noir, as well as smaller experimental acres of Italian varieties such as Nebbiolo.

So why isn't Los Alamos Valley "official"? The answer is that petitioning for an AVA isn't a priority of, or needed by, its big corporate "lairds" such as Meridian Vineyards (owned by Beringer Blass) and Corbett Canyon Vineyards (owned by The Wine Group, which also owns Franzia, Concannon, Glen Ellen, and Mogen David). They don't derive their identities from the Los Alamos Valley grapes they grow. So why bother with all the fuss and expense to create an AVA?

Nevertheless, fine wines have emerged from Los Alamos Valley. Some of Au Bon Climat's best Chardonnays, for example, used to come from the zone. Thompson Vineyard (of Bedford Thompson winery) is in Los Alamos, and their wines are lovely. But, like Cinderella before the slipper incident, Los Alamos Valley remains anonymous and unheralded. Someday, as the song says, its prince will come. But so far, he hasn't shown up.

Santa Rita Hills AVA

Santa Rita Hills is the newest and arguably most exciting vineyard zone in Santa Barbara County. Previously part of the Santa Ynez Valley AVA, growers in the zone submitted a petition to the BATF in 1997, which was formally approved in 2001. (The Chilean winery Vina Santa Rita is challenging the legality of the AVA name. Reportedly, it will accept an AVA bafflingly called "Sta. Rita Hills." At this writing there is no resolution.)

Unlike a number of California AVAs, which are mostly flags of convenience with no real wine significance, Santa Rita Hills is a true wine appellation. It separated itself from the parental Santa Ynez Valley AVA for the proper reasons of temperature (it's much cooler) and soils (considerable calcareous material). These are the very elements that make wines—and wine districts—genuinely different from each other.

The arrival of Santa Rita Hills as a separate entity has been a long time in coming. Its distinction of place was already apparent when the first edition of this book appeared in 1992. Back then, there were just two AVAs: Santa Maria Valley and Santa Ynez Valley. "Really, there should be three appellations," I observed, "the third being called something like Santa Ynez Valley West, with Highway 101 being the dividing line."

The Santa Rita Hills AVA boundary runs east-west from about three miles east of Lompoc until it reaches a large bend in the Santa Ynez River about five miles west of Highway 101.

It's a hilly terrain with numerous microclimates and soil variations. All of it is cool, although some hillsides are cooler or warmer than others, depending upon exposure. The AVA boundaries are roughly fifteen miles as the crow flies from west (near Lompoc) to east (near Highway 101).

Every afternoon during the growing season a strong, cool breeze surges through the Santa Rita Hills. This powerful ocean influence penetrates into the westernmost portion of the Santa Ynez Valley just across Highway 101, such as Ballard Canyon area. But its effect is most complete and persuasive in the Santa Rita Hills.

Given its coolness, it was inevitable that Pinot Noir and Chardonnay would be the grapes of choice in Santa Rita Hills. This wasn't just speculative. After all, Santa Barbara County's most famous (and so far, best) Pinot Noir vineyard is the famed Sanford & Benedict Vineyard, founded in 1971 long before anyone had a notion about "Santa Rita Hills." Lafond Winery planted its vineyard that same year as well. They were the pioneers, followed later by Babcock Winery in 1980. Until the mid-1990s, it was just these three producers making the case for the Santa Rita Hills.

What took everyone else so long? The answer is probably that equally cool Santa Maria Valley was far easier to plant, being broad and mostly flat. It had plenty of cheaply cultivated land, ideal for the large-scale purposes of agribusiness growers and big wineries, then and now. For twenty-five years, it served everyone's purposes. There was little reason (or persuasive economics) to look further for cool-climate vineyard locations.

Santa Rita Hills had to wait until California's fine-wine ambition evolved to another level of sophistication. Because what it offers is not a dramatic climatic difference from Santa Maria Valley, but a matter of significant nuance—which derives from soil.

Soil is what sets Santa Rita Hills apart. There isn't just one soil, of course.

Part of the zone has what's called Botella clay loam or Monterey shale. It's a blackish loam soil capable of imparting a distinctive, appealing earthiness to Pinot Noir. Botella clay is what makes Sanford & Benedict Vineyard so distinctive. Newer vineyards nearby, such as Sea Smoke and Cargasacchi Vineyards, among others, claim it as their own, too.

Because of ancient marine influence, a good number of vineyards in Santa Rita Hills have sandy soils, sandy loams, and a fair amount of alluvial gravels. But intermixed in many of these soil types is a good (and rare) amount of calcareous material such as chalk and marl. Such calcareous soil makes a difference in the taste of wines, especially such "transparent" varieties as Pinot Noir. Santa Maria Valley has sandy and sandy loam soils too, but chalk and marl are absent.

By the mid-1990s, California had become conscious of cool climates in general and Pinot Noir in particular. Moreover, already established vineyard areas were becoming prohibitively expensive or were already developed. Santa Rita Hills was ripe for development. And a consumer audience itself was ripe for just the sort of nuance imparted by interesting soils, especially when conveyed by Pinot Noir.

What happened next was striking. A group of Pinot Noir obsessives decided to buy raw land in Santa Rita Hills and plant vineyards using the newly available Dijon clones, the latest rootstocks, and denser spacing.

It was just the right time and—not to be forgotten—these players had unusually deep pockets. I don't think I've seen a smaller fish tank with more "sharks" swimming in it than Santa Rita Hills. Seemingly *everybody* has big bucks—all lavished on Pinot Noir, with good-size plantings of Chardonnay and some Syrah as well. But Pinot Noir is the focus.

And how are the results? It's early days, but so far, so very good. Santa Rita Hills Pinot Noirs are collectively intensely flavored, very dark in color, and beautifully balanced by crisp acidity. Much of this is a function of an ideally cool climate and the powerful fruit flavors (red raspberry, black cherry, black raspberry, cola) of the Dijon clones almost universally planted in Santa Rita Hills.

Does the soil show? Hard to say. It certainly does in Sanford & Benedict Vineyard Pinot Noirs. But then, those vines are about thirty years old and they're not the new Dijon clones. Not least, that site has an unusually high concentration of Botella clay. So Sanford & Benedict is not necessarily a typical example of "modern" Santa Rita Hills.

However, you can fairly say that Santa Rita Hills is already among California's top Pinot Noir zones. Much still needs to be done—as local winemakers are the first to point out—about blending the various clonal lots (almost everyone vinifies separately by block and clone), as well as picking times, various oak barrel choices, and so forth. But the zone itself is indisputably a major American Pinot Noir contender.

If there's a problem with new Dijon clone vineyards like these, it's that they can be too much of a good thing. It's a classic "be careful what you wish for" situation. On the one hand, the Dijon clones are terrific. They really do make an admirable and desirable difference.

On the other hand, these same clones are almost bullying in their powerful flavors. You don't need to taste each clone separately before you get pretty good at accurately identifying them by taste, as in, "This is 113, 114, or 115. It's all about red raspberries," or "It's got the black fruits taste of clones 667 and 777." All of these clones are delicious. But they're not subtle. In consequence, too many Pinot Noirs made from them can taste too much alike, as well as one-dimensional.

Burgundy's ancient experience reveals that a vineyard can't have too many clones. Clones that might not seem to offer much, like a piccolo in an orchestra, add a redeeming grace note. Such clonal diversity is largely absent in Santa Rita Hills in the (understandable) rush to install the latest and greatest. Over time—decades, really—growers will add many more clones, and the Pinot Noirs will become more individual and less driven by the heady rush of fruit that characterizes many Dijon-dominated Pinot Noirs.

Oddly, I have been less impressed by Santa Rita Hills Chardonnays. On paper, they should be at least as successful—and similar to—those from equally cool Santa Maria Valley. Actually, given the calcareous soils, they should be even *more* interesting, with a similar fruitiness and a soil dimension, too. Yet they're not. Here again, the newly available cool-climate Dijon Chardonnay clones predominate, which may be a factor.

Where identically cool Santa Maria Valley creates lush, inviting, tropical Chardonnays of almost voluptuous fruitiness, Santa Rita Hills Chardonnays are more austere, less forthcoming, and, to some palates, more minerally.

When I discussed this with winemakers in both areas nobody disagreed with this description—but no one could explain it either. Soil seems the likely answer, with clonal differences running a distant second.

Santa Rita Hills Chardonnays are pleasing, but nowhere near as striking or persuasive as the Pinot Noirs. This may be a matter of one man's palate and nothing more. Or it might be a function of very young vines or a need for more nuanced oak treatment.

But the greatest significance—the revealing thing—about Santa Rita Hills Chardonnay is its "dog that didn't bark" quality.[7] The proof that *something* is profoundly different about Santa Rita Hills from seemingly similar Santa Maria Valley is shown by the Chardonnays. They don't taste at all alike.

Santa Barbara County Producers Worth Seeking Out (And Some Not)

Arcadian Winery—Owner-winemaker Joseph Davis sources his grapes from several locations, notably Monterey County's Pisoni and Sleepy Hollow vineyards, as well as Pinot Noirs from Bien Nacido Vineyard in Santa Maria Valley. Beautifully made Pinot Noirs and Chardonnays of considerable elegance and refinement.

Au Bon Climat—Owner-winemaker Jim Clendenen was Santa Barbara County's original superstar—and is still. Recent vintages have reached out to Talley Vineyards in Arroyo Grande for Chardonnay and Pinot Noir, in addition to regular sourcing from Bien Nacido Vineyard in Santa Maria Valley. Rich, luxurious Chardonnays. Pinot Noirs are more variable. The best bets, as always, are single-vineyard bottlings. Don't miss the Teroldego from Monterey County, which is as good as all but the best Italian versions of this rare grape variety.

Beckmen Vineyards—One of the emerging new stars of Santa Ynez Valley. The Beckmen vineyard—called Purisima Hills Vineyard—is at a higher

[8] "Is there any point to which you would wish to draw my attention?"
"To the curious incident of the dog in the night-time."
"The dog did nothing in the night-time."
"That was the curious incident," remarked Sherlock Holmes.
From *Silver Blaze* by Sir Arthur Conan Doyle, 1892

elevation than its contiguous neighbor, Stolpman Vineyard. Beckmen might conceivably be seen as a warmer version of the Santa Rita Hills, as it catches a good bit of those cooling breezes and shares a similar soil. So far, the star varieties are Grenache and Syrah. In fact, some of the finest Syrahs seen in Santa Barbara County bear the Purisima Hills Vineyard designation. This is easily one of the stellar estates in Santa Barbara County and capable of being ranked among California's best in the near future.

Closer to home, it will be enjoyable to see how Beckmen's wines fare against its contiguous neighbor Stolpman, much like tasting, say, La Tâche against its immediate neighbor, Richebourg. Both are formidable.

Bedford Thompson—Cabernet Franc is the feature attraction for this taster at Bedford Thompson. Located in what might be called a "fringe" zone—technically it's in the Los Alamos Valley on Alisos Canyon Road—Bedford Thompson's vineyard is in that nexus where Santa Maria Valley segues into Santa Ynez Valley. (Rancho Sisquoc occupies a similar situation.) Although lovely cool-climate Syrah is also grown, it's a sterling Cabernet Franc that really sets this vineyard apart.

The Brander Vineyard—No producer has carried the banner for Santa Ynez Valley Sauvignon Blanc longer or better than owner-winemaker Fred Brander. A lover of Bordeaux and its varieties, Brander also issues Cabernet Sauvignon. But it's Sauvignon Blanc—in several versions—that shows just how ideal Santa Ynez Valley is for this variety. The austere, oak-free bottling aptly named Au Naturel is an exemplar of Sauvignon Blanc at its purest and most rewarding.

Brewer-Clifton—Winemaker Greg Brewer and Steve Clifton are prime examples of being in the right place at the right time. Their utilitarian winery is located in a compound of warehouse-type buildings in the town of Lompoc in the Santa Rita Hills. Several other wineries are located in this same warehouse cluster affectionately called "The Ghetto" by the winemakers there. (Other winery facilities in The Ghetto include Longoria, Sea Smoke, Stolpman, Presidio, and Steve Clifton's other winemaking venture, Palmina.)

Neither winemaker owns any vineyards, but their involvement with Santa Rita Hills growers (Greg Brewer is currently winemaker for Melville winery) has allowed them to purchase hard-to-obtain Pinot Noir and Chardonnay from several Santa Rita Hills vineyards. The results are impressive, especially for the Pinot Noirs, all vineyard designated. Winemaking is non-interventionist and very pure. Look especially for the Melville-sourced Pinot Noir subplot called "Carrie's Vineyard."

Santa Rita Hills-sourced Chardonnays are less persuasive to this taster, displaying a pronounced Golden Delicious apple scent in an austere, slightly mineral style. So far, they seem pleasant, but not compelling. Perhaps older vines or more bottle age will revise this judgment in the future.

Buttonwood Farm Winery and Vineyard—A longtime Santa Ynez Valley producer, Buttonwood continues to under-perform. Various varieties such as Sauvignon Blanc, Syrah, Cabernet Franc, Merlot, and Cabernet Sauvignon are uniformly lackluster.

Byron Vineyard and Winery—Created by Byron "Ken" Brown in 1984, this Santa Maria Valley winery was purchased in 1990 by the Robert Mondavi Winery. Mondavi had the wit to keep Ken Brown as winemaker, as well as invest heavily in new Pinot Noir and Chardonnay vineyards in Santa Maria Valley. Byron was one of the first Santa Maria Valley vineyard owners to experiment with various vineyard spacing densities.

The results show today. Byron Chardonnay has long been, and remains, one of the benchmark bottlings in Santa Maria Valley. Pinot Noir has improved (and changed) significantly from earlier versions, thanks to the new vineyard densities, as well as an increased reliance on older clones that perform well in Santa Maria Valley such as the Pommard clone, among others. The style verges on the oaky.

Several vineyard-designated wines are offered from Nielson Vineyard, Sierra Madre Vineyard, and Byron Vineyard.

Look also for the small-production Byron Pinot Gris, which is one of California's best. A separate label called IO is a vehicle for separate Syrah bottlings of Santa Maria Valley and Paso Robles fruit.

Brown, by the way, started his own small winery under his own name, with purchased grapes (from Santa Rita Hills) in 2003.

Cambria—A large Santa Maria Valley winery owned by Kendall-Jackson that produces ripe-tasting, excessively oaky Chardonnay and Pinot Noir. Grapes from this vineyard are also offered to others.

Single-vineyard Julia's Vineyard Pinot Noir is one of the signature wines.

It's a good Pinot Noir, but far from exceptional, never mind who's making it. Other single-vineyard bottlings include Tepusquet Vineyard, a 1,200-acre vineyard that was jointly purchased in 1987 by Kendall-Jackson and Mondavi and subsequently divided, with Mondavi taking 340 acres. At this writing Mondavi is now seeking to sell its portion.

Carhartt Vineyard—A tiny, ten-acre vineyard family winery in the heart of Santa Ynez Valley with very low yields and beautiful, austere winemaking. Superb Merlot and Syrah are produced in minute quantities in the family barn. Carhartt is one of the best-kept secrets in Santa Ynez Valley.

Carina Cellars—This is a tiny production of Syrah made under contract by winemaker Joey Tensley using the proprietary name Iconoclast. Attractive but nothing special so far.

Clos Pepe Estate—An ambitious Santa Rita Hills vineyard (and winery) that's striving for serious Pinot Noir and Chardonnay. Their grapes are mostly sold to other producers such as Longoria, Brewer-Clifton, Siduri, and Hitching Post, among others.

Devoted to sustainable agriculture, Clos Pepe Pinot Noirs have so far proved less striking than several other Santa Rita Hills vineyards. In its early days, Clos Pepe hasn't performed as well as others, with several Pinot Noirs in several different winery hands all tasting a bit diluted in the mid-palate with slightly weedy flavors.

The vineyard may be more stressed than others, as the owners are devoted to non-interventionist sustainable agriculture. Or it may be the particularities of the vineyard location. Or the vineyard "kid" just needs more time.

As the number of vintages available to taste is tiny, it's only fair to say that while others shone in the excellent 2001 vintage, they did not. But there are plenty more vintages to come. To watch, for sure.

Cold Heaven—Morgan Clendenen, who is married to Jim Clendenen of Au Bon Climat, specializes in Viognier to some very good ends. Several named-vineyard versions exist, such as Le Bon Climat (in the family vineyard near the town of Sisquoc in Santa Maria Valley) and Vogelzang Vineyard in Santa Ynez's Happy Canyon area. The best Viognier, however, comes from Sanford & Benedict Vineyard in Santa Rita Hills, showing yet again the exceptional worth of that unique vineyard.

Curtis Winery—An offshoot of Firestone Vineyards that specializes in

Rhône varieties such as Syrah and Viognier, among others. The results so far are promising, with Syrah from the estate-owned Crossroads Vineyard showing real quality. To watch.

Fess Parker Winery and Vineyard—One of the most popular winery tourist stops in Santa Ynez Valley, the Fess Parker wines are slowly improving from their original frank commercialism. Parker smartly installed a vineyard in Santa Rita Hills (labeled Ashley's Vineyard), ensuring him a supply of good quality Pinot Noir grapes, which the winery is handling professionally, if not yet at quite the same level as some others. But the prospects are good. Chardonnay is textbook Santa Maria Valley in its lushness. Syrah from Rodney's Vineyard in Santa Ynez is also a fine effort.

Fiddlehead Cellars—Winemaker Kathy Joseph is one of the pursuers of Pinot Noir in Santa Rita Hills with her 133-acre vineyard called, rather confusingly, Fiddlestix. She also makes Pinot Noir from Oregon-grown grapes and Sauvignon Blanc from Santa Ynez Valley. But it's the Fiddlestix Vineyard (across the road from Sanford & Benedict) that has attracted the most attention. Napa Valley's Beringer Blass is an equal partner in the Fiddlestix Vineyard. As elsewhere in Santa Rita Hills, no expense has been spared in the vineyard and the early results are, not surprisingly, very fine indeed. A winery to watch closely.

Firestone Vineyard—For decades and still today, Firestone Vineyard, founded in 1972, has been the showcase winery of Santa Ynez Valley. But virtually since its inception, they have not successfully transformed their 550 acres of vines into anything other than a commercial, presumably profitable but decidedly banal array of wines. The winery torch has been passed from founder Brooks Firestone to a new generation, his son Adam. The question is, will the torch get lit?

Flying Goat Cellars—A small private label for Foley Estates winemaker Norm Yost. Specializing only in Pinot Noir, Flying Goat buys grapes from several sources, including Dierberg Vineyard in Santa Maria Valley, which is newly planted to the new Dijon Pinot Noir clones. Yost is a talented winemaker and both Flying Goat and Foley Estates prove it.

Foley Estates Vineyard and Winery—One of the leading contenders for top Santa Rita Hills winery, Foley Estates is the creation of William P. Foley II, who is chairman and CEO of Fidelity National Financial, Inc., the country's largest title insurance company. He also is a major shareholder of the restaurant company that owns the Carl's Jr. hamburger chain.

Foley first purchased the former J. Carey Cellars from Firestone Vineyard in 1997 and renamed it Lincourt (q.v.). It uses Santa Ynez Valley fruit.

The real jewel is what Foley calls his Santa Rita Hills vineyard: Rancho Santa Rosa. Planted in the late 1990s, the first fruit appeared in 2001. Already, the wines are exceptional—at least the Pinot Noir—as well as, surprisingly, the Syrah. Of the vineyard's 223 acres, the largest portion (136 acres) is given over to Chardonnay, with seventy-nine acres devoted to Pinot Noir and just eight acres planted to Syrah in the warmest pocket at the base of the slope.

The winery concedes that, in retrospect, they planted too much Chardonnay and too little Pinot Noir. This will no doubt be corrected, as the Pinot Noir is superb and the Chardonnay, like others from Santa Rita Hills, is not quite as compelling. The Syrah has been impressive, especially the inaugural 2001 bottling, with the 2002 less rewarding only because the yield was too high.

Pinot Noir is king here, made in a beautifully detailed style with no intrusive oakiness or excessive, flashy fruitiness. Of all the Santa Rita Hills wineries, Foley has a shot at leading a very sophisticated and competitive pack.

Foxen Vineyard—The "Foxen Boys," as co-owners Dick Doré and Bill Wathen are affectionately known, are stalwarts of Santa Maria Valley winemaking. Located in a rustic barn along Foxen Canyon Road, the winery has issued a series of fine Pinot Noirs, Chardonnays, and Syrahs.

For this taster, their signature wine is the one that brings them the least attention and profit: Cabernet Franc. Grown in their estate vineyard called Tinaquaic, Foxen Cabernet Franc is easily one of California's finest, bar none. I bought a case of the great 1994 vintage and it's still in superb condition, and still evolving. Also superb is Foxen's Cabernet Sauvignon.

The Gainey Vineyard—An ambitious winery that evolved from its original inception as a Santa Ynez Valley horse ranch (many others have since given way to vineyards). Today, Gainey is really two wineries, reflecting the difference between what they call their Home Ranch in Santa Ynez Valley and their new vineyard in Santa Rita Hills, Santa Rosa Hills vineyard. The Santa Ynez property rightly focuses on Sauvignon Blanc, Merlot, and Cabernet Franc while the Santa Rita Hills vineyard is mostly about Pinot

Noir and Chardonnay. All of the wines are well made, but a bit too oaky for this taster. A big, rich Chardonnay is perhaps the winery's most acclaimed effort and it, too, is an opulent, oaky affair.

Hartley-Ostini Hitching Post Wines—Frank Ostini is the owner of the Hitching Post restaurant in Santa Ynez Valley, a mecca for red meat lovers. Gray Hartley is a former professional fisherman. The two paired up in 1979 as amateur winemakers and went professional in 1984 under the Hitching Post label. Like so many other small wineries in Santa Barbara County, they buy grapes from multiple vineyards, notably Sanford & Benedict.

Pinot Noir is the focus and the wines vary in quality, as much from the source of the grapes as anything. Ostini and Hartley are good winemakers. Some excellent Syrah is also issued, especially from Purisima Mountain Vineyard (see *Beckmen*). It's the old story: You're only as good as your grapes. When the grapes come from Sanford & Benedict or Purisima Mountain, this duo delivers top-quality wine.

Jaffurs Wine Cellars—Owner-winemaker Craig Jaffurs (a former aerospace cost analyst) has a passion for Rhône varieties, and his winery specializes in them. Jaffurs owns no vines, but is fortunate enough to secure grapes from the likes of Melville, Stolpman, Purisima Mountain, and Thompson vineyards. That's a swell roster. And the wines reflect it, too. Lovely Syrahs as well as good Viognier are produced. To watch closely.

Lafond Winery and Vineyards—One of the pioneers of Santa Rita Hills, with their vineyard dating to 1971, Lafond has yet to make wines that really sing, at least to me. Good, solid, honest wines and winemaking are present, but nothing dazzling. Let's hope that the increased Santa Rita Hills competition will improve their game.

LinCourt Vineyards—When William P. Foley II (see *Foley Estates*) bought the former J. Carey Cellars from Firestone Vineyard, he renamed it LinCourt. Chardonnay, Syrah, and Pinot Noir are made from grapes purchased from several vineyards, notably Dierberg Vineyard in Santa Maria Valley. Good wines, but not in the same league as Foley Estates.

Longoria Wines—Richard "Rick" Longoria has one of the longest track records of any winemaker in Santa Barbara County, starting as a cellar foreman for Firestone in 1976. He subsequently worked at Chappellet in Napa Valley, then returned to Santa Ynez Valley to become winemaker for J. Carey

Cellars. Next he was briefly the winemaker for Rancho Sisquoc and finally had a long run as winemaker for Gainey. Finally in 1998, he went out on his own, with a small winery currently located in the warehouse "ghetto" in Lompoc.

Longoria is a fastidious winemaker. Involved with the formal creation of Santa Rita Hills as an AVA, his connections give him access to multiple Santa Rita sources such as Clos Pepe and Mt. Carmel vineyards. Longoria has his own eight-acre vineyard in Santa Rita Hills called Fe Ciega ("blind faith"). The first crop appeared in 2001.

Numerous bottlings are offered, including Syrah, Merlot, and, upcoming, some Tempranillo. Inevitably, not every wine is extraordinary. But there are few, if any, wineries in Santa Barbara County where you'll get better odds of finding really fine wines than at Longoria.

Lucas & Lewellen Vineyards—Promoters of Los Alamos Valley, Louis Lucas (one of the pioneer vineyard managers in Santa Barbara County from the early 1970s) and former Santa Barbara County Superior Court Judge Royce Lewellen created their winery in 1996. Most of their grapes are sold to others.

Lucas is a classic farmer: He's got 400 acres of vines in Los Alamos Valley, and he happily grows twenty-four different varieties. When I last talked with him, he was committed to Italian varieties such as Nebbiolo. Plans are ambitious, with an anticipated 50,000-case winery. Their own wines, so far, are mostly commercial in quality.

Margerum Wine Company—The (serious) hobby winery of Doug Margerum, owner of the Wine Cask restaurant and wine shop in Santa Barbara. No store has a wider selection of Santa Barbara County wines than the Wine Cask, and the store's futures offerings of special-barrel lots of Santa Barbara County wines draw a national audience.

Margerum's own wines are promising, especially the Syrahs from Purisima Mountain Vineyard in Santa Ynez and Vogelzang Vineyard, as well as good Sauvignon Blancs from Happy Canyon-area vineyards Westerly and Vogelzang. Worth watching.

Melville—A Santa Rita Hills vineyard and winery that's of noteworthy ambition. Owner Ron Melville and his two sons, Chad and Brent, along with high-profile winemaker Greg Brewer, are seeking to make a case for Santa Rita Hills wines.

As elsewhere, Pinot Noir is their best wine, with an impressive array of eleven different clones. But their 110-acre vineyard also has a significant holding (about twenty acres) of Syrah, with nine different clones. The Syrah, however, did not impress this taster. One wonders if their site is simply too cool. Time will tell.

Chardonnay, again like others in Santa Rita Hills, is "typical": lean, slightly mineral, linear. Really, it's the Pinot Noir that sings at Melville. Look especially for the subplot bottling called Carrie's, as well as another labeled Terraces. This is a producer to watch very closely.

Mosby Winery—Owner-winemaker Bill Mosby is one of Santa Barbara's great iconoclasts. Located near, but not in, the Santa Rita Hills appellation, Mosby is dedicated to Italian grape varieties. He grows some in his own vineyard near the winery; other grapes come from Los Alamos Valley or farther afield. All are works in progress, just like Italianate wines everywhere else in California. Here you can find renditions of such Italian grape varieties as Cortese, Teroldego, Sangiovese, Dolcetto, and Lagrein, among others. Not all are successful, as Bill Mosby himself concedes, but he is dogged. And one can only applaud his sincerity and commitment—and keep tasting. It would be a mistake to tour the area and not visit Mosby.

Andrew Murray Vineyards—A complicated thirty-five-acre hillside vineyard subdivided by soil and exposure into twenty-six steep hillside subplots, this Santa Ynez Valley winery is dedicated to Syrah, with accompanying interests in other Rhône varieties such as Marsanne, Roussanne, Viognier, and Grenache. The vineyard is one of Santa Barbara County's most unusual, located at perhaps the highest elevation (1,500 feet) of any site in Santa Ynez Valley. Although warm, its elevation offsets that.

Andrew Murray Vineyards is still a work in progress, but there's little question that Syrah is the ticket. Already closely followed by California's Rhônistas, this winery will surely make its mark as the vineyard is located in a singular site.

The Ojai Vineyard—Although located in the Ojai Valley in Ventura County, south of Santa Barbara, it's fair to say that owner-winemaker Adam Tolmach is still, both in spirit and in the bottle, a Santa Barbara County winemaker. After all, he was a winemaking partner with Jim Clendenen at Au Bon Climat until he decided to sell his share and start his own winery in Ojai in 1983. To this day, most of Ojai's 6,000-case production is sourced from

Santa Barbara County.

What matters though is quality. And in this respect Santa Barbara County should be delighted to call Tolmach one of their own: Ojai Vineyard's wines are superb. Indeed, few producers anywhere in California are finer. Seemingly everything Tolmach touches is among the best of its type. He buys Chardonnay from Talley's Rincon Vineyard in Arroyo Grande. It's as good as any version I've tasted. Ditto for single-vineyard Pinot Noirs from Bien Nacido in Santa Maria, Clos Pepe in Santa Rita Hills, and Pisoni in Santa Lucia Highlands, as well as Syrahs from Stolpman in Santa Ynez, Bien Nacido in Santa Maria, and Thompson in Los Alamos.

The Ojai Vineyard's house specialty is Roll Ranch (owned by Richard and Suzanne Roll), a seven-acre vineyard in Ojai at 700 feet in elevation that specializes in Syrah, with a little Viognier. Tolmach is a Syrah fan (he makes as many as eight different Syrahs in a single vintage in some years). Roll Ranch is one of his best, a dense, rich, firmly structured Syrah that shows a warm-climate touch of leather and pepper. Winemaking doesn't get much more artisanal and perfectionist than at Ojai Vineyard.

Qupé—Bob Lindquist, the owner-winemaker of Qupé (the Chumash Indian word for poppy, pronounced kew-pay) has almost singlehandedly made a case for California Syrah. In the 1980s, when Syrah was virtually unknown in California in general and Santa Barbara County in particular, it was Lindquist who encouraged the owners of Bien Nacido Vineyard in Santa Maria Valley to plant the variety. And it was Qupé that put it on the wine map, along with other Rhône grapes. Today, Qupé has a (rightly) loyal clientele for its various bottlings of Syrah, Viognier, Grenache (wonderfully sourced from Purisima Mountain Vineyard), Marsanne, and always successful Chardonnay.

Rancho Sisquoc Winery—The image of an underachieving gifted child comes to mind with Rancho Sisquoc Winery, which is owned by the Flood family of San Francisco, whose fortune derives from the fabled Comstock Lode silver mine in Nevada. You can see the Flood Building on Market Street in San Francisco, the tallest building west of the Mississippi when it was built in 1906. Rancho Sisquoc is just a tiny part of a 37,000-acre ranch. It's the largest single private landholding in Santa Barbara County.

Rancho Sisquoc's vineyard site is possibly unique. Located at a nexus just where the cool Santa Maria Valley ends and the warm Santa Ynez Valley begins (technically Rancho Sisquoc is in the Santa Maria Valley AVA), it's in own climatic world. Most of what is produced by Rancho Sisquoc's 141 acres of vines is contracted to other wineries such as Robert Mondavi. Only a small portion is dedicated to their label.

Rancho Sisquoc has long dwelled at a commercial level. Lately, though, there are faint stirrings of ambition, but not enough to vault the wines to meet the competition. No one who visits the property can doubt the capacity of this vineyard to create singular wines, if its owners so chose. Cabernet Franc is the "genius grape" here, as various vintages have long demonstrated it to be stellar. Really, it's all about ambition and rigor—or rather, the lack of it.

Rideau Vineyard—Former insurance broker Iris Rideau opened her winery in a historic adobe house in Santa Ynez Valley in 1997 and in an amazingly short time made it one of the most popular winery tourist stops in Santa Barbara County. It's all very personal. Non-wine-geek types feel at home at Rideau, something the New Orleans-born Rideau has encouraged with singular success. The wines are good enough, but not exceptional—but the welcome is.

Rusack Vineyards—One of the up-and-comers in Santa Ynez's Ballard Canyon zone, Rusack Vineyards is the 1995 creation of Geoff and Alison Rusack. The twenty-four-acre vineyard is being replanted with all the bells and whistles: new clones, different grape varieties, new rootstocks, etc. Any judgment about the wines really deserves to wait until the new vines are installed and bearing, as the current production does not truly reflect future potential. At minimum, though, this is a winery worth watching.

Sanford Winery and Vineyards—The saga of Sanford Winery is one of the longest in Santa Barbara County and inextricably intertwined with its namesake, Sanford & Benedict Vineyard.

In 1971 Richard Sanford (a geographer) and Michael Benedict (a botanist) bought a 674-acre ranch in what is now Santa Rita Hills AVA and planted Pinot Noir and Chardonnay, among other grapes such as Riesling, Cabernet Sauvignon, and Merlot. In 1980 their partnership dissolved. Benedict kept the vineyard. Sanford bought a large ranch in the Santa Rita Hills called Rancho El Jabali and planted a small, seven-acre Pinot Noir and Chardonnay vineyard.

Sanford created his own winery in a warehouse in nearby Buellton. In

1990 Benedict sold the vineyard (the asking price was $3.5 million), which had since been renamed Benedict Vineyard. The new owners, Robert and Janice Atkins, live in London. They contracted with Sanford to manage the vineyard and purchase its grapes. The original name of Sanford & Benedict Vineyard was restored. (The Atkinses are now minority partners in Sanford Winery.)

Got all that? Now fast-forward to the twenty-first century. In 2001 Sanford opened a large, elegant adobe block winery in Santa Rita Hills on a 425-acre parcel, called Rancho Rinconada (Little Corner) contiguous to Sanford & Benedict Vineyard. A 130-acre vineyard was planted in 1997, devoted to Pinot Noir (seventy acres) and Chardonnay (sixty acres).

In 1999, Sanford created yet another vineyard just down the road called La Vina, with 100 acres of vines, nearly all of which are Pinot Noir. The first crop arrived in the 2003 vintage.

Today, Sanford Winery is arguably California's most ambitious Pinot Noir enterprise. A few other Pinot Noir enterprises are larger, such as Laetitia in Arroyo Grande. And others in Santa Rita Hills, such as Foley and Sea Smoke, among others, are similarly driven. But the combined production of Sanford & Benedict, La Rinconada, and La Vina vineyards is a formidable asset.

And how are the wines? In a phrase: better than ever. Where before, Sanford Pinot Noirs often veered to the excessively oaky, today Bruno d'Alfono's palate seems more finely calibrated and nuanced. Also, having a custom-made winery has made a difference, which he freely concedes. Simply having the wines in barrel in a cooler place than the old warehouse has altered their maturation and oak take-up, all for the better.

Sanford Winery is effectively an old soul in a vigorous new, young body—an enviable condition.

Sea Smoke—One of the glossy new Pinot Noir properties in Santa Rita Hills, the 100-acre Sea Smoke vineyard is in the same neighborhood as Sanford & Benedict and Fiddlestix vineyards. It has some of same Botella clay loam they have. It's also a single-purpose vineyard, devoted exclusively to Pinot Noir. Sea Smoke's owner, computer game developer Bob Davids, installed ten different clones across twenty-three different parcels, with numerous rootstocks to match the inevitable soil variations.

Two bottlings were issued in the inaugural 2001 vintage, labeled Botella and Southing. A third bottling, called Ten, is scheduled to appear, a blend of all ten clones in the vineyard. And how are the wines? Based on just these two 2001 bottlings, they are, of course, promising. The Botella label is intended as the "entry-level" Sea Smoke wine. The 2001 Botella is dark, dense, and relatively simple. The 2001 Southing bottling is more complex and layered, with black fruits and considerable oak spices.

The vines are still very young and the winemaking, inevitably, will grow more deft and nuanced with each vintage. But there's no doubting the ambition and the commitment. By any standard, Sea Smoke is a contender. Whether it will equal or surpass its neighboring competition will be highly pleasurable to judge.

Benjamin Silver Wines—A former winemaker for Zaca Mesa Winery (like seemingly everyone else in Santa Barbara County), Benjamin Silver is an unusually talented winemaker in his early thirties. As he has no vineyards of his own, he is necessarily dependent upon others for his grapes. Yet what he does with those grapes is impressive.

For example, in a lineup of multiple versions of the same vintage of Cambria's "Julia's Vineyard," the Benjamin Silver bottling was for this taster the outstanding wine of the bunch. Silver simply said that he harvested later. Even a Nebbiolo, a grape that no one has succeeded with in California so far, came closer to hitting the mark than any other I've tried. When he can obtain choice fruit (such as Cabernet Franc from Thompson Vineyard), Benjamin Silver creates superb wines.

Stolpman—Tom Stolpman (a Los Angeles lawyer), and his wife, Marilyn, bought a twenty-two-acre ranch in Ballard Canyon in Santa Ynez Valley. More than some other properties, it is a work in progress if only because Stolpman took the adventurous step of pursuing Italian varieties such as Sangiovese along with more conventional and likely-to-succeed sorts as Cabernet Sauvignon, Syrah, and Grenache.

Expanded to 170 vineyard acres of vines planted in calcareous soil, Stolpman rings the changes with multiple wines of (inevitably) varying quality. So far, the Italian varieties do not yet seem convincing to this taster, lacking varietal depth and flavor accuracy. But then, few such attempts have succeeded anywhere in California so far.

That acknowledged, Stolpman comes into the top rank with its Syrah,

Grenache, and a stunning Bordeaux-type blend called Limestone Hill Cuvée, which is one of the best such blends I've tasted from anywhere in the state. Anyone who submits that Cabernet Sauvignon & Co. have no place in Santa Ynez Valley has not tasted this wine.

It's impossible to observe Stolpman without noting its contiguous neighbor, Beckmen Vineyards. They share the same vineyard management company, very similar chalky soil, the same fierce ambition, and some similar grapes such as Grenache and Syrah. Winemaking, inevitably, is different. And their respective elevations and exposures are different too. But in some ways, like Burgundy's great vineyards, these two wineries will always be joined at the hip—and inevitably compared.

Lane Tanner—One of Santa Barbara County's starry fixtures, Lane Tanner pursues a vision of Pinot Noir that emphasizes delicacy and finesse over emphatic fruitiness and inky color. Does it work? You bet. As with all the other small producers who buy fruit, Tanner's wines reflect the quality of the source.

In recent years, her winemaking has somehow seemed more sure-handed, but that's just one taster's impression. Syrah from Purisima Hills Vineyard is first-rate, as is the Pinot Noir from Melville in Santa Rita Hills.

Tantara Winery—A new Santa Maria Valley winery plunked in the Bien Nacido Vineyard, from which they purchase fruit. With already excellent Chardonnays from Bien Nacido and Talley Vineyards, the winery seeks to specialize in Pinot Noirs sourced from numerous sites, including Bien Nacido and Dierberg in Santa Maria Valley, as well as Pisoni and Garys' vineyards in Santa Lucia Highlands in Monterey County. Certainly a winery to watch.

Tensley Winery—Thirtysomething Joey Tensley creates small lots of superb Syrah from Purisima Hills Vineyard (where Tensely once worked as an assistant winemaker), Thompson Vineyard, and Colson Canyon in Santa Maria Valley. This is Syrah seen through a Pinot Noir lens: supple, intense, fragrant, and fine-grained. Each vineyard is unmistakable from the others, in true Burgundy fashion. In an competition of bottlings from these vineyards (others buy the same fruit), Tensley is sure to be at the very top.

Westerley Vineyards—One of the new vineyards in the easternmost (and thus warmest) zone of Santa Ynez Valley called Happy Canyon, transplanted New Yorkers Neil and Francine Afromsky have planted an eight-five-acre vineyard emphasizing multiple Rhône varieties, as well as Sauvignon Blanc and Cabernet Sauvignon.

It's still early days, but the Viognier is a standout, as is the Sauvignon Blanc. It's a very good bet that this vineyard will, like nearby Vogelzang Vineyard, demonstrate the worth of the as-yet-unheralded Happy Canyon district. Probably in another decade it will seek its own AVA—and deserve it.

Whitcraft—Few winemakers are more unswerving in their dedication to non-interventionist Pinot Noir winemaking than owner-winemaker Chris Whitcraft. He will not filter or fine his wines, uses as little sulfur as possible, employs wild yeasts (as opposed to inoculating the juice with cultured yeasts), will not pump his wines, and even tries to avoid using devices that require electricity. The only thing missing is candlelight!

Does such purism make a difference? Sure it does. Whitcraft, like many other small wine producers, must secure his grapes from others, as he has no vines of his own. When those grapes are good, this sort of rigor reveals their worth. When the grapes are of lesser quality, it shows. That's the price of purity. Various bottlings of Pinot Noir blocks from Bien Nacido are offered, as well as Pinot Noirs from Hirsch Vineyard in Sonoma Coast, and Melville in Santa Rita Hills. The latter two are my personal preferences.

Whitcraft is a great Pinot Noir producer who only needs access to equally great grapes to show what he can do.

Zaca Mesa Winery—The perennial underachiever of Santa Barbara County. It's hard to feel sorry for Zaca Mesa Winery. Like Firestone Vineyard, it's been around long enough (since 1972) to literally and figuratively know better. The Cushman family has been the only owner and, like the Flood family of Rancho Sisquoc, they just haven't done the job.

True, they pioneered Syrah in Santa Barbara County back in 1978, making it the oldest planting in the county. And true, Zaca Mesa has had an astonishing array of talented winemakers who later went on to greater heights in their own wineries (Jim Clendenen, Bob Lindquist, Ken Brown, Benjamin Silver, and Daniel Gehrs, among others).

And true, every now and then, one wine or another is an undisputed winner. (It's usually a Syrah.) But there's no getting around the fact that Zaca Mesa isn't what it should be. It *should* be great. The vines are mature; the experience is present. The site is excellent. But the rigor and commitment to quality are lacking.

On my last visit in 2003, they insisted they're changing for the better. But that's been said before. Given Zaca Mesa's history, wine buyers are well advised to take a wait-and-see approach.

SANTA CRUZ MOUNTAINS

I am struck in California by the deep and almost religious affection which people have for nature, and by the sensitiveness they show to its influences . . . It is their spontaneous substitute for articulate art and articulate religion, and is perhaps, the substance out of which these may someday be formed afresh.

—George Santayana, *The Letters of George Santayana* (1911)

If George Santayana had chosen to become a California winegrower, he probably would have found himself drawn to the Santa Cruz Mountains. It has long been the place where an odd lot of isolated winegrowers have sensitively struggled with nature. Not for them was—or is—the easygoing fertility of Napa Valley or Sonoma County, where the Establishment has long practiced the "articulate art and articulate religion" of conventional California winegrowing.

The Santa Cruz Mountains seemingly have always been different. Part of it surely is the nature of growing grapes in pockets of isolation, which is the inevitable fate of mountain winegrowers everywhere. But partly there was—and is—an attraction of place. Certain personalities seem to seek out the Santa Cruz Mountains.

One thinks of Martin Ray, who died in 1976, as the quintessential Santa Cruz mountaineer. After pursuing big-time California winemaking by buying the Paul Masson winery from Masson himself, and subsequently selling it to Joseph E. Seagram & Sons, he created a personal winery in a site high above the Santa Clara Valley, almost voluptuously removed from everyday contact with the world. This in the 1940s, when the Santa Clara Valley abounded in apricots, not silicon chips and tract houses.

What's more, his goal was no less than Burgundian-style Pinot Noir and Chardonnay. His vines were planted in soil that grudges little more than one ton to the acre. Ray was famously combative, a zealot's zealot. Such a personality could not then, or now, get along in Napa Valley's clubby atmosphere any more than a wolverine could splash about with a family of otters. The Santa Cruz Mountains were his inevitable spiritual home.

Ray has been succeeded by other equally individualistic, if not quite so irascible, producers. One need only think of the seemingly mainstream Ridge Vineyards, which actually is one of California's most visionary wineries. Or the intransigent Kathryn Kennedy Winery (whose eponymous owner refuses to sell her vineyards, despite their million-dollar-an-acre worth as residential property). Or the beam-me-up public relations genius of Randall Grahm of Bonny Doon Vineyard, whose wines, wit, and innovation are the epitome of California wine sophistication.

There is a Santa Cruz Mountains AVA. It is mostly mountainous, bordered by the Pacific Ocean on the west and by the valley floor of the Santa Clara Valley (a.k.a. the Silicon Valley) on the eastern, or inland, side. If you envision the Santa Cruz Mountains AVA as all the mountainous territory between Half Moon Bay in the north and the town of Santa Cruz to the south, you'd pretty much have it right.

Actually, the Santa Cruz Mountains AVA is more complicated than the official line-drawing. Because it is so mountainous, and because of the profound influence of the Pacific Ocean, which forms its entire western border, there really are multiple, unofficial AVAs lurking within the general designation.

Vegetation is a giveaway. When you see Santa Cruz Mountains Vineyards, carved out of dense, towering redwoods just a few miles inland from the town of Santa Cruz, you know you're seeing an utterly different grape-growing site than the wind-scoured hillsides of the Monte Bello Ridge, which overlooks Palo Alto on the eastern side of the AVA. Both are Santa Cruz Mountains AVA, yet one landscape seems tropical, the other lunar.

In time, this overly large AVA will be subdivided, probably along the lines of an ocean-influenced zone to the west and a (Santa Clara) valley-influenced zone in the east. This already has begun, with the creation of the Ben Lomond Mountain AVA, which incorporates an ocean-influenced section of Santa Cruz County. Bonny Doon Vineyard is the most prominent winery in the Ben Lomond Mountain AVA. So far, few wines have been released bearing this designation, so its actual wine significance remains unclear.

At present, the Santa Cruz Mountains wineries and vineyards are either clustered on the ridgeline above and around the inland town of Saratoga (Ridge, Mount Eden, Kathryn Kennedy, Klein) or widely dispersed in the woods above and around the town of Santa Cruz (David Bruce, Ahlgren, Roudon-Smith, Hallcrest).

Nevertheless, there is a commonality among all true Santa Cruz Mountains vineyards: low yields. Vineyards in these hills regularly (some might say chronically) report vineyard yields of one ton per acre. A yield of two tons is much pursued, but only sporadically achieved. Mount Eden Vineyard, Martin Ray's old vineyard, gets an average of one ton per acre. Santa Cruz Mountains Vineyard has never gotten more than sixteen tons of grapes from its thirteen-acre vineyard. Ridge Vineyards' famous Monte Bello vineyard, planted to Cabernet Sauvignon, rarely achieves more than two tons per acre.

Such low yields, apart from their dire economic consequences, are both the bane and blessing of the best Santa Cruz Mountains wines. Although low yields are always desirable, it can reach a point of diminishing returns, in every sense. Too much concentration of flavor, too much extraction, and too little juice all make a wine unbalanced. Otherwise compelling flavors can seem outsized, even grotesque. But when proportion is achieved, Santa Cruz Mountain wines can deliver a profundity found nowhere else in California. (This is why I think George Santayana would have chosen the place.)

These low yields, as much as anything, explain one important-to-remember fact about Santa Cruz Mountains producers: Nearly all of them make wine from grapes grown elsewhere. Only a handful of producers in the Santa Cruz Mountains AVA make wines exclusively from grapes grown in the AVA, let alone only from their own vineyard. After all, Santa Cruz County—which comprises most, although not all, of the AVA—has just 300 acres of vineyards. (All of the Santa Cruz Mountains have about 1,000 acres of vines.) The AVA also reaches into San Mateo County to the north and incorporates a long sliver of Santa Clara County to the east.

Ridge Vineyards, for example, has long been acclaimed for its adventurousness in using grapes grown seemingly everywhere in California. In part it *was* adventurousness. But it also was necessity. The same is true for Bonny Doon Vineyard, where owner Randall Grahm has reached as far north as Oregon to purchase Pinot Noir grapes. As Jeffrey Patterson, the winemaker of Mount Eden Vineyards, freely admits, "If we didn't make Chardonnay from Edna Valley grapes, we couldn't afford to make our estate-bottled Chardonnay."

As a result, more than with most wineries in California, one must pay particular attention to the labels of Santa Cruz Mountains wineries if one seeks the expression of place. The wineries are scrupulous in this matter. Here again, Ridge Vineyards turned a necessity into a trademark: Its instantly recognizable label was designed, in large part, to accommodate and convey precisely this sort of information.

As for the Santa Cruz Mountain wines, three stand out: Cabernet Sauvignon, Chardonnay, and Pinot Noir. At their best, all three share a remarkable degree of concentration, no doubt thanks to the absurdly low yields. Also, again at their best, a savor of the earth is present. Whether this is from soil composition, as it might be with the Franciscan shale of the Monte Bello Ridge, or from thin, rocky soils allied with high (1,400 to 2,300 feet) elevations, is not immediately apparent. One thing is, though: The Santa Cruz Mountains can create wines that deliver a real distinction of place.

This distinction is most apparent in the Chardonnays. The best ones are intense and stony. The intensity derives from sunlight and low yields; the stoniness is a function of acidity from higher elevations coupled with a smack of the earth. To see the distinction of Santa Cruz Mountains Chardonnay, compare Mount Eden Vineyard's luxuriant Edna Valley Chardonnay, with its equally concentrated but far more austere estate-grown Chardonnay.

The Cabernets are similarly large-scale yet restrained. Concentration is both its asset and potential undoing. The low yields can topple a wine into flabbiness, which seems to occur with some frequency in Santa Cruz Cabernets. That said, the best versions are resinous, in the most attractive sense of the word.

Pinot Noir is problematic, as always. The concentration makes it difficult to achieve the requisite delicacy that sets apart the best Pinot Noirs. However, there exists an earthiness in Santa Cruz Pinot Noirs that speaks of place. Coupled with winemaking that strives for delicacy in the delivery of these flavors, the area has real promise as a source of Pinot Noir that evokes a sense of somewhereness.

Santa Cruz Mountains is currently experiencing a spurt of growth from a most unlikely source: ultra-expensive McMansions sited on plots of two or three acres. Keep in mind that a good portion of the Santa Cruz Mountains appellation is affected by the vast wealth generated by Silicon Valley.

Traditional winegrowing areas such as Saratoga (where Mount Eden and Cooper-Garrard wineries, among others, are located) are major residential areas for Silicon Valley's well-paid elite. They buy two- or three-acre lots for millions of dollars and then put up preposterously large "Tuscan" homes on the sites. But there's typically an acre or so of land remaining. It's now the fashion to install a "micro-vineyard" on that acre, which is tended by companies that do nothing but manage just such one-acre micro-vineyards.

In fact, one of Santa Cruz Mountains' most promising new wineries, Clos LaChance, is based entirely on creating such micro-vineyards, servicing them, and contracting for the grapes. It costs about $30,000 an acre to install the vineyard, the winery reports, and they charge the homeowners an annual $4,000 to $5,000 maintenance fee and Clos LaChance buys the grapes for $6,000 an acre. If the homeowners want, Clos LaChance will produce a private bottling and labeling of the homeowner's wine.

The idea had proved so popular that a residential development, called CordeValle, with thirty-six three-acre sites in San Martin, was designed with micro-vineyards as part of the plan. (San Martin is a suburb in the valley-floor flatland midway between San Jose and Gilroy, well away from Santa Cruz Mountains AVA.) Not coincidentally, Clos LaChance has its winery in San Martin. It is installing and managing the development's micro-vineyards (at no charge to the residents), as well as processing the grapes for the Clos LaChance label. The homeowners will not participate in any winery profit; like homeowners situated along golf courses, they simply gaze upon the cultivated beauty of the greenery.

The result of dozens of these micro-vineyards, especially in choice Santa Cruz Mountains AVA locales such as Saratoga, is that there are now, ironically, more grapes available today from historically renowned Santa Cruz Mountains vineyard sites than when these residential sites were undeveloped and still agrarian. Who could have predicted it?

Santa Cruz Mountains Producers Worth Seeking Out (And Some Not)

Ahlgren Vineyard—A tiny winery that, despite its approximately 1,500-case-a-year production, still brings in grapes from all over, including Syrah (Monterey County and Paso Robles) and Sémillon (Livermore Valley). The most impressive wines here are, not surprisingly, from Bates Ranch in Santa Cruz Mountains. Look especially for an excellent Cabernet Sauvignon, as well as a rarely seen Merlot from Bates Ranch. A Bates Ranch Cabernet Franc (with 25 percent Cabernet Sauvignon) is, at minimum, intriguing. Production of all of these is necessarily in small quantities.

Beauregard Vineyards—One of the few producers to use the Ben Lomond Mountain designation on their label for their estate-grown wines, as well as from other vineyards in the area around the town of Bonny Doon. Look for a rich, succulent Chardonnay from Beauregard Ranch, as well as nearby Meyley Ranch (managed by the Beauregard family), also in the Ben Lomond Mountain AVA. Cabernet Sauvignon from Beauregard Ranch is intense, strong, and promising. Yet another fine Chardonnay, with comparable citrus notes (which seems to be a Beauregard trademark) comes from their estate, Bald Mountain Vineyard, which lies astride the Ben Lomond and Santa Cruz Mountains AVAs. Worth noting is an excellent Hirsch Vineyard Pinot Noir from Sonoma Coast, from which Beauregard (by virtue of an old friendship with owner David Hirsch) is fortunate to be able to purchase grapes. Beauregard is a winery very much on the rise.

Burrell School Vineyards—A small estate started in 1991 that specializes only in Santa Cruz Mountains-grown wines, a rarity in Santa Cruz Mountains. Because of this, production is necessarily tiny. Look for lovely, rich, intense, metallic Chardonnay, a distinctive only-in-Santa Cruz Pinot Noir that has a taste of the soil rarely found elsewhere in California, as well as promising Syrah and Cabernet Franc. Like so many other small Santa Cruz Mountains wineries, Burrell School is still refining its winemaking, but this is a winery that will make its mark.

Byington Winery—A small Santa Cruz winery that, like nearly everyone else, makes most of its wines from grapes purchased outside of the area. Byington's own eight acres of vines are planted to Pinot Noir, which are not irrigated, resulting in classic Santa Cruz Mountains low yields. It's good

Pinot Noir that, like others from the area, requires several years of cellaring before it will fully blossom, revealing earthy notes.

Chardonnay from Sangiacomo Vineyard in Carneros is also offered, as is a Sémillon/Sauvignon/Viognier blend called Alliage (French for alloy). Worth noting is an excellent Santa Cruz Mountains-grown Cabernet Sauvignon from Bates Ranch. Byington is fast becoming one of the better producers in Santa Cruz Mountains.

Bonny Doon Vineyard—In a state chockablock with me-too wineries and accountants masquerading as winemakers (or vice versa), owner-winemaker Randall Grahm of Bonny Doon Vineyard stands out as an original. A confessed contrarian, Grahm is unabashedly European in his orientation. Originally entranced by Burgundy, he attempted to mimic Burgundian soils by plowing ten tons of limestone per acre into his Pinot Noir plot. (The Pinot Noir vines have since given way to other varieties.)

Then, Grahm became entranced by Rhône Valley varieties such as Syrah, Grenache, Roussanne, Viognier, Marsanne, and Mourvèdre. Then he went on to Italianate grapes as Nebbiolo and Sangiovese, as well as producing grappa.

All of these interests, and others such as fruit infusions (fruit juice such as raspberry blended with brandy), are issued with unequalled panache. He does everything with what the Italians call *la bella figura*—a beautiful style. No wine labels anywhere are wittier; no one writes more worldly or polished winery newsletters. No one markets his wines more bravely. Witness Grahm's most recent foray into issuing his wines with screw caps rather than corks, launched with "funerals" for the cork in New York and London.

What is less apparent to the casual observer is that, despite Grahm's devil-may-care counterculture image (he *is* from Santa Cruz after all), Bonny Doon is far more than a hippie boutique winery. Bonny Doon's production is now about 250,000 cases a year. And Grahm gets very good prices for his wines, too. Few California wineries have been more successful, especially when you consider that Bonny Doon is off the beaten tourist tracks of Napa and Sonoma.

Above all, the wines are good. This is what saves Grahm from being merely a huckster, however sophisticated. He does deliver. The Grenache bottling called Clos de Gilroy after the source of the grapes (Gilroy usually being known as the garlic capital of the world) would make a Rhône resident proud. His Châteauneuf-du-Pâpe replica, called Le Cigare Volant (the French term for a flying saucer—in this case a flying cigar), is lovely wine, although the folks in Châteauneuf-du-Pâpe still don't have much cause for concern. And so it goes. What Robert Mondavi is to the business of California fine wine, Randall Grahm is to California's fine-wine spirit—with a nod to Mondavi's business acumen for extra measure.

David Bruce Winery—For many observers, David Bruce and his wines are emblematic of what some might call Santa Cruz Mountains madness. Bruce is far from mad, although he is affably idiosyncratic. He makes his living as a dermatologist, but wine gripped him while he was still in medical school. He certainly is heir to the Martin Ray tradition, if not the temperament. And he does go back: Bruce founded his winery in 1964.

The identification of Santa Cruz Mountains madness with Bruce by longtime California wine fanciers no doubt is the result of a two-decade-long series of genuinely bizarre wine issuing (some might say emanating) from Bruce's winery-in-a-barn tucked amid the trees. For some, these wines were wondrous: late-harvest Zinfandels of a scale previously unimagined, huge, oaky Chardonnays, and strange but nevertheless intriguing Pinot Noirs. It was Bruce, I believe, who created California's first white Zinfandel, back in 1964. He was fiddling with Grenache long before the so-called Rhône Rangers galloped into fashion.

The wines were purposely made with as little handling as possible, an intellectually attractive notion that too often results in great variability and some downright bad bottles. Bruce made those, too. By the late 1970s, the mention of Santa Cruz winemaking almost automatically brought forth a vision of Bruce's wines.

Today, you wouldn't know such a tumultuous past existed, at least not to taste the current wines. After a run of surprisingly meek wines, Bruce is back in top form with wines that are typically lovely expressions of place. Inevitably, as they are sourced from all over California, quality varies. But the Petite Sirahs stand out, as do the Pinot Noirs and Cabernets. Today, David Bruce Winery is better than ever.

Cinnabar Vineyards and Winery—If David Bruce Winery was an icon of the old ways of Santa Cruz Mountains winegrowing, then Cinnabar is the gleaming model of the "new" Santa Cruz Mountains, with its handsome, well-equipped winery and aging caves. Located in the hills above Saratoga, the first vintage from Cinnabar's twenty-four-acre vineyard appeared in 1986. Only Cabernet Sauvignon and Chardonnay are produced. Regrettably, the winemaking style has evolved into wines that are, despite the impressive raw material of their grapes, far too oaky and heavy-handed. This is a pity, as Cinnabar's vineyards are first-rate. Santa Cruz Mountains has so few native vineyards of any size that to suffocate these grapes under an excess of new French oak is a far greater loss than when the same mistake occurs—as it often does—in Napa or Sonoma.

Clos LaChance—Owned by Bill and Brenda Murphy (LaChance is co-owner Brenda Murphy's maiden name), Clos LaChance specializes in creating Santa Cruz Mountains wines that are gleaned, like a honeybee methodically working from one flower to the next, from nearly two dozen micro-vineyards sited in the backyards of multimillion dollar residences in the hills above Silicon Valley. Many of these residences are located in areas that, before Prohibition, were highly regarded for the quality of their grapes.

Not surprisingly, Clos LaChance is issuing excellent wines, notably a strong, dimensional Cabernet Sauvignon as well as excellent, rich, deep, absolutely typical (in the best sense) Santa Cruz Mountains Chardonnay. Look also for a fine single-vineyard Pinot Noir from Erwin Vineyard near Loma Prieta.

As Clos LaChance continues to expand, it's worthwhile to pay close attention to the appellation on the label as an increasing amount of fruit is being sourced outside Clos LaChance's original focus, the Santa Cruz Mountains AVA. This is one of the area's most ambitious wineries, which is all to everybody's good.

Cooper-Garrard Vineyards—An estate near Saratoga that has long farmed in the area now covered by twenty-eight acres of vines. The estate-grown Cabernet Sauvignon and Cabernet Franc are the best bets here, offering characteristic Santa Cruz Mountains earthiness and density. Look also for a fairly new Syrah, which holds considerable promise. A winery to watch.

Cronin Vineyards—Although located in Woodside, a small, bucolic town near Palo Alto, the tiny Cronin Winery (2,000 cases annually) has made an outsized mark for its multiple Chardonnays. In classic Santa Cruz-area fashion, the grapes come from all over, notably from Ventana Vineyards in Monterey. Two others are from Napa Valley and Sonoma's Alexander Valley. A recent edition is a Santa Cruz Mountains Chardonnay, from Cronin's own one-acre plot of vines. Also made, in inevitably small quantities, is a Cabernet/Merlot blend, one from Santa Cruz Mountain AVA and another from Napa Valley grapes.

Fellom Ranch Vineyards—If place means anything in wine—allied, of course, with competent winemaking—then Fellom Ranch Vineyards can be counted among the most promising wineries in California. The reason is simple: Its twelve-acre vineyard is contiguous with Ridge Vineyard's Monte Bello Vineyard, the source of one of California's finest Cabernets. Although the Fellom Ranch Cabernet is not the equal of Ridge Montebello, it's still a distinctive, more-than-worthy competitor (at a much lower price, too). Also look for an excellent Zinfandel.

Thomas Fogarty Winery—Where many of the Santa Cruz-area wineries were, and are, shoestring operations, Thomas Fogarty Winery is anything but down at the heels. Named after its owner, a cardiovascular surgeon who invented a lucrative medical device (a type of catheter), among other patents, the winery occupies a stunning hillside site on the ridgeline overlooking the Santa Clara Valley. Everything is present a winery could want, including a commercial kitchen of the sort usually found only in successful restaurants. The wines, however, are less impressive.

Here again, grapes are brought in from all over to augment the twenty-four-acre estate vineyard. A Sauvignon Blanc from Amador County can be found, as well as a Monterey County Chardonnay and Gewürztraminer from the ubiquitous Ventana Vineyard, a Carneros-grown Pinot Noir, and a Napa Valley Pinot Noir. All of these are sound, unexceptional wines.

The Santa Cruz renditions are somewhat better, notably the Chardonnay, which displays the stoniness and finely etched flavors characteristic of Santa Cruz Mountains Chardonnays. The Santa Cruz Pinot Noir is less attractive, suffering from heavy-handedness found all too often in Santa Cruz Mountain Pinot Noirs.

Hallcrest Vineyards—Worth noting because it is the revival of a once-famous name. Hallcrest was founded in the 1940s by a San Francisco corporate attorney named Chaffee Hall. He lavished considerable personal attention on his wines, functioning as his own winemaker. Hall issued only two wines, both made from his vineyard at the crest of a hill above the town of Felton, hence the Hallcrest name.

Cabernet Sauvignon and Riesling were the Hallcrest specialties, each identified as coming from Santa Cruz County and presented in a bottle wrapped in wire-mesh. The wines were highly regarded in the 1950s. Hallcrest ceased operation in 1969. In 1976 it reopened under the now-defunct name Felton-Empire. It, in turn, dissolved, and the vineyard and winery were sold in 1988. The new owners restored the Hallcrest name. Grapes now come from all over, with some good Riesling emerging from the estate's five-and-a-half-acre vineyard.

Kathryn Kennedy Winery—Another tiny Santa Cruz Mountains winery, it has several distinctions. One of them is that this winery surely cannot continue indefinitely. Kathryn Kennedy is a woman of formidable stubbornness, as one of her sons, who is the winemaker, feels free to point out. Her stubbornness is this: The eight-acre vineyard is sited on residentially zoned land that, depending on the economy, sells for between $500,000 and $1 million an acre—undeveloped. What's more, Kennedy's other son is a real estate developer. But Kennedy wants no part of the great California real estate cashout. In fact, that was why, in 1973, she chose to start a vineyard to begin with, in order to prevent a road from being built near her home. But economics surely will win in the end. The current economic downturn in Silicon Valley has slowed real estate development, but that can't last forever.

The Kennedy vineyard is located in the rain shadow of a mountain, at the top of which is Mount Eden Vineyards. As a result, the vineyard is lucky to get nine inches of rain a year. Drip irrigation was installed, but even so the yields are preposterously low, sometimes as little as one-half ton per acre. It has the questionable distinction of having reported the lowest yield I've ever heard of in California: one-quarter ton per acre in 1990. Other years see a "normal" one ton per acre. (In Napa Valley, in comparison, four to five tons per acre on the valley floor is average.)

Cabernet Sauvignon is the specialty of the winery. As might be expected, it is immensely concentrated, dense, and reminiscent of Château Latour in its massiveness. It is classic Santa Cruz Mountains Cabernet. A brand-named wine called Lateral is a deft blend of roughly two-thirds Merlot and one-third Cabernet Franc (with a little Cabernet Sauvignon) from purchased grapes. It is designated "California." Also, there's an outstanding recent release called Odd Lot Cabernet blended from various Santa Cruz Mountains micro-vineyards. A truly superb Syrah has recently been issued from Santa Cruz Mountains grapes. Kathryn Kennedy is today one of California's greatest artisan wineries.

Mount Eden Vineyards—More than any other spot, the lofty Mount Eden Vineyard is the spiritual epicenter of the Santa Cruz Mountains. What is Mount Eden Vineyards today was previously the old Martin Ray vineyard, as well as his former home.

Actually, there still exists a vineyard named for Ray just below that of Mount Eden, but no wine has been issued since the 1983 vintage. The gist of the story is that after untangling the web of legal troubles caused by Ray himself, the court divided Ray's property. His family received the smaller portion of Ray's vineyard, the grapes from which now are sold to others.

Anyway, the original Ray winery was renamed Mount Eden Vineyards in 1972 and it, too, underwent a fair amount of winery tumult, with several owners and winemakers passing through before stability finally was established in the mid 1980s. Now, the winery seems set on a sure and true course.

The hillside vineyard occupies one of the most spectacular, and removed, sites of any in California, overlooking the Santa Clara Valley. From Mount Eden's 2,000-foot elevation, the remove is such that at night the densely populated Santa Clara Valley, a blanket of sparkling lights, seems more a distant galaxy than urban encroachment.

Mount Eden's vineyard is planted to Cabernet Sauvignon (the old vines were recently pulled out and replanted), Chardonnay, and Pinot Noir. All three are distinctive, intense, and characteristically Santa Cruz Mountains in their concentration and dimension.

The style of Mount Eden's wines changed significantly starting in 1981. Where before the wines veered toward giganticism, by the mid 1980s the goal clearly was toward a greater elegance and proportion.

Today, the Chardonnay is perhaps the most successful achievement. Cabernet Sauvignon, which is intrinsically more difficult to maneuver into elegance, is hulking yet graceful, like a linebacker on skates. The Pinot Noir is steadily improving, moving toward the earthy berryishness that the best Santa Cruz Mountains Pinot Noirs deliver.

Yields at Mount Eden are, like everywhere else in Santa Cruz Mountains, painfully low, typically between one and two tons an acre, tops. Winemaker and co-owner Jeffrey Patterson sensitively handles these grapes in such a manner as to barely leave a trace of his presence upon the wines. This is Santa Cruz Mountains profundity at its purest and most revealing.

Mount Eden also makes a very rewarding Chardonnay from grapes purchased from what used to be called MacGregor Vineyard in Edna Valley. (That vineyard was sold and the name has since been changed to Wolff Vineyards.) It, too, is excellent, but nowhere near as compelling as the estate-bottled Chardonnay. Comparing them is an ideal lesson in California wine somewhereness.

Few wineries in California create more profound, distinctive wines than Mount Eden. Indeed, if I were to present to a visiting European, say, the wines of just one California winery to demonstrate the originality of California wine, I'd choose Mount Eden Vineyards.

Ridge Vineyards—More than with any other California winery, keeping track of Ridge wines is seemingly a full-time job. No winery in California has made more wines, from more named locations, than Ridge—at least I don't think so. Besides, Ridge has been doing it since its founding in 1959, which gives it an edge right there.

Because Ridge, like everyone else in Santa Cruz Mountains, has always made wines from grapes grown far afield, it isn't especially associated with the area. Nevertheless, Ridge is very much Santa Cruz Mountains in spirit, as well as in several of its best wines. The spirit is revealed by the fact that anyone who set out simply to make wine from grapes hauled in from everywhere would have more wisely located near a conveniently situated freeway exit.

Instead, one arrives at the Ridge winery 2,300 feet above the Santa Clara Valley near Cupertino (the birthplace of Apple computers) only after traversing a steep, winding road that leaves you breathless with disbelief. The winery has surely been cursed by every grape-hauling truck driver in California—with reason. Any other winery would have long since relocated, but such is the cussedness of Santa Cruz Mountains winegrowers that Ridge remains where it was born.

Today, Ridge is owned by Akihito Otsuka, whose fortune derives from his Japanese pharmaceutical company. He purchased Ridge in 1986 for a reported $15 to $20 million. This was more impressive considering that Ridge owned relatively little vineyard acreage at the time, only about fifty acres. At Draper's urging, Otsuka subsequently purchased forty acres of land adjoining Ridge's Monte Bello vineyard, of which twenty-five acres are planted to vines.

More than anything, Otsuka bought a brand name, and he apparently is smart enough not to meddle with it. Ridge remains Ridge. Draper remains as winemaker. (And as a former partner, he presumably made out all right in the sale.)

As is well known, the Ridge specialty was Zinfandel and still is. Lately, though, its highest price and greatest fame is achieved by its Santa Cruz Mountain Monte Bello Cabernet Sauvignon, and rightly so. Few California Cabernets are more place-specific than this one. Fewer still are better. It simply is consistently of California's greatest Cabernets.

For a winery that dates to 1959, the Ridge style inevitably has evolved. Most of the wines from the 1970s reflect the bigger-is-better aesthetic of the time. Where before the wines were rude, now they are increasingly articulate and convincing. Scale gave way to detail; the distinctive grain of each wine became more apparent with polish.

Much less well known are Ridge Chardonnays. Indeed, there's a Ridge Monte Bello Chardonnay which is unquestionably one of California's finest renditions, rivaled only by neighboring Mount Eden Estate Chardonnay. A recent tasting of Monte Bello Chardonnay back to 1976 reveals a marvelous capacity to age (and improve), revealing the richness and stoniness that calls to mind a great Corton-Charlemagne, thanks to the limestone soil in Montebello Vineyard.

Ridge Chardonnay has a complicated history. For years there was only the Monte Bello Chardonnay. But Ridge ceased using that name in 1984. It then began issuing its Chardonnay using only the designation "Santa Cruz Mountains," which reflected purchased grapes. Then Ridge returned to the Monte Bello designation in 1996 when the former Jimsomare Vineyard was purchased and folded into Montebello Vineyard. Today, two Chardonnays are regularly offered, with Montebello easily being the better of the two, with a greater density and flavor distinction than the "Santa Cruz Mountains" bottling.

In 1991 Ridge purchased the fifty-acre Lytton Springs vineyard in Sonoma County, the source of some of its best Zinfandel. Also made is a

Mataro (the old California name for Mourvèdre), and various odd lots of wines offered to clients on the winery mailing list.

Where most other California wineries are groping to find the "latest thing," Ridge remains (profitably) true to its original calling, namely, to create source-profound wines that reveal the voice of the earth. For this reason alone, Ridge deserves to be called the conscience of California wine. It's a rare Ridge wine that isn't, at minimum, rewarding, and often, revelatory.

Santa Cruz Mountains Vineyard—Few wineries in the Santa Cruz Mountains have evolved more dramatically, and rewardingly, than this one. A specialist in Pinot Noir, owner/winemaker Ken Burnap had what might be considered a distorted vision of what Pinot Noir should be. The Pinot Noirs made before 1985 were "chainsaw wines": massive, lumbering, and devoid of Pinot Noir expression.

By Burnap's own admission, he had a change of heart, as well as palate. With each succeeding vintage, the Santa Cruz Mountain Vineyard Pinot Noirs have become steadily more delicate, without any sacrifice in flavor distinction. One of those distinctions is a strong earthiness. Now, however, it is allied with the cherry and blackberry scents and tastes that Pinot Noir should have.

The scale and strength of the wines are such that they will never be confused with Pinot Noirs from, say Carneros, but they represent an authentic expression. The yields are pure Santa Cruz Mountains: thirteen acres of Pinot Noir have never given more than sixteen tons. In 1987, for example, the yield was one-half ton per acre. With greater polish and pursuit of delicacy, this winery could create some of the most compelling Pinot Noir in California, wines of a Bonnes Mares sort of strength and longevity.

Also produced is a Santa Cruz Mountains-grown Cabernet Sauvignon from Bates Ranch, as well as a Chardonnay from the charmingly named Treasure Island Vineyard, which is one of the four vineyards of Vanumanutagi Vineyards. (The others are Jekyll, Hyde, and Kidnap Vineyards. See the Vineyard Registry for more detail.) Both are from Santa Cruz Mountains and have merit.

Thunder Mountain—Created in 1994 by Milan Maximovich (who died in 2003), Thunder Mountain specializes in purchased fruit from various Santa Cruz Mountains vineyards. Originally working out of the facility at

Byington Winery, Thunder Mountain subsequently moved to a space inside the Mirassou facility in Livermore. Several single-vineyard Chardonnays are created as well as Cabernets from Bates Ranch. Idiosyncratic wines, often a bit oaky, but equally often rewarding. Whether there will be changes at Thunder Mountain as a result of Maximovich's death is unknown.

SIERRA FOOTHILLS

I believe that the Koyukon people's extraordinary relationship to their natural community has emerged through this careful watching of the same events in the same place, endlessly repeated over lifetimes and generations and millennia. There may be more to learn by climbing the same mountain a hundred times than by climbing a hundred different mountains.
—Richard Nelson, *The Island Within*

Seeing the isolated inhabitations of ancient vineyards of the Sierra Foothills—a sweeping regional AVA that incorporates Amador, El Dorado, Nevada, Placer, Calaveras, Tuolumne, Mariposa, and Yuba counties—called to mind the passage cited above. The writer lived with a Pacific Northwest Indian tribe, the Koyukons, a people who have not moved for thousands of years. He was struck by the implications of how such a sense of place could permeate one's world view.

Nowhere else in California is there such a sense of enduring presence as in the Sierra Foothills. It isn't just the old vines, although that is the manifestation. Many of the vineyards are centenarians. Nor is it the knowledge that this, after all, is Gold Rush country, a fact celebrated and publicized at every little whistle-stop.

Instead, it is the insistent *continuance* of one tribe: Zinfandel. Today, we know that the old vineyards almost invariably contain some Petite Sirah or other robust red variety. No matter. The original winegrowers knew what they wanted, never mind the niggling particulars of grape variety. It has been cultivated in the *same* place for generations. And it continues to be, although—like the Koyukons—with a noticeable nibbling away of tradition by external influences.

One quick statistical look tells us of the constancy. In 2002, of the 2,500 acres of red wine grapes in Amador County—the heartland of the Sierra foothills—74 percent is Zinfandel. Even though the overall percentage has declined (Zinfandel accounted for 85 percent of all Amador grapevines in 1990), actually there's more Zinfandel acreage in Amador County today than there was in 1990. This is surely thanks to a renewed appreciation (and higher prices) for the grape variety.

Still, much of the Zinfandel production continues to be made into white Zinfandel—a mixed blessing. On the one hand, white Zinfandel is an insipid wine of no consequence. On the other hand, the vast success of white Zinfandel was the savior of many of California's old Zinfandel plantings. They would have long ago been ripped out had not a sweetish, rose-tinted wine using the Zinfandel name—and thus legally required to come from that particular grape—become America's favorite wine. Indeed, the demand for white Zinfandel has been so strong that the number of new Zinfandel plantings increased California's total acreage to more than 50,000 acres—one-third more than was planted in 1990.

This is not to suggest that Amador County, or any other district in the vast Sierra Foothills region, should confine itself to Zinfandel. Rather, it is to point out, admiringly, that a vocation of place is present. Many of the winery and vineyard owners are not natives. Typically, they are urbanites from Sacramento or the Bay Area. Yet, whether by birth or application, they sought out a particular tribe—Zinfandel—and willingly subscribe to its enduring practices. Nowhere else in California—not Napa or Sonoma or even the Santa Cruz Mountains—can there be found such a singular allegiance.

The saga of the Sierra Foothills is not entirely happy. Winemaking, as opposed to grape-growing, virtually disappeared in the 1950s and 1960s. After the Gold Rush years, would-be miners turned to digging in the dirt to plant vines. By 1890, the Sierra Foothills contained more than 100 wineries. As elsewhere in California, Prohibition brought it to a halt. Just one winery renewed operation, and successfully continued operating, after Repeal: D'Agostini Winery in Amador County. It remained the only winery in the area until 1970. (Today, the old D'Agostini property is Sobon Estate.)

Not for nothing has there been sniggering about Amador County as "Amateur County." Too often over the years, wines from this remote hill country have seemed, well, hillbillyish. Lately, though, the snide remarks have subsided. Amador, El Dorado, and Yuba County are being looked at anew.

This includes critical self-examination by its own growers, who are starting to come to grips with their own shortcomings. As one vineyard owner commented, "Look, we don't really know what the area can do. Our hearts are in Zinfandel, but we've got to look at other possibilities."

The "other possibilities," as elsewhere in California, are various Rhône, Piemontese, and Tuscan grape varieties: Barbera, Sangiovese, Syrah, Mourvèdre, Nebbiolo, Viognier, Marsanne, Roussanne, and the like. There's good reason—although not yet much evidence—to think that one spot or another in the numerous nooks, crannies, and elevations of this broad area can successfully support all of these varieties. Growers already have Cabernet and Sauvignon Blanc planted and producing. With few exceptions (Renaissance in North Yuba being the shining one), neither variety has emerged as anything special. The Chardonnays aren't much better either, so far.

It is Zinfandel that gives voice to the area. And for the foreseeable future, it will be Zinfandel that defines its character and fortunes. This is not only because of its widespread presence, but because of the distinction of its expression. Amador County Zinfandel, especially, is like no other in California. Considering how much Zinfandel is planted in the state (with 50,381 acres in 2002) and how widespread it is, that's quite a statement. Yet I do not think many would dispute it.

What some might wrongly dispute is the worthwhileness of what Sierra Foothills Zinfandels—really, it's Amador and El Dorado counties—have to say. Although an increasing number of growers are forcibly lightening-up their Zins, to the point of insipidity, authentic Sierra Foothills Zin is a bold, almost belligerent wine. It is almost always high in alcohol, frequently bullying past the 15 percent mark. And it can look bullying, too: Stygian-dark verging on opaque. Too often, they can be tannic, searing experiences. No wonder those who have tangled with such wines wonder whether they are worthwhile. Frankly, those wines unable to harness these forces of tannin, alcohol, and intense fruit are not.

But at their best, Amador and El Dorado Zinfandels are unique. In some ways they are reminiscent of old-fashioned Barolos in their rousing intensity of fruit, high alcohol, and hard kernel of prune and tar flavors. (The prune and tar flavors are the giveaway. No other Zinfandel in California so consistently offers them to such a degree.) Even the high alcohol levels, which can be treacherous to both winemaker and wine drinker, needn't interfere. The best wines carry it off like a graceful fat man on the dance floor. You just forget.

Fiddletown AVA, California-Shenendoah Valley AVA, and El Dorado AVA

One of the oddities of the Sierra Foothills region is that there is an El Dorado AVA (which is nearly all of El Dorado County), but no Amador AVA. This is odd because not only is Amador almost synonymous with Sierra Foothills Zinfandel, but it has more vineyard plantings than any of the other seven counties that comprise the Sierra Foothills. Instead, the only AVA entirely in Amador County is Fiddletown. The California-Shenendoah Valley AVA is astride both Amador and El Dorado Counties.

Distinguishing among the three areas is not easy, although the locals insist that differences are present. No doubt they are. But from the perspective of wine, I did not have an easy time of it. For the record, Fiddletown differs from Shenendoah Valley (there is also a Shenendoah AVA in Virginia, which is why the official name is *California*-Shenendoah Valley) by having higher elevations, cooler nighttime temperatures, and more rain. The soils in both places are the same, variations on a theme of granite and loam. Geologists refer to it as a Sierra series: red loam over decomposed granite. The El Dorado AVA is pretty much everywhere in El Dorado County with elevation levels between 1,200 feet and 3,500 feet, the zone at which grapes are grown in the area.

As for differences in Zinfandels grown in Fiddletown and Shenendoah Valley, I can only pass along this bit of intelligence from a local grower: The Fiddletown Zins tend to have tighter-knit fruit, thanks to cooler sites; the Shenendoah Zins are riper-tasting, with a strong note of black pepper. In looking over my own tasting notes, all I ever find is that business of prunes and tar, at least in the good ones.

Climatically, the Sierra Foothills are warmer than what one might imagine, given that these are, after all, the foothills of the Sierra Nevada Mountains. Inevitably, the local topography can make for significant microclimate differences. More than in many places, the angle of the sun's rays on the slope—exposure—can be critical, especially at higher elevations.

The Sierra Foothills resembles Paso Robles in having hot days and impressively cool nights. The difference is found in elevation and the more rapid drop in temperature a higher elevation delivers. For example, the town of Auburn in Placer County is only twenty miles from Placerville, in neighboring El Dorado County. Many of the El Dorado County vineyards are located near Placerville.

Auburn is at a lower elevation: 1,234 feet compared to Placerville's 1,925 feet. The effect is not revealed in their average maximum temperatures during June, July, August, and September: Auburn averages a maximum of ninety degrees Fahrenheit; Placerville averages eighty-eight degrees Fahrenheit.

Instead, the effect is discovered in the average minimum temperatures. Where Auburn averages a four-month minimum temperature of fifty-eight degrees Fahrenheit, higher-elevation Placerville gets significantly cooler at night by an average minimum of forty-nine degrees Fahrenheit. The length of the growing season reveals all: Auburn has a 260-day season; Placerville has a 182-day growing season.

Elevation also determines rainfall. The rate of increase in precipitation on the western slope of the Sierra Nevada is about one inch of precipitation for every seventy-five feet to 100 feet in elevation. This works up to the 6,000-foot level. So, for example, Auburn at 1,234 feet averages 33.5 inches of precipitation annually. Placerville, 691 feet higher up, gets forty-one inches a year or an additional 7.5 inches. The formula holds: one inch of precipitation for every ninety-two feet in elevation. Just for perspective, keep in mind the following:

• Fiddletown AVA is roughly at 1,600 feet to 1,800 feet in elevation.

• Shenendoah Valley is at 1,400 feet to 1,800 feet in elevation.

• Madrona Vineyards (east of Placerville) is the highest-elevation vineyard in California at 3,000 feet.

• The vineyard of Renaissance Vineyard and Winery in the North Yuba (County) AVA is between 1,700 feet and 2,300 feet in elevation.

Sierra Foothills Producers Worth Seeking Out (And Some Not)

Amador Foothill Winery—If I were to trot out an exemplary Sierra Foothill Zinfandel, I would look first at Amador Foothill Winery. Its various

Zinfandels represent Amador Zin at its best: pungent and powerful yet astonishingly graceful. Look for superb Zin from the ancient (planted in 1868) Grand-pere Vineyard, a vineyard that creates surprisingly delicate Zinfandel (see *Santino Winery*) of striking flavors. Utterly different is the Ferrero Vineyard Zin, all chocolate, prunes, and tar. Cabernet Sauvignon has been grafted over to Sangiovese. These are consistently superb Zinfandels.

Baldinelli Vineyard—This seventy-acre vineyard produces strong, rich, classic Zinfandel from the Shenendoah AVA. Look for the Reserve bottling. Sauvignon Blanc and Cabernet Sauvignon are ordinary.

Boeger Winery—A large range of mostly ordinary wines, including a pleasant but undistinctive Chardonnay. Promising Riesling. Good Zinfandel from Walker Vineyard grapes in El Dorado AVA. Oddly, Boeger brings in Zinfandel grapes from Nichelini Vineyards in Napa Valley, which are ironically nowhere near as good as what's available in the Sierra Foothills. Also a local Merlot, Barbera, and Cabernet Sauvignon. Many experiments; few successes.

Domaine de la Terre Rouge—One of the believers in Rhône varieties, this winery has demonstrated successfully that various Rhône grapes such as Syrah and Grenache have a legitimate place in the Sierra Foothills. Here you find "warm climate" Syrah expressions, such as whiffs of leather and black pepper. Fine, well-crafted wines that are becoming more accomplished with every vintage.

Ironstone Vineyards—One of the most ambitious—at least in terms of money spent—wineries in the Sierra Foothills. Located in Murphys, east of Stockton, Ironstone created a lavish winery with expansive tunnels. It is, if nothing else, an unquestionable statement of belief in the future of Sierra Foothills wines. The results, so far, are mixed. After all, apart from Zinfandel, the vocation of Sierra Foothills has still yet to be established. Best bets are the estate-grown Cabernet Franc and Cabernet Sauvignon (a blend of estate-grown with grapes from Lodi). A good part of Ironstone's production is sourced from outside the Sierra Foothills, although one expects that this will change over time. To watch.

Karly—Variable wines. Karly produces one of the better Sauvignon Blancs from local grapes, but the best bet is the Sadie Upton Zinfandel: tannic, dense, with that prune-y Amador taste. Sadie Upton, now deceased, owned the vineyard, which was planted in 1923.

Lava Cap Vineyards—One of Sierra Foothills' best producers, Lava Cap in Placerville (El Dorado County) excels with estate-grown Cabernet Sauvignon, Cabernet Franc, and—no surprise—Zinfandel. Look also for a rather brutish, but still rewarding, Petite Sirah. Not all of Lava Cap's wines come from their own grapes, but nearly everything is sourced from vineyards in Sierra Foothills, making Lava Cap's wines truly representative of the zone. Already a fine winery, there's surely more to come from this ambitious producer.

Montevina Wines—Montevina used to be a powerhouse name in Amador County, issuing the sort of dynamite Zinfandels that brought attention to the area. It was the first new winery built in the area after Prohibition, in 1970. The winery was sold in 1988 to the Trinchero family of Sutter Home, which originally made its name creating equally bold Zinfandels from, ironically, Amador County grapes. Today, of course, Sutter Home—a major tourist destination in Napa Valley—is synonymous with white Zinfandel.

You would think that the Trinchero interest and capital would trigger a renaissance at Montevina, but so far the wines remain just a cut above what might be called "commercial." They're good enough, but hardly the sort of accomplishment that would set off a new Gold Rush in the Sierra Foothills.

Renaissance Vineyard and Winery—Renaissance is one of the most unusual and exciting wineries in California. It *is* the North Yuba AVA, as there are no other vineyards in the tiny designation. Even in California, which is inured to tales of big money launching big wine projects, Renaissance has raised a few eyebrows. Some were lifted in skepticism and even suspicion. Renaissance, you see, is the creation of a religious (really, more philosophical) group called the Fellowship of Friends. Founded in the Bay Area in the 1960s, it now is international, if small.

The Fellowship of Friends decided to create a winery as an expression of their aesthetic ideals and beliefs. The vineyard and winery development cost $16 million back in the 1980s. Like the Mormons, the members tithe 10 percent of their gross incomes to the Fellowship. Clearly, they have well-heeled adherents.

As can be imagined in a place such as California, the idea of a little-known religious group establishing a seemingly fantastical winery in the middle of nowhere (believe me, North Yuba County is most people's idea of nowhere) gave rise to visions of cults, communes, and controversy. As far as I could see, Renaissance is patently bourgeois—an overtly intellectual community that subscribes to the philosophical teachings of Gurdjieff and Ouspensky. No commune is within sight. A few hundred members live permanently in the area, but virtually none resides on the "campus."

To be sure, Renaissance is more than a winery, although that circular facility is the most prominent building, as it is located on a knoll overlooking all the other buildings. It exists as a focal point and gathering place for its far-flung membership. So there are community buildings, auditoriums, even a small but well-run restaurant. (It happily takes real American cash from both members and ordinary folk from the area.) The campus is, however, a sight to see, with sparkling white, neo-Classical buildings scattered about the 1,250-acre retreat. Simply put, it is gorgeous. And utterly, preposterously, out of place. (Just down the road is a biker bar that would make even Clint Eastwood think twice.)

But it's the wines that matter and this is really what makes Renaissance so exciting. The wines come from a looming set of hillsides that curve around the retreat. The hills are terraced from top to bottom. All 365 acres are drip irrigated, which requires 200 miles of pipe. (And 200 miles of grueling terracing.) The soil is granitic. Upon viewing the vineyards as the car turned a corner, I said out loud (to myself), "It looks like Hermitage."

Because the Fellowship is nonprofit, and because it does not expect the winery to repay its development costs, the winery personnel were in no hurry to get to market. They still aren't. Ten different grape varieties were planted in 1976. No wine of any sort was released until 1988, even though wines were made as soon as the vines reached bearing age in 1979. It was decided to winnow the plantings to just three: Cabernet Sauvignon, Riesling, and Sauvignon Blanc. Some experimental plots of various other varieties remain.

More than anything else, Renaissance is reminiscent of a monastic order, specifically Cistercian—at least with respect to its winemaking focus. (The Benedictines were more luxury-loving, as is, apparently, the Fellowship of Friends.) As the Cistercians did in Burgundy and Germany, the Renaissance "fellows" have planted grapes in an area with no history of fine wine. And they have done so as an expression of aesthetic ideals. Moreover, the time perspective appears multigenerational, in the same way that a monastery transcends the lifespan of its inhabitants yet essentially does not change. After all, the winery is paid for and no one expects any payback.

No commercially motivated enterprise would pursue such isolated, hard-to-cultivate slopes or spend such capital in an area so far removed from wine-growing commerce. For that matter, no commercially motivated enterprise would have done so 500 years ago, either. Back then the impulse was to make manifest religious ideals. This is why the Cistercian monks and nuns carved vineyards on untested, often inaccessible slopes, many of which are today the most famous vineyards in Burgundy and the Mosel-Saar-Ruwer. Renaissance, in its fashion, is a late-twentieth-century expression of a similar, if differently put, impulse.

Renaissance continues to struggle to find its wine identity. The grapes are undoubtedly superb. And throughout its history the style has always veered admirably toward the austere. Cabernet Sauvignon has consistently performed best, although Renaissance Riesling is always rewarding. Zinfandel has proved problematic, while Syrah fails to convince—so far.

Although it's difficult for an outsider to be sure, it appears that one of Renaissance's problems rests less with its winemaking and more with its frequently changing management. A lack of what, in a private enterprise, would be called a corporate culture, seems to burden Renaissance's wine vision. The fact that Renaissance is, effectively, a collective effort seems to preclude a consistent, focused, overriding vision that comes far more easily when a single owner is at the helm. This isn't to say that it can't be achieved, just that it's more difficult in this situation.

Still, the granitic soil and high elevation (1,700 to 2,300 feet) means that there are no other wines like these in the Sierra Foothills. And, to this day, there are few vineyards like those of Renaissance anywhere in California. Although its achievement is slow in coming, I remain convinced that Renaissance has in its vineyard the potential to someday become one of California's finest wine estates. So far, though, it has fallen short of its apparent potential.

Renwood Winery—Zinfandel is the ticket here. Indeed, Renwood specializes in no fewer than six proprietary and vineyard-designated Zinfandels: Old Vine, Grandmère, Fiddletown, Grandpère, D'Agostini Bros., and Jack Rabbit Flat.

These are all lovely Zinfandels, made in an old-fashioned style using a basket press. Look especially for the Grandpère and Grandmère vineyards. Also, Renwood is issuing some of Sierra Foothills' most promising Barbera. Renwood is improving with every vintage while remaining "true to its school."

Santino Winery—One of the leading wineries in the Sierra Foothills. The Santino specialties are two: various named-vineyard Zinfandels and Amador-grown Barbera. The Zinfandels keep improving steadily. Look for Grandpère Vineyard (see *Amador Foothill Winery*), Oleta Vineyard, and Eschen. The Barbera keeps improving in direct proportion to the steadily decreasing amount of Zinfandel added to it. A pure, 100 percent Barbera tasted from the barrel was lovely. The Zinfandels are excellent, classical Amador.

Shenendoah Vineyards—A range of wines is offered, only a few of them noteworthy. The Special Reserve Zinfandel is good, solid Amador County. The Orange Muscat is a beauty. But the standout wine is the Cabernet Franc from a three-acre plot.

Sobon Estate—Only the Estate Zinfandel, from century-old vines, leaps out among the array of offerings. It is characteristic Amador Zin, all prunes and tar and strength—but good.

The Sobon winery picnic area has one of the more unnerving messages: "Watch for snakes."

Stevenot Vineyards—A winery in transition, trying very hard to upgrade its quality, Stevenot represents what's both good and simultaneously frustrating about Sierra Foothills wineries. In the struggle to reach out beyond Zinfandel—as well as to go beyond the "Amateur County" image—many Sierra Foothills wineries are reassessing their winemaking and indeed their own palates. Stevenot is one of them.

Owner Barden Stevenot, whose great-grandfather emigrated from Alsace to join the California Gold Rush in the Sierras, first purchased an old ranch in Calaveras County in 1974. His first wines appeared a few years later. The winery continued in its leisurely fashion for decades, issuing promising bottles of no great consistency.

Finally, in 1999, Stevenot purchased an adjoining 198-acre ranch and planted seventy-two acres of vines, bringing the winery's total to ninety-four vineyard acres. Nine different grape varieties are grown.

Clearly this new planting presages a new era for Stevenot. So far,

Stevenot's best wines are its Zinfandel, Cabernet Sauvignon, and Cabernet Franc. But the new vineyard promises more and better. A winery to watch closely.

Story Vineyard—Among Amador Zinfandel fans, Story continues to attract a following, especially for its Private Release Zinfandel. Not for the faint of heart, but nevertheless, authentic Amador Zinfandel production. One wishes for a bit more refinement, though.

VINEYARD REGISTRY

One of the frustrations—at least for me—of California wine is finding a single-vineyard name on a label, only to discover that no further information about that vineyard is available, either on the back label or in wine books. The following Vineyard Registry is an attempt to redress this.

The basis for inclusion is simple: The vineyard name must currently appear on a wine label or have appeared in recent years. The information is necessarily compressed: Where is the vineyard located? Who owns it? How big is it? Which grapes are planted? Which wineries cite the name on their labels? No attempt is made to judge the quality of the vineyard.

Inevitably, such a listing has shortcomings. One is an inevitable incompleteness. No sooner does the Vineyard Registry seem plausibly complete than I come across yet another vineyard designation. Also, unless a vineyard name is used on a label, it will not appear below. This means that many estate-bottled wines—for example, wines made only from vineyards owned by the winery—do not appear. The Vineyard Registry simply seeks to provide a little information—a who, what, and where—about the snowballing number of vineyard names cited on California wine labels.

Vineyards whose names begin with La, Los, Le, Les, L, etc., can be found under L. Napa County vineyards fall within the Napa Valley AVA unless otherwise specified.

Adams Knoll Vineyard (Alexander Valley AVA)—8 acres at the 180–230-foot elevation off Alexander Valley Road in the Alexander Valley. Cabernet Sauvignon (planted 1998–1999). Owners: Rick and Kathy Adams. *Winery Using Name*: Murphy-Goode.

Adastra Vineyard (Carneros AVA)—20 acres at the 20–100-foot elevation on Las Amigas Road in the Napa Valley, next to Beckstoffer Vineyards. Chardonnay, Merlot (planted 1990, 1994, 1995), Pinot Noir (planted 1994, 1995). Owners: Chris and Naomi Thorpe. *Winery Using Name*: Adastra.

Alden Vineyards (Alexander Valley AVA)—300 acres at the 1,275–1,575-foot elevation east of Asti in the Mayacamas Mountains, northeast of Geyserville. Merlot (planted 1989–1992, 1999), Cabernet Franc (planted 1992–1998), Cabernet Sauvignon (planted 1988, 1990–1991, 1994, 1998). Owner: Alden Family. *Winery Using Name*: Rodney Strong Vineyards.

Alegria Vineyards (Russian River Valley AVA)—27 acres located south of Healdsburg in Sonoma County, just south of the intersection of Old Redwood Highway and Limerick Lane. Zinfandel, Petite Sirah, Alicante, Bouschet (planted 1890), Zinfandel and Sangiovese (planted 1950), Zinfandel (planted 1987, 1997), Cabernet Franc, Syrah (planted 1991), Sangiovese, Dolcetto (planted 1992). Owners: Bill and Betsy Nachbaur. *Wineries Using Name*: Rosenblum Cellars, Russian Hill, Acorn Winery. Note: Carrying on tradition of field blend.

Alexander's Crown Vineyard (Alexander Valley AVA)—77 acres located at the southern end of the Alexander Valley. Cabernet Sauvignon, Merlot, Cabernet Franc (planted 1971). Owner: Klein Family. *Winery Using Name*: Rodney Strong Vineyards.

Alioto Vineyard (Rutherford AVA)—1.1 acres located on the Rutherford Bench, across from Flora Springs. Cabernet Sauvignon (planted 1998). Owner: M. Alioto. *Winery Using Name*: Amici Cellars.

Ambassador's Vineyard (Santa Ynez Valley AVA)—20 acres located in the heart of the Santa Ynez Valley, atop a mesa plateau, adjacent to Firestone Vineyard Winery. Syrah (planted 1990). Owner: Firestone Family. *Winery Using Name*: Curtis Winery.

Arrowood Estate Vineyard (Sonoma Valley AVA)—10 acres located on a hillside slope, roughly one mile from the Glen Ellen turnoff. Cabernet Franc (planted 1987), Petit Verdot (planted 1987), Viognier (planted 1994), Merlot (planted 1996), Syrah (planted 1997, 1998). Owners: Richard L. Arrowood and Alis Demers Arrowood. *Winery Using Name*: Arrowood Vineyards and Winery.

Alden Vineyards (Alexander Valley AVA)—300 acres at the 1,275–1,575-foot elevation east of Asti in the Mayacamas Mountains, northeast of Geyserville. Merlot (planted 1989–1992, 1999), Cabernet Franc (planted 1992–1998), Cabernet Sauvignon (planted 1988, 1990–1991, 1994, 1998). Owner: Alden Family. *Winery Using Name*: Rodney Strong Vineyards.

Alexander's Crown Vineyard (Alexander Valley AVA)—77 acres located at the southern end of the Alexander Valley. Cabernet Sauvignon, Merlot, Cabernet Franc (planted 1971). Owner: Klein Family. *Winery Using Name*: Rodney Strong Vineyards.

Arroyo Vista Vineyard (Arroyo Seco AVA)—39.5 acres located on the west side of 14th Avenue in Greenfield, Monterey County. Chardonnay (planted 1988). Owners: Lohr Family, Aby Hook. *Winery Using Name*: J. Lohr Vineyards and Wines.

Arthur Rue Vineyard (Anderson Valley AVA)—1 acre located on the southeast floor of the Anderson Valley, a half-mile outside of Boonville, between Highway 128 and Anderson Valley Way. Cabernet Franc, Merlot (planted 1997). Owners: John & Sann Schultz. *Winery Using Name*: Raye's Hill.

Bacigalupi Vineyards #1 (Russian River Valley AVA)—60.5 acres located on Westside Road in Healdsburg. Zinfandel, Pinot Noir (clones: Old Wente, Pommard, 777, 667, 115, 2-A), Chardonnay (old clone and Old Wente), Petite Sirah (Foppiano clone). Planted: unknown, but may date back to late 1800s. One block planted in 2003. Owners: Charles and Helen Bacigalupi. *Wineries Using Name*: Foppiano Vineyards, Pezzi King, Williams Selyem, Armida.

Bacigalupi Vineyards #2 (Russian River Valley AVA)—40.66 acres located on two benches above the Russian River between 100–150 feet. Chardonnay (planted 1965–1982), Pinot Noir (planted 1965). Owners: Charles and Helen Bacigalupi. *Wineries Using Name*: Rudd Estate, Keegan Cellars.

Backus Vineyard (Oakville AVA)—21.5 acres located southeast of the intersection of Silverado Trail and Oakville Crossroad in Sonoma County. Cabernet Sauvignon (planted 1975, 1997). Owner: Joe Phelps. *Winery Using Name*: Joseph Phelps Vineyards.

Balletto Vineyards (Russian River Valley AVA)—210 acres located next to the Laguna de Santa Rosa wildlife area in Sonoma County. Pinot Gris, Chardonnay, Pinot Noir (planted 1999). Owners: John and Teresa Balletto. *Wineries Using Name*: DeLoach, Balletto.

Balyeat Ranch (Chiles Valley AVA)—15 acres located at the 1,000-foot elevation in the upper Chiles Valley. Sauvignon Blanc (Musqué), Zinfandel

(Primitivo). Planted 1994–1998. Owner: Rachael Balyeat. *Wineries Using Name*: Green and Red Vineyard, Page Mill Winery.

Barlow Vineyards (Napa Valley AVA)—40 acres located a half-mile south of Dunaweal Lane on the Silverado Trail between St. Helena and Calistoga. Cabernet Sauvignon (planted 1992, 1995), Merlot (planted 1994, 1996), Zinfandel (planted 1997). Owners: Warren and Jeanne Smith Barr, Ann Smith. *Winery Using Name*: Barlow Vineyards.

Barricia Vineyard (Sonoma Valley AVA)—30 acres located on the Sonoma Valley floor, on Sonoma Highway near Madronne Road. Zinfandel (originally planted 1840s, replanted 1995, 1998, 1999), Merlot (planted 1995), Cabernet Sauvignon (planted 1998), Petite Sirah (planted 1998), Cabernet Franc (planted 1986). Owners: Patricia Herron and Barbara Olesen. *Wineries Using Name*: Ravenswood, Gundlach Bundschu, Buena Vista, Kenwood.

Beckstoffer Las Amigas Vineyard (Carneros AVA)—139 acres located on Las Amigas Road, Napa. Merlot, Pinot Noir, Chardonnay (planted 1964, 1995–1999). Owners: Beckstoffer Vineyards. *Wineries Using Name*: Signorello, Acacia, Merryvale, Provenance, Behrens & Hitchcock, Stag's Leap Wine Cellars, Juslyn.

Beckstoffer To-Kalon Vineyard (Oakville AVA)—89 acres located on Highway 29 at Walnut Avenue in Oakville, Napa Valley. Cabernet Sauvignon (clones 4, 6, 337), Cabernet Franc (originally planted 1868, current planting 1994–1997). Owners: Beckstoffer Vineyards. *Wineries Using Name*: Paul Hobbs Winery, Provenance, Atalon, Juslyn, Behrens & Hitchcock, Schrader Cellars, Carter Cellars, Karl Lawrence, Calistoga Lodge. Note: This is a portion of Napa pioneer Hamilton Crabb's original To-Kalon Vineyard first planted in 1868, the larger part of which is owned by Robert Mondavi Winery.

Beckstoffer Vineyard IV (St. Helena AVA)—25 acres located on Sulphur Springs Road in St. Helena, Napa Valley. Cabernet Sauvignon (clone 4, 6, 337). Planted 1978–2001. Owners: Beckstoffer Vineyards. *Winery Using Name*: Guenoc.

Beckstoffer Vineyard X (Oakville AVA)—45 acres located on St. Helena Highway in Napa Valley. Cabernet Sauvignon (clones 4, 7, 6, 337), Merlot (planted 1997–1999). Owners: Beckstoffer Vineyards. *Winery Using Name*: Merryvale.

Bella Oaks Vineyard (Rutherford AVA)—17 acres on bale loam soil located in the Rutherford Appellation. Cabernet Sauvignon (planted 1974, 1991). Owners: Barney and Belle Rhodes. *Winery Using Name*: Heitz Wine Cellars.

Bennett Valley Vineyards (Bennett Valley AVA)—20 acres located at the 550-foot elevation in Bennett Valley, near Matanzas Creek winery. Syrah, Grenache, Sauvignon Blanc, Roussanne (planted 2001). Owner: Young family. *Winery Using Name*: Pax.

Bien Nacido Vineyard (Santa Maria Valley AVA)—825 acres located between the 100–850-foot elevation off Santa Maria Mesa Road in Santa Barbara County. Chardonnay, Pinot Noir, Syrah, Merlot, Cabernet Sauvignon, Rousanne, Pinot Gris, Pinot Blanc, Refusco, Tocai Friuliano, Barbera, Nebbiolo, Petit Verdot, Viognier, Pinot Meunier (planted 1973–2003). Owner: Miller Family. *Wineries Using Name*: Byron, Tantara, David Bruce, Au Bon Climat, Fetzer, Foxen, Qupé, Bonny Doon, Wild Horse, Parker, Steele, Andrew Murray.

Bingham Ranch (Napa Valley AVA)—15 acres located on Foothill Boulevard in Calistoga, on the Napa Valley Plain, south of Lincoln Avenue. Cabernet Sauvignon, Merlot, Zinfandel, Petit Sirah (planted 1890–present). Owners: Helen A. Metcalf, Peter S. Hurd. *Winery Using Name*: Edgewood Winery.

Black Sears Vineyard (Howell Mountain AVA)—23 acres located at the 2,400-foot elevation on Summit Lake Drive. Zinfandel (planted 1974), Cabernet Sauvignon (planted 1987). Owners: Jerre Sears and Joyce Black Sears. *Wineries Using Name*: Howell Mountain Vineyards, Black Sears, Highland, Elyse, D-Cubed.

Blanches Vineyard (Livermore Valley AVA)—14 acres located at the 700-foot elevation, at the east end of the Livermore Valley, at Cedar Mountain Winery. Chardonnay, Cabernet Sauvignon, Pinot Noir (planted 1986). Owners: Linda and Earl Ault. *Winery Using Name*: Cedar Mountain Winery. Note: Yield at 3 tons per acre.

Blue Rock Vineyard (Alexander Valley AVA)—36 acres at the 400-foot elevation west of Silver Oak Winery. Cabernet Sauvignon, Cabernet Franc, Merlot (planted 1982–2004). Owners: Kenneth & Cheryl Kahn. *Wineries Using Name*: Benziger, Blue Rock.

Boa Ventura de Caires Vineyard (Livermore Valley AVA)—3 acres located at the 800-foot elevation on Tesla Road in the Livermore Valley. Cabernet Sauvignon (clone 8). Planted 2002. Owners: Brett and Monique Caires. *Wineries Using Name*: Boa Ventura, Steven Kent Vineyards.

Boa Vista Vineyards (El Dorado AVA)—3.5 acres located at the 2,600-foot elevation, four miles east of Placerville on Carson Road. Syrah (planted 1997), Barbera (planted 1999). Owners: Brad & Kandi Visman. *Winery Using Name*: Oakstone Winery.

Bowman Vineyards (California-Shenendoah Valley AVA)—24 acres at the 1,500-foot elevation in the heart of the Shenandoah Valley on Valley Drive in Plymouth. Zinfandel (planted 1974, 1980). Owners: Chuck and Richard Bowman. *Wineries Using Name*: Folie a Deux Winery, TKC Winery, French Hill Winery. Note: Dry farmed since planting.

Brokenleg Vineyard (Anderson Valley AVA)—5 acres located at the 1,000-foot elevation on a ridge on the northeastern side of the valley on Nash Mill Road. Zinfandel, Syrah (planted 1992). Owners: Steve and Jody Williams. *Wineries Using Name*: Handley Cellars, Claudia Springs.

Butow Organic Vineyards (Redwood Valley AVA)—28 acres located at the 650-foot elevation in the Redwood Valley, on the west fork of the Russian River. Syrah (planted 1979), Cabernet Sauvignon (planted 1964). Owners: Clara, John, and Judye Butow. *Winery Using Name*: Frey Vineyards. Note: Certified organic.

Calzada Ridge Vineyard (Santa Ynez Valley AVA)—¼ acre located on a ridge at the 875-foot elevation in the Santa Ynez Valley, about two miles south of Los Olivos. Viognier (planted 1995). Owners: Richard and Pamela Harris. *Winery Using Name*: Calzada Ridge.

Campbell Ranch Vineyard (Sonoma Coast AVA)—26 acres located at the 700-foot elevation on Soda Springs Road in the town of Annapolis. Pinot Noir (clones 115, 777, 667), Syrah (clone 877). Planted 2000, 2002, 2003. Owners: Steve and Rex Campbell. *Winery Using Name*: Hammel Wines.

Camp Meeting Ridge (Sonoma Coast AVA)—35 acres located between the 1,200–1,350-foot elevation north of Jenner on Seaview Road, above Fort Ross. Chardonnay (planted 1991, 1997), Pinot Noir (planted 1991–1993, 1997). Owners: Walt and Joan Flowers. *Wineries Using Name*: Flowers, Kistler.

Carneros Lake Vineyard (Carneros AVA)—198 acres located on Duhig Road, Napa. Merlot, Pinot Noir, Chardonnay (1963, 1995–1998). Owners:

Beckstoffer Vineyards. *Winery Using Name*: Liparita.

Carol's Vineyard (St. Helena AVA)—31.5 acres located south of Pratt Avenue in St. Helena, bordered on the east by the Napa River. Cabernet Sauvignon, Petit Verdot, Sauvignon Blanc (planted 1998). Owner: Lohr Family. *Winery Using Name*: J. Lohr Vineyards and Wines.

Catfish Vineyard (Clear Lake AVA)—7.3 planted acres located at the 1,375-foot elevation on the Kelseyville bench in Lake County. Zinfandel, Alicante Bouchet, Cinsault, Carignane, Cabernet Sauvignon, Syrah, Petite Sirah (planted 1901). Owner: Jed Steele. *Winery Using Name*: Steele Wines.

Catie's Corner Vineyard (Russian River Valley AVA)—18 acres located on Jones Road in Windsor. Viognier, Syrah, Pinot Noir. Owners: Rich, Saralee, and Catie Kunde. *Wineries Using Name*: Christopher Creek, St. Francis, Copain, Whetstone Wine Cellars, Eric Ross.

Chardonnay Vineyards (Carneros AVA)—100 acres located on Milton Road in Napa. Chardonnay (planted 1974, 2000–2001), Pinot Noir (planted 1975, 1995, 1997), Merlot (planted 1996). Owners: Chardonnay Vineyards Partnership, Califrance Corporation, General Partner. *Wineries Using Name*: Mumm Cuvée Napa, Sterling Vineyard, Acacia Winery, Kazmer & Blaise Cellars.

Charles Heintz Vineyard (Russian River Valley AVA)—100 acres at the 900-foot elevation, 8 miles from the Pacific Ocean near Occidental. Syrah (planted 2002), Chardonnay (planted 1982), Pinot Noir (planted 1998). Owner: Charles Heintz. *Wineries Using Name*: Littorai, Williams Selyem, DuMol, Dutch Bill Creek.

Charlotte's Home Vineyard (Alexander Valley AVA)—36 acres located at the southern end of the Alexander Valley along the Russian River. Sauvignon Blanc (planted 1971). Owner: Klein Family. *Winery Using Name*: Rodney Strong Vineyards.

Château Felice (Chalk Hill AVA)—24 acres located between the 400–500-foot elevation on hillsides in Healdsburg on Chalk Hill Road. Cabernet Sauvignon, Merlot, Cabernet Franc, Zinfandel, Syrah, Chardonnay (planted 1998). Owners: Barry and Phyllis Rodgers. *Winery Using Name*: Château Felice.

Chelli Vineyards (Russian River Valley AVA)—12 acres located on Wood Road in the Russian River Valley. Zinfandel, Alicante, Palomino, Petite

Sirah, Carignon (planted approximately late 1800s). Owners: Lloyd and Dee Chelli. *Winery Using Name*: Hartford Family Winery Highwire Zinfandel.

Chimney Rock Vineyards (Stags Leap District AVA)—110 acres located in the Stags Leap District. Cabernet Sauvignon, Merlot, Cabernet Franc, Petit Verdot (planted 1992, 2002). Owner: Chimney Rock Winery. *Winery Using Name*: Chimney Rock Winery.

Christensen Family Vineyard (Russian River Valley AVA)—3 acres located on Fulton Road just south of Fulton. Syrah (Clone 7). Planted 1998–1999, 2001. Owners: Paul G. and Sharon Christensen. *Winery Using Name*: Siduri/Novi.

Christine Woods (Anderson Valley AVA)—54 acres located in the Anderson Valley on Highway 128. Chardonnay, Pinot Noir (planted 1984). Owners: Vernon and Josephine Rose. *Winery Using Name*: Christine Woods. Note: Dry farmed.

Cilurzo Vineyard & Winery (Temecula AVA)—5 acres at the 1,410-foot elevation, five and a half miles east of Highway 15 on Calle Contento in Temecula. Petite Sirah (planted 1978). Owners: Vincenzo and Audrey Cilurzo. *Winery Using Name*: Cilurzo Vineyard & Winery.

Clara's Vineyard (Mendocino AVA)—15 acres located at the 600–750-foot elevation, seven miles north of Hopland on Nelson Ranch Road. Cabernet Sauvignon (planted 1993). Owner: Nelson Family. *Wineries Using Name*: Dunnwood Vineyards, Hopland Hills Winery, Folie a Deux Winery.

Clos des Knolls Vineyard (El Dorado AVA)—2 acres located at the 1,300-foot elevation in western El Dorado County, near Gold Hill/Luneman Roads. Cabernet Sauvignon, Emerald Riesling (planted 1988), Merlot, Cabernet Franc, Sauvignon Blanc, Zinfandel, Petite Sirah, Pinot Noir (planted 1989), Sémillon, Pinot Blanc (planted 1990), Symphony, Pinot Noir (planted 1992), Petit Verdot, Viognier, Dolcetto, Sangiovese, Malvasia Bianca, Mourvèdre, Pinot Noir (planted 1993), Pinot Noir, Symphony, Syrah, Mourvèdre (planted 1994), Cabernet Sauvignon (planted 2003). Owner: Bob Leidigh. *Winery Using Name*: Château Leidigh. Note: Château Leidigh, LLC, was recently bonded and began producing its first commercial wine in 2003. The wines are all estate bottled.

Cloverdale Ranch (Alexander Valley AVA)—47 acres at the northern end of the valley, east of the Russian River. Cabernet Sauvignon, Merlot. Owner:

Pellegrini family. *Winery Using Name*: Pellegrini Family.

Crackerbox Vineyard (Livermore Valley AVA)—1.5 acres on Buena Vista Avenue in Livermore Valley. Sangiovese (clone 2). Planted 1998. Owners: John Canfield and Courtney Cooke. *Wineries Using Name*: Crooked Vine, Mitchell Katz Winery.

Crane Ranch/Rolly Akers Vineyard (Napa Valley AVA)—9 acres located on Dry Creek Road on the western bench between Napa and Yountville. Cabernet Sauvignon, Merlot, Syrah (planted 1991, 1996, 2000). Owners: Michael and Chyrle Crane. *Wineries Using Name*: Crane Brothers, Hill-climber.

Crossroads Vineyard (Santa Ynez Valley AVA)—6 acres located in Santa Ynez Valley, at the corner of Foxen Canyon Road and Zaca Station Road, across the street from Curtis Winery. Syrah (planted 1997). Owner: Firestone Family. *Winery Using Name*: Curtis Winery.

D'Agostini Brothers Vineyard (California-Shenendoah Valley AVA)—40 acres located on Shenendoah Road in Plymouth, Amador County. Zinfandel (planted 1921). Owners: D'Agostini Brothers. *Winery Using Name*: Renwood.

Dalraddy Vineyard (Chiles Valley AVA)—10 acres in the Chiles Valley District of Napa. Zinfandel (planted 1970s–1980s). Owners: Elizabeth and Charlotte Williamson. *Winery Using Name*: Fife Vineyards.

Damiano Vineyard (Sierra Foothills AVA)—3.2 acres at the 2,500-foot elevation, located in Placer County, 15 miles north of Auburn in the Ophir Valley. Viognier. (planted 1997, 2002). Owner: Damiano Family. *Wineries Using Name*: Hawley, Lambert Bridge.

Darcie Kent/Altamont Vineyard (Livermore Valley AVA)—15 acres located at the 800-foot elevation on the middle bench of Crane Ridge in the Diablo Mountain Range, near the eastern edge of the Livermore Valley AVA and San Francisco Bay AVA. Merlot (planted 1992). Owners: David and Darcie Kent. *Wineries Using Name*: Mutt Lynch, Darcie Kent.

Deaver Ranch/Vineyards (Amador County)—300 acres located between the 1,000–1,800-foot elevations in the middle of the Shenendoah Valley. Zinfandel, Sangiovese, Petite Sirah (planted 1850s–present). Owner: Deaver Family. *Wineries Using Name*: Sutter Home, Montevina, Deaver.

Dr. Crane Vineyard (St. Helena AVA)—24 acres located on Crane Avenue in St. Helena, Napa Valley. Cabernet Sauvignon (clones 4, 6, 337),

Cabernet Franc, Petit Verdot (originally planted 1859, current planting 1996–1998). Owners: Beckstoffer Vineyards. *Wineries Using Name*: Paul Hobbs Winery, Behrens & Hitchcock, Juslyn, Marshall Vineyards. Note: This is a portion of Napa pioneer Dr. George Belden Crane's 300-acre vineyard originally planted in 1859.

Dollarhide Ranch/Rutherford Estate (Napa Valley AVA)—480 acres located between the 600–775-foot elevation in the Pope Valley. Cabernet Sauvignon (planted 1983–2002), Sauvignon Blanc (planted 1983–2002), Chardonnay (planted 1985), Merlot (planted 1984, 1998), Sémillon (planted 1984, 1998), Malbec (planted 2003), Cabernet Franc (planted 1985). Owner: Robert Skalli. *Winery Using Name*: St. Supéry.

Don Miguel Vineyard (Russian River Valley AVA)—50 acres located on Graton Road, in the Green Valley sub-appellation, in Sebastopol. Chardonnay (planted 1986), Pinot Noir (planted 1988). Owner: Marimar Torres. *Winery Using Name*: Marimar Torres Estate. Note: Planted at 2,000 vines per acre density. Organic.

Don Raffaele Estate (Napa Valley AVA)—7 acres located 300 feet above the valley floor in the southeast corner of Mount Veeder. Merlot (planted 1992), Cabernet Sauvignon (planted 1998). Owners: Peter and Frances Chiarella. *Winery Using Name*: Crane Family Vineyards.

DuPratt Vineyard (Mendocino Ridge AVA)—12.5 acres located at the 1,400-foot elevation in the mountains of southwestern Mendocino County. Zinfandel (planted 1916), Chardonnay (planted 1983), Pinot Noir (planted 1983, 2001). Owners: John and Elizabeth Sheela. *Winery Using Name*: Steele Wines. Note: Vineyard is in conversion period for organic certification. Zinfandel is dry farmed.

Durell Vineyard (Sonoma Valley AVA/Carneros AVA)—190 acres located between the 100–450-foot elevation in the southwest foothills of Sonoma Valley. Chardonnay, Pinot Noir, Syrah, Cabernet Sauvignon, Cabernet Franc, Merlot (planted 1983–1999). Owners: William and Eleanor Price. *Wineries Using Name*: Château St. Jean, Castle, Edmunds St. John, Steele Wines, Kistler, Patz & Hall.

Dutton Ranch—775 acres in 49 different locations throughout Sonoma County, Sonoma Coast, Russian River Valley, and Green Valley. Chardonnay, Pinot Noir, Merlot, Zinfandel, Syrah, Pinot Gris, Pinot Blanc, Sauvignon

Blanc, French Colombard (planted 1920s–2003). Owners: Gail, Steve and Joe Dutton. *Wineries Using Name*: Capiaux Cellars, Conn Valley Winery, David Noyes, Davis Family, DuMol Wine Company, Dutton-Goldfield, Ehlers Grove, Hartford Court Winery, Hunter Wine Cellars–Chasseur, J. Fritz Winery, Keegan Cellars, Kistler Vineyards, Lewis Cellars, Lost Canyon, Merryvale Vineyards, Nickel & Nickel, Patz & Hall, Russian Hill Estates, Rutz Cellars, Sebastiani Vineyards, Sebastopol Vineyards, Terra Valentine.

Eaglepoint Ranch (Ukiah Valley AVA)—84 acres at the 1,800-foot elevation on the east side of the Ukiah Valley above the Talmage bench, at the far northwest end of the Mayacamas Mountains. Zinfandel (planted 1975), Petite Sirah (planted 1976, 2000), Cabernet Sauvignon (planted 1983), Sangiovese (planted 1994), Syrah (planted 1989, 1994, 2001), Grenache (planted 2000–2001). Owner: Scharffenberger Family. *Wineries Using Name*: Eaglepoint Ranch Winery, Seghesio, Edmeades, Rosenblum, Navarro, Kendall-Jackson, Martin Ray, Claudia Springs, Sean Thakery, Copain, Fieldstone, Pepi, Stonehedge.

Eden Rock/St. Eden Vineyard (Oakville AVA)—12 acres on Oakville Crossroad in Oakville, Napa. Cabernet Sauvignon, Merlot, Cabernet Franc, Petit Verdot (planted 1993, 2000). Owner: C Richard Kramlich. *Winery Using Name*: Bond.

Eisele Vineyard (Napa Valley AVA)—39 acres located on benchland near the northern end of Napa Valley, just east of Calistoga. Cabernet Sauvignon (planted 1991, 1994, 1998, 2000, 2001, 2002), Sauvignon Blanc (planted 1991, 1993), Syrah (planted 1991, 1993, 1994, 1996, 2000). Owners: Bart and Daphne Araujo. *Winery Using Name*: Araujo Estate.

Elisabeth and Henry's Vineyard (Sonoma Coast AVA)—11 acres located at the 100-foot elevation near the intersection of Highway 101 and River Road, just above the Russian River Valley. Pinot Noir (planted 1995). Owner: Henry Siebert. *Winery Using Name*: Paradise Ridge Winery.

Elizabeth Vineyards (Redwood Valley AVA)—77 acres at the 1,000–1,100-foot elevation on the upper east bench of the Redwood Valley in Mendocino County on Colony Drive. Sauvignon Blanc (planted 1973), Zinfandel (planted 1973, 1996, 1997, 2000), Petite Sirah (planted 2000), Cabernet Sauvignon (planted 1999). Owner: Betty A. Foster. *Wineries Using Name*: Elizabeth Vineyards, Fieldbrook Winery.

Ellen's Block (Russian River Valley AVA)—1.5 acres at Russian Hill Winery on Slusser Road in the Russian River Valley. Syrah (planted 1998). Owners: Ellen Mack and Edward Gomez. *Winery Using Name*: Russian Hill.

Esola Vineyard (Shenendoah Valley AVA)—Located on Shenendoah School Road in Plymouth, Amador County. Zinfandel (planted 1924, 1930). Owner: Lena Esola. *Wineries Using Name*: Amador Foothill, Carneros Creek, Frenz.

Fagan Creek Vineyard (Napa Valley AVA)—10 acres located at the 350-foot elevation in Jamieson Canyon, at the southern end of the valley, east of Carneros. Pinot Noir (planted 1983, 1997–2003). Owners: Ken Nerlove and Greg Gahagan. *Winery Using Name*: Elkhorn Peak.

Faith Vineyard (Santa Ynez Valley AVA)—7 acres located at the 900-foot elevation, off Figueroa Mountain Road, in Los Olivos. Sangiovese, Sauvignon Blanc (planted 1998, 1999). Owners: John and Chris Jones. *Wineries Using Name*: Foxen, Duo.

Fanucchi Wood Road Vineyard (Russian River Valley AVA)—17 acres located on Wood Road in Fulton. Trousseau Gris (planted 1981), Zinfandel (planted 1906). Owner: A. Fanucchi. *Wineries Using Name*: Fanucchi Vineyards, Hartford/Hartford Court (Zinfandel), Windsor (Trousseau Gris).

Farella-Park Vineyard (Napa Valley AVA)—26 acres located between the 200–500-foot elevation between Coombsville Road and Hagen Road, at the base of the Vaca Mountains. Cabernet Sauvignon (planted 1975, 1995–2000), Merlot (planted 1979, 1993–1997), Sauvignon Blanc (planted 1998), Syrah (planted 2000). Owner: Farella family. *Winery Using Name*: Franus Cellars.

Ferrington Vineyard (Anderson Valley AVA)—30-plus acres located near Boonville. Sauvignon Blanc, Chardonnay, Pinot Noir (planted 1980s–2003). Owner: Kurt Schoeneman. *Wineries Using Name*: Handley Cellars, Williams Selyem Winery.

Fife Estate Vineyard (Spring Mountain District AVA)—14 acres located at the 1,800-foot elevation on Spring Mountain. Bordeaux varieties, Petite Sirah (planted 1999–2001). Owner: Fife family. *Winery Using Name*: Fife Vineyards.

Folkendt Vineyard (Livermore Valley AVA)—12 acres located at the 900-foot elevation in the Crone Ridge area of the Livermore Valley. Cabernet

Sauvignon, Chardonnay (planted 1993). Owner: Nick Nardolillo. *Wineries Using Name*: Steven Kent Winery, White Crane Winery.

Fox Peak Vineyard (Atlas Peak AVA)—3 acres located at the 1,500-foot elevation on Atlas Peak Road. Cabernet Sauvignon. Owners: Michael Parmenter and Kiky Lee. *Winery Using Name*: Fox Peak.

Gabrielle's Vineyard (Napa Valley AVA)—7 acres located at the 480-foot elevation on east 3rd Avenue in Napa, near Star Hill Winery. Cabernet Sauvignon (planted 1997–2000). Owner: KFGF Family Partners Ltd. *Winery Using Name*: Stag's Leap Wine Cellars.

Galles Vineyard (Livermore Valley AVA)—2.7 acres located 100 feet above the Livermore Valley floor. Cabernet Sauvignon (planted 2000). Owners: Harry Galles and Linda Nidever-Galles. *Winery Using Name:* Retzlaff Vineyards.

Garys' Vineyard (Santa Lucia Highlands AVA)—50 acres located at the 350-foot elevation in Monterey County. Pinot Noir, Syrah (planted 1997). Owners: Gary Pisoni and Gary Franscioni. *Wineries Using Name*: Lucia, Roar, Siduri, Novy, Testarossa, Pessango, Morgan, Truckee River, Vision, Lorca, Miner, Loring, Muira, Tantara, Ryan, Capiaux.

Gibson Ranch (Mendocino AVA)—32.5 acres at the 460-foot elevation in the Sanel Valley in Hopland. Sangiovese, Merlot, Chardonnay (planted 1986–1989). Owner: Robert Gibson. *Winery Using Name*: Miner Winery.

Golden Vineyards (Mendocino AVA)—21.5 acres located on East Side Road in Hopland, in Mendocino County. Syrah (planted 1994). Owners: Joe and Julie Golden. *Winery Using Name*: Renard Winery. Note: Certified biodynamic.

Gold Hill Vineyard (El Dorado AVA)—50 acres at the 1,400-foot elevation in the Sierra Foothills on Vineyard Lane off Cold Springs Road, north of Placerville overlooking the American River Valley in Coloma. Chardonnay, Cabernet Sauvignon, Merlot, Cabernet Franc, Syrah, Barbera, Viognier, Zinfandel (planted 1982, 1984, 1998). Owner: Hank Battjes. *Wineries Using Name*: Mokelumne Hill, Re Mulej, Mt. Vernon.

Goodchild Vineyard (Santa Maria Valley AVA)—67 acres located between the 500–800-foot elevation adjacent to the Santa Maria River in Santa Barbara County. Chardonnay, Pinot Noir, Pinot Gris (planted 1977–2003). Owners: Jill and Louis Lucas, Royce Lewellen. *Wineries Using*

Name: Lucas & Lewellen, Ruscack, Sunstone, Steele.

Grandpère Vineyard (California-Shenendoah Valley AVA)—19 acres located on Steiner Road in Amador County, behind Renwood Winery. Zinfandel, Barbera (planted 1868). Owner: Renwood Winery. *Winery Using Name*: Renwood Winery. Note: Oldest known clone of Zinfandel in the United States.

Green Island Vineyards (Napa Valley AVA)—138.83 acres located on Green Island Road, American Canyon, across the Napa River from Los Carneros AVA. Chardonnay, Pinot Noir (planted 1996–1997, 1999, 2001). Owners: Green Island Vineyards, Will Nord. *Winery Using Name*: Nord Estate Wines.

Greenwood Ridge Vineyards (Mendocino Ridge AVA)—16 acres at the 1,400-foot elevation six miles west on Philo Greenwood Road. White Riesling (planted 1972, 1988), Merlot (planted 1988), Cabernet Sauvignon (planted 1972), Pinot Noir (planted 1996). Owner: Green family. *Winery Using Name*: Greenwood Ridge Vineyards.

HB Vineyard (Rutherford AVA)—30 acres on St. Helena Highway, between Robert Mondavi and Niebaum-Coppola. Cabernet Sauvignon, Cabernet Franc, Merlot (planted 1990). Owners: Peju family. *Winery Using Name*: Peju Province.

Hahn Chualar Canyon Vinyard (Monterey AVA)—44 acres located on Chualar Canyon Road in Chualar. Pinot Noir (planted 1997). Owner: Nicki Hahn. *Winery Using Name*: McIntyre. Note: Dry farmed.

Hallauer Vineyard (Santa Ynez Valley AVA)—10 acres near Solvang in the Santa Ynez Valley in Santa Barbara County. Shiraz, Sangiovese, Cabernet Franc (planted 1999). Owner: Wolfgang C. Hallauer, M.D. *Winery Using Name*: Hallauer Vineyard.

Hames Valley Vineyards (Hames Valley/Monterey AVA)—700 acres in southern Monterey County. Cabernet Sauvignon, Merlot, Cabernet Franc (planted 1989), Sauvignon Blanc, Petit Verdot (planted 1999). Owners: Bob and Shelley Denney. *Wineries Using Name*: Hames Valley Vineyards, Pessagno Winery.

Handley Cellars Estate Vineyard (Anderson Valley AVA)—25 acres surrounding Handley Cellars Winery in the Anderson Valley. Pinot Noir, Chardonnay, Gewürztraminer (planted 1986–2000). Owners: Raymond and

Louise Handley. *Winery Using Name*: Handley Cellars.

Handley Vineyard (Dry Creek Valley AVA)—20 acres located at the southern end of the Dry Creek Valley on Westside Road. Chardonnay, Sauvignon Blanc, Viognier, Syrah (1978, 1999–2001). Owners: Raymond and Louise Handley. *Winery Using Name*: Handley Cellars.

Harris-Kratka Vineyard (Alexander Valley AVA)—16 acres located near the junction of Highway 128 and Chalk Hill Road at the south end of the Alexander Valley. Zinfandel, Carignane, Petit Sirah (planted 1999–2001). Owners: Marshall Harris, Cheri Kratka. *Winery Using Name*: Rosenblum Cellars.

Hayne Vineyard (St. Helena AVA)—52 acres located on Sulphur Springs Avenue in St. Helena. Zinfandel (planted 1903–1905), Petite Sirah (planted 1953–1955), Cabernet Sauvignon (planted 1995–present). Owners: William A. Hayne, Elliot A. Hayne, Martha Hayne Talbot, Sarah Hayne Simpson. *Wineries Using Name*: Turley Wine Cellars, Chase Family Cellars, Elyse Winery.

Heartwood Vineyard (Alexander Valley AVA)—3 acres at the 600-foot elevation, near Hannah Winery. Cabernet Sauvignon (planted 1995). Owners: Ed and Sandy Beddow. *Winery Using Name*: Château Souverain.

Herrerias Vineyards (Sonoma County AVA)—32 acres located on Adobe Road in Petaluma, near the border of Sonoma Coast and Carneros AVA. Pinot Noir (planted 2000). Owners: Ronald and Eva Herrerias. *Wineries Using Name*: Blackstone, Adobe Road.

Herrick's Howell Mountain Vineyard (Howell Mountain AVA)—One acre located at the 1,680-foot elevation on Brookside Drive, near White Cottage Road. Cabernet Sauvignon (planted 2000). Owners: Bob and Sandy Herrick. *Winery Using Name*: Behrens & Hitchcock Winery.

Hidden Spring Vineyard (Alexander Valley AVA)—36 acres located on Asti Road in Cloverdale. Cabernet Sauvignon, Cabernet Franc, Merlot, Viognier (planted 1989, 1993, 2000). Owners: Keith, Joanne, and Paden Collard. *Winery Using Name*: Hart's Desire Wines.

Hilltop Vineyard (Paso Robles AVA)—68 acres located between the 720–810-foot elevation east of Airport Road and north of Tower Road. Cabernet Sauvignon, Petit Verdot (planted 1990, 1999). Owners: Lohr family, Ron Rankin. *Winery Using Name*: J. Lohr Vineyards and Wines.

Hinnrichs Vineyards (Santa Ynez Valley AVA)—5 acres at the 550-foot elevation, located midway between Solvang and Buellton. Syrah (planted 1999). Owner: Bob Hinnrichs. *Winery Using Name*: Andrew Murray Vineyards.

Hoatzin Vineyard (Rutherford AVA)—10.36 acres located between Mee and Gaileron Lanes in the Napa Valley, midway between Rutherford and St. Helena. Chardonnay, Merlot (planted 1991). Owners: Jim and Margaret Watson. *Winery Using Name*: Aetna Springs Cellars.

Hoenselaars Vineyard (Sonoma Coast AVA)—3 acres located at the 500-foot elevation near the intersection of Highway 101 and River Road, overlooking the Russian River Valley. Zinfandel, Syrah, Petite Sirah (planted 1998). Owners: Dr. Walter Byck and Marijke Byck-Hoenselaars. *Winery Using Name*: Paradise Ridge Winery.

Hornberger Vineyards (Rutherford AVA)—14 acres located on South Whitehall Lane in St. Helena, one mile north of Rutherford. Cabernet Sauvignon (planted 1968, 1992, 1998, 1999, 2000). Owners: Robert and Mary Hornberger. *Wineries Using Name*: Beaulieu, St. Clements (Beringer).

Hudson Vineyards (Carneros AVA)—Hudson Vineyards operates two non-contiguous vineyards, Home Ranch with 105 acres, Shadow Ranch with 75 acres, located north of Highway 121 in northeastern Carneros. Chardonnay, Syrah, Merlot, Pinot Noir, Pinot Gris, Cabernet Franc, Grenache, Sauvignon Blanc, Viognier, Barbera, Durif (Petite Sirah), Roussanne (planted 1984–1999). Owner: Lee Hudson. *Wineries Using Name*: Kistler, Ramey Wine Cellars, Kongsgaard Wine, Havens Wine Cellars, Neyers Vineyards, Nickel and Nickel, Arietta.

Hyde Vineyard (Carneros AVA)—150 acres located at the 100-foot elevation on Carneros Highway in Napa between Carneros Highway and Old Sonoma Road. Chardonnay, Pinot Noir, Sauvignon Blanc, Sémillon, Merlot, Cabernet Franc, Cabernet Sauvignon, Syrah (planted 1979). Owner: Larry Hyde. *Wineries Using Name*: Paul Hobbs, Kistler, Patz & Hall, Ramey, Selene, HdV, Whitethorn, Mondavi.

Ink Grade Vineyard (Howell Mountain AVA)—3-acre block of port wine grapes located in the Napa Valley. Tinta Cao, Touriga National, Souzao, Tinta Amarela, Tinta Madeira, Bastardo (planted 1992). Owner: Heitz Wine Cellars. *Winery Using Name*: Heitz Wine Cellars.

Jack Rabbit Flat (California-Shenendoah Valley AVA)—10-acre block within Fox Creek Vineyards. Zinfandel (planted approximately 1925). Owner: Fox family. *Winery Using Name*: Renwood.

Jane's Vineyard (Russian River Valley AVA)—193 acres located west of Santa Rosa. Sauvignon Blanc (planted 1998), Chardonnay, Pinot Noir (planted 1972). Owner: Klein family. *Winery Using Name*: Rodney Strong Vineyards.

Jeriko Vineyards (Sanel Valley AVA)—105 acres located one-half mile north of Hopland on east and west sides of Highway 101 in Mendocino County. Chardonnay (clone 4), Cabernet Sauvignon (planted 1986, replanted 1997), Pinot Noir (planted 1997), Merlot (planted 1998), Sangiovese (planted 1997), Syrah (planted 1998). Owner: Daniel Fetzer. *Winery Using Name*: Jeriko Estate.

Keefer Ranch (Green Valley)—48 acres in the Green Valley sub-appellation. Chardonnay (planted 1989, 1996), Pinot Noir (planted 1996, 2001). Owner: Marcy Keefer. *Wineries Using Name*: Flowers, Armida, Spelletitch, Failla, Siduri, Tandem, Red Car.

Keever Vineyards (Yountville AVA)—4.5 acres located on the west side of Highway 29, just south of the Veterans Home. Cabernet Sauvignon, Cabernet Franc (planted 2000, 2002). Owners: Bill and Olga Keever. *Winery Using Name*: Keever Vineyards (first release 2005).

Kelleher Family Vineyard (Oakville AVA)—13 acres located two miles north of Yountville. Cabernet Sauvignon (planted 1996). Owners: Kelleher Family Trust, Don and Donna Kelleher. *Winery Using Name*: Kelleher Family Vineyard.

Kenefick Ranch (Napa Valley AVA)—125 acres located south of Calistoga, across the street from Araujo Winery. Cabernet Sauvignon, Merlot, Cabernet Franc, Petit Verdot, Malbec, Sauvignon Mustique, Syrah (1920s, 1990s–present). Owners: Thomas, Caitlin, and Chris Kenefick. *Wineries Using Name*: Behrens & Hitchcock, Carinni, Rosenblum Cellars.

Klopp Ranch (Russian River Valley AVA)—25 acres located in the Russian River Valley. Pinot Noir (planted 1989, 1991, 1995, 1999). Owners: Ted and Kathy Klopp. *Winery Using Name*: Merry Edwards.

Krupp Vineyard (Atlas Peak AVA)—31 acres located at the 1,350-foot elevation, 6.4 miles up Soda Canyon Road, just east of Stag's Leap. Cabernet

Sauvignon (planted 1992), Merlot (planted 1993), Malbec (planted 2002), Tempranillo (planted 2002). Owners: Jan and Janice Krupp. *Wineries Using Name*: Veraison, Van Asperen, Lonen.

L'Ancien Verger Vineyard (Russian River Valley AVA)—7 acres located between the 420–500-foot elevation on an outcropping of the Wilson Grove Formation, off Occidental Road. Chardonnay (planted 1998), Pinot Noir (planted 2000). Owner: James Manoogian. *Winery Using Name*: Stryker Sonoma.

La Porte Cochere Vineyard (Russian River Valley AVA)—3.75 acres located in the Russian River Valley on the Northern Santa Rosa Plain, west of Fulton. Chardonnay (planted 1990). Owners: Faye and Dick Youngs. *Winery Using Name*: Girard Winery.

La Ribera Vineyards (Mendocino AVA)—150 acres located five miles south of Talmage on East Side Road, along the Russian River in southern Mendocino County. Cabernet Sauvignon (planted 1988, 1992, 2000), Carignane (planted 1950s), Chardonnay (planted 1980, 1981, 1988, 1992, 1996, 1997, 1998, 2000, 2004), Chenin Blanc (planted 1995, 2003), Merlot (planted 1996), Muscat Canelli (planted 1995), Sauvignon Blanc (planted 1988, 1995, 1996, 2004), Syrah (planted 2001), Zinfandel (planted 1950s). Owners: Thornhill family. *Winery Using Name*: Husch Vineyards.

Larkmead Vineyards (Napa Valley AVA)—120 acres located between St. Helena and Calistoga, adjacent to Highway 29. Cabernet Sauvignon, Merlot, Cabernet Franc, Petit Verdot, Malbec, Syrah, Zinfandel, Tocai Friuliano, Sauvignon Blanc (planted 1880s–present). Owners: Larkmead Vineyards, Cameron and Kate Baker. *Wineries Using Name*: Larkmead Vineyards, Stony Hill.

Larner Vineyards (Santa Ynez Valley AVA)—33.45 acres located around the 600-foot elevation in the Purisima Hill range on Ballard Canyon Road. Mourvèdre (planted 1999), Syrah (planted 1999–2001), Viognier (planted 1999), Malvasia Bianca (planted 1999–2000), Grenache (planted 2000). Owner: Larner family. *Wineries Using Name*: Drew Family Cellars, Palmina, Benjamin Silver Wines, Herman Story Wines, Bonacorssi, Tensley, Shadow Canyon Cellars, Ceres Wine Cellars, Jelly Roll, Samsara.

Lauterbach Hill (Russian River Valley AVA)—15 acres located near Martinelli Winery. Pinot Noir (planted 1996), Syrah (planted 1998). Owners:

Stew Lauterbach and Barb Swary. *Wineries Using Name*: Pax, Lauterbach Hill.

Les Chenes Estate Vineyards (San Francisco Bay AVA)—5 acres located at the 900-foot elevation in the Livermore Valley two miles east of Greenville Road, off Tesla Road. Syrah (planted 1999). Owners: Candice and Richard Dixon. *Winery Using Name*: Tenuta.

Lewelling Vineyards (St. Helena AVA)—13 acres at the 240-foot elevation, located on Lewelling Lane southwest of St. Helena. Cabernet Sauvignon (planted 1974, 1996), Merlot (planted 1988). Owners: Doug, David, and Alan Wight. *Wineries Using Name*: Lewelling Vineyards Wine Co., Trinchero Winery, Edgewood Estate.

Little Vineyards and Family Winery (Sonoma Valley AVA)—25 acres located between Valley of the Moon Winery and BR Cohn Winery. Zinfandel (planted 1975), Syrah (planted 1996), Cabernet Sauvignon (planted 1994), Pinot Noir (planted 1997). Owners: Joan and Rich Little. *Wineries Using Name*: Little Vineyards and Family Winery, Ravenswood.

Livingston Moffett (Rutherford AVA)—10 acres on a western hillside between Zinfandel and Whitehall Lanes in St. Helena. Cabernet Sauvignon (planted 1968, 1990, 1998, 2000, 2001). Owners: John and Diane Livingston. *Winery Using Name*: Livingston Moffett.

Lockwood Vineyard (San Lucas AVA)—1,850 acres located at the southern tip of Monterey County. Chardonnay, Sauvignon Blanc, Merlot, Cabernet Sauvignon, Syrah (planted 1989). Owners: R.P. Toeppen, Phil Johnson, Butch Lindley. *Wineries Using Name*: Shale Ridge Vineyard, Hidden Mesa Vineyard, Lawson Ranch Vineyard, Desolation Flats Vineyard.

Lone Oak Vineyard (Sonoma Valley AVA)—10 acres located at the 400 foot elevation in the soon-to-be-named Bennett Valley AVA, near Mantanzas Creek Winery in Santa Rosa. Sauvignon Blanc, Grenache Noir, Syrah (planted 1999). Owners: Joe and Gail Judge. *Winery Using Name*: Lone Oak Vineyard.

Lorenzo Vineyards (Russian River Valley AVA)—10 acres on Piezzi Road, north of Occidental Road in the Russian River Valley. Chardonnay (Wente clone). Planted 1973. Owner: John Bazzano. *Winery Using Name*: Landmark and Chasseur/Hunter Wine Cellars.

Los Chamizal Vineyards (Sonoma Valley AVA)—90 acres located between the 300–800-foot elevation, one mile northeast of Sonoma. Zinfandel, Cabernet Sauvignon, Cabernet Franc, Syrah, Mourvèdre, Grenache, Chardonnay (planted 1976, 1995–present). Owners: Peter and Margaret Haywood. *Wineries Using Name*: Haywood, Mayo.

Martha's Vineyard (Oakville AVA)—35 acres located on valley floor west of Highway 29, near Oakville. Cabernet Sauvignon (planted early 1960s, 1994). Owner: Martha's Vineyard Ltd. Partnership. *Winery Using Name*: Heitz Wine Cellars.

McDowell Valley Vineyards (McDowell Valley AVA)—313 acres located between the 750–1,100-foot elevation, three miles east of Hopland in Mendocino County. Syrah, Grenache (planted 1919), Zinfandel, Cabernet Sauvignon, Petite Sirah, Chardonnay, Sauvignon Blanc (planted 1948). Owners: Bill and Vicky Crawford. *Wineries Using Name*: Fetzer, McDowell.

M. Griffin Vineyard (Russian River Valley AVA)—31.23 acres located on Westside Road in Healdsburg. Valdiguie (planted 1959), Riesling (planted 1970), Gewürztraminer (planted 1979), Chardonnay (planted 1979–1983), Cabernet Sauvignon (planted 1998), Pinot Noir (planted 1998). Owner: L. Martin Griffin, Jr. *Winery Using Name*: Hop Kiln Winery.

Mead Ranch Vineyards (Atlas Peak AVA)—59 acres located at the 1,750-foot elevation, five miles up Atlas Peak Road past William Hill Winery, in the Atlas Peak sub-AVA. Cabernet Sauvignon (planted 1988, 1991), Zinfandel (planted 1960s–1975). Owners: Mead Ranch, Jane Mead. *Wineries Using Name*: Turley Wine Cellars, Storybook Mountain Vineyards, Villa Mt. Eden Winery.

Mitsuko's Vineyard (Carneros AVA)—224 acres located on Withers Road, off Los Carneros Avenue south of Highway 121. Chardonnay, Merlot, Cabernet Sauvignon, Pinot Noir, Sauvignon Blanc, Syrah (planted 1989–1991). Owners: Jan and Mitsuko Shrem, Clos Pegase Winery. *Winery Using Name*: Clos Pegase Winery.

Mohr-Fry Ranches (Lodi AVA)—20.72 acres located on North West Lane in Lodi. Zinfandel (planted 1901), Alicante Bouschet (planted 1922). Owner: Mohr Enterprises, Ltd. *Wineries Using Name*: Mohr-Fry, Chouinard Vineyards, St. Amant Winery, Crystal Valley Cellars.

Mojon's Bench Vineyard (Alexander Valley AVA)—2.3 acres located in the Alexander Valley. Merlot (planted 1994–1995). Owner: Schwartz family.

Winery Using Name: Mojon's Bench.

Moulds Family Vineyard (Oak Knoll AVA)—4 acres located on Dry Creek Road, just below the Mt. Veeder AVA. Cabernet Sauvignon (clone 337, planted 2000). Owners: Steve and Betsy Moulds. *Winery Using Name*: Behrens & Hitchcock.

Mount Veeder Estate (Domaine Chandon) (Mt. Veeder AVA)—68 acres located at the 2,000-foot elevation on Mt. Veeder Road. Chardonnay (planted 1985, 1998), Cabernet Sauvignon (planted 1997–1999), Syrah (planted 2003). Owners: LVMH Moët & Hennessey Louis Vuitton. *Winery Using Name*: Domaine Chandon.

Nagasawa Vineyard (Sonoma Coast AVA)—8 acres located at the 500-foot elevation, near Highway 101 and River Road, above the Russian River Valley. Chardonnay, Sauvignon Blanc (planted 1985), Zinfandel, Syrah, Petite Sirah (planted 2002). Owners: Dr. Walter Byck and Marijke Byck-Hoenselaars. *Winery Using Name*: Paradise Ridge Winery.

Nevins Vineyard (Alexander Valley AVA)—17 acres at the 400-600-foot elevation, near the Chalk Hill Road and Highway 128 intersection. Merlot, Cabernet Sauvignon (clones 7, 337, 4453). Planted 1993. Owners: Bruce and Sindy Nevins. *Winery Using Name*: Dutcher Crossing Winery.

Nova Vineyards (Clear Lake AVA)—37 acres located at the 1,500-foot elevation in Lake County, near Catfish Vineyard in Kelseyville. Zinfandel (planted 1965). Owners: Jim T. Smith, Jill L. Smith, Milton and Ellen Heath. *Wineries Using Name*: Burgess Cellars, Wild Hog Vineyard, Davis Bynum Winery, Sunce Winery, X-Winery, Sunset Cellars, Hallcrest Vineyards, The Organic Wine Works.

Nunes Vineyard (Russian River Valley AVA)—35 acres located at the edge of the bench, a gentle slope of 20 feet from Old Redwood Highway to Highway 101. Pinot Noir (Dijon clones 114, 115, 667, 777). Planted 2000. Owners: Fred and Wendy Nunes. *Winery Using Name*: Sonoma Coast Vineyards.

Oak Savanna Vineyard (Santa Ynez Valley AVA)—25.5 acres located at the 1,500-foot elevation at the 7.75 mile marker on Foxen Canyon Road in Santa Barbara County. Syrah, Sangiovese, Tempranillo, Viognier (planted 2001), Chardonnay (planted 1972). Owner: Sandy Hill. *Wineries Using Name*: Oak Savanna Vineyard and Oak Savanna Cellars, 1000 Hills.

Oehlman Vineyard (Russian River Valley AVA)—12 acres located on Vine

Hill Road in Sebastapol. Pinot Noir (Martini and Pommard Clones). Planted 1998, 1994–1995. Owner: Karl Oehlman. *Winery Using Name*: Hawley.

Old Hill Ranch (Sonoma Valley AVA)—24 acres originally planted in 1851, then replanted in 1885. Zinfandel, Grenache, Alicante Bouchet, Petite Sirah, Mourvèdre, Carignane, Pelourcin, Tannat, Tempranillo, Charbono (replanted six acres in 1990, 14 acres are still original plantings from 1885). Owner: Anne Teller. *Wineries Using Name*: Bucklin, Ravenswood.

Old Windmill Vineyard (Russian River Valley AVA)—5.79 acres located on Westside Road in Healdsburg. Zinfandel (planted 1979). Owner: L. Martin Griffin, Jr. *Winery Using Name*: Hop Kiln Winery.

Old Yokayo Rancho #1 & #2 (Mendocino AVA)—Two vineyards totalling 30 acres, located at the 1,400- and 2,000-foot elevations in eastern Mendocino County in the Ukiah Valley. Syrah (#1). Planted 1990. Syrah, Cabernet Sauvignon (#2). Planted 1998. Owners: Pam and Paul Jepson, Patrick Rodgers. *Winery Using Name*: Fife Vineyards.

Olivet Grange Vineyard (Russian River Valley AVA)—10.45-acre parcel located at 3930 Piner Road, Santa Rosa, CA at the corner of Olivet and Piner Roads, west of Santa Rosa and southwest of Healdsburg. The property is adjacent to the Papera and Mancini Vineyards and is two parcels away from the Olivet Lane Estate owned by the Pellegrini Family. Pinot Noir (777, 667, 115 on 420A), Pinot Noir (114 and 115 on 101-14MG), Pinot Gris (146 on 420A, 1,165 vines). Planted 2000. Owners: Kathleen and Simon Inman. *Wineries Using Name*: Inman Family Wines, Siduri Wines.

Olivet Lane Vineyard (Russian River Valley AVA)—69 acres on sloping benchland in the Russian River Valley. Pinot Noir, Chardonnay (planted 1975–1976). Owner: Pellegrini family. *Wineries Using Name*: Pellegrini, Merry Edwards, Gary Farell, Westmar.

Pacini Vineyard (Mendocino AVA)—28 acres at the 825–875-foot elevation on the Talmadge Bench in Mendocino County. Zinfandel, Petite Sirah, Carignane, Cinsault (planted 1937–1939). Owner: Jed Steele. *Winery Using Name*: Steele Wines.

Page Nord Vineyards (Napa Valley AVA)—23.96 acres located on Trubody Lane between Napa and Yountville. Syrah, Cabernet Sauvignon (planted 1997). Owners: Page and Nord Family Vineyards. *Wineries Using Name*: Novy Family Wines, Mayo Family Wines, Behrens & Hitchcock,

August Briggs.

Palisades Vineyard (Napa Valley AVA)—18 acres located two miles north of Calistoga, adjacent to Highway 29, on the banks of Horns Creek. Petite Sirah, Syrah (originally planted 1904, current plantings 1968, 1977, 1997). Owners: Anne Carver and Denis Sutro. *Winery Using Name*: Carver Sutro Wines.

Paraiso Vineyards (Santa Lucia Highlands AVA)—227 acres between the 250–800-foot elevation in the southern end of the appellation, above the junction of Foothill Road and Paraiso Springs Road in Monterey County. Riesling (planted 1973), Pinot Noir (planted 1973, 1988, 2000), Chardonnay (planted 1973, 1983, 2002), Syrah (planted 1989, 1994, 2000, 2002), Souzao (planted 1997), Viognier (planted 2002), Roussanne (planted 2002). Owners: Richard and Claudia Smith and family. *Wineries Using Name*: Paraiso, Morgan, Pelerin, Campion, Tudor, La Rochelle.

Parmelee-Hill Vineyards (Sonoma Valley AVA/Sonoma Coast AVA)—52 acres located between the 100–400-foot elevation in the southwest foothills of Sonoma Valley in the Sonoma Valley/Sonoma Coast AVAs. Chardonnay, Pinot Noir, Syrah, Zinfandel, Merlot (planted 1994–1998). Owners: Stephen and Gwen Hill. *Wineries Using Name*: Edmunds, St. John, Steele Wines, Castle.

Pelkan Ranch & Vineyard Company (Knights Valley AVA)—65 acres at the 700- to 1,100-foot elevation in the Mayacamas Mountains, located between Foss Hill Road and Spencer Lane in Sonoma County at the southeast end of Knights Valley AVA. Cabernet Franc, Merlot, Syrah, Grenache, Cabernet Sauvignon (planted 1989, 1996, 2000.) Owner: John R. Pelkan. *Wineries Using Name*: Sterling Vineyards, Joel Gott.

Perry Family Vineyard (St. Helena AVA)—One acre located on Rockland Drive in St. Helena near Lodi Lane, 400 feet above Highway 29. Cabernet Sauvignon (planted 1998). Owners: Jim and Sandra Perry. *Winery Using Name*: Grace Family Vineyards.

Philary Vineyards (Napa Valley AVA)—500 vines (planted 3 by 3) located at the 1,000-foot elevation in the southern end of the Napa Valley. Syrah (planted 1996, 1998). Owners: Philip and Hilary Brodey. *Winery Using Name*: J.C. Cellars. Note: Everything done by hand, no machinery or equipment used.

Pickberry Vineyards (Sonoma Mountain, Sonoma Valley, Sonoma County AVA)—30 acres located at the 640-foot elevation on Enterprise Road, on the north slope of Sonoma Mountain. Cabernet, Cabernet Franc, Merlot (planted 1982–1983, 1986). Owners: Cris and Lorna Strotz. *Winery Using Name*: Ravenswood.

Ponzo Vineyard (Russian River Valley AVA)—40 acres located on Redwood Highway in Healdsburg, next to Foppiano in the Russian River Valley. Zinfandel. Planted 1910–1935. Owner: Phil Ponzo. *Wineries Using Name*: Hart's Desire, Ridge, Nickel & Nickel.

Ron & Cheryl Pourroy Vineyard (Alexander Valley AVA)—10 acres located in the southern Alexander Valley. Zinfandel (old vine), Cabernet Sauvignon (planted 1994–2000). Owners: Ron & Cheryl Pourroy. *Wineries Using Name*: White Oak, Hanna Winery.

Primitivo Vineyard (Russian River Valley AVA)—7.24 acres located on Westside Road in Healdsburg in the Russian River Valley. Zinfandel (planted 1991). Owner: L. Martin Griffin. *Winery Using Name*: Hop Kiln Winery.

Progeny Vineyard (Mt. Veeder AVA)—17.5 acres located at the 1,600-foot elevation on Mt. Veeder Road. Petite Sirah, Cabernet Sauvignon (planted 1998). Owner: Betty O'Shaughnessy. *Wineries Using Name*: Beringer, St. Clement.

Quail Hill Vineyard (Russian River Valley AVA)—42 acres in the Russian River Valley on Frei Road between Highway 116 and Guernville Road in the heart of the Laguna Ridge area. Pinot Noir (planted 1972, 1996–1997, 2000), Chardonnay (planted 1974). Owners: Lynn and Mara Fritz. *Winery Using Name*: Lynmar.

Quartz Hill Vineyard (El Dorado AVA)—5 acres located at the 2,200-foot elevation three miles north of Placerville on Mosquito Road overlooking the south fork of the American River. Merlot (planted 1977–1998), Petite Sirah (planted 1999). Owners: Bob and Margot Scharpf. *Winery Using Name*: Thomas Coyne.

Raboli Vineyards (Livermore Valley AVA)—85 acres located in the Livermore Valley hills, adjacent to Wente Brothers Winery and Vineyard, southeast of San Francisco Bay. Cabernet Sauvignon, Mourvèdre, Tempranillo, Zinfandel (planted 1915, 1999). Owners: Con and Marlene Raboli, Robert McGlinchey. *Wineries Using Name*: Murrieta's Well, Livermore Valley, and

Estate Vineyards.

Rancho Chimiles (Napa Valley AVA)—23.5 acres located at the 900–1,000-foot elevation between the Wooden and northern Gordon valleys, also 14.5 acres at the 600-foot elevation in the Wooden Valley. Cabernet Sauvignon (planted 1988), Zinfandel (planted 1998), Sauvignon Blanc, Sauvignon Musque, Sémillon (planted 1995). Owner: Terrence Wilson family. *Wineries Using Name*: Franus (Peter Franus Wine Co.), Stag's Leap.

Rancho Del Oso (Howell Mountain AVA)—20 acres located at the 1,800-foot elevation on Friesen Drive in Angwin. Cabernet Sauvignon (planted 1997). Owner: Betty O'Shaughnessy. *Winery Using Name*: Beringer.

Rancho La Rinconada Vineyard (Santa Rita Hills AVA)—129.5 acres, located 11 miles west of Highway 101 on Santa Rosa Road, flanked by the Santa Rita Hills on the north and the Santa Rosa Hills to the south. Chardonnay, Pinot Noir (planted 1997). Owners: J. Richard Sanford. *Winery Using Name*: Sanford Winery and Vineyards.

Rancho Salina Vineyard (Sonoma Valley AVA)—30 acres between the 750–1,000-foot elevation on the western slopes of the Mayacamas Range, two miles north of Sonoma Plaza. Cabernet Sauvignon, Cabernet Franc, Merlot. Owner: Domenic J. Paino. *Wineries Using Name*: Ravenswood, Imagery (Benziger), Sonoma Creek (Larson Family Winery).

Rancho Sarco Vineyards (Napa Valley AVA)—36.95 acres on Monticello Road, a half mile east of Silverado Trail. Chardonnay (planted 1992–1993), Cabernet Sauvignon (planted 2000), Syrah (planted 2000, 2002). Owner: Rancho Sarco Vineyards, Will Nord. *Wineries Using Name*: Tulocay Winery, Jeff Runquist Wines.

Randle Hill Vineyard (Yorkville Highlands AVA)—13 acres located in southern Mendocino County. Sauvignon Blanc (planted 1982), Sémillon (planted 1989). Owner: Edward Walls. *Winery Using Name*: Yorkville Cellars.

Rauger Vineyard (Napa Valley AVA)—1 acre located south of St. Helena on the valley floor, near Flora Springs and Corison Wineries. Syrah (planted 1989). Owners: Rich Auger, Mary Radu. *Winery Using Name*: Topaz Wines.

Redhead Vineyard (Mendocino AVA)—13 acres located at the 1,400-foot elevation above Lake Mendocino. Zinfandel, Petite Sirah (planted 1978). Owner: Fife Vineyards. *Winery Using Name*: Fife Vineyards.

Reichel Vineyard (Alexander Valley AVA)—20 acres at the 2,300–2,500-

foot elevation, located on Pine Mountain Road in Cloverdale. Cabernet Sauvignon, Cabernet Franc (planted 1985, 2001). Owners: Charles and Corinne Reichel. *Winery Using Name*: Byington Vineyards and Winery.

Rennie Vineyard (Yorkville Highlands AVA)—16.5 acres located between 1,000–1,300-foot elevation in southern Mendocino County. Merlot, Cabernet Sauvignon, Cabernet Franc, Malbec, Petit Verdot (planted 1990). Owner: Edward Walls. *Winery Using Name*: Yorkville Cellars.

Renwood Vineyards (Shenendoah Valley AVA/Amador AVA)—6 acres on Upton Road in Plymouth. Viognier, Syrah (planted 1995). Owner: Renwood Winery. *Winery Using Name*: Renwood.

Reuling Vineyard (Russian River Valley AVA)—13 acres by the Russian River in Forestville, just east of Green Valley. Pinot Noir and Chardonnay (planted 2000-2003). Owners: Tim and Jackie Reuling. *Wineries Using Name*: Aubert Wines, Peter Michael Winery.

Ritchie Vineyard (Russian River Valley AVA)—65 acres located on a hillside near the Sonoma Coast. Chardonnay, Sauvignon Blanc, Pinot Noir (planted 1972). Owner: Kent Ritchie. *Wineries Using Name*: Aubert, Scot Paul, Taft.

River Oaks Vineyard (Alexander Valley AVA)—800 acres located in the Alexander Valley. Cabernet Sauvignon, Chardonnay, Merlot, Sauvignon Blanc, Malbec, Cabernet Franc, Tempranillo, Petit Verdot. Owner: Clos du Bois. *Winery Using Name*: Clos du Bois.

Robert Young Vineyards (Alexander Valley AVA)—317 acres located on the east side of the Alexander Valley, on Red Winery Road in Geyserville. Chardonnay, Merlot, Cabernet Sauvignon, Cabernet Franc, Pinot Blanc, Shiraz, Sauvignon Blanc, White Riesling, Melon, Petit Verdot, Zinfandel, Malbec, Viognier. Owner: Robert Young family. *Wineries Using Name*: Château St. Jean, Murphy-Goode.

Robinwood Vineyard (St. Helena AVA)—8 acres located on Sulphur Springs Avenue in St. Helena. Cabernet Sauvignon (planted 1971). Owner: Cowan family. *Winery Using Name*: Rutherford Ranch.

Rockpile Vineyard (Rockpile AVA)—28 acres located at the 2,000-foot elevation at the western end of the Rockpile AVA in Sonoma County. Cabernet, Merlot, Petit Verdot (planted 1991), Cabernet, Syrah (planted 1999), Merlot (budded over to Syrah in 2002 and 2003). Owners: Rod and Cathy

Park. *Wineries Using Name*: St. Francis, JC Cellars, Paradise Ridge.

Rosella's Vineyard (Santa Lucia Highlands AVA)—50.1 acres located at the 400-foot elevation in Monterey County. Chardonnay, Pinot Noir (planted 1996), Pinot Noir, Syrah (planted 1999), Pinot Noir (planted 2000). Owners: Gary and Rosella Franscioni. *Wineries Using Name*: Roar, Siduri, Testarossa, Miner, Vision, Bernardus, Loring, Morgan, Novy, Lorca.

Rosemary's Vineyard (Temecula AVA)—20 acres located at the 1,460-foot elevation in the Temecula Valley wine country at Wilson Creek Winery and Vineyards. Cabernet Sauvignon, Chardonnay (planted 1970), Zinfandel (grafted over in 1995). Owners: Gerry and Rosemary Wilson. *Winery Using Name*: Wilson Creek Winery.

Rubaiyat Vineyard (Sonoma Mountain AVA)—3 acres at the 500-foot elevation on the northern slope of Sonoma Mountain on Sonoma Mountain Road. Syrah/Shiraz (planted 1998). Owners: Thomas K. Smith and Jaleh Smith. *Winery Using Name*: Loxton Cellars.

Ruhl Vineyard (Yountville AVA)—15.58 acres located on Washington St. in Yountville. Chardonnay, Merlot (planted 1994), Cabernet Sauvignon (planted 1999). Owner: Al Ruhl Trust. *Wineries Using Name*: Frank Family Vineyards, Rombauer, Louis Martese.

Rutherford Estate (Rutherford AVA)—35 acres located between Highway 29 and the Napa River. Merlot (planted 1990, 1996), Cabernet Sauvignon (planted 1990, 1996), Petit Verdot (planted 1996). Owner: Robert Skalli. *Winery Using Name*: St. Supéry.

Sanford and Benedict Vineyard (Santa Rita Hills AVA)—134.2 acres located 10 miles west of Highway 101 on Santa Rosa Road, flanked by the Santa Rita Hills on the north and the Santa Rosa Hills to the south. Pinot Noir, Chardonnay, Viognier, Pinot Grigio, Gewürztraminer (planted 1971). Owners: Robert and Janice Atkins. *Wineries Using Name*: Au Bon Climat, Bonaccorsi Wines, Longoria Wines, Hitching Post Wines, Cold Heaven, Di Bruno, Talinda Oaks.

Sangiacomo Vineyard (Carneros AVA)—1,000 acres located south of the city of Sonoma. Chardonnay, Pinot Noir, Merlot (planted 1969–2003). Owner: Sangiacomo family. *Wineries Using Name*: Acacia, Goodman, Ravenswood, Richardson, Solitude, Steele Wines.

Saralee's Vineyard (Russian River Valley AVA)—275 acres located on

Slusser Road in Windsor, four miles west of Highway 101. Chardonnay, Dolcetto, Gewürztraminer, Grenache, Malvasia Bianca, Marsanne, Merlot, Meunier, Pinotage, Pinot Blanc, Pinot Gris, Pinot Noir, Rousanne, Sauvignon Blanc, Syrah, Viognier (planted 1989). Owners: Rich and Saralee McClelland Kunde. *Wineries Using Name*: Arrowood, Baystone, Joseph Swan, Alderbrook, Wild Hog, Dry Creek.

Sblendorio Estate & Vineyard (Livermore Valley AVA)—5 acres located on Mines Road in the Livermore Valley. Chardonnay (planted 1996), Zinfandel (planted 1997–1998), Petite Sirah (1998). Owners: Sblend and Beth Sblendorio. *Wineries Using Name*: Crooked Vine, Livermore Valley Cellars, Concannon Vineyard.

Schmidt Ranch (Oakville AVA)—35 acres located on the west side of Highway 29. Cabernet Sauvignon, Merlot, Syrah, Sangiovese, Petit Verdot (planted 1991). Owner: W. Clarke Swanson. *Winery Using Name*: Swanson Vineyards and Winery.

Sea Smoke Vineyards (Santa Rita Hills AVA)—100 acres located on south facing slopes on the north side of the Santa Ynez River Canyon, just east of Mt. Carmel Vineyard in Santa Barbara County. Pinot Noir (24 blocks, 10 clones, 3 rootstocks). Planted 1999. Owner: Bob Davids. *Wineries Using Name*: Sea Smoke, Foxen.

Silacci Vineyards (Monterey AVA)—22 acres located two miles north of the Santa Lucia Highlands AVA in Salinas on River Road. Pinot Noir (Pisoni, 667, 777, 828). Planted 1999–2002. Owners: Gary Pisoni, Robert Silacci, Loren Cloninger, Joe and Phil Boskovich. *Wineries Using Name*: Cloninger Cellars, Pisoni, Passangno, Miuri.

Silva Vineyard (Arroyo Seco AVA)—49 acres located on the corner of Thorne Road and Arroyo Seco Road in Monterey County. Pinot Gris, Pinot Noir (planted 1998). Owners: Edward and Eyvlen Silva. *Winery Using Name*: McIntyre.

Silverado Trail Vineyard (Rutherford AVA)—7 acres located on Silverado Trail at the Rutherford Ranch Winery, between Howell Mountain and Atlas Peak. Cabernet Sauvignon (planted 1975). Owner: Zaninovich Family. *Winery Using Name*: Rutherford Ranch Winery.

Silver Mountain Vineyard (Santa Cruz Mountains AVA)—12 acres located at the 2,100-foot elevation, near Miller Hill and Skyland Roads.

Chardonnay (planted 1981), Merlot (planted 1993), Pinot Noir (planted 2002). Owner: Jerold O'Brien. *Winery Using Name*: Silver Mountain Vineyards. Note: Certified organic.

Solari Vineyards (Napa Valley AVA)—110 acres located on Bennett Lane, approximately three miles west of Calistoga. Cabernet Sauvignon, Merlot, Cabernet Franc, Sauvignon Blanc, Muscat Canelli, Zinfandel, Sangiovese, Petite Sirah (planted 1979–2002). Owner: Solari Family. *Wineries Using Name*: Robert Pecota Winery, Sterling Vineyards.

Sophia's Vineyard (Temecula AVA)—Five acres along Monte de Oro Road in Temecula. Cabernet Sauvignon (clone 337). Planted 1999. Owners: Palumbo Family. *Winery Using Name*: Palumbo Family Vineyards and Winery.

Spaulding Vineyard (Diamond Mountain District AVA)—17 acres located between the 600–1,000-foot elevation off Kortum Canyon Road above Calistoga. Cabernet Sauvignon, Merlot (planted 1971–1973). Owners: James and Barbara Spaulding. *Winery Using Name*: Stonegate.

Spottswoode Estate Vineyard (St. Helena AVA)—38 acres located on the western edge of St. Helena. Cabernet Sauvignon, Cabernet Franc, Savignon Blanc, Petit Verdot (1882, 1990s). Owner: Mary Weber Novak. *Winery Using Name*: Spottswoode.

Stagecoach Vineyard (Atlas Peak AVA/Napa Valley AVA)—493 acres located between the 900–1,700-foot elevation on the south side of Pritchard Hill. Cabernet Sauvignon, Merlot, Cabernet Franc, Petit Verdot, Syrah, Malbec, Chardonnay (planted 1996–2000). Owners: Jan Krupp, Bart Krupp, Ronald Family Trust, Bob Notine, Avalon Partnership, Panorama Holding. *Wineries Using Name*: Paul Hobbs, Palmieri, Veraison, Miner, Erich Russell, Stonehedge.

Stagecoach-Krupp Vineyard (Atlas Peak AVA)—Stagecoach block is 6 acres, Krupp block is 5.43 acres. Cabernet Sauvignon (Krupp block planted 1992, Stagecoach block planted 1996). Owner: Dr. Jan Krupp. *Winery Using Name*: Rutherford Ranch.

Stage Gulch Vineyards (Sonoma Coast AVA)—90 acres located on Stage Gulch Road near Adobe Road, midway between Petaluma and Sonoma in the Petaluma Gap. Chardonnay (planted 1991, 1992, 1997, 1998), Pinot Noir (planted 1991, 1997, 1998), Merlot (planted 1994, 1995, 1998), Syrah (planted 1992). Owners: Jens and Connie Kullberg. *Wineries Using Name*:

Rosenblum Cellars, Lost Canyon Winery.

Stanly Ranch Vineyard (Carneros AVA)—200 acres located on the site of the historic Stanly Ranch at the end of Stanly Lane in Napa. Pinot Noir, Chardonnay, Pinot Gris (planted 1971–2001). Owners: Beringer Blass Wine Estates, Stanly Ranch Vineyards. *Wineries Using Name*: Beringer, Abiouness.

Star Vineyard (Rutherford AVA)—67 acres near Route 128 and Highway 29. Chardonnay (planted 1978–1999), Pinot Noir (planted 1991–1999), Merlot (planted 1999), Cabernet Franc (planted 1999), Cabernet Sauvignon (planted 1991–1999). Owner: Reginald B. Oliver. *Winery Using Name*: St. Clement.

Student Vineyard (Napa Valley AVA)—6 acres located at the southeast corner of the city of Napa. Chardonnay, Cabernet Franc, Petit Verdot, Merlot, Muscat, Syrah, Sauvignon Blanc, Viognier, Pinot Noir, Cabernet Sauvignon. Owners: Napa Valley College, Viticulture and Winery Technology. *Winery Using Name*: Winesmith.

Stuhlmuller Vineyard Properties (Alexander Valley AVA)—150 acres located on West Soda Rock Lane, 2.6 miles east of Alexander Valley Road, fronting the Russian River, at the confluence of the Alexander Valley, Chalk Hill, and Russian River appellations. Chardonnay, Cabernet Sauvignon, Cabernet Franc, Zinfandel, Petit Verdot, Syrah. Planted 1979–2002. Owners: Roger, Carmen, Fritz, and Annie Stuhlmuller. *Wineries Using Name*: Château Souverain, Armida, Dutcher Crossing, Page Mill, Cronin, O'Connor, Stuhlmuller Estate.

Sullivan Vineyards (Rutherford AVA)—23 acres located behind Franciscan Winery, on Galleron Road. Merlot (planted 1979, 1995, 1997), Cabernet Sauvignon (planted 1990, 1998, 2000, 2002). Owner: Sullivan Family Estate Partnership. *Winery Using Name*: Sullivan Vineyards.

Sunny View (Russian River Valley AVA)—15 acres on Guerneville Road. Pinot Noir (Pommard, 667, 777 clones), Viognier (planted 1999). Owners: Ellen Mack and Edward Gomez. *Winery Using Name*: Mayo Family Winery.

Tara Vineyard (Russian River Valley AVA)—6 acres located at Russian Hill Winery. Pinot Noir (planted 1998). Owners: Ellen Mack and Edward Gomez. *Winery Using Name*: Russian Hill Winery.

Three Palms Vineyard (Napa Valley AVA)—83 acres located on the Silverado Trail, four miles south of Calistoga. Cabernet Sauvignon, Merlot, Cabernet Franc, Malbec, Petit Verdot (planted 1968–1992, replanted 1992–2003). Owners: Sloan and John Upton. *Wineries Using Name*: Duckhorn Vineyards, Sterling Vineyards.

Tietjen Vineyard (Rutherford AVA)—7.5 acres located on Niebaum Lane, west of Highway 29 on the bench. Cabernet Sauvignon (planted 1986, replanted 1993–1998). Owners: Hugh Tietjen and Patricia McDonald. *Wineries Using Name*: Elyse, Monticello.

Tina's Vineyard/De La Montanya Vineyards (Russian River Valley AVA)—11 acres located in the heart of the Russian River Valley, in Sonoma County. Pinot Noir (planted 1997). Owners: Dennis and Tina De La Montanya. *Wineries Using Name*: Walter Hansel Family Vineyards, De La Montanya Vineyards and Winery.

Top Block (Russian River Valley AVA)—3 acres adjacent to Russian Hill Winery on Slusser Road. Syrah (Estrella clone), Viognier (planted 1998). Owners: Ellen Mack and Edward Gomez. *Winery Using Name*: Russian Hill Winery.

Trailside Vineyard (Rutherford AVA)—85 acres in the Rutherford appellation. Cabernet Sauvignon (planted 1990). Owners: Heitz Wine Cellars. *Winery Using Name*: Heitz Wine Cellars.

Trentadue Vineyard (Alexander Valley AVA)—150 acres located between Healdsburg and Geyserville, off Highway 101 East. Carignane, Cabernet Sauvignon, Merlot, Petit Sirah, Syrah, Sangiovese, Zinfandel, Chardonnay (planted 1896–2000). Owners: Leo and Evelyn Trentadue. *Winery Using Name*: Ridge.

Trenton Station Vineyard (Russian River Valley AVA)—140 acres located on Old Trenton and River Roads. Viognier, Syrah, Pinot Gris, Pinot Noir, Zinfandel (planted 1999). Owners: Rich and Saralee McClelland Kunde. *Wineries Using Name*: Joseph Swan Vineyards, Lost Canyon Winery.

Trio C Vineyard (Yountville AVA)—76.21 acres on Finnell Road, just east of Yountville. Chardonnay (planted 1991–1992), Merlot (planted 1991, 1992, 1994), Cabernet Sauvignon (planted 1998). Owners: Trio Vineyards, Will Nord. *Wineries Using Name*: Galleron, Audubon Cellars.

Triska Crane Ridge Vineyards (San Francisco Bay AVA)—18.5 acres located at the 750-foot elevation on Crane Ridge on Cedar Mountain Drive in Livermore. Merlot (planted 1994). Owners: Maria and Mark Triska. *Winery Using Name*: Eckert Estate Winery.

Trout Gulch Vineyards (Santa Cruz Mountains AVA)—19 acres located at the 700-foot elevation in Aptos. Chardonnay, Pinot Noir (planted 1982–1988). Owner: Meinard Hanggi. *Wineries Using Name*: Trout Gulch Vineyards & Beauregard Vineyards, Burrell School Vineyards.

Turtle Creek Vineyard (Russian River Valley AVA)—3.78 acres located on Westside Road in Healdsburg. Zinfandel (planted 1996). Owner: L. Martin Griffin. *Winery Using Name*: Hop Kiln Winery.

Vadasz Vineyards (Sonoma Valley AVA)—70 acres located about a mile west of Carneros, at the base of Sonoma Mountain. Pinot Noir, Syrah, Sauvignon Blanc, Cabernet Sauvignon (planted 1998), Sauvignon Blanc (planted 2000), Chardonnay, Malbec, Cabernet Sauvignon (planted 2001). Owners: Les and Judy Vadasz. *Winery Using Name*: Moon Mountain.

Vanumanutagi Vineyard (Santa Cruz Mountains AVA)—9.2 acres located at the southern most tip of the appellation at the 850-foot elevation off of Redwood Retreat Road. Chardonnay (planted 1981). Owner: Leo Ware. *Winery Using Name*: Clos LaChance Winery.

Ventana Vineyard (Arroyo Seco AVA)—400 acres located between the Arroyo Seco River and Los Coches Road west of Highway 101 between Soledad and Greenfield. Chardonnay, Cabernet Sauvignon, Merlot, Syrah, Sauvignon Blanc, Riesling, Gewürztraminer, Chenin Blanc, Orange Muscat, Pinot Noir, Cabernet Franc, Grenache Noir. Planted 1972–present. Owners: J. Douglas and LuAnn Meador. *Wineries Using Name*: Ventana Vineyards, Cain, J.C. Cellars.

Vesenaz Vineyard (Dry Creek Valley AVA)—5.5 acres located on the benchlands of Dry Creek Valley, near the intersection of Dry Creek Road and Canyon Road. Syrah, Zinfandel (planted 1997). Owners: Fred and Janet White. *Winery Using Name*: Selby Winery.

Vineyard Georges III (Rutherford AVA)—265 acres on Conn Creek Road in Rutherford, Napa Valley. Cabernet Sauvignon (clones 4, 6, 7, 8, 337). Originally planted 1928, current planting 1990–1998. Owners: Beckstoffer Vineyards. *Wineries Using Name*: Clos du Val, Delectus, Merryvale, Provenance. Note: Planted prior to 1895 by E.A. Rutherford.

Vineyard 29 (Napa Valley AVA)—3.5 acres located on Highway 29, one mile north of St. Helena. Zinfandel, Cabernet Sauvignon, Cabernet Franc (planted 1989). Owners: Chuck and Anne McMinn. *Wineries Using Name*: Vineyard 29, Aida.

Vogt Vineyard (Howell Mountain AVA)—14 acres located at the 1,650-foot elevation on Bell Canyon Road on Howell Mountain. Cabernet Sauvignon, Merlot (planted 1996–1997). Owners: Stephen and Nita Vogt. *Winery Using Name*: Nickel and Nickel.

Volker Eisele Vineyard (Chiles Valley AVA)—60 acres located on Lower Chiles Valley Road. Cabernet Sauvignon (planted 1991–1999), Cabernet Franc (planted 1995), Sémillon (planted 2000–2001), Sauvignon Blanc (planted 2000–2001), Merlot (planted 1992, 1994). Owners: Volker and Liesel Eisele. *Winery Using Name*: Volker Eisele Family Estate.

Weir Family Vineyard (Napa Valley AVA)—12 acres located on the Southern Silverado Trail, one mile south of the Stags Leap AVA. Cabernet Sauvignon (planted 1997). Owners: Ernie and Irit Weir. *Winery Using Name*: Hagafen.

Whaler Vineyard (Mendocino AVA)—8 acres located at the edge of the Talmadge Ridge, above Eastside Road in Ukiah. Zinfandel, Syrah (planted 1980s–1990s). Owners: Russell and Anne Nyborg. *Wineries Using Name:* Fife Vineyards, Whaler Vineyards.

Windy Oaks Estate, Schultze Family Vineyard (Santa Cruz Mountains AVA)—15 acres at the 1,000-foot elevation, off Hazel Dell Road, overlooking the Monterey Bay, in Corralitos. Pinot Noir (planted 1996, 1997, 2000, 2001), Chardonnay (planted 1997). Owners: Judy & Jim Schultze. *Wineries Using Name*: David Bruce Wine Club, Windy Oaks Estate.

Winston Hill Vineyards (Rutherford AVA)—30 acres on Silverado Trail that rises to the 800-foot elevation. Cabernet Sauvignon, Sangiovese, Cabernet Franc, Merlot (planted 1993–1994). Owner: Richard Frank. *Wineries Using Name*: Frank Family Vineyards, Winston Hill Vineyards.

Wolff Vineyard (Edna Valley AVA)—55 acres on Orcutt Road, mid-valley. Chardonnay (planted 1976, 1982). Owners: Jean-Pierre and Elka Wolff. *Winery Using Name*: Mount Eden Vineyards.

Zabala Vineyards (Arroyo Seco AVA)—1,334 acres located on Los Coches Road in Soledad, in Monterey County. Chardonnay (planted 1972-1998), Pinot Noir (planted 2000), Syrah (planted 2000), Sauvignon Blanc (planted 2001), Chardonnay (planted 2001). Owner: Zabala family. *Wineries Using Name*: Picchetti, Mirassou.

Zahtila Vineyards (Napa Valley AVA)—3.25 acres located at the 700 foot elevation at the base of Oat Hill, east of Calistoga, 100 yards north of Silverado Trail on Highway 29. Zinfandel (planted 1976, 1996, 2000). Owner: Laura Zahtila. *Winery Using Name*: Zahtila Vineyards.

Zanini Ranch (Fiddletown AVA)—18 acres located on Olstrum Road in Fiddletown. Zinfandel (planted approximately 1979). Owners: Ray and Helen Zanini. *Winery Using Name*: Renwood.

Ziegler Vineyards (Dry Creek Valley AVA)—18.8 acres located on the east bank of Dry Creek, where Dry Creek Road meets Lyton Springs Road. Merlot, Pinot Noir, Chardonnay (planted 1978). Owner: Ziegler family. *Winery Using Name*: Burnett Ridge.

BIBLIOGRAPHY

Adams, Leon D. *The Wines of America, Second Edition Revised.* New York: McGraw Hill, 1978.

Amerine, Maynard A. "Chardonnay in California." In *The Focus on Chardonnay Journal,* Spring 1990. Windsor: Sonoma-Cutrer Vineyards, Inc., 1990.

Amerine, Maynard A. and Roessler, Edward B. *Wines: Their Sensory Evaluation.* San Francisco: W.H. Freeman and Co., 1976.

Anderson, Bette Roda. *Weather in the West.* Palo Alto: American West, 1975.

Anonymous. *The Making of Wines in California: Trials Experienced by the Industry.* San Francisco Chronicle, January 3, 1897.

Asher, Gerald. *An Englishman's Perspective of California and Her Wines.* In *Bulletin of the Society of Medical Friends of Wine,* Vol. 18, No. 1. San Francisco: The Society of Medical Friends of Wine, February 1976.

Bailey, Harry P. *The Climate of Southern California.* Berkeley: University of California Press, 1966.

Barry, Roger G. and Chorley, Richard J. *Atmosophere, Weather and Climate, Fourth Edition.* London: Methuen, 1982.

Berry, Elizabeth. "The Importance of Soil in Fine Wine Production." In *Journal of Wine Research,* Vol. 1, No. 2. Abingdon, Oxfordshire: Carfax/The Institute of Masters of Wine, 1990.

Blue, Anthony Dias. *American Wine—A Comprehensive Guide,* rev. New York: Harper and Row, 1988.

California Agricultural Statistics Service. *California Grape Acreage,* annual editions from 1980 to 1990. Sacramento: California Agricultural Statistics Service.

Conaway, James. *Napa: The Story of an American Eden.* Boston: Houghton Mifflin, 1990.

Darlington, David. *Angels' Visits: An Inquiry Into the Mystery of Zinfandel.* New York: Henry Holt and Co., 1991.

Donley, Michael W.; Allan, Stuart; Caro, Patricia; and Patton, Clyde P. *Atlas of California*. Culver City: Pacific Book Center, 1979.

Felton, Ernest L. *California's Many Climates*. Palo Alto: Pacific Books, 1965.

Galet, Pierre. Translated and adapted by Lucie T. Morton. Ithaca: Cornell University Press, 1979.

Geiger, Rudolf. *The Climate Near the Ground*, trans. Scripta Technica Inc. Cambridge: Harvard University Press, 1965.

Gilbert, Jack. *Monolithos: Poems 1962 and 1982*. New York: Alfred A. Knopf, 1982.

Heublein Fine Wine Group. *The 1991 Data Annual: A Comprehensive Overview of the California Wine Industry*. St. Helena: Data Annual Publications, 1991.

James, William. *Some Problems of Philosophy: A Beginning of an Introduction to Philosophy*. New York: Longmans, Green and Co., 1911.

Laube, James. *California's Great Cabernets: The Wine Spectator's Ultimate Guide for Consumers, Collectors, and Investors*. San Francisco: Wine Spectator Press, 1989.

Laube, James. *California's Great Chardonnays: The Wine Spectator's Ultimate Guide for Consumers, Collectors, and Investors*. San Francisco: Wine Spectator Press, 1990.

Melville, John. *Guide to California Wines*. Garden City: Doubleday, 1955.

Merwin, W.S. *Opening the Hand*. New York: Atheneum, 1983.

Muscatine, Doris; Amerine, Maynard A.; and Thompson, Bob, editors. *The University of California/Sotheby Book of California Wine*. Berkeley: University of California Press/Sotheby Publications, 1984.

Nelson, Richard. *The Island Within*. San Francisco: North Point Press, 1989.

Pinney, Thomas. *A History of Wine in America: From the Beginnings to Prohibition*. Berkeley: University of California Press, 1989.

Pronsolino, Eileen and Bell, Niel. "Anderson Valley: Winegrowing and Winemaking History." In *Sketches From Anderson Valley*. Boonville: Anderson Valley Historical Society, 1989.

Reynolds, Richard D. *Squibob: An Early California Humorist*. San Francisco: Squibob Press Inc., 1990.

Robinson, Jancis. *Vintage Timecharts: The Pedigree and Performance of Fine Wines to the Year 2000*. New York: Weidenfeld and Nicolson, 1989.

Roby, Norman S. and Olken, Charles E. *The New Connoisseurs' Handbook of California Wines*. New York: Alfred A. Knopf, 1991.

Santayana, George. *The Letters of George Santayana*, edited by Daniel Cory. New York: Charles Scribner's Sons, 1955.

Schoonmaker, Frank. "The Red Wines of America: A Report." in Allen, H. Warner. *Natural Red Wines*. London: Constable, 1951.

Schoonmaker, Frank and Marvel, Tom. *American Wines*. New York: Duell, Sloan and Pearce, 1941.

M. Shanken Communications Inc. *The U.S. Market for California Varietal Wine: Impact Databank Review and Forecast 1990 Edition*. New York: M. Shanken Communications Inc., 1990.

Thompson, Bob. *Notes on a California Cellarbook: Reflections on Memorable Wines*. New York: Beech Tree/William Morrow, 1988.

Thompson, Bob. *The Simon and Schuster Pocket Guide to California Wines*, rev. New York: Simon and Schuster, 1990.

Thompson, Bob and Johnson, Hugh. *The California Wine Book*. New York: William Morrow, 1976.

Turner, Frederick Jackson. "The Development of American Society." In *America's Great Frontiers and Sections: Frederick Jackson Turner's Unpublished Essays*, edited by Wilbur R. Jacobs. Lincoln: University of Nebraska Press, 1965.

INDEX